ISBN 978-90-04-25754-2

Full text of the lecture published in July 2013 in the *Recueil des cours*, Vol. 361.

Cover illustration : "Law gavel on a chess board with pieces" (© zimmytws).

# HAGUE ACADEMY OF INTERNATIONAL LAW

*A collection of law lectures
in pocketbook form*

AIL-POCKET

2013

Competence-Competence
in the Face of Illegality in Contracts
and Arbitration Agreements

# Competence-Competence in the Face of Illegality in Contracts and Arbitration Agreements

RICHARD KREINDLER

## TABLE OF CONTENTS

Introduction. . . . . . . . . . . . . . . . . . . . . 19

Chapter I. Definition of the subject . . . . . . . . . 26

A. Initial focus and questions . . . . . . . . . . . . 26
B. The range of questions seeking answers . . . . . 31
C. The historical setting in commercial arbitration . 44
D. The historical setting in investment-treaty arbi-
  tration. . . . . . . . . . . . . . . . . . . . . . . 49
E. Corruption in cross-border commercial life . . . 54
F. The intersection between corruption and law . . 58

Chapter II. The meaning of "illegality" . . . . . . . 61

A. Overview of the problem of illegality in its different forms . . . . . . . . . . . . . . . . . . . 61
  1. Overtly illegal contracts . . . . . . . . . . . 61
  2. Illegality and lack of assent. . . . . . . . . . 64
  3. Illicit contracts and public versus private
    parties. . . . . . . . . . . . . . . . . . . . . 66
  4. Illegality ab initio versus ex post. . . . . . . 67
B. Circumstances of the illegality. . . . . . . . . . 68
  1. Initial awareness of the illegality by all parties 68
  2. Subsequent awareness of the illegality by all
    parties. . . . . . . . . . . . . . . . . . . . . 69
  3. Illicit intention and awareness of one party . 69
  4. Reliance on the illegality as claim or defence 70
  5. Contracts of bribery versus contracts arising
    out of bribery . . . . . . . . . . . . . . . . . 70
C. Suspicion of illegality versus knowledge or
  obviousness of same . . . . . . . . . . . . . . . 70
  1. Maintaining impartiality and equal treatment 71
  2. Dilatory tactics and allegations of illegality . 72
  3. Mutual denial of illegality . . . . . . . . . . 72
D. Initial attempts at definitions of "corruption"
  and "bribery". . . . . . . . . . . . . . . . . . . 73
E. International and transnational efforts to
  define "bribery" . . . . . . . . . . . . . . . . . 75
F. The temporal dimension of illegality. . . . . . . 81

G. Different national legislative approaches to the definition of illegality . . . . . . . . . . . . . . 92

   1. "Facilitation payments", "speed money" and "grease payments" . . . . . . . . . . . . 92
   2. Differences in the definition of elements of corrupt conduct . . . . . . . . . . . . . . . . 95
   3. Differences in the dividing line between corrupt and non-corrupt intermediaries . . . . . 97

H. Illegality and investment arbitration . . . . . . . 103

Chapter III. The context of private international law versus public international law . . . . . . . . . . . 106

A. Introduction . . . . . . . . . . . . . . . . . . . . 106

   1. International commercial arbitration based on contractual privity . . . . . . . . . . . . . . . 106
   2. International investment arbitration based on contractual privity . . . . . . . . . . . . . . . 109
   3. International investment arbitration based on a BIT or MIT, without contractual privity . . 112

B. The meaning of public policy in international arbitration . . . . . . . . . . . . . . . . . . . . . 114

   1. Limitations to party autonomy . . . . . . . . 114
   2. The meaning and function of public policy in international arbitration . . . . . . . . . . . . 116
   3. The function of public policy in international arbitration generally . . . . . . . . . . . . . . 121

     *(a)* Public policy limitations to arbitration as a means of dispute settlement . . . . . 123
     *(b)* Public policy limitations to the applicable substantive and procedural law . . . 128
     *(c)* Public policy limitations to the existence and enforcement of an award . . . . . . . 134

        (i) Court practice in the United States . 140
        (ii) Court practice in France . . . . . . 143
        (iii) Court practice in England . . . . . 144
        (iv) Court practice in Germany . . . . . 145
        (v) Court practice in Switzerland . . . . 146

   4. The existence and role of public policy for the international arbitrator . . . . . . . . . . . . . 149

     *(a)* The absence of a *lex fori* and the role of public policy . . . . . . . . . . . . . . . 149

*(b)* Criticism of an "international" or "trans-national" public policy . . . . . . . . . . 151

*(c)* Rebuttal to the criticism of an "interna-tional" or "transnational" public policy . . 153

5. Corruption and bribery in public and private international law . . . . . . . . . . . . . . . . 155

*(a)* Prevailing opinion on bribery as a matter of customary law . . . . . . . . . . . . . 156

*(b)* Widespread condemnation of bribery by tribunals . . . . . . . . . . . . . . . . . 159

*(c)* Criticism of the existence of a transa-tional public policy prohibition against bribery. . . . . . . . . . . . . . . . . . . 161

Chapter IV. The question of the applicable law or laws 167

A. International commercial arbitration and the applicable law . . . . . . . . . . . . . . . . . . 167

1. *Lex contractus* as manifestation of party autonomy . . . . . . . . . . . . . . . . . . 168

2. *Lex contractus, lex arbitri* and the place of performance . . . . . . . . . . . . . . . . 169

3. The connectedness of the law of place of performance . . . . . . . . . . . . . . . . 170

4. Violation of universal public policy versus local public policy. . . . . . . . . . . . . 174

B. International investment arbitration and the appli-cable law . . . . . . . . . . . . . . . . . . . . 181

1. The autonomy of the parties to choose the law in international investment disputes . . 182

2. Party autonomy and the law of the host State 185

3. The law of the investor or the law of a third State . . . . . . . . . . . . . . . . . . . 186

4. The investment agreement as a self-contained legal system . . . . . . . . . . . . . . . 187

5. Rules of law versus bodies of law. . . . . . 191

6. The choice of "international law" . . . . . . 194

7. International law as a component of domestic law. . . . . . . . . . . . . . . . . . . . 201

8. International law in the "absence" of its choice by the parties. . . . . . . . . . . . 204

9. Consequences of non-application of proper law — nullity . . . . . . . . . . . . . . . 212

10. Corruption and illegality in an investment treaty-based choice of law. . . . . . . . . 218

C. Commercial versus investment arbitration: reconciling illegality and applicable law . . . . .  222

Chapter V. Corruption allegations, suspicions, findings and admissions . . . . . . . . . . . . . . . . . .  224

A. The different contexts in which corruption plays a role . . . . . . . . . . . . . . . . . . . . . . .  224
  1. Overview of the problem of illegality in its different forms . . . . . . . . . . . . . . . . .  224
  2. Different kinds of illegality . . . . . . . . . .  225
    *(a)* Overtly illegal contracts . . . . . . . . .  225
    *(b)* Illegality and lack of assent . . . . . . .  227
    *(c)* Illicit contracts and public versus private parties . . . . . . . . . . . . . . . . . . .  230
    *(d)* Illegality *ab initio* versus *ex post* . . . . .  231
  3. Different factual circumstances of illegality .  231
    *(a)* Initial awareness of the illegality by all parties . . . . . . . . . . . . . . . . . . .  232
    *(b)* Subsequent awareness of the illegality by all parties . . . . . . . . . . . . . .  232
    *(c)* Illicit intention and awareness by only one party . . . . . . . . . . . . . . . . . . .  233
    *(d)* Reliance on the illegality as a claim or defence . . . . . . . . . . . . . . . . .  233
    *(e)* Contracts of bribery versus contracts arising out of bribery . . . . . . . . . . .  234
  4. Suspicion of illegality versus knowledge or obviousness of the same . . . . . . . . . . .  234
    *(a)* Maintaining impartiality and equal treatment . . . . . . . . . . . . . . . . . . .  235
    *(b)* Dilatory tactics and allegations of illegality . . . . . . . . . . . . . . . . . . . .  235
    *(c)* Mutual denial of illegality . . . . . . . .  236

B. Illegality and jurisdictional limitations . . . . . .  237
  1. Competence-competence . . . . . . . . . . .  237
    *(a)* Commercial arbitration . . . . . . . . . .  237
    *(b)* Investment treaty arbitration . . . . . . .  243
  2. Illegality and separability of the arbitration agreement . . . . . . . . . . . . . . . . . . .  244
    *(a)* Commercial arbitration . . . . . . . . . .  244
    *(b)* Investment treaty arbitration . . . . . . .  248

3. Arbitrability. . . . . . . . . . . . . . . . . . 249
   *(a)* Commercial arbitration . . . . . . . . . 249
   *(b)* Investment treaty arbitration . . . . . . . 250
4. Corruption issues and competence, separability and arbitrability. . . . . . . . . . . . . . 251

Chapter VI. The burden of proof and the standard of
proof of illegality . . . . . . . . . . . . . . . . . 252

A. Introduction . . . . . . . . . . . . . . . . . . . 252
B. Burden of proof generally . . . . . . . . . . . 254

  1. Commercial context. . . . . . . . . . . . . . 254
  2. Investment treaty context . . . . . . . . . . . 255
  3. General approaches to burden of proof and
    its allocation . . . . . . . . . . . . . . . . . 257

C. Burden of proof and corruption . . . . . . . . 259

  1. General challenges . . . . . . . . . . . . . . 259
  2. Parallel litigation, arbitration or investigations 260

    *(a)* Absence of contractual privity . . . . . . 262
    *(b)* Existence of contractual privity. . . . . . 264
    *(c)* Issues related to the seat and/or applicable
      arbitral rules. . . . . . . . . . . . . . . . 267
    *(d)* Degree of relatedness and relevance . . . 270

  3. Approaches to proof in commercial and
    public law arbitration . . . . . . . . . . . . . 273
  4. Approaches to proof in investment treaty
    arbitration . . . . . . . . . . . . . . . . . . . 276
  5. Similarities and differences in commercial
    and investment approaches to proof . . . . . 279

Chapter VII. Attribution of illegal actions and knowledge of the State . . . . . . . . . . . . . . . . . 281

A. Introduction . . . . . . . . . . . . . . . . . . . 281
B. Attribution generally in international arbitration
involving States . . . . . . . . . . . . . . . . . 282
C. The intersection between corruption and attribution . . . . . . . . . . . . . . . . . . . . . . . . 286

Chapter VIII. The rights and duties of the arbitrator . 294

A. Introduction . . . . . . . . . . . . . . . . . . . 294
B. Conceptual challenges and issues related to
rights and duties generally . . . . . . . . . . . 294

  1. Rights of the international arbitrator . . . . . 294

2. Duties of the international arbitrator . . . . . 296

(a) Duties of the arbitrator and party autonomy . . . . . . . . . . . . . . . . . . . 296
(b) Duties of the arbitrator and public policy 297
(c) Standards of procedural international
public policy . . . . . . . . . . . . . . . 299
(d) Policy-related concerns, including enforceability . . . . . . . . . . . . . . . . . . . 312

3. The arbitrator's investigative rights and
duties in the context of corruption . . . . . . 316
4. Should or must an arbitrator always decide
illegality *when alleged*? . . . . . . . . . . . 317

(a) Degree or lack of reviewability of the
award . . . . . . . . . . . . . . . . . . . 319
(b) The limited extent and quality of review
of the award. . . . . . . . . . . . . . . . 320
(c) The unlikelihood of review or annulment
of the award. . . . . . . . . . . . . . . . 321
(d) The quality of the award and its subsequent scrutiny . . . . . . . . . . . . . . . 321
(e) The precedential value or use of the award 322
(f) Social engineering within the constraints
of the arbitral mandate . . . . . . . . . . 322
(g) Toleration of illegality as a discouragement for future conduct. . . . . . . . . . 323
(h) Pressure and moral suasion on the reviewing instance . . . . . . . . . . . . . . . . 324
(i) The undesirable option of resignation. . . 324
(j) The arbitrator and the appointing authority 325
(k) Informing the penal authorities of the illegality . . . . . . . . . . . . . . . . . . . 334

5. How should or must the arbitrator treat illegality *when admitted*? . . . . . . . . . . . . 337
6. Should or must the arbitrator, *sua sponte*,
decide illegality when *not* alleged?. . . . . . 339

Chapter IX. Legal consequences of a finding or
admission of corruption . . . . . . . . . . . . . . 352

A. Introduction . . . . . . . . . . . . . . . . . . . 352
B. Jurisdiction and admissibility versus the merits:
general conceptual challenges . . . . . . . . . . 354

1. Issues common to commercial and investment treaty context . . . . . . . . . . . . . 355

     *(a)* Time and cost of adjudication . . . . . . 355
     *(b)* Assessment of the issue at an early, uninformed stage . . . . . . . . . . . . 356
     *(c)* The right of the arbitrator to confirm his authority. . . . . . . . . . . . . . . . . 357
     *(d)* Waiver of objections by the party . . . . 358
     *(e)* Characterization of the objection or defence . . . . . . . . . . . . . . . . . 359
     *(f)* Tribunal considerations in making the characterization . . . . . . . . . . . . . 359
     *(g)* Bifurcation and the further arbitral proceedings. . . . . . . . . . . . . . . . . 360

  2. Differences between commercial and investment treaty context . . . . . . . . . . . . . 362

     *(a)* Perspectives on time and cost of adjudication . . . . . . . . . . . . . . . . . . 362
     *(b)* Trends in requesting and granting requests for bifurcation. . . . . . . . . . . . . . 362
     *(c)* The applicable law or laws . . . . . . . . 363
     *(d)* Privity of contract versus "consent" . . . 364
     *(e)* Distinguishing jurisdiction and admissibility. . . . . . . . . . . . . . . . . . . . 365

C. Jurisdiction and admissibility versus the merits: the illegality and corruption context . . . . . . 370

  1. Issues common to the commercial and investment treaty context . . . . . . . . . . . . . 370

     *(a)* Jurisdiction and admissibility as early-stage problems . . . . . . . . . . . . . . 370
     *(b)* The form of decision and the further merits proceedings . . . . . . . . . . . 371
     *(c)* Proof and law . . . . . . . . . . . . . . 373

  2. Differences between the commercial and investment treaty context . . . . . . . . . 373

     *(a)* Reciprocal allegations of corruption . . . 373
     *(b)* Legality of the investment as a gateway issue. . . . . . . . . . . . . . . . . . . 374
     *(c)* Enforceability of the award and corruption 379

D. Legal consequences and effects of a positive finding of illegality or corruption . . . . . . . 379

  1. The investment treaty context and claimant investor illegality . . . . . . . . . . . . . . 380

*(a)* Legality as a prerequisite for jurisdiction
and consent . . . . . . . . . . . . . . . . .   380
*(b)* Jurisdiction and estoppel based on "unclean hands"  . . . . . . . . . . . . . . .   390
*(c)* The Unclean Hands Doctrine and "equal
fault" or "mutual fault" . . . . . . . . . .   403
*(d)* Arbitrability and acts of bribery  . . . . .   407

2. The commercial arbitration context and
claimant illegality. . . . . . . . . . . . . . .   412

*(a)* Possible denial of benefits of arbitration
agreement, resulting in lack of *jurisdiction*?. . . . . . . . . . . . . . . . . . . .   412
*(b)* Where the contract was "made" illegally,
is jurisdiction affected? . . . . . . . . . .   413
*(c)* Inadmissibility or voidness on the basis
of "unclean hands" . . . . . . . . . . . .   413
*(d)* Inadmissibility or voidness on the basis
of breach of public policy . . . . . . . .   415

Chapter X. Justifications, excuses and defences for
illegal conduct . . . . . . . . . . . . . . . . . . . .   417

A. Introduction  . . . . . . . . . . . . . . . . . . .   417
B. Conceptual challenges generally . . . . . . . . .   417

1. Issues common to the commercial and investment treaty context . . . . . . . . . . . . . .   417
2. Differences between the commercial and
investment treaty context . . . . . . . . . . .   419

C. The specific context of illegality and corruption   420

1. Issues common to the commercial and investment context  . . . . . . . . . . . . . . . .   420
2. Differences between the commercial and
investment treaty context . . . . . . . . . . .   420

D. Specific defences in the context of illegality and
corruption  . . . . . . . . . . . . . . . . . . . .   421

1. Unintentional acts of bribery by the claimant or respondent . . . . . . . . . . . . . .   421
2. "Facilitation payments" by the claimant to
the respondent  . . . . . . . . . . . . . . .   422
3. Lawfulness of activity of the claimant in the
respondent host State as an excuse . . . . . .   423
4. Unlawfulness of activity of the claimant in
the respondent host State as a justification. .   424

    5. Self-help or self-defence, duress, economic necessity by the claimant . . . . . . . . . . 427
    6. Justification or excuse on the basis of alleged widespread corruption . . . . . . . . . . . 431
    7. Economic necessity as the defence by the State to request for a bribe from the claimant 433

Chapter XI. Standards of review of arbitral awards in the corruption context. . . . . . . . . . . . . . 435

  A. Introduction . . . . . . . . . . . . . . . . . 435
  B. Public policy-related enforceability issues in the corruption context . . . . . . . . . . . . . . . 438

    1. Which public policy?. . . . . . . . . . . . 438

      *(a)* Public policy at the seat or as defined by the seat, if any . . . . . . . . . . . . 438
      *(b)* Public policy at the place or places of attempted enforcement, if any . . . . . . 440

    2. Competing mandates of public policy and finality . . . . . . . . . . . . . . . . . . 441

      *(a)* *Westacre*. . . . . . . . . . . . . . . . 441
      *(b)* *Soleimany* . . . . . . . . . . . . . . . 445
      *(c)* *Hilmarton* . . . . . . . . . . . . . . . 449
      *(d)* Reconciling *Westacre, Soleimany* and *Hilmarton* . . . . . . . . . . . . . . . 451

    3. Public policy as a content- or results-oriented approach . . . . . . . . . . . . . . . . . 454

  C. Conclusion . . . . . . . . . . . . . . . . . . 458

Bibliography . . . . . . . . . . . . . . . . . . . . 472

About the author . . . . . . . . . . . . . . . . . . 487

  Biographical note . . . . . . . . . . . . . . . . 487
  Principal publications . . . . . . . . . . . . . . 488

## INTRODUCTION

Competence-competence[1] on the one hand and bribery and corruption[2] on the other have, for different reasons, been mainstays of international dispute resolution thought and practice for the longest time[3]. Yet in recent decades and even just the last few years, their intersection has become increasingly important, and problematic.

Important in the sense that competence-competence have become increasingly rooted and accepted in legal thought and practice across national and cultural borders[4], including in the previously hesitant common law

---

[1] E. Gaillard and J. Savage (eds.), *Fouchard, Gaillard, Goldman on International Commercial Arbitration*, The Hague, Kluwer Law International, 1999, paras. 650 *et seq.*

[2] An overview on the issues of bribery and corruption in international arbitration is given by A. Sayed, *Corruption in International Trade and Commercial Arbitration*, The Hague, Kluwer Law International, 2004.

[3] F. G. de Cossio, "The Compétence-Compétence Principle, Revisited", *Journal of International Arbitration*, Vol. 24 (2007), p. 231, states that competence-competence is "[o]ne of the most venerable and important principles of arbitration law". Corruption and bribery moved into the spotlight in 1963 with an ICC award issued by sole-arbitrator Gunnar Lagergren. In his award, Judge Lagergren declined jurisdiction because the parties had agreed to bribe Argentine officials and therefore "forfeited any right to ask for assistance of the machinery of justice (national courts or arbitral tribunals) in settling their disputes". *Mr. X, Buenos Aires* v. *Company A*, ICC Case No. 1110, *Arbitration International*, Vol. 10 (1994), p. 293.

[4] G. B. Born, *International Commercial Arbitration*, The Hague, Kluwer Law International, 2009, pp. 855 *et seq.*

sphere[5]. And important in the sense that, regrettably, forms of illegality extending to corruption and bribery have found their way more and more into international dispute resolution[6]. Problematic — and here hopefully lies the contribution of these lectures — in the sense that while competence-competence has generally found a uniform definition and acceptance[7], in an age of increasing globalization and cross-pollination, what is illegal is not always clear[8]. And what consequences illegality can, should or must have for the authority of the arbitrator to adjudicate an international dispute is likewise not always apparent.

---

[5] Regardless of contentual differences, the principle of competence-competence is accepted and known in common law jurisdictions. In the United States, the contemporary approach towards competence-competence is grounded in large part in the Supreme Court's decision *First Options of Chicago, Inc.* v. *Kaplan*, 514 US 938 (1995). Regarding the development of competence-competence in England, see P. Gross, "Competence of Competence: An English View", *Arbitration International*, Vol. 8 (1992), pp. 205 *et seq.*

[6] See for example A. Crivellaro, "Arbitration Case Law on Bribery: Issues of Arbitrability, Contract Validity, Merits and Evidence", in K. Karsten and A. Berkeley, *Arbitration, Money Laundering, Corruption and Fraud*, Dossiers — ICC Institute of World Business Law (September 2003), pp. 109 *et seq.*

[7] See, among many, N. Blackaby and C. Partasides with A. Redfern and M. Hunter, *Redfern and Hunter on International Arbitration*, 5th ed., Oxford, Oxford University Press, 2009, para. 5.99 ("However, the usual practice under modern international and institutional rules of arbitration is to spell out in express terms the power of an arbitral tribunal to decide upon its own jurisdiction or, as it is often put, its competence to decide upon is own competence").

[8] See for example M. Hwang and K. Lim, "Corruption in Arbitration — Law and Reality", *Asian International Arbitration Journal*, Vol. 8 (2012), p. 4.

These lectures seek to define the problem and provide acceptable solutions where possible, all the while attempting to derive support from a mixture of stringent dogmatic approach and pragmatic attention to real-life expectations and conduct. More so than in many other areas of private international law and international dispute resolution, the intersection between the authority of the arbitrator and the possible illegality of the subject matter or parties' conduct poses a particular challenge[9].

That challenge is to postulate proper solutions under the law, including principles of transnational or international law[10], to conduct which can take on a multiplicity of appearances due to various cultural understandings of what is legal and what is not in commercial life. The pat statement, if also correct, that bribery and corruption are not only illegal but also offend transnational or international public policy[11] does not relieve the arbitrator, or these lectures, from the burden of scrutinizing that statement doctrinally and exploring its consequences in a period of ever-increasing globalization of means of doing business.

Accordingly, these lectures address the question of competence-competence and illegality in contracts and

---

[9] M. A. Raouf, "How Should International Arbitrators Tackle Corruption Issues?", *ICSID Review — Foreign Investment Law Journal*, Vol. 24 (2009), p. 119.

[10] N. Blackaby and C. Partasides with A. Redfern and M. Hunter, *supra* footnote 7, paras. 3.140 and 3.166.

[11] ICC Case No. 1110, *supra* footnote 3, p. 293. ("Such corruption is an international evil; it is contrary to good morals and to an international public policy common to the community of nations"). According to G. Bottini, "Legality of Investments under ICSID Jurisdiction", in M. Waibel *et al.* (eds.), *The Backlash against Investment Arbitration*, Kluwer Law International, 2010, p. 299, "there is a growing consensus that corruption is against the international *ordre public*".

arbitration agreements generously and broadly, in ways which transcend the actual title.

*First*, they examine not only competence-competence in the strict sense of the largely accepted definition of the term[12], but also extend the discussion to other aspects of the potential authority of the arbitral tribunal which are not necessarily encompassed by the term, and which may be seen as extending broader or narrower prerogatives to the arbitrator. These include arbitrability[13], separability[14] and jurisdiction[15].

*Second*, they examine illegality largely, but not exclusively, in the context of corruption, and intentionally treat important manifestations of illegality such as fraud[16], including fraud in the factum[17] and fraud in the inducement[18], only in passing and by comparison. This treatment is a reflection of choice and economy, but also of the intention to address the most commercially and legally relevant illegality of our times, namely bribery both in the public and the private sphere.

*Third*, they examine corruption and bribery in the international sphere. They thereby intentionally do not have the ambition of treating the tension between arbitral powers and illegality in exclusively domestic law and a domestic arbitration context. This would inevitably lead to an anecdotal and piecemeal result. At the same time, the lectures are mindful of, and seek to benefit from, the simple fact that particularly in international commercial arbitration, the challenge resides

---

[12] See *supra* footnote 7.
[13] See *infra* Chapter V.B.3.
[14] See *infra* Chapter V.B.2.
[15] See *infra* Chapter V.B, Chapter IX.B and Chapter IX.C.
[16] See *infra* Chapter II.D.
[17] See *infra* Chapter II.A.4.
[18] *Ibid*.

precisely in the intersection between the agreement to a particular national substantive law including mandatory norms on the one hand[19] and the possible application of some other national or supranational norms on the other[20].

*Fourth*, they examine and indeed compare and contrast international commercial arbitration and international investment and investment treaty-based arbitration. Consideration of this topic without inclusion of investment arbitration, whose importance has escalated in the short time period of roughly the last 20 years[21], would be an indefensible disregard of one of the main and most publicly accessible sources of case law and commentary on the subject, namely illegality in relation to foreign investors and government officials.

*Fifth*, as a consequence these lectures also examine arbitration agreements both in the conventional sense of an arbitration clause in a commercial contract between parties having "privity"[22] and arbitration agreements in the sense of an investment treaty between a foreign investor and a host State without such "privity"

---

[19] G. B. Born, *supra* footnote 4, pp. 2159 *et seq.*

[20] A. Sayed, *supra* footnote 2, p. 2.

[21] One can regard *Asian Agricultural Products Ltd. (AAPL)* v. *Republic of Sri Lanka*, ICSID Case No. ARB/87/3, Final Award, 27 June 1990, *ICSID Review — Foreign Investment Law Journal*, Vol. 6 (1991), pp. 526 *et seq.*, as the beginning of the "boom" of investment arbitration. In its award, the arbitral tribunal stated in paragraph 18 that "the present case is the first instance in which the Centre has been seized by an arbitration request exclusively based on a treaty provision and not on implementation of a freely negotiated arbitration agreement . . .". With respect to the importance of investment arbitration, see C. McLachlan, L. Shore and M. Weiniger, *International Investment Arbitration — Substantive Principles*, Oxford, Oxford University Press, 2007, para. 1.07.

[22] See *infra* Chapter III.A.1.

but on the basis of a bilateral or multilateral State-to-State treaty or agreement for the mutual protection of foreign investments generally[23] or in a particular field such as energy[24].

On the basis of the foregoing, these lectures are both broad and narrow, depending on the particular intersection between competence and illegality being addressed, but in ways which may provide greater coherence and guidance than has prevailed up to now. Indeed it is precisely the lack of sufficient coherence with which this subject has been addressed that makes it important and topical. It is hoped that these lectures can contribute to providing further coherence in those areas where it is possible and desirable, identifying the areas where it is not necessarily possible or desirable, and suggesting a structure for consideration of future developments.

To that end, the structure of the lectures is as follows:

Chapter I. Definition of the subject;

Chapter II. The meaning of "illegality";

Chapter III. The context of private international law versus public international law;

Chapter IV. The question of the applicable law or laws;

Chapter V. Corruption allegations, suspicions, findings and admissions;

Chapter VI. The burden of proof and the standard of proof of illegality;

Chapter VII. Attribution of illegal actions and knowledge of the State;

Chapter VIII. The rights and duties of the arbitrator;

---

[23] See *infra* Chapter III.A.3.

[24] See *infra* Chapter I.D regarding the importance and development of energy-related Investment Arbitration.

Chapter IX. Legal consequences of a finding or admission of corruption;

Chapter X. Justifications, excuses and defences for illegal conduct; and

Chapter XI. Standards of review of arbitral awards in the corruption context.

## CHAPTER I

## DEFINITION OF THE SUBJECT

### A. Initial Focus and Questions

The competence-competence of the arbitral tribunal in the face of illegality in contracts and particularly arbitration agreements represents the intersection between two of the most important aspects of international dispute resolution in our time, in both private and public international law. Indeed generally speaking and in the context of these lectures, it represents a welcome and not always present opportunity to combine private and public international law analysis to attempt to achieve a synthesis.

A focus solely on private international law would unacceptably turn a blind eye to transnational and international public policy and to the entire domain of public international claim claims, particularly in investment protection-related arbitration. A focus only on public international law, as tempting as this might be under the rubric of globalization of public policy, would of course absurdly shut out claims arising under a national material law, almost the entirety of international commercial arbitration, and those aspects of commercial arbitration which may be relevant for investment treaty claims.

Those two key aspects of international dispute resolution today are on the one hand the authority of the arbitral tribunal and on the other hand the role of corruption in international commercial life. They come together at the latest when aspects of commercial life are sought to be interjected into international commercial or treaty protection claims to be resolved by arbitration.

On the level of the authority of the arbitral tribunal, even before we address the context of illegality we are confronted with a myriad of possible tensions, the discussion of which would exceed the present scope.

Suffice it to say that in present-day concepts and practice of domestic and especially international arbitration, the arbitrator has both rights and duties in the most basic sense. They are to be aligned in some effective and enforceable way with the rights and duties of the parties whose agreement, or putative agreement, gave rise to his role in the first place.

Those rights and duties are reflected in the most basis sense in such statutory frameworks as the UNCITRAL Model Law on International Commercial Arbitration[25], such institutional arbitration rules as those of the International Chamber of Commerce[26] and the International Centre for Settlement of Investment Disputes[27], and such guidelines as the International Bar Association (IBA) Rules on the Taking of Evidence in International Arbitration[28]. The arbitrator's and the parties' respective rights and duties may clash: where does the discretion of the tribunal to conduct the proceedings[29] and take evidence[30] as it sees fit and with due speed and efficiency conflict with the rights of the parties to the right to be heard[31], equal treatment[32] and

---

[25] http://www.uncitral.org/pdf/english/texts/arbitration/ml-arb/07-86998_Ebook.pdf.

[26] http://www.iccwbo.org/products-and-services/arbitration-and-adr/arbitration/icc-rules-of-arbitration.

[27] https://icsid.worldbank.org/ICSID/StaticFiles/basic-doc/CRR_English-final.pdf.

[28] http://www.ibanet.org/Publications/publications_IBA_guides_and_free_materials.aspx#takingevidence.

[29] E.g. Art. 19 (2), UNCITRAL Model Law.

[30] E.g. Arts. 17 (2) *(d)*, 27, UNCITRAL Model Law.

[31] E.g. Art. 24, UNCITRAL Model Law.

[32] E.g. Art. 18, UNCITRAL Model Law.

general respect for their party autonomy[33] including regarding the procedure itself?

Is the arbitrator a servant of the parties, both because he thanks his office to a creature of contract[34] and because the parties can attempt to remove him from office under certain circumstances[35] during the course of the arbitration? Or rather is the arbitrator, notwithstanding and subject to those two indisputable facts, fully in charge of the arbitration and the way in which he investigates the facts — as long as the right to be heard, equal treatment and any other enforceability standards, particularly under the law of the seat, are not violated?

This potential for clash is one of the most important and intriguing challenges of our times in the area of international arbitration, all the more so because of the increasing number of competing standards, customs, expectations and therefore outcomes resulting from cross-border commerce and dispute resolution. As recently as 20 or 30 years ago in some quarters a sense reigned that the arbitral tribunal was firmly in charge once the parties had passed the baton to it and could even unilaterally take steps to try to settle the dispute. The sense of balance has likely changed, and this is for the better.

The powers and rights in the arbitrator's quiver have not been reduced either in law or in practice in recent years. Rather, they may be seen as having been tempered by the increasing pro-active of parties and counsel inspired by Anglo-American concepts of the adversarial philosophy of dispute resolution[36]. Party

---

[33] E.g. Art. 19 (1), UNCITRAL Model Law.

[34] E. Gaillard and J. Savage (eds.), *supra* footnote 1, paras. 1102 *et seq.*

[35] See e.g. the possibility of challenging the arbitrator pursuant to Arts. 12 (2), 13, UNCITRAL Model Law.

[36] See generally M. R. Freedman, *Lawyers' Ethics in an Adversary System*, Indianapolis, Bobbs-Merrill, 1975.

autonomy, which existed no less firmly on paper 30 years ago than today, has been bolstered by party and counsel expectations of involvement in the process and procedure. This has been coupled with an increasing vigilance in monitoring the conduct of the proceedings for any enforceability defects under the law of the seat or the law of a putative place of recognition and enforcement [37].

The rise in importance of investment protection arbitration particularly under the auspices of ICSID, with its pronounced accessibility and transparency as compared with most commercial arbitrations [38], has served to accelerate this process in some respects. Investment-treaty based arbitrations are typically an amalgam of different nationalities including nationalities unrelated to the parties. The rules of procedure in many such arbitrations are less rote than under national laws of arbitration including the UNCITRAL Model Law. Preliminary objections to jurisdiction and admissibility are raised by State respondents with regularity [39]. Both partial and final awards are challenged in annulment proceedings which themselves receive more notoriety than comparable set aside proceedings before most leading national courts. The result is that while parties usually wish competent and indeed robust arbi-

---

[37] C. Chatterjee, "The Reality of the Party Autonomy Rule in International Arbitration", *Journal of International Arbitration*, Vol. 20 (2003), p. 557, states that the party autonomy rule has been replaced by a lawyer autonomy rule.

[38] On the World Bank's website, one can find relevant aspects of the various ICSID arbitrations (Parties, Counsels, Arbitral Tribunals, Awards, etc.); https://icsid.worldbank.org/ICSID/Index.jsp. See also C. McLachlan, L. Shore and M. Weiniger, *supra* footnote 21, paras. 3.42 *et seq*.

[39] On the basis of Article 41 of the ICSID Arbitration Rules.

trators, parties are also more vigilant than ever about
ensuring that party autonomy does not disappear once
the arbitral tribunal is seised with the file.

Against this fascinating and complicated backdrop,
the question of the authority of the arbitral tribunal
generally becomes even more complex once issues of
illegality, including corruption and bribery, are interjected. The arbitral tribunal, both in commercial arbitration and in investment-treaty disputes although in
different ways, must consider the existence, nature and
extent of its authority, of its rights. These include the
authority of the arbitrator to address and to make binding decisions related to disputes in which corruption is
alleged, suspected, admitted or otherwise proven.

Depending upon the circumstances, each one or
only one of these elements — allegations, suspicions,
admissions or proof — may be present. Each one may
affect differently the analysis of the existence, nature
and extent of authority to investigate and to make decisions of a binding nature. The task becomes all the
more difficult when one considers that indicia of corruption and bribery, and indeed most forms of illegal
conduct, are not carried out in the open, but rather are
usually intentionally and often assiduously concealed,
disguised, distorted or destroyed to remove all traces[40].
Depending upon the applicable rules and law and the
backgrounds of the parties and arbitrators, the arbitral
tribunal may come to different conclusions as to how
far its authority goes to investigate and to rule on cor-

---

[40] The *United Nations Anti-Corruption Toolkit*, 3rd ed.,
2004, p. 464 *sub* Tool #34: "Senior officials actively
engaged in corruption are often in a position to impede
investigations and destroy or conceal evidence, . . .". The
entire text of the *United Nations Anti-Corruption Toolkit*
can be retrieved from http://www.unodc.org/pdf/crime/
corruption/toolkit/corruption_un_anti_corruption_toolkit_s
ep04.pdf.

ruption issues. This will be the case especially when based on "mere" suspicion and even suspicion shared by the arbitrators.

It may be challenging enough already for an arbitrator to decide how far its investigative prerogatives extend, and whether they are delimited by the allegations and prayers for relief of the parties themselves[41]. Where those allegations and prayers for relief raise issues of corruption, or where they do not do so but the arbitral tribunal suspects corruption as part of the mix, the extent of the arbitrator's authority may be in question. To add to the complexity, in international disputes and particularly investment protection arbitrations based in public international law, the question arises of which substantive and procedural legal standards apply to the extent of the investigative rights and duties.

## B. The Range of Questions Seeking Answers

These lectures seek to raise and answer the following questions in the context of the foregoing landscape:

*First, how can, should or must an arbitral tribunal conduct itself in the face of suspected illegality of a contract in relation to which it is meant to adjudicate a dispute?*

Depending upon the applicable law, rules and other context, the arbitral tribunal may have discretion, or it may have discretion with a hortatory component

---

[41] R. Kreindler, "Aspects of Illegality in the Formation and Performance of Contracts", in A. J. van den Berg (ed.), *International Commercial Arbitration: Important Contemporary Questions*, ICCA Congress Series, 2002, London, Vol. 11, Kluwer Law International, 2003, pp. 225 *et seq.*

("should")[42], or the arbitral tribunal may have no choice and in fact be obligated to take or not take certain action[43]. Furthermore, apart from the statutory or other agreed landscape, the answer to how the arbitrator should conduct himself may depend on the following: whether the illegality is suspected by a party, suspected by a party and also the arbitral tribunal, or suspected solely by the arbitrator without any party reference to illegality.

Where a party suspects or purports to suspect illegality on the side of the opposing party and includes such allegations in its prayers for relief and statement of case, then the issue, whether true or not, is presumably firmly part of the *petita* and will need to be addressed by the arbitrator — lest he fail to comply with his mission[44]. Where a party does not make such an allegation and the arbitrator independently harbours a suspicion of illegality, then the question arises of whether the arbitral prerogative to investigate the facts and circumstances with all appropriate means[45] extends to a suspicion not raised by any party. The risk might be one of *ultra petita* and not *infra petita*[46], but with no less dire consequences for the enforceability[47] of the award.

---

[42] R. Kreindler, "Public Policy and Corruption in International Arbitration: A Perspective for Russian Related Disputes", *Arbitration*, Vol. 72 (2006), pp. 242 *et seq.*; A. Sayed, *supra* footnote 2, p. 33.

[43] M. Hwang and K. Lim, *supra* footnote 8, pp. 18 *et seq.*

[44] *World Duty Free Company Limited* v. *The Republic of Kenya*, ICSID Case No. ARB/00/7, Award, 4 October 2006, available at http://ita.law.uvic.ca/documents/WDFv.KenyaAward.pdf.

[45] M. Hwang and K. Lim, *supra* footnote 8, pp. 18 *et seq.*

[46] R. Kreindler, *supra* footnote 41, pp. 235 *et seq.*

[47] Art. V (1) *(c)* of the 1958 Convention on the Recognition and Enforcement of Foreign Arbitral Awards:

Furthermore, query whether the answer to these questions may be seen as depending on the nature and characterization of the relationship between the arbitrator and the parties or between the arbitrator, the parties and the arbitral institution, if any.

In commercial arbitrations based on a conventional arbitration clause, the investigative and inquisitorial rights and duties of the arbitrator vis-à-vis the parties are usually defined loosely and generously, as mentioned above[48].

The wide discretion expressly bestowed on the arbitrator, for example under the UNCITRAL Model Law[49] or the ICC Rules of Arbitration[50], provides a generous basis for the arbitrator to "follow his nose" respecting suspicions of corruption.

But again he or she may do so only within the confines of due process, equal treatment and public policy, and of course only to the extent, antecedently,

---

"Recognition and enforcement of the award may be refused at the request of the party against whom it is invoked, only if that party furnishes to the competent authority where the recognition and enforcement is sought, proof that: . . . The award deals with a difference not contemplated by or not falling within the terms of the submission to arbitration, or *it contains decisions on matters beyond the scope of the submission to arbitration* . . ." (Emphasis added.)

See also Art. 34 (2) *(a)* (iii), UNICTRAL Model Law, with almost the same wording.

[48] See *supra* footnote 42 and footnote 43.

[49] Art. 19 (2), UNCITRAL Model Law:

"Failing such agreement, the arbitral tribunal may, subject to the provisions of this Law, conduct the arbitration in such manner as it considers appropriate. The power conferred upon the arbitral tribunal includes the power to determine the admissibility, relevance, materiality and weight of any evidence."

[50] Art. 22, ICC Rules of Arbitration.

the requirements of competence[51] and arbitrability[52] are fulfilled.

Essentially uniquely, many German commentators have postulated a contract between and among the arbitrators, the parties and the institution, if any[53]. This notion, which appears to have lost momentum in recent years and since the 1998 entry into force of the German Arbitration Act contained in the Tenth Book of the German Civil Procedure Code[54], has not found acceptance in most other jurisdictions. For purposes of the investigative powers of the arbitral tribunal in the face of illegality, it is submitted here that even accepting such notion, it does not clearly add to or bolster the prerogatives of the arbitrator. The one possible exception might be the extent to which the arbitrator has a right or even a duty to inform the arbitral institution of a suspicion or finding of illegality, irrespective of whether the parties have themselves raised such issue, as part of a disclosure obligation to the institution. This question will be addressed later below, while the conclusion is that the duty, if any, to notify the institution

---

[51] R. Mirzayev, "International Investment Protection Regime and Criminal Investigations", *Journal of International Arbitration*, Vol. 29 (2012), p. 83.

[52] G. B. Born, *supra* footnote 4, pp. 771 and 803.

[53] J. Münch, Vorbemerkung zu den §§ 1034 *et seq.*, *Münchener Kommentar zur Zivilprozessordnung*, 3rd ed., Munich, Beckverlag, 2008, para. 5; W. Voit, Sec. 1035, *Musielak Kommentar zur Zivilprozessordnung*, 9th ed., Munich, Verlag Franz Vahlen, 2012, Rn. 22; P. Schlosser, Vorbemerkungen vor § 1025, *Stein/Jonas Kommentar zur Zivilprozessordnung*, 22nd ed., Tübingen, Mohr Siebeck, 2002, para. 7; B. von Hoffman, "Der internationale Schiedsrichtervertrag — eine kollisionsrechtliche Skizze", *Festschrift für Ottoarndt Glossner zum 70. Geburtstag*, Heidelberg, Verlag Recht und Wirtschaft, 1993, pp. 143 *et seq.*

[54] Secs. 1026-1066, German Civil Procedure Code.

will not depend upon whether a contract in the German sense is deemed to exist.

Furthermore, the nature and characterization of the relationship between the arbitrator and the parties or between the arbitrator, the parties and the arbitral institution, if any, may take on a different hue in the case of treaty-based disputes. In an arbitration "without privity" in which the agreement to arbitrate between the foreign investor and the host State is based on an arbitration agreement in a State-to-State investment treaty to which the investor was not a party, may the investigative powers of the tribunal thereby have a different scope, whether greater or lesser?

In a typical ICSID Convention arbitration arising out of a bilateral investment treaty providing for ICSID, the express authority to investigate illegality is arguably not particularly different than in a commercial arbitration. Under the ICSID Convention and the ICSID Arbitration Rules[55], essentially the arbitral tribunal will have comparable authority. As to whether the arbitral tribunal will have a comparable duty to investigate, here the answer will not be found in the applicable rules any more directly than it is contained in commercial arbitration rules such as those of the ICC, namely not at all.

Still a further question will arise, addressed below, of whether the foundation of treaty-based jurisdiction, namely a deemed consent by the host State respondent to ICSID arbitration by any foreign investor with whom it has no privity, could affect the extent of the treaty-based arbitral tribunal's right or duty to investigate illegality and how he should conduct himself. Here too, as discussed below[56], how the tribunal con-

---

[55] See *supra* footnote 27.
[56] Concerning the rights and duties of the tribunal in the face of illegality, see *infra* Chapter VIII.

ducts itself includes what is its assessment of competence, arbitrability, severability and admissibility. The
answers to these questions — for example, are there
grounds for a jurisdictional or admissibility objection
based on illegality — by the tribunal in the illegality
context may indeed be different for a treaty-based
tribunal than for a commercial arbitrator relying on a
standard arbitration clause in a contract.

*Second, how should an arbitral tribunal behave
where illegality is admitted or is otherwise manifest?*

As stated previously, depending upon the applicable
law, rules and other context, the arbitral tribunal may
have a right or a duty to investigate allegations of corruption and may have a right or a duty to draw particular consequences from the existence of such allegation for the conduct of the proceedings[57]. And again,
apart from the statutory or other agreed landscape, the
answer to how the arbitrator should conduct himself
may depend on whether the illegality is suspected by
a party, suspected by a party and also the arbitral tribunal, or suspected solely by the arbitrator without any
party reference to illegality.

Is a meaningful distinction to be drawn where the
corruption or bribery is not alleged and not suspected,
but rather is admitted or is otherwise manifest?
Invariably, an admission of illegality, assuming the
veracity of the admission, would render moot the right
or duty of the arbitrator to investigate whether there is
an illegality. At the same time, the admission and the
acceptance of it as true would not absolve the arbitrator
of any duty which he might have to draw consequences
from the admission, including respecting his own competence, the arbitrability of the claim, the separability
of the arbitration agreement and the admissibility of
the underlying claim on the merits.

---

[57] R. Kreindler, *supra* footnote 42, p. 246.

If the arbitrator has discretion as to such consequences, his discretion may be limited by the simple
fact that the illegality is admitted for all to see. If the
arbitrator has no discretion as to the consequences to
be drawn and indeed a consequence may be the ousting
of his own further jurisdiction, then his discretion may
extend solely to the confirmation of the absence of
such jurisdiction, pursuant to the competence-competence doctrine.

As for the particular consequences, it will be discussed below[58] how they may differ depending upon
whether the admission of illegality is by the claimant
party, the respondent party, or for that matter both parties respectively. One of the intriguing aspects of the
intersection between arbitration and illegality is the
possibility, depending on the circumstances, for a party
to raise and admit its own illegality as a justification,
excuse or defence, particularly with the goal of negat-
ing the competence of the tribunal or the admissibility
of the underlying claim or both. And once again, particularly in this area of jurisdiction or admissibility the
answers to these questions by the tribunal in the illegality context may indeed be different for a treaty-
based tribunal than for a commercial arbitrator relying
on a standard arbitration clause in a contract[59].

*Third, should the nature or severity of a would-be
illegality make a difference to the assessment by the
arbitrator of certain core issues?*

Just as we will see that the definition of illegality
and even of corruption or bribery is not uniform and

---

[58] See *infra* Chapter II.B.
[59] See J. W. Yackee, "Investment Treaties & Investment
Corruption: An Emerging Defense for Host States",
*Virginia Journal for International Law*, Vol. 52 (2012),
pp. 734 *et seq.*, who raises several points which are
relevant for ICSID tribunals addressing the question of
corruption in BIT-based arbitrations.

that one person's illegality is another person's innocu-
ous "influence peddling"[60], so too illegality in the
context of arbitration disputes may be egregious, it
may be *de minimis*[61] or it may be somewhere in
between. The question arises of whether any illegality,
as long as it has been characterized as such, should be
considered in the same way for purposes of any consequences for jurisdiction, for the separability of the
agreement to arbitrate from the illegal contract, for the
arbitrability of claims arising out or related to the
underlying illegality, for the admissibility of such
claims, and for the decision whether to assess those
very consequences only as an issue of the "full merits"
or instead early on as a preliminary pre-merits issue.

It may be considered that there is a threshold or tripwire of illegality, which, once it is passed, should give
rise to the same consequences for each of these questions. It may instead be considered that even if there is
such a tripwire, certain conduct may be more egre-
giously illegal than other, and that such difference can
or should be taken into account in considering the
consequences for competence and the like. Finally, in

---

[60] A. Sayed, *supra* footnote 2, p. 199 with footnote
561. According to H. Raeschke-Kessler and D. Gottwald,
"Corruption", in R. Muchlinski *et al*. (eds.), *The Oxford
Handbook of International Investment Law*, New York,
Oxford University Press, 2008, p. 587, influence peddling
means giving, offering or promising of an undue advantage to a person who then sells his influence to the
Government.
[61] One can, for example, refer to the Kenyan
"Harambee" system which "ha[s] its root in the African
culture where societies made collective contribution
toward individual or communal activities". *World Duty
Free* v. *Kenya*, *supra* footnote 44, para. 134. However, the
arbitral tribunal in that case found that this system could
not justify bribes given to government officials, *ibid*.,
para. 170.

international arbitration it may be considered that the fact that one and the same conduct constitutes an illegality under one body of law but not under another should be considered in the assessment of the tribunal, for example, illegality under the law at the place of performance but legality under the law at the seat of arbitration — or vice versa[62].

Again, in the context of investment-treaty arbitration or other arbitrations in which there is an overlay between public international law principles and local law (e.g., of the host State), illegality may lie under the one standard but not under the other. In such cases, the arbitral tribunal will be called upon to decide whether the one result supersedes the other and if so with what consequences. In the investment area, there will also be the notable difference that in ICSID arbitration, unlike commercial arbitration, there is no juridical seat with its own *lex arbitri*, whereas in commercial arbitration as well as in investment arbitrations which do have a seat the question of illegality will invariably need to be examined under the law of arbitration.

Irrespective of which school of thought one subscribes to as to whether the arbitrator has a true duty to render an enforceable award or rather simply a best efforts obligation[63], in the case of a seat the arbitrator has one clear port of call for enforceability, the *lex arbitri*. An illegality which triggers a ground for annulment of the award under the *lex arbitri*, and particularly a violation of public policy thereunder, will pose an immediate challenge, whereas an illegality under the law of a possible place of enforcement elsewhere

---

[62] R. Kreindler, *supra* footnote 41, pp. 248 *et seq*.

[63] A summary regarding this issue can be found at G. J. Horvath, "The Duty of the Tribunal to Render an Enforceable Award", *Journal of International Arbitration*, Vol. 18, 2001, pp. 135 *et seq*.

may be seen as less compelling and even ignorable. By
contrast, in an ICSID arbitration without a juridical
seat, the arbitrator has the — less clear — port of call
for enforceability of the annulment grounds under the
ICSID Convention[64]. While those annulment grounds
are express and few, they are not only unrooted from a
national *lex arbitri* including that of the host State, but
also do not include an express ground of violation of
public policy. The challenges posed by this situation
will also be addressed below as well[65].

*Fourth, when should the issue of competence or
jurisdiction hinge on whether the illicitness arguably
"tainted" the underlying contract* ab initio, *as opposed
to an illegality arising or becoming apparent only in
the course of later performance of the contract?*

The circumstances which affect the assessment of
competence or lack thereof may exist from the inception of the underlying contract (e.g., where a party was
not an original signatory[66]) or arise subsequently during the lifetime and performance of the contract (e.g.,
where a non-signatory is later deemed to have succeeded to or become a beneficiary of the signatory to
the contract[67]). Thus the elements necessary for jurisdiction or admissibility may exist at the time of entry
into effect of the contract but subsequently change, or
they may arise only after the entry into effect of the
contract as a result of a change.

On the level of illegality, similarly the circumstances giving rise to alleged or proven illegality may
be present from the beginning of the contract and

---

[64] Art. 52, ICSID Convention.
[65] See *infra* Chapter XI.
[66] E. Gaillard and J. Savage (eds.), *supra* footnote 1,
para. 724.
[67] N. Blackaby and C. Partasides with A. Redfern and
M. Hunter, *supra* footnote 7, para. 2.51.

indeed relate to the very inception of the same, or they may be linked to the later performance. The question arises of whether this temporal distinction makes a difference for the possible consequences relating to competence, arbitrability, separability and admissibility. In commercial arbitration, for example, the distinction is made between fraud in the factum and fraud in the inducement, with differing results for the nullity of the arbitration agreement contained within the main contract[68]. In investment arbitration, the distinction is made between illegality in the procuring of an investment and illegality in the maintaining of the same, and here too there may be differences, although not necessarily for the same reasons, as discussed below[69].

*Fifth, given suspected or manifest illegality, which rules of law or standards of law should apply as to whether and how to proceed respecting jurisdiction, separability, arbitrability and the merits of the dispute?*

Not only will a suspicion or finding of illegality depend on which substantive law standard is applied to the question, but so too the consequences which may flow from that illegality may differ depending on which law applies to the consequences. In international commercial arbitration, the suspicion or finding of illegality may impact on the coming into effect or the continued existence of the arbitration agreement as distinct from the underlying contract.

While the underlying contract will often be governed by a particular substantive law chosen by the parties, it does not necessarily follow that the arbitration agreement which may be tainted by that illegality

---

[68] G. B. Born, *supra* footnote 4, pp. 714 *et seq.* See also *infra* Chapter II.A.4.

[69] See *infra* Chapter II.F.

will be governed by the same law[70]. Usually, the parties will not have subjected the arbitration agreement expressly to a substantive law, and certainly not to a law different than the substantive law governing the contract. However, questions can arise where either the parties did not include a governing law clause for the main contract at all or, as is often the case, they agreed to apply the substantive law of one country to the contract and chose a seat of arbitration and thereby the *lex arbitri* of another country[71]. In the case of illegality, the conduct complained above may be illegal under the *lex causae* but not under the *lex arbitri* or vice versa, or the contract may be illegal under both laws but result in different consequences for jurisdiction, separability, arbitrability and the merits depending on the law[72].

Still different situations may arise in the investment treaty area, where particularly in ICSID arbitration there is no *lex arbitri* to begin with and the *lex causae* may be a mixture of public international law and local law principles which themselves are irreconcilable in

---

[70] E. Gaillard and J. Savage (eds.), *supra* footnote 1, para. 412. See with respect to determining the applicable law for the arbitration agreement P. Bernardini, "Arbitration Clauses: Achieving Effectiveness in the Law Applicable to the Arbitration Clause", in A. J. van den Berg (ed.), *Improving the Efficiency of Arbitration Agreements and Awards: 40 Years of Application of the New York Convention*, ICCA Congress Series, 1998, Paris, Vol. 9, Kluwer Law International, 1999, pp. 198 *et seq.* Bernardini also states that

"[e]xperience of negotiation of international contracts and of international arbitration shows that the issue of the law applicable to the arbitration clause receives no specific attention by the drafters of an international contract". *Ibid.*

[71] G. B. Born, *supra* footnote 4, pp. 470 *et seq.*
[72] G. B. Born, *supra* footnote 4, p. 425.

terms of what is illegal and what are the consequences once found illegal. Furthermore, even once the applicable law has been ascertained and the illegality established, the consequences for jurisdiction, separability, arbitrability and the merits may be different than in a comparable commercial arbitration, among other reasons because there is no conventional arbitration agreement and there is no classical contract involved.

*Sixth, what are the legal consequences of a finding of corruption?*

Indeed this is the elephant in the room and this is the question which has informed each and every prior question. It assumes that the arbitral tribunal has the authority to make a binding decision based on the illegality, at a minimum to deny its own competence. It assumes that the arbitrator has established that the illegality has a minimum severity or threshold to be relevant to the outcome. It assumes that irrespective of whether the illegality arose at the beginning or only later in the relationship, consequences can be drawn. And it assumes that the arbitrator has established which rules of law apply to the determination of the consequences.

It also assumes that the result can be allowed irrespective of whether it differs from the result in application of another law, such as the law of the place of performance, the law at a putative place of enforcement or even the substantive law chosen by the parties. It even assumes that the arbitral tribunal for particular reasons may intentionally disregard the choice of law especially if it concludes that the choice itself was a charade or an abuse of party autonomy designed to render legal what would otherwise be illegal. These questions are addressed at length below[73].

---

[73] See *infra* Chapter IV.

*Seventh, what are the standards for review of an arbitral award which has assigned such legal consequences?*

From the perspective of the consumer of arbitration, an arbitral award which is not enforceable is not worth the paper it is written on. Accordingly, enforceability of the award is the goal and the end game, and this is no less true for the arbitrator. In that end game, we assume that the arbitrator has established illegality, has established the applicable law, has established the consequences under that law, and has drawn those consequences in his award. It also assumes that the result indeed differs from the result in application of another law, such as the law of the place of performance, the law at a putative place of enforcement or even the substantive law chosen by the parties.

At the end of the day, all that matters is whether this award rendered on such a basis survives. "Survives" in terms of annulment under the law of arbitration at the seat of arbitration, in terms of annulment where there is no conventional seat of arbitration such as ICSID disputes, and in terms of opposition to recognition and enforcement at a different locale away from the seat of arbitration. Here too more coherence in the possible approaches has been wanting and an aim of these lectures is to assess whether and how such additional coherence is possible.

## C. *The Historical Setting in Commercial Arbitration*

It has been 50 years since an acute focus was placed, perhaps for the first time, on how an arbitral tribunal can, should or must conduct itself in the face of suspected or manifest illegality of a contract. The issue of illegality of contract in the context of arbitration has been examined from time to time over the last several decades.

However, it was particularly the award in ICC Case No. 1110 (1963), rendered by Gunnar Lagergren, which cast a sharp focus on issues of competence-competence and severability of the arbitration agreement in the face of a suspected or manifestly illegal contract[74].

The award has frequently been construed to stand, *inter alia*, for the proposition that disputes involving allegations of corruption are non-arbitrable, and even that an arbitrator must resign his mandate in the face of a manifestly illegal contract, without rendering an award of any kind on jurisdiction or the merits:

> "the agreement between the parties contemplated the bribing of Argentine officials . . . [p]arties who ally themselves in an enterprise of the present nature must realize that they have *forfeited any right to ask for assistance of the machinery of justice* (national courts or arbitral tribunals) in settling their disputes." (ICC Case No. 1110, *supra* footnote 3, at 282 (emphasis added).)

At the same time, the award enunciated

> "a general principle of law recognized by civilized nations that *contracts which seriously violate bonos mores or international public policy are invalid or at least unenforceable* and that they cannot be sanctioned by courts or arbitrators" (*ibid.*, at 293 (emphasis added)).

---

[74] ICC Case No. 1110, *supra* footnote 3. The Award was reprinted for the first time in full in J. G. Wetter, "Issues of Corruption before International Arbitral Tribunals: The Authentic Text and True Meaning of Judge Gunner Lagergren's 1963 Award in ICC Case No. 1110", *Arbitration International*, Vol. 10 (1994), pp. 277 *et seq.*

Since that time, various arbitral awards, national court rulings[75] and commentaries[76] have come to light respecting illegality in the formation and performance of contracts containing an agreement to arbitrate. Subsequent awards have largely rejected Lagergren's perceived notion of non-arbitrability. They have upheld the right of the arbitrator to exercise jurisdiction to rule on the merits of a dispute involving an illegal or allegedly illegal contract.

In such cases, the tribunal has often rejected the defence of voidness for, for example, corruption on the

---

[75] See, e.g., Tribunal Fédéral [Swiss Federal Tribunal], *National Power Corporation* v. *Westinghouse*, 2 September 2003, BGE 119 II 380, refusing to set aside an award dated 19 December 1991 which had found allegations of corruption not to have been proven; the highest Swiss court described as outdated the notion that disputes concerning allegations of corruption are not arbitrable. All "BGE"-judgments are available at http://www.bger.ch/index/juridiction/jurisdiction-inherit-template/jurisdiction-recht/jurisdiction-recht-leitentscheide1954.htm.

[76] Among the various commentators who have addressed issues of illegality of contract in a variety of forms are A. S. Kosheri and P. Leboulanger, "L'arbitrage face à la corruption et aux trafics d'influence", *Revue de l'arbitrage* (1984), pp. 3 *et seq.*; P. Mayer, "Le contrat illicite", *Revue de l'arbitrage* (1984), pp. 205 *et seq.*; P. Lalive, "Ordre public transnational (ou réellement international) et arbitrage international", *Revue de l'arbitrage* (1986), pp. 329 *et seq.*; B. Oppetit, "Le paradoxe de la corruption à l'épreuve du droit du commerce international", *Journal du droit international* (1987), pp. 5 *et seq.*; P. Mayer, "La règle morale dans l'arbitrage international", *Etudes Pierre Bellet* (1991), pp. 379 *et seq.*; V. Heuzé, "La morale, l'arbitre et le juge", *Revue de l'arbitrage* (1993), pp. 179 *et seq.*; Y. Derains, "La lutte contre la corruption — Le point de vue de l'arbitre international", *Contribution au Congrès AIJA*, Montreux, 1996; J. Rosell and H. Prager, "Illicit Commissions and International Arbitration: The Question of Proof", *Arbitration International*, Vol. 15 (1999), pp. 329 *et seq.*

basis that the defendant failed to substantiate the corruption claim[77]. These awards, rulings and commentaries, emanating from varied jurisdictions and legal cultures, have displayed more elements of anecdotalism than of convergence. They have by no means given rise to a complete consensus or reconcilability of views.

Moreover, the evolution in thinking respecting the arbitrator's rights and duties in connection with illegality of contract[78] has been accompanied by a profusion of new or amended bodies of national arbitration legislation and adoption of the UNCITRAL Model Law in whole or part in certain active arbitration locales. Finally, over the last several years a number of States have acceded to multilateral conventions condemning illegal contracts, corruption, bribery of public officials, etc.

These accessions have arguably contributed to, or confirmed, the development of certain national and transnational concepts of public policy in abhorrence of illegality of contracts. Prominent among such conventions, which have arguably contributed to a certain generalization of condemnation of corruption particularly in the public domain, are the 1997 OECD

---

[77] See, e.g., ICC Award No. 4145 (1984), *Establishment of Middle East State* v. *South Asian Construction Company*, *XII Yearbook Commercial Arbitration*, 1987, pp. 97 *et seq.*; ICC Award No. 6286 (1991), *U.S. Partner* v. *German and Canadian Partners*, *XIX Yearbook Commercial Arbitration*, 1994, p. 141, para. 22.

[78] In the first edition (1986) of Redfern & Hunter, *Law and Practice of International Commercial Arbitration*, Lagergren's decision in ICC Case No. 1110, *supra* footnote 3, was held to be commendable, on the basis that *ex turpi causa actio non oritur*; in the third edition (1999), para. 3-28 at p. 153, the authors stated that in the intervening 13 years the outcome and practice were likely to be different.

Convention on Combating Bribery of Foreign Public Officials in International Business Transactions[79], the 1999 Conventions of the Council of Europe[80], and the 2000 United Nations Convention against Transnational Organized Crime[81].

---

[79] The Convention on Combating Bribery of Foreign Public Officials in International Business Transactions (DAFFE/IME/BR(97)20) was signed on 17 December 1997, and came into effect on 15 February 1999. All of the 34 OECD members as well as additionally Argentina, Brazil, Bulgaria, Colombia, Russia and South Africa have adopted the Convention (Status as of 13 February 2013, retrieved from http://www.oecd.org/corruption/oecdantibriberyconvention.htm). See also M. Pieth, L. A. Low and P. J. Cullen, *The OECD Convention on Bribery — A Commentary*, Cambridge, Cambridge University Press, 2007.

[80] The Criminal Law Convention on Corruption, CETS No. 173, opened for signature on 27 January 1999, entered into force on 1 July 2002 and is ratified by 43 countries (Belarus as the only non-member State of the Council of Europe). The Additional Protocol to the Criminal Law Convention on Corruption, CETS No. 191, opened for signature on 15 May 2003, entered into force on 1 February 2005 and is ratified by 29 member States. The Civil Law Convention on Corruption, CETS No. 174, opened for signature on 4 November 1999, entered into force on 1 November 2003 and is ratified by 34 countries including Belarus as the only non-member State of the Council of Europe. (Status as of 12 February 2013; retrieved from http://www.conventions.coe.int/Treaty/Commun/Liste Traites.asp?CM=8&CL=ENG).

[81] The United Nations Convention against Transnational Organized Crime of 15 November 2000 entered into force on 29 September 2003 and has 147 signatories as well as 174 parties. There are three protocols also of 15 November 2000 supplementing this Convention: Protocol to Prevent, Suppress and Punish Trafficking in Persons, Especially Women and Children (entered into force on 25 December 2003; signatories: 117, parties: 154), Protocol against the Smuggling of Migrants by Land, Sea and Air (entered into force on 28 January 2004; signa-

## D. *The Historical Setting in Investment-Treaty Arbitration*

While it has been 50 years since an acute focus was placed on how a commercial arbitral tribunal is to conduct itself in the context of illegality[82], it is only more recently that this intersection between the two has played a role in investment treaty arbitration. While investment treaty arbitration and more loosely investment protection arbitration has existed for longer than 50 years[83], of course its major growth has arisen in the context of bilateral investment treaties providing for investor-State arbitration. And while the first bilateral investment treaty is now considered to be the 1959 treaty between the Federal Republic of Germany and Pakistan[84], since replaced by the 2009 treaty between Germany and Pakistan[85], the rise of investment arbitra-

---

tories: 122, parties: 135), and Protocol against the Illicit Manufacturing of and Trafficking in Firearms, Their Parts and Components and Ammunition (entered into force on 3 July 2005; signatories: 52, parties: 97). (Status as of 12 February 2013; retrieved from http://www.unodc.org/unodc/en/treaties/CTOC/signatures.html).

[82] See *supra* Chapter I.C.

[83] The introduction of investment arbitration is regarded as a change in paradigm in international investment law, cf. J. W. Salacuse and N. P. Sullivan, "Do BITs Really Work? An Evaluation of Bilateral Investment Treaties and Their Grand Bargain", *Harvard Internationall Law Journal*, Vol. 46 (2005), p. 88; S. W. Schill, "Private Enforcement of International Investment Law: Why We Need Investor Standing in BIT Dispute Settlement", in M. Waibel *et al.* (eds.), *The Backlash against Investment Arbitration*, Kluwer Law International, 2010, pp. 29 *et seq*.

[84] The Treaty for the Promotion and Protection of Investments (with Protocol and exchange of notes) was signed on 25 November 1959 and entered into force on 28 April 1962; 457 *UNTS* 23.

[85] The "Agreement on the Encouragement and Reciprocal Protection of Investments" between Pakistan and

tion is largely attributable to the ICSID Convention in 1965[86] and even more so to the first wave of ICSID arbitrations brought against the Republic of Argentina in connection with its "pesification" crisis in 2000[87].

Since that first wave, investment treaty arbitration and in particular ICSID arbitration have increased steadily in numbers and in notoriety[88], and other investment-treaty based arbitrations have likewise arisen, particularly in the context of the 1994 Energy Charter Treaty ("ECT")[89]. As of 31 December 2012, 419 arbitrations had been lodged at ICSID since 1965,

---

Germany was signed on 1 December 2009. It was ratified by Pakistan in 2010 and by Germany on 8 July 2011. See http://www.pakistan.diplo.de/Vertretung/pakistan/en/05_Business_Economy/1_ExternalEconomicPromotion/Invest_Schutz_Abk_Seite.html.

[86] The Convention on the Settlement of Investment Disputes between States and Nationals of Other States was opened for signature on 18 March 1965 and entered into force on 14 October 1966. As of 25 July 2012, 158 States signed and 147 States have ratified the Convention. See the List of Contracting States and Other Signatories of the Convention, available at https://icsid.worldbank.org/ICSID/FrontServlet?requestType=ICSIDDocRH&actionVal=ContractingStates&reqFrom=Main.

[87] P. Di Rosa, "The Recent Wave of Arbitrations against Argentina under Bilateral Investment Treaties: Background and Principal Legal Issues", *The University of Miami Inter-American Law Review*, Vol. 36 (2004), pp. 41 *et seq*.

[88] S. W. Schill, *supra* footnote 83, p. 30.

[89] The Energy Charter Treaty was signed on 17 December 1994 together with the Protocol on Energy Efficiency and Related Environmental Aspects (PEEREA). They entered into force in April 1998. As of February 2013, the ECT had been signed or acceded to by 51 States, the European Union and Euratom. All of them ratified the ECT except Australia, Belarus, Iceland, Norway and the Russian Federation. See http://www.encharter.org/index.php?id=7.

of which 350 since 2000 and 247 since 2005[90], and under the ECT 33 since 1994 and 28 since 2005[91]. Some of these arbitrations were brought in connection with a foreign investment contract between the investor and the host State or a State instrumentality, while the vast majority of these arbitrations were brought solely on the basis of a BIT or the ECT "without privity", such that the agreement to arbitrate was sought in the BIT itself and not in any direct contract between investor and host State.

This fact is relevant, as will be addressed below[92], in the context of the distinction which needs to be made in the context of illegality between arbitration agreements which may be "tainted" by an alleged or found illegality in a main contract, on the one hand, and illegality related to an investment for which there is no such conventional contract, on the other hand. To the extent the fate of the main contract infected by illegality may or may not be shared by the related if also separate arbitration agreement, it can be relevant that by contrast in most investment treaty-based claims there is no such relationship to begin with, since there is no such contract but rather "only" the treaty itself.

In parallel with the gradual uptick in treaty-based arbitrations in the 1980s and 1990s and the increasing momentum after 2000 beginning with the claims against Argentina, two further developments are of relevance. First, in parallel with the rise in the number of claims, an increasing number of States negotiated, or

---

[90] The ICSID Caseload — Statistics, Issue 2013-1, available at https://icsid.worldbank.org/ICSID/FrontServlet?requestType=ICSIDDocRH&actionVal=CaseLoadStatistics.

[91] See the list of cases under the ECT provided by the Energy Charter Secretariat, available at http://www.encharter.org/index.php?id=213 (accessed on 13 February 2013).

[92] See *infra* Chapter V.B.2.

renegotiated, bilateral investment treaties which invariably provided for one or the other form of dispute resolution by arbitration, ICSID or otherwise. In the case
of Germany, for example, which to this day has entered
into more BITs than any other country with China a
close second[93], Germany entered into 34 BITs in the
period 1959 to 1980, 77 in the period 1981 to 2000,
and 25 in the period 2001 to 2012[94], of which 17 represented renegotiated BITs with such countries as
Pakistan and China[95]. The landscape of available BITs
grew exponentially, and with it the potential for international arbitration between foreign investors and host
States.

The second notable development was in turn the end
of the Cold War in 1989-1990, the rise of newly independent States from the former Soviet Union and
within its sphere, and the shifting of the former classical North-South and East-West basis for foreign direct
investment to a new landscape of general globalization
in all directions of the compass. The result was an
increase in foreign direct investment generally, particularly into previously inaccessible or neglected or otherwise inhospitable markets such as the former Soviet

---

[93] As of June 2012, Germany entered into 136 BITs
while China entered into 128 BITs; United Nations Conference on Trade and Development (UNCTAD), "World
Investment Report 2012: Towards a New Generation of
Investment Policies", Annex Table III.1, p. 199. As of the
end of 2011, there are 2,833 BITs in total; *ibid.*, p. XX
(the report is available at http://www.unctad-docs.org/
files/UNCTAD-WIR2012-Full-en.pdf).

[94] See the Table of BITs, dated 27 April 2012, provided
by the German Federal Ministry of Economics and
Technology, available at http://www.bmwi.de/BMWi/
Redaktion/PDF/B/bilaterale-investitionsfoerderungs-und-
schutzvertraege-IFV,property=pdf,bereich=bmwi2012,
sprache=de,rwb=true.pdf.

[95] *Ibid.*

States, the People's Republic of China[96] and Latin America[97].

This development was further accelerated by the entry of such States into BITs and MITS, and by an increase in foreign direct investment particularly in the energy- and tourism-related areas. Furthermore, the United States itself entered into the North American Free Trade Agreement (or NAFTA) with Canada and Mexico in 1994[98], which in turn spawned various treaty-based arbitrations and related case law and commentary. By 2010, some 37 NAFTA arbitrations had been commenced of which 16 were pending[99].

In tandem with the foregoing developments, a perceptible increase in focus on issues of cross-border corruption and bribery developed. On the one hand, numerous externalities indicated a perceptible growth in intolerance for corruption to access such newly opened markets, as discussed below[100].

On the other hand, a realization developed that cor-

---

[96] See for the FDI inflows to China between 1990 and 2005, "Rising FDI into China: The Facts behind the Numbers", UNCTAD Investment Brief, No. 2, 2007, p. 2. Available at http://unctad.org/en/Docs/iteiiamisc20075_en.pdf.

[97] See for the development in Latin America, "Foreign Direct Investment in Latin America and the Caribbean — 2011", Economic Commission for Latin America and the Caribbean (ECLAC), p. 6, Figure 1. Available at http://www.eclac.cl/publicaciones/xml/2/46572/2012-182-LIEI-WEB.pdf.

[98] The North American Free Trade Agreement (NAFTA) between the United States, Canada and Mexico entered into force on 1 January 1994. The text is available at http://www.nafta-sec-alena.org/en/view.aspx?conID=590.

[99] Material on cases filed against each of the NAFTA parties since 1994 are accessible at http://www.state.gov/s/l/c3439.htm.

[100] See *infra* Chapter III.

ruption, while of course not a new phenomenon, continued to play a role or even an increased role in precisely this exercise of penetrating such new markets.

### E. Corruption in Cross-Border Commercial Life

There is no question but that illegality, and in particular corruption and bribery, pose important and fascinating challenges both on the level of private international law and public international law, and thus represent a unique combination for the purposes of these Hague lectures.

Bribery of public officials, "intermediaries", "business consultants", "middlemen", "black boxes", "influence peddling", "pots de vin"[101], "money laundering", "dawn raids"[102], US Foreign Corrupt Practices Act[103], UK Bribery Act[104], Transparency International[105],

---

[101]  *Engl.* "bribe".

[102]  See in this context the Judgment of the European Court of Justice (Grand Chamber), C-550/07 P, 14 September 2010 (*Akzo Nobel Chemicals and Akcros Chemicals* v. *Commission*) in which the Court assesses a case in which Commission officials carried out an investigation at the applicants' premises.

[103]  The FCPA was enacted in 1977 and due to certain amendments in 1998 the anti-bribery provisions now also apply to foreign firms and persons who cause an act in furtherance of corrupt payments to take place within the territory of the United States; for further details see http://www.justice.gov/criminal/fraud/fcpa/.

[104]  The UK Bribery Act came into force on 1 July 2011, introducing the new corporate offence for failing to prevent bribery on behalf of a commercial organization.

[105]  The NGO was founded by the former World Bank official Peter Eigen in 1993; for further information see http://www.transparency.org.

Enron [106], WorldCom [107] — all of these terms and concepts have figured with increasing frequency and familiarity on the front pages of newspapers and magazines as well as the internet on a daily basis for several years, and increasing with frequency with each new year. Allegations and findings of bribery — "private to public" and "public to private", "private to private" and "public to public", — have become an ever increasing element of commercial life, involving both developing and developed countries, investors and public officials, East and West, North and South.

In tandem with this development, and further accentuating it, the current period of financial instability involving increasingly interlinked regional and global markets has played its role, and gives rise to the question of whether corruption is the cause or rather the

---

[106] In 2001, Enron, once ranked No. 7 by Fortune 500, filed the largest bankruptcy at that time (cf. P. M. Healy and K. G. Palepu, "The Fall of Enron", *Journal of Economic Perspectives*, Vol. 17 (2003), pp. 3 *et seq.*). The dimensions and aftermath of the Enron case induced discussions on management ethics, see e.g. M. C. Henderson, M. G. Oakes and M. Smith, "What Plato Knew about Enron", *Journal of Business Ethics*, Vol. 86 (2009), pp. 463 *et seq.*; S. Premeaux, "The Link between Management Behavior and Ethical Philosophy in the Wake of the Enron Convictions", *Journal of Business Ethics*, Vol. 85 (2009), pp. 13 *et seq.*

[107] The dimensions of WorldCom's bankruptcy in 2002 even exceeded Enron's. In answer to these scandals and irregularities at other big companies the Sarbanes-Oxley Act of 2002 was enacted, which is called "the biggest reform of corporate governance since the federal security laws were enacted seventy years ago" (R. Hefendehl, "Enron, WorldCom, and the Consequences: Business Criminal Law between Doctrinal Requirements and the Hopes of Crime Policy", *Buffalo Criminal Law Review*, Vol. 8 (2004), pp. 51 *et seq.*).

effect of certain kinds of financial instability. Studies have already sought to show that corruption in the context of foreign direct investment can actually undo or at least dramatically reduce the intended salutary macroeconomic effects of investment for a lesser developed country [108].

Furthermore, both in developing countries and developed countries, corruption affects the greatest developmental needs, such as infrastructure including telecoms and construction, energy including nuclear power, natural resource development including oil and gas, and intellectual property including pharmaceuticals. It is precisely these areas among others that are often monopolistically controlled, supervised or otherwise regulated by public authorities in developing and developed countries alike. It is precisely these areas that have proven to be among the most susceptible to legal conflict and in turn to international arbitration. And it is also these areas among others which have accounted for allegations or findings of corruption involving public officials in recent years. Indeed measured by the so-called Transparency International Corruption Perceptions Index (0=highly corruption, 10=very clean), in the year 2010 some three-quarters of 178 countries assessed scored below 5 [109], indicating that corruption was systemic, endemic and not going away soon.

Thus the 2010 Global Corruption Barometer identified the scale and scope of corruption as "staggering": four in ten polled businessmen participating responded that they had been asked to pay bribe to public author-

---

[108] Cf. e.g. P.-G. Méon and K. Sekkat, "Does Corruption Grease or Sand the Wheels of Growth?", *Public Choice*, Vol. 122 (2005), pp. 69 *et seq.*

[109] The Corruption Perceptions Index Report can be downloaded at http://www.transparency.org/cpi2010/results.

ities and five in 10 estimated that corruption raised project costs by at least 10 per cent[110]. According to the 2009 Global Corruption Report, in developing countries alone public officials had received bribes believed to total between US$20 and 40 billion annually[111]. That amount was estimated to equal some 20 to 40 per cent of official development assistance worldwide. The side effects of such corruption, apart from lining the pockets of a select few, include exploitative work conditions, slave labour, child labour, discrimination, energy shortages and diversions, environmentally hazardous practices, unsafe medical drugs and practices, and defective and unsafe infrastructure[112].

The negative correlation between levels of foreign direct investment and corruption in a particular country has also been studied and established[113]. Thus an increase in corruption can have the same negative effect on inward FDI as raising the tax rate by several percentage points[114]. Empirical evidence suggests that

---

[110] Transparency International, Global Corruption Barometer 2010, accessible at http://www.transparency.de/fileadmin/pdfs/Wissen/Korruptionsindices/GCB_2010.pdf.

[111] http://www.acrc.org.ua/assets/files/zvity_ta_dos lidzhennya/global_corruption_barometer_2009_web.pdf.

[112] Corruption induces inequality and poverty, cf. http://go.worldbank.org/6UZ4XEP700.

[113] See e.g. A. Al-Sadig, "The Effects of Corruption on FDI Inflows", *Cato Journal*, Vol. 29 (2009), pp. 267 *et seq.*

[114] "For example, in a benchmark estimation, an increase in corruption from the level of Singapore to that of Mexico would have the same negative effect on inward foreign investment as raising the marginal corporate tax by fifty percentage points." (S.-J. Wei, "Negative Alchemy? Corruption and Composition of Capital Flows", OECD Development Center Working Paper No. 165 (2000), p. 8.)

corruption lowers investment and retards economic growth to a significant extent[115].

In short, the reasons for studying the intersection between corruption and agreements to resolve disputes related to commercial dealings alleged to be corrupt are manifest, and transcend a purely academic interest. The need for coherence in the dogmatic approaches to the issue ideally should assist in addressing real-life approaches to dispute resolution.

If the approaches to dispute resolution are coherent, then perhaps the approaches to contractual and other mechanisms for dispute resolution will be more coherent. If the mechanisms are more coherent, then dispute avoidance may be enhanced and in any event adjudication of matters which unavoidably become disputes may be more predictable.

## F. *The Intersection between Corruption and Law*

In short, corruption cannot be discussed without considering the law and the law is increasingly being affected by allegations and findings of corruption. Indeed it is submitted that there is likely to be little incentive on the part of a host State to change corrupt practices in its public or private sector as they impact on foreign direct investment if that host State continues to receive that investment anyway and/or the host State is able to continue to escape the legal consequences of tolerating or even participating in such corrupt practices.

Conversely, foreign investors may avoid investing in particular countries with poor governance and high corruption, resulting perhaps in a decline of cross-

---

[115] C. J. Robertson and A. Watson, "Corruption and Change: The Impact of Foreign Direct Investment", *Strategic Management Journal*, Vol. 25 (2004) p. 393.

border corruption involving that country but also cutting it off from valuable and needed foreign investment. Furthermore, if foreign investors lose the protection of being able to seek redress through arbitration in a neutral forum when they themselves succumb to and engage in corruption, then perhaps such investors may become more hesitant to invest in States where corruption is endemic.

The intersection is of course not the same in the case of commercial versus investment treaty arbitration. Not all international commercial contracts relate to foreign investment although by and large, depending on how one defines investment, any cross-border transaction might be seen as promoting investment even in the absence of a host State. Furthermore, commercial arbitration is based on a commercial contract of privity, so that the party in the shoes of an "investor" has consciously and expressly addressed dispute resolution if it has included an arbitration agreement.

This does not however necessarily mean that the parties to a commercial arbitration agreement have reflected on the possible ramifications of corruption between them on the validity of the contract or the arbitration agreement. In the case of treaty-based investment claims brought in arbitration, it is fair to say that most investors including even sophisticated multinational companies are not necessarily aware of the existence of an investment treaty which might entitle them to seek ICSID or other international arbitration against the host State in the case of a dispute.

While such awareness is increasing as a result of the growth in notoriety of investment arbitration and leading to intentional structuring of investments to achieve maximum benefits of a particular nationality and a particular BIT regime, this is more the exception than the rule. Most foreign investors large and small probably have little consciousness of the ability to sue the host

State itself in an international forum in application of public international law principles based on such protections as "fair and equitable treatment" and "prohibition against discrimination".

Accordingly, if the consciousness is indeed so low, then surely the awareness of the possible deleterious effects of engaging in corruption on the investor's ability to survive an objection to jurisdiction or admissibility over the claim is even lower, or non-existent. Likewise, if the consciousness of many or most public officials including at the bottom rung is low, then too the awareness of the possible negative effects of government-sponsored corruption for a defence against a claim for treaty protection is low too. In short, the link between the awareness of the economic downsides of engaging in corruption and the negative legal consequences in a later dispute is tenuous at best.

The tenuousness of the link does not bode well for using the effect of corruption on arbitration as a means to discourage corruption generally. Having said that, the relative unfamiliarity of the citizenry with the law should not serve as grounds to have no law, or not to refine the law as it exists.

Ultimately, better defining and harmonizing the legal principles applicable to corruption in the context of international arbitration can certainly better serve the cause of reining in corruption, stimulating FDI, and ultimately improving the lot of the citizenry and the transparency of the government apparatus.

CHAPTER II

THE MEANING OF "ILLEGALITY"

A. *Overview of the Problem of Illegality
in Its Different Forms*

Which kinds and forms of "illegality" concern us in the present context, and which not? There are several levels of differentiation and distinction which must be made from the arbitrator's perspective. There may be many forms and shades of illegal and illicit contracts. Not all of them necessarily enjoy generally uniform condemnation and not all of them necessarily constitute "bribery" or "corruption", to which we will turn as our main focus shortly. Not all of them should necessarily be seen as consequently causing the nullity of the related agreement to arbitrate or otherwise undermining the authority of the arbitral tribunal to adjudicate the underlying claim.

*1. Overtly illegal contracts*

*First*, one must distinguish between certain categories of "overtly illegal contracts" and other categories which may be less overtly illegal in nature.

Contracts which are overtly illegal are those whose subject matter or purpose is generally considered to offend "public morality"[116]. The offence of public morality arises as a result of a consensus based upon,

---

[116] See e.g. Y. Lahlou and M. Matousekova, "Le role de l'arbitre dans la lutte contre la corruption", *Revue du droit des affaires internationales*, Vol. 6 (2012), p. 622.

for example, (i) the vast majority of national legal systems, (ii) evolving notions of transnational or international public policy[117], (iii) emerging *lex mercatoria* considerations[118], or even (iv) local mandatory laws or *lois de police*[119]. We shall return to this concept of consensus again in the narrower context of bribery *per se* below[120].

Among such categories, particularly at the transnational level, are *(a)* facilitation or promotion of drug trafficking, *(b)* terrorism, *(c)* subversion, *(d)* prostitution, *(e)* child abuse, *(f)* slavery, and *(g)* other forms of human rights violations[121]. Generally, contracts relating to such subject matters may be considered to possess an overt illegality. That overt illegality or illicitness would render any contract null and void *ab initio* according to the vast majority of national laws and any other rules of law meant to withstand the scrutiny of national or international public policy[122].

---

[117] P. Lalive, *supra* footnote 76, pp. 329 *et seq*.

[118] Cf. O. Lando, "The Lex Mercatoria in International Commercial Arbitration", *International and Comparative Law Quarterly*, Vol. 34 (1985), p. 753:

"Arbitrators of different nationalities who have applied the *lex mercatoria* in collegiate arbitral tribunals have not experiences great difficulties in reaching consensus. . . . Most arbitrators have common ethics and common notions of how business should be conducted. That leads them in the same direction."

[119] P. Mayer, "Mandatory Rules of Law in International Arbitration", *Arbitration International*, Vol. 2 (1986), p. 275: "[A] mandatory rule (loi de police in French) is an imperative provision of law which must be applied to an international relationship irrespective of the law that governs that relationship."

[120] See *infra* Chapter III.B.3.a.

[121] ILA, "Final Report on Public Policy", *TDM*, Vol. 1 (2004), para. 28.

[122] G. B. Born, *supra* footnote 4, p. 755.

Other categories of illicit contracts may be "less overtly illegal". Where the contract or associated conduct is less obviously contemptible, the challenge of the arbitrator to determine the extent of jurisdiction, arbitrability, severability, etc. in fact becomes potentially more difficult, and not less so. Such contracts include various forms of broker, sponsoring, agency, consultancy and intermediary agreements. Such agreements are invariably associated with the payment of a commission for some — often ill-defined or even non-existent — consideration or performance [123].

The reasons why the arbitrator's task here may be more difficult than in the case of an overtly illegal contract include the fact that such commission arrangements may be perfectly legal, or in any event not expressly proscribed, in some countries [124]. A further difficulty is the distinction, amongst such contracts, between those relating to the payment of a "commission" to a public official and those relating to the payment of a commission to a private entity.

Particularly in the case of a bribe or other corrupt practice vis-à-vis a public official, the egregiousness of the conduct may be seen to rise dramatically. At the same time, a noticeable trend in recent years, as reflected in certain international conventions and national legislation, is the expanding of the focus to include not only private to public corruption, but also private to private. Bribing a public official remains the classic example of illegality here, but bribing a private person has been recognized as potentially being just as pernicious even if it lacks the element of a breach of the public trust [125].

---

[123] A. Argandoña, "Private-to-Private Corruption", *Journal of Business Ethics*, Vol. 47 (2003), pp. 255 *et seq.*

[124] H. Raeschke-Kessler and D. Gottwald, *supra* footnote 60, p. 587.

[125] A. Argandoña, *supra* footnote 123, p. 254.

## 2. *Illegality and lack of assent*

*Second*, one must consider illicit contracts which are manifestly illegal not necessarily because of their overtly offensive nature or purpose, but rather because they simply never came into effect as purported. A graphic example is a contract which the defendant claims, perhaps truthfully, never to have signed or otherwise assented to[126]. An even more graphic example is a claim that the signature or other alleged manifestations of assent are in fact forgeries[127].

If such defence is true, the contract invariably becomes null and void *ab initio*[128]. This result of nullity is indeed not unlike the first category of overtly offensive contracts involving drug trafficking, prostitution, etc.[129] A principal difference between the two

---

[126] See e.g. the decision of the Tribunal Fédéral [Swiss Federal Tribunal] rendered on 31 May 2002, Case No. 4P.102/2001 and *Bothell* v. *Hitachi Zosen Corp.*, 97 F. Supp. 2d 1048, 1051-1053 (WD Wash. 2000).

[127] Courts are divided over the question whether the same degree of clarity and certainty is required to demonstrate that an arbitration agreement has been formed as is required for the formation of substantive commercial contracts, cf. G. B. Born, *supra* footnote 4, pp. 644 *et seq.*

[128] *Ipcon Collections LLC* v. *Costco Wholesale Corp.*, No. 11-3944-cv(L) (2d Cir. 2012).

[129] Cf. N. Blackaby and C. Partasides with A. Redfern and M. Hunter, *supra* footnote 7, para. 2.97, holding that the validity of the arbitration agreement

> "must depend on the reason for which the contract is found to be null and void . . . [giving as an example 'that's not my signature']. No amount of insistence upon the autonomy of the arbitration clause can make it valid if the respondent was not a party to it",

citing the so-called *Pyramids* case, Award in ICC Case No. 3493 (1983), *S.P.P. (Middle East) Ltd.* v. *Arab Republic of Egypt*, *International Legal Materials*, Vol. 22 (1983), p. 767, para. 46 (also available at *IX Yearbook Commercial Arbitration*, 1984, pp. 111 *et seq.*); the Cour

categories, of course, is that the drug smuggling contract is deemed null and void even where all contracting parties assented to it. The forged contract, on the other hand, is deemed null and void because of the lack of mutual assent, and not — or not solely — by reason of its underlying subject matter.

From the perspective of the arbitrator's (possible) jurisdiction, separability and arbitrability, should there be a difference between the illicit drug smuggling contract and the illicit forged contract[130]? In fact, it may

---

d'appel of Paris upheld a claim by the award debtor Egyptian Government that it was not a party to the underlying contract, with the result that the award made on the basis that it was in fact a party was set aside in France: CA Paris, 12 July 1984, *République Arabe d'Egypte* v. *Southern Pacific Properties Ltd., Journal du droit international*, Vol. 112 (1985), p. 129, *International Legal Materials*, Vol. 23 (1984), p. 1048.

In fact, the *Pyramid*s case did not stand so much for the proposition of "that's not my signature" in the sense of a forgery or falsification. Rather, its focus was whether the term "approval, agreement and ratification" of an arbitration clause implied an intention to become a party to that clause. Extension of the arbitration agreement signed by a State-owned entity to the State is a wholly different matter than the illegality of a contract containing an arbitration clause by virtue of forgery or falsification of an assent to that contract or arbitration clause. It is the latter, the forgery or falsification scenario, which concerns us here.

[130] A relatively recent example of a prominent international arbitration dispute involving contentions of forgery, in this case forged documents submitted as evidence, was the territorial dispute between the State of Bahrain and the State of Qatar submitted to the International Court of Justice in The Hague: ICJ, case concerning *Maritime Delimitation and Territorial Questions between Qatar and Bahrain (Qatar* v. *Bahrain)*, Judgment of 16 March 2001, *International Legal Materials*, Vol. 40 (2001), p. 847. In that case, decided on the merits after a prolonged jurisdictional phase, claimant Qatar submitted, and then later retracted, various allegedly falsified historical documents

be that in the case of both contracts, unless the illicitness is manifest, it must still be proven, through submissions, to the satisfaction of the tribunal. The allegation of illegality based on smuggling or forgery is, at least initially, only a claim, or defence, and must be proven.

In all such cases where proof is still to be adduced, the tribunal must normally have jurisdiction to establish the facts of the case and take evidence. In those cases where no proof is needed because the illegality is manifest, the question of whether the tribunal has jurisdiction to make any ruling over the dispute will normally depend on whether the illicitness, additionally, leads to the voidness of the separate arbitration agreement.

### 3. Illicit contracts and public versus private parties

*Third*, within the category of less overtly illegal contracts such as commission agreements, the arbitrator may need to distinguish between commission agreements providing for payment to a private party ("influence peddling") and those providing for payment to a public official ("bribery") [131]. In the latter

---

respecting the 1939 award to Bahrain of the disputed Hawar islands lying between Bahrain and Qatar. The official judgment has been criticized for the fact that the ICJ judgment did not make any evaluation of the series of events related to the submission and later retraction of the allegedly forged documents: see, e.g., "Faking It: Eversheds, Freshfields and the ICJ Forgeries", *Legal Business*, Issue 114 (May 2001), pp. 66-71. This ICJ case may be seen as relating to illegality in the formation and performance of contract as well as in the conduct of the arbitration proceedings themselves, which is a separate subject altogether.

[131] Cf. in German law, a decision of the Bundesgerichtshof [German Federal Court of Justice], 8 May 1985 — IV a ZR 138/83, *Neue Juristische Wochenschrift*, 1985, pp. 2405 *et seq.*, holding that

case, the aim of the commission payment is customarily to secure a contract award or other advantage from an agent of a State by means of what is normally considered "bribery" [132]. In the former case, the commission payment may have somewhat the same nature and purpose, but not seek to corrupt an instrumentality of a Government. Should this distinction matter as to whether the arbitrator has jurisdiction over a dispute relating to such a commission agreement?

Depending upon the jurisdiction, "influence peddling" vis-à-vis public officials may be illegal, but not be sanctionable in the *private* domain as long as it does not implicate a public official. Whether influence peddling even in the private domain is sanctionable will depend upon the particular form of action taken and the applicable law [133].

### 4. *Illegality* ab initio *versus* ex post

*Fourth*, the arbitral tribunal may be called upon to make hairline distinctions between fraud in the induce-

---

"an agreement by which a foreign public official promises in criminal fashion to carry out a particular official act in exchange for payment of a bribe is void under Section 138 German Civil Code *[Sittenwidriges Geschäft]*. The same must apply for a contract between an interested party and an intermediary when its sole or main purpose consists of establishing an agreement to pay a bribe to the responsible public official and to forward this payment to him and when the bribe is included in the commission promised to the intermediary."

[132] Among the recent prominent cases of alleged bribery of public officials which became subject to arbitration included the sale of certain French naval frigates to the Republic of Taiwan by the French Thomson CSF via a Swiss "intermediary": *Frontier AG & Brunner Sociedad* v. *Thomson CSF*, ICC Case No. 7664, Award, 31 July 1996.

[133] A. Argandoña, *supra* footnote 123, pp. 255 *et seq.*

ment of the contract and so-called fraud in the factum. Fraud in the inducement may result in the illegality *ex post* of the contract[134]. Fraud in the factum may result in its illegality *ab initio*[135].

Should the arbitrator apply a different standard respecting arbitrability and separability when the contract is deemed to have become illegal "only later", as opposed to the case where there was never any contract at all? Does it not make a difference whether the alleged fraud is manifest, as opposed to requiring the parties first to be put to their proof?

## B. Circumstances of the Illegality

Wholly apart from the foregoing potential distinctions, the arbitrator may be confronted with a wide range of *factual* circumstances which could affect the issues of jurisdiction, arbitrability and separability.

### 1. Initial awareness of the illegality by all parties

*First,* whether the subject matter is overtly offensive or, rather, more of a "gray area" illegality, both parties were manifestly aware of the illegality *ab initio*. Both parties may have known of and intended the illicit nature and illicit purpose of the contract. Both parties may have known of and intended the inclusion of an agreement to arbitrate precisely to shield adjudication of any disputes from national courts which would strike down the contract as illegal.

The arbitrator must decide issues of arbitrability and separability in the context of an illegality going to the heart of both the underlying contract and the arbitration agreement. If the arbitrator does so, however, is

---

[134] R. Kreindler, *supra* footnote 41, p. 213.
[135] *Ipcon Collections LLC* v. *Costco Wholesale Corp.*, No. 11-3944-cv(L) (2d Cir. 2012).

he an "accomplice" to the illicit effort to shield adjudication from the national courts?

## 2. *Subsequent awareness of the illegality by all parties*

*Second*, both parties executed the contract on the assumption that it was licit in nature, and only subsequently became aware of the illegality in the course of performance. By extension, both parties included the agreement to arbitrate on the basis that it was a legitimate dispute resolution mechanism for a legitimate underlying contract.

The arbitrator must decide in the context of illegality of the main agreement. He must also decide in the context of whether the severity of the illegality should prevent him from affirming his jurisdiction on the basis of the arbitration agreement. How severe must the illegality be for the arbitrator no longer to be able to exercise jurisdiction on the basis of arbitrability and separability?

## 3. *Illicit intention and awareness of one party*

*Third*, one party is aware of the illegality *ab initio*, working, for example, through a third-party "intermediary", while the other party is unaware of the illegality. The first party did not necessarily fraudulently induce the second party to enter into the contract, but it may have induced it to enter into the contract under false pretences. Is this not the same thing?

The arbitrator must assess the extent to which one party's good-faith reliance on the legality of the contract may influence his assessment of arbitrability and separability. Just because one of the two parties had an illicit intention, does this deprive the other party acting in good faith and in reliance on the licitness of the contract from having his day before the arbitrator?

## 4. *Reliance on the illegality as claim or defence*

*Fourth*, the party seeking relief in the arbitration himself committed the illegality. He seeks the benefit of an arbitral award upholding the illegality. The defendant, who is being sued for manifest non-performance, seeks to use the illegality as a means to forestall judgment against it. The arbitral tribunal may be confronted with a situation where the illegality is sanctionable under only one of several potentially applicable bodies of law.

Should the tribunal condone the illegality in order to find against a clearly defaulting defendant, or should it deny its own jurisdiction due to the illegality even though the defendant will thereby be able to abscond despite its non-performance? What if the non-performance relates to a part of the contract which may be legal and severable from the remaining, illicit portions of the contract?

## 5. *Contracts of bribery versus contracts arising out of bribery*

*Fifth*, the underlying contract is not alleged to represent an agreement to pay a bribe, but rather is a contract which is alleged to have arisen and been made possible as a result of an antecedent payment of an illegal bribe involving the same parties.

The tribunal must distinguish between the two contracts and decide whether its jurisdiction is in any way undermined by the circumstances which gave rise to the contract.

### C. *Suspicion of Illegality versus Knowledge or Obviousness of Same*

Each of the above possible permutations may be affected by the extent to which the arbitral tribunal has a "mere" suspicion that illegality obtains, as opposed to a firm knowledge based on the obviousness or manifest nature of the same.

Particularly in such cases, how far should arbitrators go to determine whether the contract submitted to them has been procured or performed by illegal means, or otherwise suffers from some illicitness which may render (i) it null and void, (ii) perhaps the arbitration agreement null and void, and (iii) the arbitrator defunct?

In the case of "mere" suspicion, the conviction with which the tribunal decides whether it is in a position to assert jurisdiction and render an award may be influenced by the "degree" of suspicion involved. In particular, the following issues may arise for the tribunal in the case of a suspicion falling short of concrete knowledge or admission of the illegality:

## 1. Maintaining impartiality and equal treatment

*First*, arguably the existence of a "mere" suspicion will place special challenges on the tribunal to maintain the requisite level of impartiality and/or independence and to ensure equal treatment. This may be the case particularly where the suspicion of illegality attaches to only one party, and not to all parties jointly. As a matter of the applicable arbitral rules, the *lex arbitri* and any other potentially relevant standards, the arbitrators have a duty, for example, to maintain such impartiality and to treat the parties equally[136].

To the extent the tribunal suspects illegality on the part of one party but not of all, it must ensure that it does not allow unsubstantiated or even half-substantiated indicia of impropriety on one side to influence its even-handedness in conducting the arbitration. This is a matter of impartiality and independence. It is also

---

[136] See, e.g., Arts. 12, 18, UNCITRAL Model Law.

an issue of equal treatment, due process and a balanced affording to both sides of an opportunity to present the respective case. The extent of such "opportunity" will depend upon the applicable arbitral rules and *lex arbitri* [137].

## 2. Dilatory tactics and allegations of illegality

*Second*, where the suspicion is based primarily or solely on a "mere" allegation of illegality by the *defendant*, the tribunal may see fit to be marginally more rigorous and circumspect in its readiness to conclude that such an illegality exists. Quite apart from the not infrequent occurrence of a dilatory defendant espousing arguments primarily for the purpose of postponing or derailing completely the day of judgment, a mere allegation of illegality by the defendant should not immediately make non-arbitrable a contract which is otherwise on its face arbitrable.

The marginally greater rigour brought to bear on the defendant may not in any way offend the arbitrator's duty of equal treatment and due process under the relevant rules and curial law. In the case of a counter-claim, it may well be that it is the claimant who then relies on a partial illegality as its defense to any liability under the counterclaim.

## 3. Mutual denial of illegality

*Third*, it may be that *both* parties deny that the underlying contract is illegal and at least the claimant

---

[137] UNCITRAL Model Law, Art. 18, provides for "a full opportunity of presenting his case" whereas ICC Rules, Art. 22 (4), speaks, in the context of *clôture de la procédure*, of "a reasonable opportunity to present its case".

insists on its arbitrability. Should the tribunal's "mere" suspicion of a true illegality be more readily put to rest by the fact that both parties "agree" that the contract is not illegal? Or should the tribunal inquire nevertheless into the grounds for its continuing suspicion?

The fact that both parties deny an underlying illegality does not necessarily make any less compelling the grounds for the tribunal's suspicion to the contrary; indeed the fact or manner of mutual denial may actually fire the tribunal's suspicions all the more. The mutual denial may be a concerted effort to shield the illegality from the tribunal. Alternatively, it may be an attempt to seek resolution of the dispute from a private tribunal in circumstances where a national court would not be receptive.

### D. *Initial Attempts at Definitions of "Corruption" and "Bribery"*

While there may be differences of opinion as to what kinds of conduct constitute corruption, there should be little disagreement as to the notional legal definition of corruption.

"Corruption" derives from *corrumpere*, "to break". Thus corruption has been defined as a situation in which "agents and public officers break the confidence entrusted to them"[138]. It has also been defined as the "perversion or destruction of integrity in the discharge of public duties by bribery or favour; the use or existence of corrupt practices, esp. in a state, public corporation, etc."[139]. Transparency International has defined corruption as the "abuse of entrusted power for private

---

[138] C. Nicchols *et al.*, *Corruption and Misuse of Public Office*, 2nd ed., Oxford, Oxford University Press, 2011, para. 1.01.

[139] *Oxford English Dictionary*.

gain"[140]. And a "bribe" has been defined as an act "to influence corruptly, by a reward or consideration, the action of (a person), to pervert the judgment or corrupt the conduct by a gift"[141].

A further approach to corruption and bribery has been to posit two broad categories: (i) "according to rule" corruption, whereby a bribe is paid to receive preferential treatment for something that the bribe receiver is required to do by law[142] and "against the rule" corruption, whereby a bribe paid to obtain services that the bribe receiver is prohibited from providing[143]. Furthermore, most modern States consider the definition of corruption and bribery to extend to all persons induced to act corruptly in discharge of duties, whether public or private. Thus corruption may include a private person bribing a public person, a public person bribing a private person, a public person bribing a public person and a private person bribing a private person[144].

---

[140] Transparency International FAQs on Corruption, available at http://www.transparency.org/whoweare/organisation/ faqs_on_corruption.

[141] *Oxford English Dictionary*.

[142] See Art. 15 *(a)* of the United Nations Convention against Corruption, *International Legal Materials*, Vol. 43 (2004), p. 37, which entered into force on 14 December 2005:

> "The promise, offering or giving, to a public official, directly or indirectly, of an undue advantage, for the official himself or herself or another person or entity, *in order that the official act or refrain from acting in the exercise of his or her official duties* . . ." (Emphasis added.)

[143] The differentiation between "according to rule" corruption and "against the rule" corruption is the approach chosen by Transparency International.

[144] H. Raeschke-Kessler and D. Gottwald, *supra* footnote 60, pp. 587 *et seq.*

Corruption is also to be distinguished from fraud, and it is primarily the former which is the subject of these lectures even while fraud may constitute corruption and corruption may also constitute fraud. At the same time, they are legally distinct. Fraud hasbeen defined as the knowing misrepresentation of the truth of a material fact to induce another to act in a manner detrimental to his interests [145].

In common parlance, we sometimes speak of the "five fingers of fraud", namely that (i) a person made a material false statement, (ii) he knew the statement to be false, (iii) he intended to deceive the victim, (iv) the victim justifiably relied on the false statement, and (v) the victim was damaged [146]. As stated, we may also distinguish between fraud in inducement to enter into a contract, which may result in illegality *ex post*, as opposed to fraud in entering into a contract, which may result in illegality *ab initio*. The former is sometimes associated with the "gun held to the head" while the latter is sometimes represented by the protestation of "That's not my signature!" [147]

### E. *International and Transnational Efforts to Define "Bribery"*

In the present day, there is a wide range of international conventions which condemn and interdict bribery, as do the national laws of various States. Thus, a number of instruments negotiated, signed and ratified under the aegis of the Organisation for Economic Co-

---

[145] B. A. Garner (ed.), *Black's Law Dictionary*, 9th ed., West Group, 2009, "fraud" (p. 731).

[146] *Lincoln Land FS* v. *Mau (In re Mau)*, 293 BR 919, 923 (Bankr. CD Ill. 2003).

[147] See, e.g., P. V. Tytell, "The Detection of Forgery and Fraud", in A. J. van den Berg, *supra* footnote 41, p. 315.

operation and Development (OECD) have the express aim and purpose of prohibiting acts constituting bribery[148].

Foremost here is the OECD Convention on Combating Bribery of Foreign Public Officials in International Business Transactions[149]. Further international conventions prohibiting bribery include the Inter-American Convention against Corruption (1996)[150], European Union Convention on the Fight against Corruption Involving Officials of the European Communities or Officials of Member States (1997)[151], Council of Europe Criminal Law Convention on Corruption (1999)[152], Council of Europe Civil Law Con-

---

[148] "Organisation for Economic Co-operation and Development: Council Recommendation on Bribery in International Business Transactions, May 27, 1994", *International Legal Materials*, Vol. 33 (1994), p. 1389; "Organisation for Economic Co-operation and Development: Council Recommendation C (96) 27/Final on the Tax Deductability of Bribes to Foreign Public Officials of Apr. 11, 1996", *International Legal Materials*, Vol. 35 (1996), p. 1311.

[149] OECD Convention on Combating Bribery of Foreign Public Officials in International Business Transactions, *supra* footnote 79.

[150] Inter-American Convention against Corruption, 29 March 1996, *International Legal Materials*, Vol. 35 (1996), p. 727, available at http://www.oas.org/juridico/english/treaties/b-58.html.

[151] European Union Convention on the Fight against Corruption Involving Officials of the European Communities or Officials of Member States, 26 May 1997, Official Journal (C 195), pp. 2 *et seq*. The Convention has entered into force on 28 September 2005. Its full text is available at http://eur-lex.europa.eu/LexUriServ/LexUriServ.do?uri=CELEX:41997A0625%2801%29:EN:HTML. For an overview see http://europa.eu/legislation_summaries/fight_against_fraud/fight_against_corruption/l33027_en.htm.

[152] Council of Europe Criminal Law Convention on Corruption, *supra* footnote 80.

vention on Corruption (1999)[153], and African Union Convention on Preventing and Combating Corruption (2003)[154]. The most recent and universal effort toward combating bribery within the international context is the United Nations Convention against Corruption (hereinafter "UN Anti-Corruption Convention"), which as of 24 December 2012 has 140 Signatories and 165 States parties[155].

As stated earlier, corruption and bribery have been most closely associated and preoccupied with public officials and the public domain. For example, a definition of bribery is prescribed in the UN Anti-Corruption Convention[156] and the OECD Anti-Bribery Convention[157] respectively. Both conventions can and should be purposefully considered in order to ascertain an appropriate delimitation or definition of the prohibition against bribery in international law.

Thus, Article 15 *(a)* of the UN Anti-Corruption Convention defines "bribery of national public officials" in relevant part as follows:

---

[153] Council of Europe Civil Law Convention on Corruption, *supra* footnote 80.

[154] African Union Convention on Preventing and Combating Corruption, 11 July 2003, *International Legal Materials*, Vol. 43 (2004), pp. 5 *et seq.*, available at http://www.africa-union.org/root/au/Documents/Treaties/Text/Convention%20on%20Combating%20Corruption.pdf.

[155] United Nations Convention against Corruption, *supra* footnote 142. For information on the number of States that have ratified the Convention, see United Nations Office on Drugs and Crime, United Nations Convention against Corruption — Ratification Status, available at http://www.unodc.org/unodc/en/treaties/CAC/signatories.html (last accessed 18 February 2013).

[156] United Nations Convention against Corruption, *supra* footnote 142.

[157] OECD Convention on Combating Bribery of Foreign Public Officials in International Business Transactions, *supra* footnote 79.

"[W]hen committed intentionally:

*(a)* The promise, offering or giving, to a public official, directly or indirectly, of an undue advantage, for the official himself or herself or another person or entity, in order that the official act or refrain from acting in the exercise of his or her official duties."

Similarly, Article 1 (1) of the OECD Anti-Bribery Convention defines bribery in relation to "foreign public officials" in relevant part as follows (emphasis added):

"[The conduct] of any person intentionally to offer, promise or give any undue pecuniary or other advantage, whether directly *or through intermediaries, to a foreign public official*, for that official or for a third party, *in order that the official act or refrain from acting in relation to the performance of official duties*, in order to obtain or retain business or other improper advantage in the conduct of international business."

For purposes of the definition of "bribery", Article 16 (1) of the UN Anti-Corruption Convention is essentially identical to Article 1 (1) of the OECD Anti-Bribery Convention[158].

---

[158] United Nations Convention against Corruption, Art. 16 (1) (bribery of foreign public officials and officials of public international organizations) provides:

"Each State Party shall adopt such legislative and other measures as may be necessary to establish as a criminal offence, when committed intentionally, the promise, offering or giving to a foreign public official or an official of a public international organization, directly or indirectly, of an undue advantage, for the official himself or herself or another person or entity, in order that the official act or refrain from acting in the

Statutory definitions of bribery in most national criminal laws to which I have had exposure are also essentially the same or to similar effect. Indeed, bribery is sanctioned by the criminal law of most, if not all, countries [159].

The foregoing definitions of "bribery" consider it from the perspective of corruption by the payer of a public-sector bribe as opposed to by the payee or recipient. Such conduct can of course also constitute corruption and bribery. The mirror image of Article 15 of the UN Convention, but applicable only to national public officials, is the intentional solicitation or acceptance by a national or foreign public official directly or indirectly of an undue advantage for the official himself or herself or another person or entity in order that the official act or refrain from acting in the exercise of his or her official duties [160]. This direction obviously

---

exercise of his or her official duties, in order to obtain or retain business or other undue advantage in relation to the conduct of international business."

[159] See, e.g., Secs. 304, 307 Strafgesetzbuch [Austrian Penal Code] [StGB]; Art. 337, Código Penal [Brazilian Penal Code] [CP]; Arts. 301-307a, Bulgarian Criminal Code; Art. 250, Chilean Criminal Code; Secs. 160-162, Czech Criminal Code; Sec. 122, Danish Criminal Code; Secs. 331-336, Strafgesetzbuch [German Criminal Code] [StGB]; Korean Act on Preventing Bribery of Foreign Public Officials in International Business Transactions; Sec. 276a, Norwegian Penal Code; Art. 10, Japanese Unfair Competition Prevention Law — Supplementary Provisions; and Arts. 267, 268, Slovenian Penal Code.

[160] Art. 16 (2), United Nations Convention against Corruption:

"Each State Party shall consider adopting such legislative and other measures as may be necessary to establish as a criminal offence, when committed intentionally, the solicitation or acceptance by a foreign public official or an official of a public international organization, directly or indirectly, of an undue advan-

covers the situation in which the public official either accepts the offer of bribery by a private person or the public official or requests or demands the same on the official's own initiative.

Furthermore, the definition of illegality in the sense of bribery has been expanded to include conduct exclusively in the private sector, without involvement of a public official. Thus Article 21 of the UN Convention defines corruption by the *payer* of a private sector bribe as intentionally promising, offering or giving directly or indirectly of an undue advantage to any person who directs or works, in any capacity, for a private sector entity for the person himself or herself or for another person in order that he or she, in breach of his or her duties, act or refrain from acting[161]. In turn, corruption by the recipient of a private-sector bribe is defined as intentional solicitation or acceptance directly or indirectly of an undue advantage by any person who directs or works, in any capacity, for a private sector entity[162].

The procedural and substantive challenges posed by these definitions are apparent, all the more so in the context of international commercial or investment treaty arbitration which likely involves a multiplicity of bodies and principles of law which may be applied. The evidentiary challenges can likewise be daunting.

*First*, "intent" must be shown generally. *Second*, the "promising, offering, giving or receiving" of an undue advantage must be proven, whether "directly or indi-

---

tage, for the official himself or herself or another person or entity, in order that the official act or refrain from acting in the exercise of his or her official duties."

[161] Art. 21 *(a)*, United Nations Convention against Corruption.

[162] Art. 21 *(b)*, United Nations Convention against Corruption.

rectly". *Third*, an "undue advantage" must be shown in situations where the advantage or the "undue" nature of the advantage are not always apparent, especially as bribery is typically masked, concealed or otherwise disguised. *Fourth*, the private or public capacity of the person giving or receiving the undue advantage may be critical, particularly as will be seen in the case of a person whose action is to be attributed to a public authority. *Fifth*, the conduct of acting or refraining from acting in breach of a duty must be proven.

In short, it can be well imagined that corruption on either the payer or the payee end and either in the public or the private sector may be more difficult to allege and prove than initially meets the eye. Only if and when an allegation of corruption reaches a critical level of plausibility or veracity would it then normally achieve the potential of triggering consequences for the arbitral tribunal in the ways already broadly outlined and discussed in detail below.

## F. The Temporal Dimension of Illegality

A further dimension of the attempt to define illegality for our purposes relates to the timing of the alleged or proven illegality, and in turn whether that timing may impact on the possible consequences for the authority of the arbitral tribunal. In particular, we may usefully distinguish between *pre-*contract or pre investment illegality and *post-*signing or post-investment illegality. Again, the distinction is rendered further problematic by the fact that in most investment treaty-based arbitrations involving illegality we will not necessary have a contract *per se* in which an agreement to arbitrate is contained.

With regard to pre-contract or pre-investment illegality, apart from the possible distinction between fraud in the inducement and fraud in the factum mentioned earlier[163], the arbitral tribunal may wish to assess certain factual questions which may in turn depend on the applicable law.

*First*, query to what extent the alleged illegality constituted a *sine qua non* in order to obtain the contract/investment. If the illegality was incidental to or had no connection to the contract or investment, then the tenuousness of the connection may make it more difficult to link the illegality to a discretion or even duty to draw certain consequences for competence, arbitrability, admissibility, etc. On the other hand, if the illegality was at the very heart of the contract or the investment or the contract or investment would not have materialized but for the illegality, then the connection is anything but tenuous.

*Second*, the problem nonetheless may still arise of whether the illegality, even if connected, preceded the contract or investment so clearly and drastically in time that there might be no contract or investment to establish. Particularly in the case of an investment meant to fulfil the definition of investment invariably found in BITs, query whether the incipient illegality could result in no investment having come about at all. It is submitted here that to the extent illegal investor conduct is contrary to international law and should render an investment by that investor illegal, as discussed below[164], the relevant point in time at which the investor must still have conducted itself legally in order to maintain the investment's legality and not compromise jurisdiction is the date of the institution of the arbitral proceedings. In this regard, both the ICSID Convention and the ECT are silent regarding the date on which the requirements for the existence and exercise of jurisdiction must be met.

---

[163] See *supra* Chapter II.A.4.
[164] See *infra* Chapter II.H.

However, the requirement that the date in question is the date of the institution of arbitral proceedings can and should be derived from accepted principles of international adjudication. As stated by Professors Dolzer and Schreuer, for example,

"[i]t is an accepted principle of international adjudication that, in the absence of treaty provisions to the contrary, the relevant date for purposes of jurisdiction is the date of the institution of proceedings" [165].

This general principle has also been affirmed in *Vivendi II* in the context of an investment arbitration:

"It is [a] generally recognized [principle] that the determination of whether a party has standing in an international judicial forum, for purposes of jurisdiction to institute proceedings, is made by reference to the date on which such proceedings are deemed to have been instituted. ICSID Tribunals have consistently applied this Rule." [166]

---

[165] R. Dolzer and C. H. Schreuer, *Principles of International Investment Law*, Oxford, Oxford University Press, 2008, p. 41 (citing the following cases for this principle: *Questions of Interpretation and Application of the 1971 Montreal Convention arising from the Aerial Incident at Lockerbie (Libyan Arab Jamahiriya v. United States of America)*, Preliminary Objections, 27 February 1998, *ICJ Reports 1998*, p. 130, available at http://www.icj-cij.org/docket/files/89/7249.pdf; *Arrest Warrant of 11 April 2000 (Democratic Republic of the Congo v. Belgium)*, 14 February 2002, *ICJ Reports 2002*, p. 13, available at http://www.icj-cij.org/docket/files/121/8126.pdf).

[166] *Compania de Aguas del Aconquija, P.A. & Vivendi Universal P.A.* v. *Argentina (Vivendi II)*, ICSID Case No. ARB/97/3 (formerly *Compañía de Aguas del Aconquija, S.A. and Compagnie Générale des Eaux v. Argentine Republic*), Decision on Jurisdiction, 14 November 2005, para. 60, available at http://ita.law.uvic.ca/documents/AgueasVivendijurisdictiondecision.pdf (dismissing Argentina's objections to Claimant's *jus standi*).

This principle has been cited or applied approvingly by various other ICSID arbitral tribunals in different contexts[167]. Thus, it can and should be viewed as an established principle that the investment must have been maintained in accordance with international law and thus not tainted by a concomitant or subsequent illegal act at the time the arbitral proceedings related to such investment are instituted. Thus a claimant investor alleged to have committed an illegality which might deprive the tribunal of jurisdiction would have had to maintain its investment in accordance with international law, without any concomitant or subsequent acts of bribery, up until the date it initiated this ICSID arbitration.

*Third*, query to what extent the alleged illegality was undertaken in order to improve the terms and conditions of the contract or investment or to expedite or facilitate approval of the terms and conditions. Here, the illegality did not make the contract or investment possible *per se* and they would have arisen without the illegality, but the reason for the illegality relate to facilitation or expedition of the investment or of certain terms.

On the one hand, it could be said that such motivation does not go to the but-for existence of the contract or investment, and that therefore the illegal conduct does not go to the heart of the issue. On the other hand, it could be said that particularly in a typical competitive bid situation the motivation indeed goes to the root of the transaction, and that the transaction would have looked entirely different, or would not have been obtained in the first place, absent the conduct.

With regard to "facilitation," one need look no farther than the US FCPA from 1977, the pioneer of

---

[167] See R. Dolzer and C. H. Schreuer, *supra* footnote 165, p. 41, for further references.

national legislation respecting control and sanctioning of cross-border corruption involving public officials, to see that the FCPA itself allows for certain kinds of facilitation payments to be made without triggering a finding of corruption or a related sanction[168]. By contrast, the much more recent and in some respects more stringent UK Bribery Act from 2010 expressly prohibits such facilitation payments[169]. While certain forms of facilitation payments may be seen as being more "influential" than others, particularly depending on the absolute amount of the payment or the relative value of the payment to the particular recipient, query whether strictly speaking there is a continuing justification in today's concept of corruption for the FCPA exception. In any event, in this respect the FCPA is no longer the model for best practice in combating corruption today, although its pragmatic approach to such payments may not be wrong in the overall scheme.

As stated, we may usefully distinguish between *pre-*contract or pre-investment illegality and *post-*signing or post-investment illegality. Bribery or corruption may

---

[168]  15 USC § 78dd-1 *(b)* states:

"Subsections *(a)* and *(g)* of this section shall not apply to any facilitating or expediting payment to a foreign official, political party, or party official the purpose of which is to expedite or to secure the performance of a routine governmental action by a foreign official, political party, or party official."

[169] This expressly follows from the 2011 "Guidance about procedures which relevant commercial organisations can put into place to prevent persons associated with them from bribing (section 9 of the Bribery Act 2010)", Annotation to Section 7, para. 45, available at http://www.justice.gov.uk/downloads/legislation/bribery-act-2010-guidance.pdf.

As was the case under the old law, the Bribery Act does not (unlike US foreign bribery law) provide any exemption for such [faciliation] payments.

have nothing to do with the procurement of the contract or investment, based simply on the fact that the impugned conduct took place *after* the contract was entered into or the investment was effected. However, here too the arbitral tribunal may wish to assess certain factual questions which may in turn depend on the applicable law.

Whether the conduct took place after the contract was entered into may be ascertainable in most cases but the same cannot necessarily be said for an investment without privity of contract. Since in an investment protection context the existence of an "investment" must be shown[170], there may be the challenge of showing when the investment arose in a situation where the illegality may be alleged to have thwarted the coming into being of the investment in the first place. On the one hand, but for the illegality the investment would have come about. On the other hand, without a pre-existing investment of at least some tangibility query whether a subsequent illegality had any effect on the investment and whether the illegality, even if shown, should influence the exercise of authority of the tribunal over an investment which never saw the light of day.

Moreover, the mere fact that the alleged illegality occurred after the contract or the investment arose does not necessarily mean that the illegality is not related to or even at the heart of the reason for being of the contract or investment. The illegality may have been promised, offered, contemplated, anticipated or otherwise linked to the contract or investment, and then simply postponed or delayed in terms of its actually being effectuated. This temporal disconnect need not

---

[170] See for the definitions of "investment" under various Treaties, C. McLachlan, L. Shore and M. Weiniger, *supra* footnote 21, paras. 6.04 *et seq.*

mean that the contract or investment was not directly or indirectly related to the later alleged illegality.

Furthermore, the foregoing leads to the further question of the legal issue of a "link" between the acts of bribery on the one hand and the investment and/or the investment dispute on the other hand. As stated by me elsewhere [171], it is submitted that illicit acts attributable to an investor can and should render its investment illegal. At the same time, any requirement for establishing a "link" between the illicit act and the investment or the investment dispute should not be overstated: a direct or indirect link should suffice as long as there is not a total lack of connectedness between the two [172].

Where the alleged illegality shows no real connectedness, if only because it occurred significantly later than the time of entering into being of the contract or investment, then different questions may be posed. The issue will not be whether a contract or particularly investment ever really existed or even had a hope of existing, because it did exist, perhaps for some extended period of time. Rather, the issue will be whether the alleged illegal conduct *post*-signing or post-investment in order to amend the terms and conditions or in order to renew or extend the terms and conditions of the contract or investment should have consequences for the arbitrator's competence and other authority to adjudicate. The answer in most cases should be relatively straightforward at least in the

---

[171] See *infra* Chapter II.H.

[172] In the context of the Unclean Hands Doctrine, see G. Fitzmaurice, "The General Principles of International Law Considered from the Standpoint of the Rule of Law", *Recueil des cours*, Vol. 92 (1957), p. 119 ("an illegality by one State cannot justify a totally unconnected illegality by another"). In my opinion, this rationale should be applied in the same fashion in relations between States and non-State investors.

abstract: yes, a contract or investment is meant to be protected against illegality not only in its inception, but also in its maintenance.

In the case of investment protection claims, the foregoing leads to the related question of whether the investor must *maintain* the legality of its original investment as of the date of commencing proceedings. Here too the answer must be yes. Accordingly, failure or refusal to do so can and should result in the lack of jurisdiction over claims under that investment by reason of non-compliance with the applicable international law. Only an investor who is in compliance with international law at the time of the institution of the proceeding should be entitled to enjoy protection under, for example, the ECT.

While international law is generally applicable only between States, it is a well-established principle in investment arbitration law that the investor's investment itself must also comply with international public policy, which, as discussed further below [173], forms part of international law [174]. The investor is making and maintaining the investment subject to protections under either an investment contract or a bilateral investment and/or a multilateral investment treaty, which in turn trigger the application of international law.

It can be derived therefrom that the investor must comply with international law and public policy while making and maintaining the investment. This also derives from the concept that if the investor is granted subjective rights under international law, it also has a

---

[173] See *infra* Chapter III.B.

[174] See, e.g., the general reasoning in *Inceysa Vallisoletana S.L.* v. *Republic of El Salvador*, ICSID Case No. ARB/03/26, Award, 2 August 2006, paras. 245 *et seq.* Available at http://ita.law.uvic.ca/documents/Inceysa_Valli soletana_en_001.pdf; *World Duty Free* v. *Kenya, supra* footnote 44, para. 157.

subjective *duty* to comply with the general principles and legal standards of, for example, the ECT, as the ECT is in turn governed by international law[175].

On the basis of this principle as well as the objectives of the ECT and international law, the investor's obligation to comply with international law is *ongoing*. That ongoing obligation relates not only to the making of the investment, but also to the maintenance of the investment. The ongoing compliance with international law is a reciprocal obligation that can and should be derived from the objective and purpose of the respective treaty and from international law. In accord with this principle of an obligation of legality of conduct on the part of the investor, the majority of the arbitral tribunal in the original award in *Fraport* v. *Philippines* stated, in a somewhat different factual context, in relevant part:

> "As for policy, BITs oblige governments to conduct their relations with foreign investors in a transparent fashion. *Some reciprocal if not identical obligations lie on the foreign investor.*"[176]

---

[175] For the position that the investor is granted subjective rights under international law in the context of investment arbitration, see P. Muchlinski, "'Caveat Investor'? The Relevance of the Conduct of the Investor under the Fair and Equitable Treatment Standard", *International & Comparative Law Quarterly*, Vol. 55, 2006, pp. 535, 547, 557 ("a duty to conduct the investment, once it has been undertaken, in a reasonable manner"). See also R. Happ, *Schiedsverfahren zwischen Staaten und Investoren nach Artikel 26 Energiechartavertrag*, 2000, p. 138; O. Spiermann, "Individual Rights, State Interests and the Power to Waive ICSID Jurisdiction under Bilateral Investment Treaties", *Arbitration International*, Vol. 20 (2004), p. 185 with footnote 24.

[176] *Fraport AG Frankfurt Airport Services Worldwide* v. *The Republic of the Philippines*, ICSID Case No. ARB/03/25 (L. Yves Fortier, Bernardo M. Cremades

Whether the investment is *made* illegally or *maintained* illegally should not be viewed as an outcome-determinative distinction. The general purpose of a bilateral or multilateral investment treaty is to give protection only to legal investments not tainted by corruption. It is submitted that if protection were denied only for investments that were made illegally and not to those that were maintained illegally, investors could be incentivized to maintain protection by forming the investment legally and committing criminal acts at a later stage.

Accordingly, it would be inconsistent for international law to sanction corruption but still protect a corrupt investment if the corruption were committed in order to maintain the investment instead of initially in order to procure it. With respect to the deleterious effects of corruption, it makes no difference whether the corruption occurs at the time of procurement or while maintaining or seeking to maintain the investment at a later time. Furthermore, only investors complying with basic principles of international law promote growth that would be sustainable *without* ongoing bribery[177].

Thus, it would be contrary to international law and public policy if investors were permitted to commit illegal acts such as corruption in order to maintain their investment and still take advantage of either contract-based or particularly treaty-based protections for their

---

and W. Michael Reisman), Award, 16 August 2007, para. 402 (emphasis added); available at http://ita.law.uvic.ca/documents/FraportAward.pdf.

[177] On the growing international consensus that corruption hinders economic growth and seriously undermines the credibility of public institutions, see E. de Laurentiis, "Institutional Strengthening of Public Sector Procurement", in D. Bradlow and A. Escher (eds.), *Legal Aspects of Foreign Direct Investment*, The Hague, Kluwer Law International, 1999, p. 244.

investments in conformity with applicable standards of international law. Indeed, a failure to maintain the investment legally should normally result in a failure to remain in conformity with those standards. Consequently, it can and should be concluded that an investor who does not maintain the investment in compliance with international law thereby loses protections under the applicable investment protection treaty which it might otherwise enjoy.

The foregoing is from the perspective of alleged or proven illegality by the *investor*, who is invariably the claimant in an investment protection dispute and not vulnerable to claims or counterclaims by the host State respondent, other than a claim for the costs of arbitration. The focus on this perspective is thus intentional, and not at all meant to turn a blind eye to or seem less concerned with the prospect of illegality by the host State respondent, or by the respondent contracting party in a commercial contract dispute. Indeed the consequences of the respondent's illegal conduct are a significant question which is addressed in detail below[178].

Finally, query where it is of any relevance for assessing the possible consequences of the illegality for the tribunal's authority whether the investment was originally made in compliance with the applicable law. It is submitted that the answer is no: the relevant time for determining the legality of the investment for purposes of the existence of jurisdiction is the date of the institution of proceedings. If at the time the proceedings were instituted the investment had already become illegal due to the claimant's antecedent related acts of bribery, then the original lack of illegality, for example when the investment was first made, would not undo the subsequent illegality at the time the arbitral procedure was invoked.

---

[178] See *infra* Chapter VII.

## G. *Different National Legislative Approaches to the Definition of Illegality*

That divergent approaches exist with respect to certain basic elements of conduct in international commerce is relevant if and when an arbitral dispute arises and competing arguments under national law on the one hand and transnational principles on the other are made, or between one national law and another national law.

As mentioned earlier [179], depending upon the commercial or investment context and the applicable laws, including the *lex arbitri* (if any) and the *lex causae* as well as the law of putative enforcement, whether something is illegal may depend on which law applies. Thus whether the competence and authority of the arbitral tribunal may depend on the same question. And whether the decision made by the tribunal, to uphold or to deny its jurisdiction, is enforceable will also depend on the same question. To say that the outcome may be seen as a moving target, even as to a basic question of corruption, is thus not an overstatement.

### 1. *"Facilitation payments", "speed money" and "grease payments"*

The comparison already made between the FCPA in the United States and the very recent UK Bribery Act with respect to so-called facilitation payments brings into sharp focus the fact that even while international instruments such as at the UN and OECD level have sought to harmonize definitions of illegality, national instruments have often consciously gone their own way. The area of "facilitation payments", "speed money" or "grease payments" is a graphic example.

---

[179] See *supra* Chapter I.B.

Facilitation payments have been defined recently as follows: "Payment made with the purpose of expediting or facilitating the provision of services or routine government action which an official is normally obliged to perform."[180]

Facilitation payments are specifically permitted, subject to defined limits, in Australia[181], Canada[182],

---

[180] UK Law Commission, "Reforming Bribery — A Consultation Paper", Consultation Paper No. 185 (2007), p. 291, para. F.5 of Appendix F. Available at http://lawcommission.justice.gov.uk/docs/cp185_Reforming_Bribery_consultation.pdf.

[181] See the facilitation payments defence in Article 70 (4) of the 1995 Australian Criminal Code Act. On 15 November 2011, the Australian Minister for Home Affairs launched a Public Consultation Paper with the topic of "Assessing the 'facilitation payments' defence to the Foreign Bribery offence and other measures". Available at http://www.crimeprevention.gov.au/Financialcrime/Documents/v2Public%20consultation%20paper%20-%20amendments%20to%20bribery%20offences%20%20corrected%20version%2018%20November%202011.pdf. According to the Australian Government's Attorney-General's Department (Crime Prevention), "[t]he consultation was conducted during the period from November 2011 to February 2012". It also states that the Australian "[g]overnment will take into consideration all the submissions received when determining the next steps to be taken in relation to the issues raised in the consultation paper". See http://www.crimeprevention.gov.au/Financialcrime/Pages/Briberyofforeignpublicofficials.aspx.

[182] See the exception for facilitation payments in Subsection 3 (4) of the 1999 Corruption of Foreign Public Officials Act (46-47 Elizabeth II, Bill S-21). However, on 5 and 12 February 2013, the Senate of Canada has conducted two readings of the Fighting Foreign Corruption Act (60-61 Elizabeth II, Bill S-14) which *inter alia* aims to repeal Subsection 3 (4) and its faciliation payments exception. The text and the status of the Fighting Foreign Corruption Act can be retrieved from http://www.parl.gc.ca/LegisInfo/BillDetails.aspx?Language=E&Mode=1&billId=5960855. (Last access on 19 February 2013.)

New Zealand[183], South Korea[184] and particularly the United States[185]. They are not specifically prohibited under the OECD Bribery Convention[186]. They are

---

[183] See Sec. 105C (3) of the New Zealand Crimes Act 1961:

> "This section does not apply if — *(a)* the act that is alleged to constitute the offence was committed for the sole or primary *purpose of ensuring or expediting the performance by a foreign public official of a routine government action; and (b) the value of the benefit is small.*" (Emphasis added.)

[184] Korean Act on Combating Bribery of Foreign Public Officials in International Business Transactions.

[185] 15 USC § 78dd-1 *(b)*; see *infra* at footnote 168.

[186] However, in the Commentaries on the Convention on Combating Bribery of Foreign Public Officials in International Business Transactions, Art. 1, para. 9:

> "Small 'facilitation' payments do not constitute payments made 'to obtain or retain business or other improper advantage' within the meaning of paragraph 1 and, accordingly, are also not an offence. Such payments, which, in some countries, are made to induce public officials to perform their functions, such as issuing licenses or permits, are generally illegal in the foreign country concerned. Other countries can and should address this corrosive phenomenon by such means as support for programmes of good governance. However, criminalisation by other countries does not seem a practical or effective complementary action."

Additionally, the Council adopted on 26 November 2009, the Recommendation for Further Combating Bribery of Foreign Public Officials in International Business Transactions which *inter alia* states:

> "Member countries should: (i) undertake to periodically review their policies and approach on small facilitation payments in order to effectively combat the phenomenon; (ii) encourage companies to prohibit or discourage the use of small facilitation payments in internal company controls, ethics and compliance pro-

specifically prohibited under the UK Bribery Act[187] and most other national laws[188].

## 2. *Differences in the definition of elements of corrupt conduct*

Perhaps even more fundamental to the challenge of grasping a definition of illegality in the context of international disputes is the fact that certain differences exist, in national law, on the level of the constitutive elements of corrupt conduct. Thus once again depending on which national law or other sources of law apply to the question of illegality in a commercial or investment arbitration, the initial analysis of whether illegality lies may differ, and thereby influence the decision on the extent of the arbitral tribunal's power.

A graphic example of this difference in constitutive elements is to be found within one and the same legal culture, the common law family. Thus the very word "corruptly" is used *expressis verbis* in the relevant statutes in the United States[189] and Singapore[190] with-

---

grammes or measures, recognising that such payments are generally illegal in the countries where they are made, and must in all cases be accurately accounted for in such companies' books and financial records."

[187] See *supra* at footnote 169.
[188] C. Nicchols *et al.*, *Corruption and Misuse of Public Office*, 2nd ed., Oxford, Oxford University Press, 2011, paras. 4.120-4.121.
[189] 15 USC §78dd-1 *(a)* and *(g)*, §78dd-2 *(a)* and *(i)* as well as §78dd-3 *(a)*.
[190] Especially Sec. 5 of the Singaporean 1993 Prevention of Corruption Act:

"Any person who shall by himself or by or in conjunction with any other person — *(a) corruptly* solicit or receive, or agree to receive for himself, or for any other person; or *(b) corruptly* give, promise or offer to any person whether for the benefit of that person or of

out any express statutory definition of the term. By contrast, the more recent UK Bribery Act of 2010 has taken a different approach.

The term "corruptly" is not expressly required as part of the statutory definition of guilt in the case of bribery: Section 1 (2) *(a)* requests the intention of "the advantage — (i) to induce a person to perform improperly a relevant function or activity, or (ii) to reward a person for the improper performance of such a function or activity".

Pursuant to Section 4 (1) *(a)*, a relevant function or activity "is performed improperly if it is performed in breach of a relevant expectation" to which belong good faith [191], impartiality [192] and adherence to the position of trust [193].

In the event of an arbitral dispute as to whether illegality lies and which law applies to the definition of corruption, it would not be far-fetched for the outcome of the analysis to differ where the respective statutes employ different terms respecting the constitutive elements.

Arguments built around "good faith", "impartiality", "breach of trust" etc. will resonate differently with different triers of fact, even if there is general agreement that bribery is wrong and illegal. What is "good faith" dealing is subject to interpretation, all the more so given that not every legal culture or system even has a concept, in statute or case law or both, of "good faith".

---

another person, . . . shall be guilty of an offence . . ." (Emphasis added.)

For a detailed view of the meaning of "corruptly" under the Prevention of Corruption Act, see C. Ong *et al.*, "The Meaning of 'Corruptly'", *Singapore Academy of Law Journal*, Vol. 11, 1999, pp. 147 *et seq.*

[191] Sec. 3 (3), UK Bribery Act.
[192] Sec. 3 (4), UK Bribery Act.
[193] Sec. 3 (5), UK Bribery Act.

### 3. *Differences in the dividing line between corrupt and non-corrupt intermediaries*

A further complication may arise where the conduct at issue is clearly defined and demonstrated, and the facts surrounding it are not even in dispute, but the nature of the act or the actor associated with the conduct is in question. The reason for the debate could be that depending upon the legal standard applied to the nature of the act or the actor, the conduct could be considered corrupt or not corrupt.

The intermediary agreement or the agreement providing for "trading in influence" or "influence peddling" demonstrates this challenge. Such agreements do not necessarily violate *domestic* law, depending on the jurisdiction. A case in point is the law of the one country whose substantive law and/or arbitration law serve more frequently than perhaps any other as a perceived satisfactory compromise in commercial cross-border contracts and dispute resolution mechanisms: Switzerland.

Interestingly, under Swiss obligations law as codified and also interpreted by jurisprudence there is no *per se* prohibition against intermediary agreements, "agency contracts" or "brokerage contracts". Thus, pursuant to Article 412 (1) of the Swiss Code of Obligations ("CO"),

> "A brokerage contract is a contract whereby the broker is instructed to alert the principal to an opportunity to conclude a contract or to facilitate the conclusion of a contract in exchange for a fee."

Furthermore, pursuant to Article 412 (2), CO, "The brokerage contract is generally subject to the provisions governing simple agency contracts" (Art. 412 (2), CO (which includes Arts. 394-406, CO)).

While these provisions will not render an outright bribery payment legal if subject to Swiss law, by their terms they could legitimize numerous forms of intermediary, business consultant and lobbying arrangements in which the person being paid is being paid for the performance of informing the principal of an "opportunity" or of facilitating entering into a contract related to such opportunity, and nothing more. This begs the question of how and by what means the person in the "broker's position" came to learn of such opportunity, the extent of efforts undertaken to do so, the same questions with regard to "facilitation", and the amount of the fee and its proportionality to the extent and value of the efforts undertaken. It is these questions, among others, which have challenged arbitral tribunals confronted with such kinds of contracts in commercial contracts in which Swiss law has had possible application, and would legitimize such arrangements where another law might not do so.

The initial challenge is of course the nature of such a contract or arrangement, quite apart from whether it involves private entities, public entities or both. Is the contract or arrangement legal influence peddling or is it illegal corruption? While the analysis, as in any case of allegations of corruption or bribery, will depend on the facts and the extent to which the associated evidentiary burdens have been met, as discussed in detail below[194]. At the same time, where Swiss obligations law applies, it is telling that an arbitral tribunal may first come to the conclusion that such arrangements are in principle legal, as did the tribunal in the well-known decision of the highest court in Switzerland in *Hilmarton* v. *Omnium* in 1990 in review of an international commercial arbitration award rendered under the ICC Rules at a Geneva seat in application of Swiss law:

---

[194] See *infra* Chapter VI.C.3 and Chapter VI.C.4.

"[T]he use of intermediaries to follow a dossier within an administration is allowed in our legal system. The negotiation through intermediaries of a contract with the State administration, if no doubtful activities are developed, is part of the activities normally and by definition developed by brokers, like the negotiation of contracts between private persons." [195]

What are "doubtful activities" will then be a further question, but the arrangement *per se* will not be illegal, as already held by the underlying arbitral tribunal two years earlier: to be illegal, the brokerage contract requires proof that both parties actually intended for the intermediary to bribe or otherwise exercise improper influence over a third party or that the agreement was performed in this manner — *Hilmarton (Agent)* v. *Omnium/Algeria*, ICC Case No. 5622 (1988) [196]. This conclusion too is notable, because it means that if Swiss substantive law is applied to the arrangement, "influence" *per se* is not illegal as long as it is not "improper". What is improper influence will need to be alleged, proved and found on a case-by-case basis.

The influence of Swiss law in this regard cannot be underestimated, both because of the importance of Switzerland as a choice of law and choice of seat of arbitration in many commercial disputes and because of the influence of Swiss obligations law on the drafting of certain other laws of obligations, for example,

---

[195] Tribunal Fédéral [Swiss Federal Tribunal], *Omnium de Traitement et de Valorisation — OTV* v. *Hilmarton*, judgment of 17 April 1990, *XIX Yearbook Commercial Arbitration*, 1994, p. 222 para. 25.

[196] The arbitral award of 1988 is published in *XIX Yearbook Commercial Arbitration*, 1994, pp. 105 *et seq.*

that of Turkey[197]. It is also notable because, as will be discussed below[198], arbitral awards rendered at a Swiss seat or under Swiss law or both are then subject to recognition and enforcement outside of Switzerland, most particularly under the New York Convention. There the question will arise of whether an award based on a finding of legal brokerage activity is susceptible of refusal of enforcement for violation of public policy under the local law of attempted enforcement. Finally, as also addressed below, it is important in investment treaty-based arbitrations in which public international law principles may apply, for example under Article 42 (1) of the ICSID Convention[199]. The tribunal must assess whether a brokerage arrangement, particularly involving some activity possibly attributable to the host State, is legal under the applicable law while an annulment tribunal under Article 52 (1) *(b)* of the ICSID Convention must assess a possible violation of the manifest excess of powers standard[200].

Returning to the focus of Swiss law in international commercial arbitration, various tribunals applying

---

[197] A. Oguz, "The Role of Comparative Law in the Development of Turkish Civil Law", *Pace International Law Review*, Vol. 17 (2005), p. 380.

[198] *Infra* Chapter XI.

[199] "The Tribunal shall decide a dispute in accordance with such rules of law as may be agreed by the parties. In the absence of such agreement, the Tribunal shall apply the law of the Contracting State party to the dispute (including its rules on the conflict of laws) and such rules of international law as may be applicable."

[200] "Either party may request annulment of the award by an application in writing addressed to the Secretary-General on one or more of the following grounds: *(a)* that the Tribunal was not properly constituted; *(b)* that the Tribunal has manifestly exceeded its powers; . . ."

Swiss law have upheld validity of intermediary agreements. Thus the arbitral tribunal in the well-known case of *Westacre* v. *Jugoimport*, an ICC dispute with a Geneva seat applying Swiss law, held: "Lobbying as such is not an illegal activity. Lobbying by private enterprises to obtain contracts in third countries is frequently carried on with active support from the state . . ." Having "good contacts with the people making decisions for [Yugoslavia]" did not establish the existence of bribery or other illicit activity. In fact, this "was probably why [the alleging party] secured Claimant's services" in the first place . . . (*Westacre (UK)* v. *Jugoimport (Yugoslavia)*, ICC Case No. 7047 (1994))[201].

The frankness of the tribunal's statement may be a correct and pragmatic application of Swiss law to some, and a naive and dangerous condoning of activity leading to bribery to others and the decision is by no means exceptional.

Thus in another case, ten years earlier, an ICC award rendered at a Vienna seat in application of Swiss law, the tribunal determined that this type of agreement was "perfectly valid" under Swiss law (*Agent (FL/Arab)* v. *Company (S-Korea)*, ICC Case No. 4145 (1984))[202]. The contract at issue was an intermediary agreement aimed at "convincing the Ministry and/or the World Bank team to deal with Defendant, better than with other competitors", which included enjoying "excellent connections . . . that enabled it to provide the Defendant with important information and to exert a certain influence on the decision to be taken"[203].

---

[201] *Westacre* v. *Jugoimport*, ICC Case No. 7047 (1994), Award, 28 February 1994, *ASA Bulletin*, Vol. 13 (1995), pp. 339 and 342.
[202] ICC Case No. 4145, *Collection of ICC Arbitral Awards*, Vol. II, p. 63, para. 63.
[203] ICC Case No. 4145, *Collection of ICC Arbitral Awards*, Vol. II, p. 62, para. 62.

And in another case, four years after *Westacre*, an ICC Award rendered at a Geneva seat in application of Swiss law, the tribunal held, interestingly, that precisely the existence of a certain loyalty between the public official and the family of the intermediary served to *exclude* the presence of acts of corruption:

> "The privileged and uncontested relations between the family of the claimant and the President [of the public purchasing entity] would have rather been of such a nature as to facilitate the efforts of the claimant and the obtaining of useful information, on an amicable and free basis, without any corruption being necessary or envisaged." (*Agent (North African State)* v. *Contractor (F)*, ICC Case No. 9333 (1998).)[204]

Again, from one perspective this kind of conclusion might be the ultimate in pragmatism and not searching for illegality where it does not really exist. From another perspective, however, precisely this linking between close relations and amicable obtaining of "useful information" might be considered the ultimate in either naivety or shortsightedness or both. And yet this general position has also been upheld in some circumstances by courts reviewing the enforceability of awards, including outside the sphere of Swiss law. As will be discussed in greater detail later on[205], the English Court of Appeal has acknowledged the Swiss position as a matter of the foreign *lex causae* and held that absent sufficient evidence to constitute bribery the recognition of the award in *Westacre* would not necessarily be objectionable:

---

[204] Translated by A. Sayed, *supra* footnote 2, p. 131, footnote 400. The ICC Case No. 9333 (1998) Final Award is published in *ASA Bulletin*, Vol. 19 (2001), p. 757 (quotation retrievable at p. 770).

[205] See *infra* Chapter III.B.3.c.iii.

"[A] contract for the purchase of personal influence short of bribery would not be contrary to the public policy of Switzerland and would not be contrary to public policy in Switzerland to enforce a contract that involved the commission of acts contrary to the public policy of . . . any other foreign and friendly state as opposed to being 'illegal' by the law of that state."[206]

## H. Illegality and Investment Arbitration

Finally, in our overview of attempts to define illegality, we address briefly the context specifically of investment protection-related arbitration, both ICSID and non-ICSID. Foreign direct investment, or "FDI", is regulated by a patchwork of bilateral and regional investment treaties. A common treaty requirement provides that investments must be made in compliance with the laws and regulations of the host State, or "in accordance with host State law", as discussed in greater detail below[207]. A purpose of such clauses has been held to be "to prevent the Bilateral Treaty from protecting investments that should not be protected, particularly because they would be illegal" (*Salini* v. *Morocco*, ICSID 2001)[208].

An arbitral tribunal confronted with such a clause, or even in the absence of such a clause confronted with the co-existence of host State law and public interna-

---

[206] Court of Appeal, *Westacre Investments Inc.* v. *Jugoimport-SPDR Holding Co. Ltd and Others*, 12 May 1999, XXIVa, *Yearbook Commercial Arbitration*, 1999, p. 762.

[207] See *infra* Chapter IX.C.2.b.

[208] *Salini Construttori S.p.A. & Italstrade S.p.A.* v. *Kingdom of Morocco*, ICSID Case No. ARB 00/4, Decision on Jurisdiction, 16 July 2001. Available at http://italaw.com/sites/default/files/case-documents/ita0738.pdf.

tional law principles, may be challenged to decide
whether an act constitutes corruption or bribery under
one, both or neither bases. If the outcome is different
depending upon the application, then the arbitral tribunal will also need to assess which applied law prevails, as will be discussed further below[209].

By way of example, host States have contended that
the "in accordance with host State law" provision
would already limit the definition of investment under
a BIT to the domestic notion of "investment" instead
of referring to and requiring proof of the legality of the
investment in order to be deserving of protection[210].
While this contention arises from time to time, it may
be seen as having been discredited and a consensus can
be detected to the effect that an investment made or
obtained through corruption, even if it somehow fulfilled the requirement of being in accordance with host
State law, should not generally be afforded protection
under public international law[211].

In this context, a further wrinkle is the distinction
which may need to be drawn between corruption and
other kinds of illegality for purposes of considering
whether there has been a breach of domestic law so as
to exclude investment protection. Two main categories
have been posited here: illegality *per se*, involving the
illegality of the business activity itself or of the assets
used for this purpose under domestic law[212] versus
simple breaches of *de minimis* domestic formalities, as
for example found in the case of *Tokios Tokelés* v.

---

[209] See *infra* Chapter IV.

[210] *Salini* v. *Morocco*, *supra* footnote 208.

[211] C. McLachlan, L. Shore and M. Weiniger, *supra*
footnote 21, para. 6.64.

[212] *Inceysa Vallisoletana S.L.* v. *Republic of El Salvador*, ICSID Case No. ARB 03/26, Decision on Jurisdiction, 2 August 2006, available at http://italaw.com/doc-
uments/InceysaDescription.pdf.

*Ukraine*, ICSID 2007[213]. Illegality *per se* can include breaches of fundamental principles of the domestic law, for example, by fraudulent misrepresentations or dissimulation of true ownership — *Desert Line* v. *Yemen*, ICSID 2008[214]. Accordingly, as in commercial arbitration so in investment-treaty arbitration fraud can rise to the level of corruption or bribery for purposes of the later competence-competence analysis.

---

[213] *Tokios Tokelés* v. *Ukraine*, ICSID Case No. ARB/02/18, Award, 26 July 2007 (available at http://italaw.com/sites/default/files/case-documents/ita0866.pdf.

[214] *Desert Line Projects LLC* v. *Republic of Yemen*, ICSID Case No. ARB/05/17, Award, 6 February 2008, para. 104. Available at http://italaw.com/sites/default/files/case-documents/ita0248_0.pdf.

## CHAPTER III

## THE CONTEXT OF PRIVATE INTERNATIONAL LAW VERSUS PUBLIC INTERNATIONAL LAW

### A. Introduction

The focus of these lectures' analysis of competence-competence and corruption is in both private and public international law. Specifically, it is the role of public international law, private international law and the otherwise chosen law in the context of the ability of the arbitrator to adjudicate issues of corruption, including when corruption is alleged, suspected, admitted or found to infect the underlying contract and/or even the underlying basis for arbitration, whether in the conventional commercial context or in the investment-treaty based context.

In this regard, we have three main perspectives: *(a)* international commercial arbitration based on contractual privity, *(b)* international investment arbitration likewise based on contractual privity, and *(c)* international investment arbitration based on a BIT or MIT, without contractual privity. We look at each basis in turn.

### 1. International commercial arbitration based on contractual privity

The most frequently encountered form of arbitration is commercial arbitration based on contractual privity, usually in the form of a bilateral written contract. Two aspects of this kind of contract concern us generally and in the specific context of competence-competence and corruption.

*First*, we have the conventional party-to-party choice of substantive law or, absent such a choice or a choice in a valid manner, a mechanism for determining law or rules of law. Generally, a national law or rules of law will apply to the substantive adjudication of the claims and defences under the contract, including one related to or giving rise to allegations or finding of corruption. *Second*, we have the conventional party-to-party choice of a seat of arbitration or, absent such a choice or a choice in a valid, operative and per-formable manner in the sense of Article II (3) of the New York Convention [215], a mechanism for determining the seat, and thereby the *lex arbitri*.

In respect of both the substantive law and the seat of arbitration, public policy will be an important com-ponent in at least the first two of the following three connections.

*First*, the arbitral tribunal will normally have regard for the public policy of the applied substantive law or rules of law, including so-called "international public policy" or "transnational public policy", to which we will return shortly [216]. *Second*, the public policy of the *lex arbitri* will be of concern, for purposes of the proper conduct of the arbitration at the seat of arbitra-tion and for control of the enforceability of the award under the grounds for set aside of the award under

---

[215] The New York Convention, Article II (3), provides that

"the court of a Contracting State, when seized of an action in a matter in respect of which the parties have made an agreement within the meaning of this article, shall, at the request of one of the parties, refer the par-ties to arbitration, unless it finds that the said agree-ment is null and void, inoperative or incapable of being performed".

[216] N. Blackaby and C. Partasides with A. Redfern and M. Hunter, *supra* footnote 7, para. 10.85.

the law of arbitration at the seat, for example, under Article 34 (2) *(b)* (ii) of the UNCITRAL Model Law[217]. *Third*, the arbitral tribunal may wish to have regard for the public policy of the law of enforcement of the award in a country other than at the seat, for example, under the public policy ground for refusal of recognition and enforcement under Article V (2) *(b)* of the New York Convention[218].

Whether one subscribes to the view that the arbitral tribunal has a duty to ensure the enforceability of the award or merely to take best efforts in that direction or something in between[219], the first and second of the above three standards will need to be addressed, while the third may not be and indeed may not be apparent in any event. At the same time, the parties to the arbitration may well be invoking the public policy of one or another jurisdiction away from the seat throughout the

---

[217] See Art. 34 (2) *(b)* (ii), UNCITRAL Model Law (UNCITRAL Model Law on International Commercial Arbitration, Sales No. E.08.V.4, Vienna, United Nations, 2006, available at http://www.uncitral.org/pdf/english/texts/arbitration/ml-arb/07-86998_Ebook.pdf).

[218] Pursuant to Art. V (2) *(b)* of the New York Convention

"Recognition and enforcement of an arbitral award may also be refused if the competent authority in the country where recognition and enforcement is sought finds that . . . *(b)* the recognition or enforcement of the award would be contrary to the public policy of that country."

[219] N. Blackaby and C. Partasides with A. Redfern and M. Hunter, *supra* footnote 7, para. 11.11; see e.g. Art. 41 of the ICC Rules, which provides that "the arbitral tribunal shall act in the spirit of the Rules and shall make every effort to make sure that the award is enforceable at law"; Art. 32 (2) of the LCIA Rules specifies that "the arbitral tribunal and the parties shall act in the spirit of these Rules and shall make every reasonable effort to ensure that an award is legally enforceable".

arbitration as an alleged standard of control for the tribunal. In many international commercial arbitrations, including precisely those involving corruption allegations, there may well be possible conflicts or disconnects between and among the foregoing standards which the arbitral tribunal will be called upon to resolve.

## 2. *International investment arbitration based on contractual privity*

A second, but far rarer form of arbitration is international investment arbitration based on contractual privity, again usually in the form of a bilateral written contract but additionally involving or claimed to be involving an investment which benefits from a bilateral or multilateral investment treaty. An example of such a contract which resulted in an international arbitration award involving issues of competence-competence, admissibility and corruption was *World Duty Free* v. *Kenya*[220], to which we will return frequently below[221].

Here, the same two aspects of this kind of contract concern us in the specific context of competence-competence and corruption, but with some variation as compared with conventional international commercial arbitration.

*First*, we again have the conventional party-to-party choice of substantive law or, absent such a choice or a choice in a valid manner, a mechanism for determining law or rules of law in the investment contract itself. A national law or rules of law will apply to the substantive adjudication of the claims and defences under the investment contract. At the same time, to the extent the

---

[220] *World Duty Free* v. *Kenya*, *supra* footnote 44.
[221] See, *inter alia*, the case summary below at Chapter VII.C.

investor invokes the protections of an investment treaty, he will also invoke the choice-of-law provision contained within that agreement, which may be different than the contractually agreed choice of law. That choice of law in the treaty will invariably foresee some application of public international law principles, and certainly in a manner and to an extent not possible in a conventional commercial arbitration involving a single country's substantive law.

*Second*, the investment contract may or may not have a conventional party-to-party choice of a seat of arbitration and thus may or may not have a specific *lex arbitri*. If it has a choice of a seat of arbitration, then the *lex arbitri* and its public policy will play a similar role to that of a commercial arbitration. If it does not provide for a seat of arbitration, then whether there will be a conventional seat and *lex arbitri* at all will depend on what kind of investment treaty-based arbitration is agreed upon or invoked.

In the case of an ICSID arbitration without a seat, there will be no *lex arbitri* and no "local" public policy ground for setting aside the ICSID award at the seat, but there may be a "transnational" or "international" public policy ground for annulment of the award under Article 52 (1) *(b)* of the ICSID Convention in the context of a "manifest excess of powers"[222]. In those situations where the bilateral investment treaty[223] or a

---

[222] Art. 52 (1) *(b)* of the ICSID Convention (Convention on the Settlement of Investment Disputes between States and Nationals of Other States, 575 *United Nations Treaty Series* 259, signed on 18 March 1965, entered into force on 14 October 1966, available at https://icsid.world-bank.org/ICSID/StaticFiles/basicdoc/CRR_English-final.pdf).
[223] For example, the 2003 BIT between Germany and China provides at Art. 9 (3) as follows: "The dispute shall be submitted for arbitration under the [ICSID] Convention,

multilateral investment treaty such as the ECT allows the investor to choose ICSID arbitration without a seat or, for example, UNCITRAL *ad hoc* rules arbitration with a seat[224], then the standard of public policy applicable to the corruption issues may be governed by a party agreement after the dispute has arisen and after the conduct is alleged to have taken place.

If ICSID is chosen, then Article 52 of the ICSID Convention for annulment without express reference to public policy violations will apply, and the ICSID Convention provisions respecting self-executing enforcement will also apply[225]. If the UNCITRAL Rules are chosen, then a seat of arbitration will need to be agreed or fixed, and the *lex arbitri* of that seat, for example, The Hague or Stockholm, will apply for purposes of the public policy standard for possible annulment while cross-border enforcement will be governed by the public policy standard under Article V (2) *(b)* of the New York Convention, which provides for refusal of enforcement for violation of the public policy under the national law of the enforcing court.

In respect of both the substantive law and the seat of arbitration, public policy will be an important component in the same way as described above for commercial arbitration involving based on contractual privity.

*First*, the arbitral tribunal will normally have regard for the public policy of the applied substantive law or rules of law, including so-called "international public

---

unless the parties in dispute agree on an ad-hoc arbitral tribunal to be established under the [UNCITRAL Rules] or other arbitration rules."

[224] See Art. 26 (4) *(b)*, Energy Charter Treaty (Energy Charter Treaty, 2080 *United Nations Treaty Series* 95, signed on 17 December 1994, entered into force on 16 April 1998, available at http://www.encharter.org/fileadmin/user_upload/document/EN.pdf)

[225] Art. 54 of the ICSID Convention.

policy" or "transnational public policy", to which we will return shortly[226]. A difference will be that such international or transnational norms may assume far greater and more direct importance in an investment arbitration based on a treaty than in a commercial contract. *Second*, the public policy of the *lex arbitri* will again be of concern, but only if there is a seat of arbitration, which would not be the case for an ICSID Convention arbitration. *Third*, the arbitral tribunal may again wish to have regard for the public policy of the law of enforcement of the award in a country other than at the seat, but only if there is a seat of arbitration. In an ICSID Convention arbitration, the public policy ground for refusal of recognition and enforcement under Article V (2) *(b)* of the New York Convention would be irrelevant inasmuch as the ICSID Convention itself, and not the New York Convention, would govern recognition and enforcement and the refusal thereof[227].

## 3. International investment arbitration based on a BIT or MIT, without contractual privity

We have already addressed in passing above the third category in the second category, namely the most frequent form of international investment arbitration with a corruption component, based not in a contract but solely in a BIT or MIT. Here, issues of corruption will be analysed in the context of a treaty-based choice of a substantive law or a mechanism for determining the law or rules of law.

Depending on the treaty at issue, this may be a hierarchy or mixture of national law or rules of law and principles of public international law. For example,

---

[226] N. Blackaby and C. Partasides with A. Redfern and M. Hunter, *supra* footnote 7, para. 10.85.
[227] See Arts. 54 *et seq.*, ICSID Convention.

Article 10 (6) of the 1976 Germany-Israel BIT provides that

> "the arbitral tribunal shall reach its decision on the basis of the Treaties existing between the Contracting Parties and of general international law, and taking into account the local law of the Contracting Party in which the investment is situated".

Among the decisions which have recently grappled with this issue are *Fraport* v. *Philippines*[228], *Siemens* v. *Argentina*[229] and *World Duty Free* v. *Kenya*[230]. And here depending on the treaty and the choice or election of arbitral rules, there will either be a conventional national seat and thereby national *lex arbitri* or, more frequently, ICSID Convention arbitration devoid of a national seat or national *lex arbitri*. Thus the majority of international investment arbitrations concerned with corruption allegations have had regard for so-called "international public policy" or "transnational public policy", the standards applicable to such public policy have related primarily but not exclusively to public international law and not a national law, and the arbitral tribunal's decision has been rendered, and reviewed, under the "manifest excess of powers" standard of the ICSID Convention[231].

In short, the question of the ability of the arbitrator to adjudicate issues of corruption, including when corruption is alleged, suspected, admitted or found to infect the underlying contract and/or even the underlying basis for arbitration, is a question of the sanctity and enforceability, if any, of the ultimate award. Here,

---

[228] *Fraport AG* v. *The Republic of the Philippines*, *supra* footnote 176.

[229] *Siemens AG* v. *The Argentine Republic*, ICSID Case No. ARB/02/8, Award, 6 February 2007.

[230] *World Duty Free* v. *Kenya*, *supra* footnote 44.

[231] See Art. 52 (1) *(b)* of the ICSID Convention.

depending on the context, there may be a role for public international law, private international law, and the otherwise chosen law. This is all the more so since any so-called international public policy or transnational public policy may be deemed to inform the otherwise applicable law, and be mandatorily binding.

## B. The Meaning of Public Policy in International Arbitration

As stated, most modern States consider the definition of corruption and bribery to extend to include all persons who are induced to act corruptly in the discharge of their duties, whether in the public sector or the private sector. Statutory definitions of bribery in most national criminal laws are also essentially the same or to similar effect as in Article 15, UN Convention against Corruption, and Article 1 (1) of the OECD Anti-Bribery Convention. And indeed even if bribery were not to be defined or codified as a criminal offence under an applicable national law, it may still be a violation of international law, and international law may still be deemed to be part of the applicable law, via the route of international or transnational public policy, and/or to be a control on the enforceability of any arbitral decision in set aside or annulment proceedings or enforcement proceedings, depending on the contract or treaty context.

## 1. Limitations to party autonomy

Arbitration is essentially private dispute settlement based on party autonomy. Party autonomy, however, is not without its limits. There are important limitations on party autonomy, most notably on grounds of public policy. The importance of this limitation is demonstrated by the fact that public policy is only one of two grounds expressly set forth in the New York Convention by which a court may, under its own law, refuse to enforce an arbitral award, the other being arbitrability[232]. It is this intersection of party autonomy and public policy that is of particular interest, and a special challenge, in the area of arbitration of corruption issues[233].

*First*, there may be public policy limitations to the general right to submit disputes related to corruption, and thereby possibly to criminal law, to arbitration. In the public interest, a State can reserve certain subject matters to the exclusive domain of the national courts and thereby exclude or severely circumscribe arbitrability. In the context of corruption, public policy considerations can be of particular relevance inasmuch as the issue may particularly implicate public interest, including the sovereign's desire and right to retain prosecution of criminal matters to itself.

Moreover, depending on the applicable law and the specific circumstances, public policy considerations may also render an arbitration agreement void or voidable. Since the arbitration agreement is the basis for any arbitration, at least in the commercial context, voidness or voidability of the arbitration agreement may well translate into an undermining or lack of jurisdiction of the arbitral tribunal and, hence, into a lack of basis for the arbitration proceedings overall.

*Second*, there may be public policy limitations to both the substantive and the procedural laws that may be applicable to the dispute. So-called mandatory laws may limit the parties' freedom of choice of the substantive law or laws. So-called procedural public policy,

---

[232] See Art. V (2) of the New York Convention.
[233] See generally R. Kreindler and A. Tevini, "The Impact of Public Policy Considerations", in T. D. Halket (ed.), *Arbitration of International Intellectual Property Disputes*, Juris Publishing, 2012, Chap. 9, p. 437.

overlapping in large part with concepts of due process, may restrict the arbitral tribunal's otherwise existing discretion to determine the procedural course of the arbitration.

*Third*, there may be public policy limitations to the enforcement of an arbitral award. National arbitration laws typically include public policy grounds among the grounds for challenging international arbitral awards at the seat of the arbitration, in the commercial context. Public policy violations are, as previously noted, also a ground for refusal of enforcement pursuant to Article V of the New York Convention. While they are not expressly a ground for annulment pursuant to the ICSID Convention, they can be and are so considered, most often in the context of a "manifest excess of powers".

## 2. *The meaning and function of public policy in international arbitration*

When employing the concept of public policy, we refer to the "fundamental notions of a particular legal system"[234]. At the same time, a precise definition of public policy is "notoriously difficult"[235], and the concept is also not applied in a uniform fashion. Public policy has been called "one of the most elusive and divergent notions in the world of juridical science"[236],

---

[234] B. Hanotiau and O. Caprasse, "Public Policy in International Commercial Arbitration", in E. Gaillard and D. di Pietro (eds.), *Enforcement of Arbitration Agreements and International Arbitral Awards — The New York Convention in Practice*, London, Cameron May Ltd., 2008, p. 789.

[235] *Ibid.*, p. 788.

[236] M. Ferrante, "Enforcement of Foreign Arbitral Awards in Italy and Public Policy", in *Hommage à Frederic Eisemann, Liber Amicorum*, ICC Publishing, 1978, p. 86.

and a concept so vague and fundamental that it is much easier to feel than to define[237]. It has been referred to as a "particularly fleeting" concept which "probably borrows part of its majesty from the mystery by which it is surrounded"[238].

There is a variety in the interpretation of public policy from country to country. It is precisely these differences in understanding of public policy between national laws that give meaning to public policy as a limitation to international arbitration, particularly in the commercial area. If public policy were defined the same way worldwide, no nation State would have significant grounds, for example, to refuse enforcement of awards rendered in another nation State on grounds of a violation of its own — differing — public policy[239].

In addition, public policy is also not a static concept. It differs with time, as the principles that a State considers to be fundamental to its legal and social framework evolve, and as the public policy exception as a "judicially administered legal principle is further specified and interpreted by national jurisprudence"[240]. As was already stated more than a century ago,

---

[237] G. Horsmans, "L'arbitrage et l'ordre public interne belge", *Revue de l'arbitrage* (1978), pp. 79 *et seq.* ("Il s'agit d'une notion aussi vague que fondamentale, qui se sent bien plus qu'elle ne se définit") ("This is a concept that is as vague as it is fundamental and that is felt much more than it is defined" (author's translation)).

[238] See B. Hanotiau and O. Caprasse, *supra* footnote 234, pp. 787 *et seq.*

[239] J. García de Enterría, "The Role of Public Policy in International Commercial Arbitration", *Law and Policy in International Business*, Vol. 21 (1989-1990), p. 401.

[240] *Ibid.*, p. 402.; see also D. Otto and O. Elwan, "Art. V (2)", H. Kronke *et al.* (eds.), *Recognition and Enforcement of Foreign Arbitral Awards: A Global Commentary on the New York Convention*, The Netherlands, Kluwer Law International BV, 2010, p. 368.

"public policy in every country is in a constant state of flux. It is always evolving. It is impossible to ascertain any absolute criterion. It cannot be determined within a formula. It is a conception."[241]

Moreover, there are different concepts of public policy which vary between and among countries[242]. Many countries distinguish between a wider concept of domestic public policy *(ordre public interne)*[243], which also encompasses provisions of mandatory domestic law, and the more restrictive concept of international public policy *(ordre public international)*, which

---

[241] ICJ, *Application of the Convention of 1902 Governing Guardianship of Infants (Netherlands* v. *Sweden)*, 28 November 1958, *ICJ Reports 1958*, p. 122 (dissenting opinion of Judge Sir Percy Spender). Available at http://www.worldcourts.com/icj/eng/decisions/1958.11.28_guardianship.htm.

[242] Furthermore, traditionally a distinction was also drawn between public policy as understood in common law jurisdictions versus public policy as understood in civil law jurisdictions. The civil law concept of public policy was generally broader, since it also encompassed mandatory domestic rules and elements of due process, which, for example, in the United States are protected by the due process clause of the United States Constitution. See J. García de Enterría, *supra* footnote 239, p. 395.

[243] The *"ordre public interne"* generally is not an accepted ground for refusal of recognition and enforcement of arbitral awards pursuant to the New York Convention. See, e.g., Art. 1498, New French Code of Civil Procedure, allowing for refusal of recognition only where the recognition "manifestly contradicts the ordre public international". Hence, French courts may not refuse recognition of an arbitral award considered to implicate an "international dispute" which merely violates the *ordre public interne*, but not at the same time also the *ordre public international*. On the development of the distinction between international and domestic public policy in the United States see J. García de Enterría, *supra* footnote 239, p. 389.

respects only the most basic principles of a State, such as those that are necessary for the preservation of the legal and social order[244]. In addition, there is also the concept of *transnational* public policy, which refers to the generally internatio-nally accepted core principles, which thus are part of the public policy of the majority of States[245].

Finally, one can differentiate between substantive

---

[244] See J. García de Enterría, *ibid.*, p. 396. There is the general understanding that, while all rules of *ordre public international* are included in the notion of *ordre public interne*, not all the *ordre public interne* is part of the *ordre public international*. See L. Matray and P. Martens, "Arbitrage et ordre public interne", *Revue de l'arbitrage* (1978), p. 108.

[245] See J.-B. Racine, avant-propos de Laurence Boy, préface de Philippe Fouchard, *L'arbitrage commercial international et l'ordre public*, Paris, LGDJ, 1999, pp. 353 *et seq.* However, ascertaining the existence and violation of a principle of "transnational public policy" can be at times difficult. "The existence of transnational conventions, resolutions and the like condemning a particular practice does not automatically mean that such practice is in" violation of international public policy. See R. Kreindler, "Approaches to the Application of Trans-national Public Policy by Arbitrators", *Journal of World Investment*, Vol. 4 (2003), p. 246. At the same time, such conventions have undoubtedly contributed to the evolution of a concept of international public policy that does not tolerate certain illegal contracts. See R. Kreindler, "Schiedsgerichte und Rechtsverstöße der Vertragsparteien: Das für die Beurteilung von Rechtsverletzungen anzuwendende Recht", B. Bachmann *et al.* (eds.), *Grenzüberschreitungen, Beiträge zum Internationalen Verfahrensrecht und zur Schiedsgerichtsbarkeit, Festschrift für Peter Schlosser zum 70. Geburtstag*, Mohr Siebeck Verlag, 2005, p. 431; R. Kreindler, *supra* footnote 41, p. 212. Examples for situations affecting transnational public policy include presumably contracts promoting or facilitating corruption, drug trafficking, prostitution, torture, slavery, etc. See R. Kreindler, *supra* footnote 41, p. 262.

public policy[246] and procedural public policy[247]. Legal violations of the parties usually can result only in a

---

[246] Violations of substantive public policy may arise, for example, in the context of violations of foreign exchange, antitrust, import/export, and other regulatory legal provisions as well as in the event of a violation of public morals. R. Kreindler, *supra* footnote 245, p. 442.

[247] See R. Kreindler, "Standards of Procedural International Public Policy", *Stockholm International Arbitration Review*, Vol. 2 (2008), pp. 143-144 ("Generally, to make out a standard of 'transnational substantive public policy', the modern trend favors relying upon a consensus as to its content. The presence of a consensus is in turn demonstrated especially by the body of international convention law, and also by whether there is a convergence between and among various elements. These include national laws, national case law, arbitral case law, public international law, the general principles of law, and customs and usages. On that basis, transnational substantive public policy has indeed found a place in international arbitration. . . . Is it the same for transnational procedural public policy? In many respects, yes: reference, for example, to such sources as the UNCITRAL Model Law, the New York Convention, the ILA Report on Public Policy as Bar to Enforcement of International Arbitral Awards, national arbitration laws and national case law as well as arbitral awards give ready support to a consensus of three kinds: First, that the right to a reasonable opportunity to be heard and the right to equal treatment (respecting both the constitution of the tribunal and the later proceedings) are fundamental procedural rights that may not be violated. Second, however, that violation of these rights does not necessarily automatically give rise to grounds for denial of enforceability to the award. Third, that even where violation does lead to annulment or refusal of enforcement because the violation affected the outcome of the award, that is not the whole story. Namely, violation does not necessarily trigger the separate ground of violation of public policy, in this case procedural public policy and more specifically transnational procedural public policy. In this regard, transnational procedural public policy is arguably more problematic and elusive than transnational substantive public policy").

substantive public policy defence but not in a procedural public policy defence[248].

### 3. The function of public policy in international arbitration generally

When opting for arbitration, rather than State court
proceedings, to resolve a corruption issue, the parties
generally gain the possibility to decide all aspects of
their dispute settlement mechanism as they wish. For
example, the parties may choose the applicable procedural and substantive laws, the place and language
of the arbitration, and, most of all, the individuals
empowered to make a final and binding decision about
the dispute concerned. Therefore, dispute resolution by
arbitration is dominated by party autonomy and is
largely beyond the scrutiny of national courts.

Notwithstanding, arbitration is not entirely detached
from State influence[249]. The State maintains an interest
in limiting party autonomy where private party dispute
settlement impacts the public interest. Therefore,
national and international legal frameworks for international arbitration allow for limitations to party autonomy on grounds of public policy considerations. States
may restrict the subject matters that can be submitted
to arbitration, where a *lex arbitri* applies, and they may
refuse to enforce arbitral awards if such enforcement
were negatively to affect the public interest, where
enforcement is required. This discretion of a country's
courts to enforce awards reduces the disputing parties'
ability to avoid the scrutiny of national courts by
choosing arbitration[250]. Therefore, public policy has

---

[248] See R. Kreindler, *supra* footnote 245, p. 442.

[249] In fact, arbitral awards cannot be enforced but with
the assistance of state courts, unless they are self-executing in the sense of, e.g., certain investment-based awards.

[250] See J. García de Enterría, *supra* footnote 239,
p. 390.

also been labelled as "the last point of resistance to the autonomy of international arbitration"[251]. This is no less true in international investment treaty arbitration, although for slightly different reasons.

Public policy is an accepted and legitimate limitation to international arbitration, but it is also recognized that public policy must be interpreted and applied restrictively, since a more lenient interpretation would jeopardize the effectiveness of international commercial arbitration overall[252]. The same essentially applies too to international investment treaty arbitration.

Moreover, the public policy exception must arguably also be applied more restrictively in arbitration than in litigation since, by choosing arbitration, parties voluntarily waive the protection of their own national courts[253]. In this context, United States courts, for example, have held that a party which voluntarily initiates arbitration is estopped from opposing the recognition or enforcement of a related award on public policy grounds[254]. However, overall there is no general international consensus with regard to the permissible or desirable extent of a court's public policy control[255].

One may differentiate between the following three major public policy limitations to party autonomy in

---

[251] B. Hanotiau and O. Caprasse, *supra* footnote 234, p. 787.

[252] See J. García de Enterría, *supra* footnote 239, p. 391.

[253] *Ibid.*, p. 394.

[254] *Ibid.*, p. 393. See also R. B. von Mehren and M. E. Patterson, "Recognition and Enforcement of Foreign-Country Judgments in the United States", *Law and Policy in International Business*, Vol 6 (1974), p. 63.

[255] For additional discussion, see B. Hanotiau and O. Caprasse, *supra* footnote 234, pp. 804 *et seq.*

the context of international arbitration: (i) public policy limitations to arbitration as means of dispute settlement; (ii) public policy limitations to the applicable substantive and procedural laws of the arbitration; and (iii) public policy limitations to the existence and enforcement of an arbitral award.

### (a) *Public policy limitations to arbitration as a means of dispute settlement*

Limitations to arbitration as a means of dispute settlement are embodied primarily in the concept of arbitrability of the disputed subject matter. In addition, since any commercial arbitration is premised on an agreement to arbitrate and any investment treaty arbitration on a concept of consent, public policy limitations on arbitration as a form of dispute settlement can arise from general public policy-related grounds under applicable law for the invalidity of the arbitration agreement or of the basis for consent.

*First*, in light of the nature and function of corruption as a civil, criminal or mixed civil and criminal matter, the question of arbitrability poses the greatest public policy concern. The extent to which a particular subject matter may be referred to an international arbitral tribunal, rather than to a State court for resolution, usually is a matter of public policy [256]. Since arbitration of corruption issues are generally private proceedings, but, especially in the investment context, with possible consequences to the parties involved as well as to the society at large, it can be in the public interest to

---

[256] See N. Blackaby and C. Partasides with A. Redfern and M. Hunter, *supra* footnote 7, para. 2.116; B. Hanotiau and O. Caprasse, *supra* footnote 234, p. 819; J. Lew *et al.*, *Comparative International Commercial Arbitration*, Alphen aan den Rijn, Kluwer Law International, 2003, p. 199.

reserve certain types of disputes for national courts, where proceedings are in the public domain[257].

Especially in the commercial context, a State's decision on arbitrability is generally reflective of its overall political, social and economic prerogatives, as well as of its general attitude towards arbitration[258]. Thus, depending on the country, bankruptcy, antitrust, securities, employment, patent or trademark disputes may not be arbitrable[259]. In addition, in most jurisdictions arbitration cannot be used to resolve criminal cases[260].

The scope of internationally arbitrable subject mat-

---

[257] See N. Blackaby and C. Partasides with A. Redfern and M. Hunter, *supra* footnote 7, para. 2.116. On different theoretical and conceptional approaches how to resolve the conflict between the public policy domain and the private dispute resolution domain, see W. Grantham, "The Arbitrability of Intellectual Property Disputes", *Berkeley Journal of International Law*, Vol. 14 (1996), p. 185.

[258] In other words, it must balance between the domestic importance of reserving certain public interest matters to the State courts' jurisdictions and the more general public interest to handle trade and commerce through an effective dispute settlement. Against this background, the decision respecting arbitrability may also be different in a purely national dispute as compared to an international dispute. See, e.g., N. Blackaby and C. Partasides with A. Redfern and M. Hunter, *supra* footnote 7, para. 2.114, and J. Lew *et al.*, *supra* footnote 256, p. 199. Even though restrictions on arbitrability result from underlying public policy considerations, the determination of the nature of the types of disputes that are susceptible of resolution by arbitration is not based on general public policy criteria, but rather on whether a dispute involves an "economic interest" or on the concept of "capability of the parties to reach an agreement.", J. Lew *et al.*, *ibid.*, p. 200.

[259] W. Grantham, *supra* footnote 257, p. 178. With respect to the arbitrability of anti-trust/competition law issues see, e.g., J. Beechey, "Arbitrability of Anti-trust/ Competition Law Issues — Common Law", *Arbitration International*, Vol. 12 (1996), pp. 179 *et seq*.

[260] See J. Lew *et al.*, *supra* footnote 256, p. 188.

ters has expanded over time[261]. For example, in the much-cited case of *Mitsubishi* v. *Soler*[262], the United States Supreme Court held that antitrust disputes arising out of international agreements are arbitral, thus narrowing the traditional doctrine as to the general inarbitrability of antitrust claims reflected in *American Safety Equipment Corp.* v. *J. P. Maguire & Co.*[263]

In commercial arbitration, whether a particular subject matter is arbitrable is generally determined pursuant to the law applicable to the arbitration agreement. If the parties have not agreed on such law, arbitral tribunals usually apply the law at the seat of the arbitration[264]. However, there is also the view that an arbitral tribunal must additionally take into account the law on arbitrability of the prospective place or places of enforcement[265]. This requirement

---

[261] See B. Hanotiau and O. Caprasse, *supra* footnote 234, p. 819; J. Lew *et al.*, *op. cit.*, p. 200. On the development of the concept of arbitrability of intellectual property disputes under French law, see E. Fortunet, "Arbitrability of Intellectual Property Disputes in France", *Arbitration International*, Vol. 26 (2010), pp. 282 *et seq.*

[262] *Mitsubishi Motors Corp.* v. *Soler Chrysler Plymouth Inc.*, 473 US 628 (1985). For a discussion of this case see, e.g., J. Beechey, *supra* footnote 259, p. 183.

[263] *American Safety Equipment Corp.* v. *J. P. Maguire & Co.*, 391 F. 2d 826 (2d Cir. 1968). On the development of the concept of arbitrability of intellectual property disputes under French law see E. Fortunet, *supra* footnote 261, pp. 282 *et seq.*

[264] Unlike in court litigation, there is no *lex fori* in arbitration which must be used by arbitrators for conflict of law questions. In the absence of an agreement on the subject by the parties, in international arbitration no single nation's law is *a priori* competent. See also J. García de Enterría, *supra* footnote 239, p. 433; J. Lew *et al.*, *supra* footnote 256, pp. 535 *et seq.* and R. Kreindler, *supra* footnote 245, p. 243.

[265] It has also been argued that, in addition to *lex arbitri* and the law where enforcement may be sought, the law

arguably applies since an arbitral award is not enforceable pursuant to Article V (2) *(a)* of the New York Convention if the dispute is not arbitrable according to the law of the place where enforcement is sought. Moreover, there is a generally (if not uniformly) recognized duty of arbitrators to render an award that is valid and enforceable [266].

*Second*, public policy considerations can also impact the issue of the validity of the arbitration agreement [267] or in the case of investment treaty arbitration the validity of the consent. A valid arbitration agreement is the prerequisite for any arbitration proceedings.

Depending on the law applicable to the arbitration agreement, arbitration agreements may be held to be invalid on grounds of public policy [268], although this

---

governing the IP contract in dispute and the law of the country or countries granting the relevant IP must be considered. See generally on the law applicable to the question of arbitrability R. Kreindler, "Die Schiedsfähigkeit von Streitigkeiten über die Rechtsbeständigkeit von eingetragenen Schutzrechten im internationalen Vergleich — aus US-amerikanischer Sicht", *Schiedsgerichtsbarkeit und Gewerblicher Rechtsschutz*, Bonn, Deutsche Institution für Schiedsgerichtsbarkeit e.V., DIS-MAT XIII, 2006, pp. 83 *et seq*.

[266] ICC Rules, Art. 41. See also W. Grantham, *supra* footnote 257, p. 173.

[267] B. Hanotiau and O. Caprasse, *supra* footnote 234, p. 799.

[268] For example, under German law arbitration agreements may be void as a result of the underlying contract's voidness pursuant to Sec. 138, German Civil Code. An arbitration agreement may be void *ab initio* on other grounds recognized under the applicable contract law, such as the lack of an actual agreement or the lack of the relevant form. R. Kreindler, *supra* footnote 41, p. 215. An arbitration agreement's coverage of subject matters which are inarbitrable renders that part of the arbitration agreement unenforceable not invalid.

application of public policy considerations is not common[269].

On the other hand, in light of the widely recognized principle of separability, invalidity of the underlying contract normally does not automatically translate into invalidity of the agreement to arbitrate[270]. Rather, invalidity of the arbitration agreement as a result of the invalidity of the main contract will follow only if the nature and circumstances of the main contract's invalidity inextricably apply also to the arbitration agreement, such as when a contract was obtained by threat[271]. Again, in investment arbitration the analysis

---

[269] Generally, an arbitrator should take into account that a decision to nullify a contractual agreement is a decision to deviate from the principle of *pacta sunt servanda*, which is likewise a deviation from a component of public policy. Thus, the arbitrator must balance the different elements of public policy. R. Kreindler, *supra* footnote 41, p. 225. Moreover, the arbitrator must also balance the principle of public policy with other fundamental principles applying in the arbitration, such as the concepts of competence-competence, separability, and arbitrability. *Ibid.*, p. 266. Finally, a distinction should be drawn between overt public policy violations and those violations which are less overt. *Ibid.*, p. 214.

[270] R. Kreindler, *supra* footnote 41, p. 227.

[271] *Ibid.*, at pp. 229, 254 *et seq.* By contrast, a contract obtained as a result of corruption, or facilitating the same, may not be deemed to be void *ab initio*. *Ibid.*, p. 254. See also *Westinghouse and Bruns & Roe (USA)* v. *National Power Company and the Republic of the Philippines*, ICC Case No. 6401, Award, 19 December 1991, *Mealey's International Arbitration Report* 7 (1) (1992), reprinted in 7 *International Arbitration Report*, dictum at B-13-B-14 (1992) ("There may be instances where a defect going to the root of an agreement between parties affects both the main contract and the arbitration clause. An obvious example is a contract obtained by threat"). See also the Court of Appeal's decision in *O'Callaghan* v. *Coral Racing Ltd.* of 19 November 1998, [1998] All England Reporter (D) 607, holding that an arbitration clause in an indisputably

will be somewhat different, relating to the issue of consent to arbitration, as discussed later[272].

(b) *Public policy limitations to the applicable substantive and procedural law*

Most jurisdictions have public policy limitations to the applicable substantive law in the form of statutory or case-law based mandatory laws[273]. Such mandatory

---

illegal gaming agreement could not be regarded as a valid arbitration agreement.

[272] See *infra* Chapter V.B.2.b., Chapter V.B.3.b., Chapter V.B.4.

[273] For example, Art. 7 (2) of the Rome Convention (Convention 80/934/ECC on the Law Applicable to Contractual Obligations opened for signature in Rome on 19 June 1980, entered into force on 1 April 1991, available at http://eur-lex.europa.eu/LexUriServ/LexUriServ.do?uri=CELEX:41998A0126(02):EN:HTML) provides that "[n]othing in this Convention shall restrict the application of the rules of the law of the forum in a situation where they are mandatory irrespective of the law otherwise applicable to the contract". Further, pursuant to Art. 16 of the Rome Convention, "[t]he application of a rule of the law of any country specified by *this Convention* may be refused only if such application is manifestly incompatible with the public policy ('ordre public') of the forum". Similarly, Sec. 187 of the Restatement (Second) Conflicts of Laws (available at http://www.kentlaw.edu/perritt/conflicts/rest187.html) recognizes that the chosen substantive law will not be applied in the event that it is "contrary to a fundamental policy" of the forum State. G. B. Born, *supra* footnote 4, pp. 2172 *et seq.* See also Art. 19 (1), Swiss Law on Private International Law; *Société Almira Films* v. *Pierrel*, Cour d'appel [CA] [regional court of appeal] Paris, 16 February 1989, *Revue de l'arbitrage* (1989), p. 711; aff'd, Cour de cassation [Cass.] [supreme court for judicial matters] 1ᵉ civ., *Revue de l'arbitrage* (1991), p. 625 (Fr.); G. Kegel and K. Schurig, *Internationales Privatrecht*, 9th ed., Munich, Beck Verlag, 2004, pp. 520 *et seq.*; E. Gaillard and J. Savage (eds.), *supra* footnote 1, para. 1516.

laws are an expression of positive public policy and aim at protecting the fundamental social, political or economic interests of a State[274]. They are applicable irrespective of the otherwise applicable substantive law[275]. They can thus partially or entirely render unenforceable the parties' substantive agreement, with respect to certain contractual restrictions that contradict mandatory national competition laws, with respect to contractual waivers, or choice-of-law clauses.

However, where the governing substantive law conflicts with mandatory rules, under substantive law other than the governing law, arbitrators should not disregard the governing substantive law, unless the application of such law would result in a violation of *international* public policy. It should be only in such extreme cases that party autonomy is trumped by the "higher good" of international public policy[276].

---

[274] See, e.g., Tribunal Fédéral [Swiss Federal Tribunal], 21 January 2002, *ASA Bulletin*, Vol. 20 (2002), p. 534. See P. Francescakis, "Quelques précisions sur les 'lois d'application immédiate' et leurs rapports avec les règles de conflits de lois", *Revue critique de droit international privé*, Vol. 55 (1996), p. 1.

[275] P. Mayer, *supra* footnote 119, p. 274 ("Mandatory rules of law are a matter of public policy *(ordre public)*, and moreover reflect a public policy so commanding that they must be applied even if the general body of law to which they belong is not competent by application of the relevant rule of conflict of laws"). See also *Westacre* v. *Jugoimport*, ICC Case No. 7047, *supra* footnote 201, p. 332, upheld by Swiss Federal Supreme Court, 30 December 1994 ("The parties are to be enabled to subject their legal relations to the law they choose, and to exclude the national law which would otherwise apply. Therefore, provisions of the law which is excluded can only be recognized within the chosen law to the extent that they are part of the ordre public international").

[276] R. Kreindler, *supra* footnote 245, p. 244 ("[T]he arbitrator need not apply the agreed or determined governing law if doing so would cause him or her to violate inter-

Moreover, where the mandatory law of a country other than that of the governing law or that of the seat of the arbitration is in question, such mandatory law should be applied only where there is a close link between the subject matter of the dispute and the country of that law and where the relevant mandatory law would sanction a severe violation of international public policy[277].

At the same time, where the mandatory law embodies a transnational public policy, the arbitrator should clearly give effect to it[278]. In particular, considerations

---

national public policy. In such extreme cases, party autonomy is trumped by the 'higher good' of international public policy . . . Where disregard of the mandatory public policy at [a third] Country X would itself offend international public policy, moreover, the arbitrator has a right to apply the law of Country X over and above the agreed . . . law so as to avoid offending that transcending public policy"). See also R. Kreindler, *supra* footnote 246, p. 435. On the question whether the arbitrator is to be primarily the servant of the parties or that of truth see *ibid.*, at pp. 439 *et seq.* See extensively on duties of the arbitrator when faced with issues of potential public policy violations and illegality R. Kreindler, *supra* footnote 41, p. 209.

[277] R. Kreindler, *supra* footnote 246, p. 434. See also Art. 9 of the 1991 Resolution of the Institute of International Law concerning the autonomy of the parties in international contracts between private persons or entities, reprinted in Institut de droit international, Tableau des résolutions adoptées (1957-1994), p. 413 (1992) ("If regard is to be had to mandatory provisions . . . of a law other than that of the forum or that chosen by the parties, then such provisions can only prevent the chosen law from being applied if there is a close link between the contract and the country of that law and if they further such aims as are generally accepted by the international community"), for the original French version see *Revue critique de droit international privé*, Vol. 51 (1992), p. 198.

[278] R. Kreindler, *supra* footnote 245, pp. 248 *et seq.* ("That the courts at the seat and/or at the place of

as to the enforceability of the arbitral award should not influence an arbitrator's decision whether to disregard the governing law[279]. Courts in most developed jurisdictions, however, have been reluctant to override

---

attempted enforcement abroad might have an opportunity to review and assess the illegality themselves does not make it any less imperative for the award already to have done so . . . The reviewing or enforcing court, even if it were entitled to review certain elements of the illegality essentially *de novo*, cannot possibly have the same access to the evidence as did the tribunal. In most cases, the reviewing court is not allowed to conduct such an inquiry, in any event. Therefore, the tribunal must not forsake the opportunities provided by the unique access which it has to the facts during the arbitration. . . . The arbitrator has no mandate to engage in social engineering, but it would be a mistake to assume that his or her office did not give the arbitrator a legitimate platform from which to investigate and combat public policy offenses, within the constraints of his or her mission"). On the standard of proof to be applied by the arbitral tribunal in its assessment of the illegality of a contract for public policy violations see R. Kreindler, *supra* footnote 41, pp. 223 *et seq.*

[279] R. Kreindler, *supra* footnote 245, p. 245 ("[T]he arbitrator cannot possibly be the servant to several different masters; he or she must observe generally accepted international norms, even if it is thereby likely that the award will have little prospect of cross-border enforcement in that single country. Inasmuch as Art. V (2) *(b)* of the New York Convention should be seen as a mandatory guidelines for the arbitrator, he or she must attempt to determine whether or not the broad consensus internationally is embodied in the application of the agreed substantive law"). See also Art. 2 of the Resolution on Arbitration between States, State Enterprises or State Entities, and Foreign Enterprises, adopted by the Institute of International Law on 12 September 1989, in A. J. van den Berg (ed.), *XVI Yearbook Commercial Arbitration*, Kluwer Law International, 2001, p. 238 ("In no case shall an arbitrator violate principles of international public policy as to which a broad consensus has emerged in the international community").

choice-of-law agreements on grounds of public policy[280].

As provided in some national arbitration laws, public policy has a procedural component as well as a substantive one. For example, the English Arbitration Act explicitly provides that an arbitral award may be vacated if "the award or the way in which it was procured [are] being contrary to public policy"[281]. This

---

[280] See, e.g., G. B. Born, *supra* footnote 4, pp. 2174 *et seq.*, with further references. See also Art. 9 of the 1991 Resolution of the Institute of International Law concerning the autonomy of the parties in international contracts between private persons or entities, reprinted in Institut de droit international, Tableau des résolutions adoptées (1957-1994), p. 413 (1992) ("If regard is to be had to mandatory provisions . . . of a law other than that of the forum or that chosen by the parties, then such provisions can only prevent the chosen law from being applied if there is a close link between the contract and the country of that law and if they further such aims as are generally accepted by the international community"); for the original French version see *Revue critique de droit international privé*, Vol. 51 (1992), p. 198. This approach was also confirmed, e.g., by the Swiss Federal Tribunal's decision in *Beverly Overseas S.A.* v. *Privredna Banka Zagreb*, 28 March 2001, *ASA Bulletin*, Vol. 19 (2001), pp. 807 *et seq.*

[281] English Arbitration Act, Art. 68 (2) *(g)*. See also, e.g., Art. 1065 (1) *(e)* Netherlands Code of Civil Procedure ("the award, or the manner in which it was made, violates public policy or morals"). For a definition of procedural public policy under Swiss law, see Tribunal Fédéral, [Swiss Federal Tribunal], *X Inc.* v. *Z. Corp.*, 3 April 2002, *ASA Bulletin*, Vol. 20 (2002), p. 365 ("L'ordre public procédural garantit aux parties le droit à un jugement indépendant sur les conclusions et l'état de fait soumis au Tribunal arbitral d'une manière conforme au droit de procédure applicable; il y a violation de l'ordre public procédural lorsque des principes fondamentaux et généralement reconnus ont été violés, ce qui conduit à une contradiction insupportable avec le sentiment de la justice, de telle sorte que la décision apparaît incompatible avec des

due process element of public policy, however, over-laps directly with a party's equally protected right to be heard, which also constitutes a recognized vacatur ground under most national arbitration laws[282] as well as a ground for non-enforcement pursuant to Article V (1) *(b)* of the New York Convention.

Procedural public policy, however, may also include principles of equal treatment and protections against fraud that are not covered by the right to be heard[283]. Procedural public policy, absent a particular party agreement, is determined by the law at the seat of the arbitration[284]. Vacatur or non-enforcement of an arbitral award on grounds of procedural public policy vio-

---

valeurs reconnues dans un Etat de droit") ("Procedural public policy guarantees to the parties the right to an independent judgment respecting the conclusions and the nature of the facts submitted to the arbitral tribunal in a manner conforming to the applicable procedural law; public policy is being violated when fundamental and generally recognized principles were violated, leading to an unbearable contradiction to the sense of justice such that the relevant decision appears to be incompatible with the accepted values in a State governed by the rule of law" (author's translation)). See also R. Kreindler and T. J. Kautz, "Agreed Deadlines and the Setting Aside of Arbitral Awards", *ASA Bulletin*, Vol. 15 (1997), p. 576.

[282] Cf., e.g., Art. 34 (2) *(a)* (ii) of the UNCITRAL Model Law.

[283] E. Gaillard and J. Savage (eds.), *supra* footnote 1, para. 1654.

[284] Procedural public policy is again interpreted restrictively. For example, the German Federal Supreme Court recognizes a violation of procedural public policy only in the event that "the arbitral procedure suffers from a grave defect that touches the foundation of the State and economic functions", Bundesgerichtshof [German Federal Court of Justice], 15 May 1986, *XXII Yearbook Commercial Arbitration*, 1987, p. 490, quoted in G. B. Born, *supra* footnote 4, p. 2852.

lations, however, is rare[285]. In order to constitute grounds for non-enforcement, the violation of procedural laws or rules must be severe and deprive a party of fundamental rights[286].

(c) *Public policy limitations to the existence and enforcement of an award*

A number of public policy limitations exist on the substance and procedure of an international arbitration, with some distinctions between a commercial award and a treaty-based award relating partly not but solely to the fact that an ICSID-based investment treaty award has no seat, as discussed previously. Public policy considerations are relevant not only during an arbitration proceeding, but also following the issuance of the arbitral award[287].

---

[285] P. Pinsolle and R. Kreindler, "Les limites du rôle de la volonté des parties dans la conduite de l'instance arbitrale", *Revue de l'arbitrage* (2003), p. 60. Examples of court decisions rejecting applications for non-enforcement of arbitral awards on grounds of procedural public policy violations include, for example, the following: *Fitzroy Eng'g* v. *Flame Eng'g, Inc.*, 1994 US Dist. LEXIS 17781 (ND Ill. 1994) (respecting alleged conflicts of interest of a party's counsel); Bundesgerichtshof [German Federal Court of Justice], 1 February 2001, *XXIX Yearbook Commercial Arbitration*, 2004, p. 708 (respecting procedures for the selection of arbitrators); *Nicor Int'l Corp.* v. *El Paso Corp.*, 292 F. Supp. 2d 1357 (SD Fla. 2003) (respecting the lack of presence of an allegedly necessary party to the proceedings); Oberster Gerichtshof [Austrian Supreme Court of Justice], 26 January 2005, *XXX Yearbook Commercial Arbitration*, 2005, p. 421 (respecting the submission of fraudulent evidence in the proceedings).

[286] D. Otto and O. Elwan, *supra* footnote 240, p. 389 (with further references).

[287] See, generally, R. Kreindler and A. Tevini, *supra* footnote 233, p. 461.

*First*, public policy considerations constitute possible grounds for annulment of an arbitral award at the seat of the arbitration or, in the case of an ICSID Convention award, under the ICSID annulment standard, and thus touch the existence of the arbitral award. In the case of commercial awards or investment protection awards in which a seat has been chosen, most national arbitration laws contain a public policy exception with respect to the annulment of international arbitral awards similar to that of Article V (2) *(b)*, New York Convention[288]. Furthermore, even in jurisdictions, such as the United States, that do not have statutory grounds for annulment on grounds of public policy violations, it is established jurisprudence that a court may annul an arbitral award for violations of public policy[289].

*Second*, either independently or in connection with the annulment of the arbitral award at the seat of the arbitration[290], public policy concerns can be grounds

---

[288] See, e.g., French New Code of Civil Procedure, Art. 1502 (5) ("contrary to international public policy"); German Code of Civil Procedure, Section 1059 (2) (2) *(b)* ("recognition or enforcement of the award leads to a result which is in conflict with public policy *ordre public*"); English Arbitration Act, 1996, Sec. 68 (2) *(g)* ("the award being obtained by fraud or the award or the way in which it was procured being contrary to public policy"); Swiss Law on Private International Law, Art. 190 (2) *(e)* ("The award may only be annulled . . . if the award is incompatible with public policy"); Japanese Arbitration Law, Art. 44 (1) (vii) ("the content of the arbitral award is in conflict with the public policy or good morals of Japan").

[289] See, e.g., *United Paperworkers Int'l Union* v. *Misco, Inc.*, 484 US 29, 42 (1987) and *W. R. Grace & Co.* v. *Local Union*, 461 US 757, 766 (1983); *Hurd* v. *Hodge*, 334 US 24, 34-35 (1948).

[290] Pursuant to Art. V (1) *(e)* of the New York Convention, an award which has been set aside on public policy grounds at the seat of the arbitration may be denied

for non-enforcement of an arbitral award, and thus render an arbitral award effectively meaningless, in the event that the courts of the country or countries where enforcement is sought refuse to enforce the award. Therefore, an arbitral award may be unenforceable, unless it is in compliance with the public policy of both the rendering and the enforcing State or States[291]. In certain commercial arbitration awards, such as those involving intellectual property rights which typically are protected in several countries, and enforcement thus typically is sought in more than one country, an arbitral award relating to intellectual property rights often will need to comply with the public policy of several countries[292]. The same analysis will not apply to ICSID Convention awards insofar as they are meant to be self-enforcing and are not subject to enforcement in the courts of a respective country, but at the same time the ICSID Convention annulment standards can be seen to control for violations of international or even national public policy under some circumstances pursuant to the manifest excess of powers control[293].

As for international commercial arbitration awards and those investment arbitrations which have a seat, the application of the public policy exception in all major jurisdictions typically raises largely identical problems in the context of vacatur proceedings at the seat of the arbitration as in enforcement proceedings

---

recognition and enforcement in any country where enforcement is sought.

[291] See J. García de Enterría, *supra* footnote 239, p. 404.

[292] See F. Dessemontet, "Arbitration of Intellectual Property Rights and Licensing Contracts", in E. Gaillard and D. di Pietro (eds.), *Enforcement of Arbitration Agreements and International Arbitral Awards — The New York Convention in Practice*, London, Cameron May Ltd., 2008, pp. 555 *et seq*.

[293] See Art. 52 (1) *(b)* of the ICSID Convention.

under Article V of the New York Convention[294]. For this reason, these issues can be discussed jointly. In this context, I focus on the general public policy exception that permits the courts at the seat of the arbitration or in the country where enforcement is sought respectively to annul or refuse enforcement of an award if it is found to be in conflict with the public policy of the annulment or the enforcement State[295]. Other, more specific public policy-related grounds for annulment or non-enforcement include the lack of arbitrability of the subject matter[296], the invalidity of the arbitration agreement[297], and the violation of procedural public policy and due process[298].

In practice, the following three issues typically become relevant in the context of a court's consideration of public policy in the context of annulment or enforcement proceedings.

*First*, whose or what kind of public policy applies? Generally, at least in non-ICSID arbitrations, it is the public policy of the annulment courts or, respectively, the enforcement courts that is applicable[299]. Where an

---

[294] See also P. Lalive, "Transnational (or Truly International) Public Policy and International Arbitration", in Pieter Sanders (ed.), *Comparative Arbitration Practice and Public Policy in Arbitration*, ICCA Congress Series No. 3, New York, Kluwer Law International, 1987, p. 257.

[295] E.g., UNCITRAL Model Law, Art. 34 (2) *(b)* (ii), and New York Convention, Art. V (2) *(b)*. Art. 34 (2) *(b)* (ii) of UNCITRAL Model Law is directly based on Art. V (2) *(b)* of the New York Convention.

[296] E.g., New York Convention, Art. V (2) *(a)*.

[297] E.g., New York Convention, Art. V (1) *(a)*.

[298] E.g., New York Convention, Art. V (1) *(b)*.

[299] See, e.g., Art. 34 (2) *(b)* (i), UNCITRAL Model Law ("public policy of *this* State") (emphasis added). However, exceptionally, and to the extent that this follows from the applicable conflicts rules, national courts also may give effect to the public policy of a foreign State. G. B. Born, *supra* footnote 4, p. 2623.

international arbitral award is at issue, courts in most major jurisdictions apply a more restrictive concept of "international public policy" as opposed to the broader concept of domestic public policy[300]. Pursuant to the concept of international public policy, only matters which are essential to the forum State's legal system and which are regarded as being mandatory even in international or transnational settings may constitute relevant public policy grounds[301].

---

[300] In some jurisdictions, such as France, this is even prescribed by statute. See, e.g., Arts. 1514 and 1520 French New Code of Civil Procedure. In other jurisdictions, the application of international rather than domestic public policy in these situations has been established by case law. See, e.g., Tribunal Fédéral [Swiss Federal Tribunal], 19 April 1994, BGE 120 II 155; Tribunal Fédéral [Swiss Federal Tribunal], 8 March 2006, BGE 132 III 389. See also G. B. Born, *supra* footnote 4, p. 2838. With respect to France, see also *Euro'n Gas Turbines SA* v. *Westman Int'l Ltd.*, Cour d'appel [CA] [regional court of appeal] Paris, 30 September 1993, *XX Yearbook Commercial Arbitration*, 1995, p. 202 ("a contract having as its aim and object a traffic in influence through the payment of bribes is, consequently, contrary to French international public policy as well as to the ethics of international commerce as understood by the large majority of States in the international community").

[301] *Ibid.* For example, French courts have defined the concept of international public policy as the ensemble of rules and values whose misconception of the French legal order cannot tolerate even in an international context ("l'ensemble des règles et des valeurs dont l'ordre juridique français ne peut souffrir la méconnaissance, même dans les situations à caractère international") ("the ensemble of rules and values with respect to which the French legal order cannot endure ignorance, even in situations with an international character" (author's translation)). See *SA Renosol France et autre* v. *Société Coverall North America*, Cour d'appel [CA] [regional court of appeal] Paris, 1ᵉ ch., 15 February 1996, (Fr.); *Société Cargill France* v. *SA Tradigrain France*, Cour d'appel [CA] [regional court of appeal] Paris, 1ᵉ ch., 14 June 2001,

*Second*, should the court assess merely whether the outcome of the arbitral award would be contrary to the relevant public policy (e.g., that the conduct compelled by the arbitral award or the amount of damages awarded contradicts the relevant public policy)? Or, should the court also consider whether the substantive claim granted by the award itself violates the applicable public policy (e.g., by imposing liability for failure to engage in illegal practices[302])? Overall, there is much support, especially in legal literature, for the view that at least in the context of annulment proceedings the competent courts should also look to the underlying legal claims or defences on which the grant or denial of a particular relief is based[303]. In fact,

---

*Revue de l'arbitrage* (2001), p. 805, obs. Y. Derains (Fr.). See also P. Pinsolle and R. Kreindler, *supra* footnote 285, pp. 59 *et seq.*

[302] See, e.g., the English courts' famous decision in *Soleimany* v. *Soleimany* [1999] QB 785, 800 (English Court of Appeal) which set aside an award that enforced a joint venture for the purpose of smuggling goods out of Iran in violation of Iranian customs laws ("Where public policy is involved, the interposition of an arbitration award does not insulate the successful party's claim from illegality which gave rise to it. . . . The court is in our view concerned to preserve the integrity of its process, and to *see* that it is not abused. The parties cannot override that concern by private agreement. They cannot by procuring an arbitration conceal that they, or rather one of them, is seeking to enforce an illegal contract. Public policy will not allow it").

[303] See G. B. Born, *supra* footnote 4, p. 2624; Y. Derains, "Public Policy and the Law Applicable to the Dispute in International Arbitration", in P. Sanders, *Comparative Arbitration Practice and Public Policy in Arbitration, VIIIth International Arbitration Congress, New York, 6-9 May 1986*, ICCA Congress Series No. 3, New York, Kluwer Law International, 1987, pp. 227 *et seq.* R. Kreindler, *supra* footnote 41, p. 218. See also the American Law Institute's [ALI] Recognition and Enforcement of Foreign Judgments: Analysis and Proposed

"[a]ny other result would render the public policy exception largely meaningless because the payment of money, in and of itself, is very seldom contrary to public policy or mandatory law." [304]

*Third*, the prerequisites for vacating or refusing enforcement of an international arbitral award on grounds of public policy violations are rather restrictive internationally. The competent courts are called to balance the "competing mandates" of public policy and the finality of arbitral awards [305].

On the basis of the major issues typically arising in the context of annulment and enforcement proceedings with respect to public policy at least in non-ICSID arbitrations, what follows is a short overview of court practice on these issues in selected jurisdictions, namely the United States, France, England, Germany and Switzerland.

### (i) *Court practice in the United States*

In the United States, in order to justify "vacatur" or non-enforcement of an international arbitral award, the public policy in question must be "explicit", "well-defined and dominant", and may be ascertained only "by reference to the laws and legal precedents and

---

Federal Statute of 2005 § 5 *(a)* (vi) ("[T]he judgment or the claim on which the judgment is based is repugnant to the public policy of the United States, or to the public policy of a particular state of the United States when the relevant legal interest, right or policy is regulated by state law"); *United Paperworkers International Union, AFL-CIO, et al.* v. *Misco, Inc.*, 484 US 45 n. 12 (1987); Art. 44 (1) (viii) of the Japanese Arbitration Law ("the content of the arbitral award is in conflict with the public policy or good morals of Japan").

[304] See G. B. Born, *supra* footnote 4, p. 2624. For the opposite view, e.g., that issues relating to the underlying contract should not be re-examined by courts, see D. Otto and O. Elwan, *supra* footnote 240, p. 375.

[305] R. Kreindler, *supra* footnote 41, p. 209.

not from general considerations of supposed public interests"[306]. Importantly, a reviewing court may not review the merits of the award "under the cover of public policy"[307]. As to the question whether the enforcement of the arbitral award itself would have to violate public policy or whether a public policy violation would be implicated where the underlying claims are contrary to public policy, a consensus does not appear to exist yet[308].

---

[306] See *W.R Grace & Co.* v. *Rubber Workers*, 461 US 766 (1983); *United Paperworkers International Union, AFL-CIO, et al.* v. *Misco, Inc.*, 484 US 43 (1987); *David Brown and Rita Brown* v. *Rauscher Pierce Refsnes, Inc., and William H. Brashears*, 994 F. 2d 776 and 782 (1987).

[307] Tribunal Fédéral [Swiss Federal Tribunal], *Inter Maritime Mgt SA* v. *Russin & Vecchi*, 9 January 1995, *XXIX Yearbook Commercial Arbitration*, 1997, p. 797. This position is equally assumed by US, French, English, German, and other courts. See *Brandeis Intsel Ltd.* v. *Calabrian Chem. Corp.*, 656 F. Supp. 160, 163 (SDNY 1987) ("[M]anifest disregard of law, whatever the phrase may mean, does not rise to the level of contravening 'public policy', as that phrase is used in Art. V of the Convention"); *Admart AG* v. *Stephen & Mary Birch Found., Inc.*, 457 F. 3d 302 (3d Cir. 2006) ("mistake of fact and manifest disregard of the law" not considered as grounds for reusing recognition of arbitral award); Tribunal Fédéral [Swiss Federal Tribunal], 14 November 1991, *XVII Yearbook Commercial Arbitration*, 1992, p. 283; *Andre* v. *Multitrade*, Cass. [Supreme Court for Judicial Matters] 1ᵉ civ., 23 February 1994, *Revue de l'arbitrage* (1994), p. 683 (Fr.); *Deutsche Schachtbau- und Tiefbohrgesellschaft mbH* v. *Ras Al-Khaimah Nat'l Oil Co.* (English Court of Appeal), 2 All England Law Reports, 1987, p. 779; Bundesgerichtshof [German Federal Court of Justice], 12 July 1990, *Neue Juristische Wochenschrift*, 1990, p. 3210 (Ger.); OGH [Austrian Supreme Court], 26 January 2005, *XXX Yearbook Commercial Arbitration*, 2005, p. 421 (Austria).

[308] See G. B. Born, *supra* footnote 4, p. 2626. For cases ruling that "the public policy exception is implicated when enforcement of the award compels one of the parties to

However, compared to European Union court practice, with respect to European Union competition law[309], United States courts are generally more reluctant to refuse enforcement of arbitral awards based on antitrust law violations[310]. While United States courts have generally rejected the majority of vacatur or non-enforcement applications brought on grounds of public policy violations, the public policy defence has been successful in certain other cases and thus should not be disregarded[311]. In particular, some courts have vacated arbitral awards holding that the relevant arbitral tribunal's ignorance of the *res judicata* effect of prior judgments violated the relevant public policy[312].

---

take action which directly conflicts with public policy", see *Brown* v. *Rauscher Pierce Refsnes, Inc.*, 994 F. 2d 782 (1993); *Revere Copper and Brass Inc.* v. *Overseas Private Inv. Corp.*, 628 F. 2d 83 (DC Cir. 1980), cert. denied, 446 US 983 (1980).

[309] The European Court of Justice has held that Article 81 of the Treaty establishing the European Community is part of the European Union's public policy. Therefore, an arbitral award that violates Article 81 should be refused enforcement pursuant to Article II *(b)* of the New York Convention. See Case No. C-126/97, *Eco Swiss China Time Ltd.* v. *Benetton International NV*, 1999 ECR I-3055. See in more detail C. Liebscher, "Arbitration of Antitrust Disputes", in E. Gaillard and D. di Pietro (eds.), *Enforcement of Arbitration Agreements and International Arbitral Awards — The New York Convention in Practice*, London, Cameron May Ltd., 2008, pp. 544 *et seq.*

[310] See, e.g., *Baxter Int'l, Inc.* v. *Abbott Laboratories*, 315 F. 3d 829 (7th Cir. 2003). The court held that its only duty was to ensure that the arbitral tribunal "took cognizance of the antitrust claims and actually decided them". *Ibid.*, at 832.

[311] For an extensive overview, see G. B. Born, *supra* footnote 4, pp. 2626 *et seq.*

[312] See *Aircraft Braking Sys. Corp.* v. *Local 856, Int'l Union et al.*, 97 F. 3d 159 (6th Cir. 1996) ("Arbitrators are not free to ignore the preclusive effect of prior judg-

(ii) *Court practice in France*

The public policy exception for vacatur or non-enforcement of international arbitral awards under French law is similarly limited. French courts review an arbitral award only with respect to its compatibility with the restrictive concept of international public policy[313]. As French courts have stated,

"[i]t is only permissible to have recourse to the international public policy exclusionary clause in Article 1502-5 of the New Code of Civil Procedure, now Article 1520-5 since the Decree No. 2011-48 of January 13, 2011, if enforcement of the award would intolerably frustrate our legal system. Its adverse effect must constitute a manifest violation of a rule of law that is deemed essential or of a fundamental principle."[314]

Moreover, it is not sufficient for an arbitral award to abstractly contradict public policy. Rather, the award's enforcement must specifically violate the relevant public policy[315]. Whether *res judicata* rules can constitute matters of public policy has not been handled

---

ments under the doctrines of res judicata and collateral estoppel, . . .").

[313] See P. Pinsolle and R. Kreindler, *supra* footnote 285, pp. 59 *et seq.*

[314] Cour d'appel [CA] [regional court of appeal] Paris, 18 November 2004, 132 *Journal du droit international* 357 (2005), 60932 (Fr.). Pursuant to this judgment, essential public policy principles of the French legal system include, in particular, EU competition law "since it is indisputable that the international public policy of the Member States can also have a Community source". The French arbitration law was revised by Decree No. 2011-48 of 13 January 2011.

[315] Cour d'appel [CA] [regional court of appeal] Paris, 27 October 1994, *Revue de l'arbitrage* (1994), p. 709 (Fr.).

uniformly by French courts[316]. The rare cases in which French courts have annulled or refused enforcement of arbitral awards on public policy grounds include, for example, cases involving bribery[317] and insolvency proceedings[318].

### (iii) *Court practice in England*

English courts also apply public policy exceptions very restrictively. Under English case law, non-enforcement due to public policy grounds requires that

> "there [be] some element of illegality or that the enforcement of the award . . . be clearly injurious to the public good or, possibly, that enforcement would be wholly offensive to the ordinary reasonable and fully informed member of the public on whose behalf the powers of the state are exercised"[319].

---

[316] For a judgment rejecting a public policy violation based on the tribunal's failure to apply *res judicata* rules, see Cour de cassation [Cass.] [supreme court for judicial matters] 1e civ., 5 February 1991, *Revue de l'arbitrage* (1991), p. 625 (Fr.); see also Cour d'appel [CA] [regional court of appeal] Paris, 9 June 1983, *Revue de l'arbitrage* (1983), p. 497 (Fr.). For a case vacating an arbitral award for failure to apply *res judicata* rules, see Cour d'appel [CA] [regional court of appeal] Paris, 28 September 1979, *Revue de l'arbitrage* (1980), p. 506 (Fr.).

[317] Cour d'appel [CA] [regional court of appeal] Paris, 30 September 1993, *XX Yearbook Commercial Arbitration*, 1995, p. 198 (Fr.).

[318] Cour de cassation [Cass.] [supreme court of judicial matters], civ. 1e, 5 February 1991, *Revue de l'arbitrage* (1991), p. 625 (Fr.).

[319] *Deutsche Schachtbau-und Tiefbohrgesellschaft mbH v. Ras Al Khaimah Nat'l Oil Co.*, [1987] 2 Lloyd's Law Reports, p. 254 (English Court of Appeal). See also *Westacre Inv. Inc.* v. *Jugoimport-SDPR Holding Co. Ltd.*, decided in 1997, [1998] 4 All England Law Reports, pp. 570, 593 (QB), approved in *Westacre* v. *Jugoimport*,

Where foreign arbitral tribunals have already examined — and rejected — an argument based on public policy or illegality, English courts will usually not consider such arguments at the enforcement stage again[320].

This was specifically demonstrated in the much-cited cases of *Hilmarton*[321] and *Westacre Investments Inc.* v. *Jugoimport-SDPR Holding Co.*[322], where English courts enforced foreign arbitral awards irrespective of the illegality of the underlying claims holding that the policy of giving effect to arbitral awards outweighed the policies against the illegal conduct. These cases are addressed in detail below[323].

### (iv) *Court practice in Germany*

In Germany as well, vacatur, or refusal of enforcement, of international arbitral awards on grounds of public policy violations is very much a limited exception. Pursuant to Section 1059, German Civil Procedure Code, an award may be vacated on public policy grounds only if "the arbitral award would lead to evident abuse and to grave harm to public order"[324].

---

*supra* footnote 206 (English Court of Appeal), requiring that arbitral awards would have to "ignore palpable and indisputable illegality".

[320] For a related discussion, see G. B. Born, *supra* footnote 4, p. 2850.

[321] High Court of Justice, *Hilmarton Limited* v. *Omnium de Traitement et de Valorisation S.A.*, Queen's Bench Division, 24 May 1999, *ASA Bulletin*, Vol. 17 (1999), pp. 368 *et seq.*

[322] Court of Appeal, *Westacre* v. *Jugoimport*, *supra* footnote 206, upholding the decision of the High Court in *Westacre* v. *Jugoimport*, *supra* footnote 319, pp. 570 *et seq.*

[323] See *supra* Chapter II.G.3.

[324] Bayerisches Oberstes Landesgericht [Bavarian Higher Regional Court], 25 August 2004, *Zeitschrift für Schiedsverfahren*, 2004, p. 320.

Such abuse or harm is assumed, in particular, "when an award enforces an agreement contrary to *bonos mores*, or breaches a rule which is part of the very basis of the social or economic order of a country, or in case the award was obtained by fraud"[325].

### (v) *Court practice in Switzerland*

Switzerland also pursues a particularly restrictive approach to annulment or non-enforcement on grounds of public policy violations[326]. The public policy exception is viewed as a mere reserve clause, which has only a negative function but no positive normative role. An arbitral award will thus be annulled only if the result to which it leads, rather than merely its reasoning, is incompatible with Swiss international public policy[327].

---

[325] *Supra* footnote 324.

[326] See, e.g., Tribunal Fédéral [Swiss Federal Tribunal], 8 March 2006, BGE 132 III 389 (Swiss). The public policy exception respecting *vacatur* proceedings is set out in Art. 190 (2) *(e)* of the Swiss Private International Law Act. Non-enforcement on grounds of public policy is regulated by Art. 194 of the Swiss Private International Law Act, and Art. V of the New York Convention.

[327] See Tribunal Fédéral [Swiss Federal Tribunal], *X SA* v. *Y SA*,30 January 2002, *ASA Bulletin*, Vol. 20 (2002), pp. 328 *et seq*. (Swiss) ("Il faut souligner à cet égard que l'ordre public, au sens de l'art. 190 al. 2 let. e LDIP, ne constitue qu'une simple clause de réserve ou d'incompatibilité, ce qui signifie qu'il a uniquement une fonction protectrice (ordre public négatif) et qu'il ne produit aucun effet normatif sur les rapports juridiques litigieux. . . . Au demeurant, la sentence attaquée ne sera annulée que si le résultat auquel elle aboutit est incompatible avec l'ordre public; il ne suffit donc pas que ces motifs le soient, il faut encore pouvoir tirer la même conclusion à l'égard de son dispositif") ("It needs to be underlined in this respect that public policy, in the sense of Art. 190:2 lit. e French Code on Private International Law, only is a simple reserve clause or incompatibility clause, which means that it has

Cases in which international arbitral awards were annulled or refused enforcement on grounds of public policy violations are the exception. The annulment of an international arbitral award on grounds of public policy violations occurred for the first time in 2010, where a court set aside an award issued in disregard of an already existing court judgment involving the same parties, the same dispute and the same cause of action[328].

Thus both in the context of annulment and enforcement proceedings relating to international commercial arbitral awards and those investment awards which have a classical juridical seat, there is a general consensus in most developed jurisdictions that courts must apply the public policy exception only in limited and exceptional cases. Regarding the enforcement of international arbitral awards, the requirement of a restrictive application follows directly from the New York Convention's pro enforcement bias, since the public policy exception would otherwise function as a loophole in the New York Convention[329]. In particular, it is

---

solely a protective function (negative public policy) and that it does not produce any normative effect on the legal relations in dispute. . . . Overall, an award that is challenged will be vacated only if the result to which it leads is incompatible with public policy; it is thus not sufficient that its reasoning is [incompatible], one must still be able to draw the same conclusion with respect to its operative provisions" (author's translation)).

[328] Tribunal Fédéral [Swiss Federal Tribunal], 10 April 2010, BGE 136 III 345.

[329] See J. Lew *et al.*, *supra* footnote 256, p. 721 n. 173; J. García de Enterría, *supra* footnote 239, p. 391, noting that the New York Convention is only as effective as the application of the public policy exception by the national courts of the signatory States. See also *Hebei Imp. & Exp. Corp.* v. *Polytek Eng'g Co.*, *XXIV Yearbook Commercial Arbitration*, 1999, pp. 675-677 (Hong Kong Court of Final Appeal) (HK). ("[T]he award must be so fundamentally

generally recognized that national courts may not
review the merits of an international arbitral award
based on the public policy defence[330]. Attempts by
counsel to recast substantive objections to an arbitral
award as matters of public policy violations are seldom
successful in practice.

In short, while the public policy defence is often
raised as a ground for set aside or as an objection to
enforcement of an arbitral award, and while, due to the
vagueness of the concept, the application of the public
policy defence is principally unpredictable[331], such
defence, generally, is successful only in rare cases[332].
Finally, the general public policy exception as embodied in Article V (2) *(b)* of the New York Convention is
a residual clause and has independent relevance

---

offensive to that jurisdiction's notion of justice that,
despite it being a party to the [New York] Convention, it
cannot reasonably be expected to overlook the objection");
*Halsbury's Laws of Singapore*, Vol. 2 (Re-Issue), p. 136
(Public policy exception "should be construed narrowly so
that enforcement would be refused only if the award
violates the most basic notions of morality and justice").

[330] See, e.g., *Myers, Inc.* v. *United Mexican States*, Fed.
Ct. of Canada, 31 January 2004, *XXIX Yearbook Commer-
cial Arbitration*, 2004, p. 195; *Revere Copper & Brass
Inc.* v. *OPIC*, 628 F. 2d 81 (DC Cir. 1980).

[331] The public policy exception therefore also has been
described as "a very unruly horse" so that "once you get
astride it you never know where it will carry you",
*Richardson* v. *Mellish* [1824-1834], All England Law
Reports 258 (Common Pleas).

[332] See B. Hanotiau and O. Caprasse, *supra* footnote
234, pp. 819 *et seq*. For an overview of situations in which
the recognition and enforcement of an arbitral award was
refused on grounds of public policy violations pursuant to
Art. V (2) *(b)*, New York Convention, see, e.g., D. Otto
and O. Elwan *supra* footnote 240, pp. 391 *et seq*. For an
overview of situation in which a violation of public policy,
by contrast, was denied, see *ibid.*, pp. 394 *et seq*. See also
G. B. Born, *supra* footnote 4, p. 2625.

only where one of the other, more specific grounds for refusal of recognition and enforcement, is not fulfilled[333].

### 4. *The existence and role of public policy for the international arbitrator*

#### (a) *The absence of a* lex fori *and the role of public policy*

In international arbitration and particularly commercial arbitration, there is general agreement that arbitrators have no *lex fori*, even if they usually have a *lex arbitri*[334], so that unlike the national judge, the arbitrator is not bound by a particular or national system of private international law (whether conflict rules or substantive rules), and thus not bound by the "international public policy" of any given State, except to the extent that he decides to be "bound" for purposes of ensuring enforceability.

Instead, the arbitrator in international commercial arbitration and generally also in the investment treaty context is bound to respect an overarching set of principles of truly international, or transnational, public policy. The contents of this transnational public policy may overlap with the contents of the national "international public policy" of many States, but must be distinguished. A national "international public policy" retains at least in part a particular and even "parochial" national character with national rules while a transnational public policy is truly international, independent of specific national rules or interests, and reflects

---

[333] With respect to Art. V (2) *(b)* of the New York Convention see J. García de Enterría, *supra* footnote 239, pp. 403 and 417.

[334] N. Blackaby and C. Partasides with A. Redfern and M. Hunter, *supra* footnote 7, para. 3.218.

values or perceived values and fundamental norms and interests of the international community[335].

To qualify to form part of such public policy particularly across national boundaries, no unanimity is necessarily required: "The condemnation of racial discrimination, corruption or drug trafficking need not be absolutely unanimous for it to reflect a universal moral standard."[336] And

> "[a]lthough it may not be part of the substantive law of every sovereign state, genuinely international public policy is nevertheless a reality, and it is perfectly able to operate so as to override the law which would otherwise apply, just as the local conception of international public policy would operate in a national court"[337].

This bold and far-reaching concept of transnational public policy is indeed also recognized in case law. By way of example, the English House of Lords held in *Kuwait Airways Corporation* v. *Iraqi Airways Company*, 2002, as follows:

> "This conclusion on English public policy does not reflect an insular approach. Our domestic public policy on the status of Resolution 319 does not stand alone. In recent years, particularly as a result of French scholarship, principles of international public policy (l'ordre public veritablement international) have been developed in relation to subjects such as traffic in drugs, traffic in weapons, terror-

---

[335] M. Hunter and G. Conde e Silva, "Transnational Public Policy and its Application in Investment Arbitrations", *The Journal of World Investment*, Vol. 4 (2003), pp. 374 and 378.

[336] E. Gaillard and J. Savage (eds.), *supra* footnote 1, para. 1535.

[337] *Ibid.*

ism, and so forth: . . . The public policy condemning Iraq's flagrant breaches of public international law is yet another illustration of such a truly international public policy in action."[338]

And the Swiss Federal Tribunal had made reference to a universal conception of public policy, whereby an award up for review by that court will be set aside when incompatible with public policy if it is contrary to the fundamental moral or legal principles recognized in all civilized countries ("contraire aux principes juridiques ou moraux fondamentaux reconnus dans tous les Etats civilisés"), Decision of 30 December 1994[339]. This decision is almost 20 years old, and so this concept is by no means a new phenomenon, although its application to corruption and particularly to the international investment context has increased in frequency and grown in importance in precisely the last two decades.

(b) *Criticism of an "international" or "transnational" public policy*

This bold concept of public policy, which has become increasingly anchored in international commercial and investment arbitration in these last two decades, including in the context of corruption and bribery, is not without its critics. Five particular bases of criticism can be identified and will then be rebutted.

*First*, it may be contended that the governing law, whether in commercial arbitration or investment arbitration, does not include or contain a reference to an

---

[338] *Kuwait Airways Corporation (Respondents)* v. *Iraqi Airways Company (Appellants) and Others*, Judgment, 16 May 2002, [2002] UKHL 19.

[339] Tribunal Fédéral [Swiss Federal Tribunal], 30 December 2004, *ASA Bulletin*, Vol. 13 (2004), p. 224.

amorphous transnational public policy — a concept notably not to be found in the authoritative statement of sources of international law in Article 38 (1) of the ICJ Statute:

"1. The Court, whose function is to decide in accordance with international law such disputes as are submitted to it, shall apply:

*(a)* international conventions, whether general or particular, establishing rules expressly recognized by the contesting States;

*(b)* international custom, as evidence of a general practice accepted as law;

*(c)* the general principles of law recognized by civilized nations;

*(d)* subject to the provisions of Article 59, judicial decisions and the teachings of the most highly qualified publicists of the various nations, as subsidiary means for the determination of rules of law.

2. This provision shall not prejudice the power of the Court to decide a case *ex aequo et bono*, if the parties agree thereto."

As stated by Abdulhay Sayed:

"the fictitious idea that there exists a coherent and consistent arbitral practice over many procedural and substantive issues . . . Realistically speaking, one can hardly pretend in today's world that there exists a coherent arbitral practice capable of serving as a productive source for a Transnational legal order." [340]

---

[340] A. Sayed, "The Legal Basis for Arbitrations Respecting State Contracts", Thesis (LL.M.), Harvard Law School, 1993, *Hein's Legal Theses and Dissertations*, 002-00058, p. 33.

*Second*, any effort to distance oneself from the governing law and to invoke public policy and especially transnational public policy is to be treated with great scepticism:

> "Public policy — it is an unruly horse and when once you get astride it, you never know where it will carry you. It may lead you from the soundlaw. It is never argued at all but when other points fail."[341]

*Third*, the international commercial arbitrator is obliged to be sensitive to policy, but the policy of that legal system which the parties have selected or to which the arbitrator is directed by principles of conflict of law. This applies less cleanly admittedly in investment treaty based arbitration.

*Fourth*, the concept of transnational public policy is superfluous because its quoted principles or examples, such as prohibition of bribery or of slavery, are assumed already to be contained in all national governing laws. For that reason, international commercial arbitrators at least can apply or refer only to a national or domestic notion of public policy, whereas anything else is impermissible law making.

(c) *Rebuttal to the criticism of an "international" or "transnational" public policy*

As compelling as the foregoing critiques might seem at first glance, they have not carried the day, and rightly so.

---

[341] *Richardson* v. *Mellish*, 2 Bing, p. 303 (1824), cited by W. M. Reisman, "Law, International Public Policy (So-called) and Arbitral Choice in International Commercial Arbitration", in A. J. van den Berg (ed.), *International Arbitration 2006: Back to Basics?*, ICCA Congress Series, Vol. XIII, Montreal, Kluwer Law International, 2007, p. 849.

*First*, international arbitral practice has largely abandoned strict a conflict of laws method in determining the applicable law[342]. Accordingly, in international arbitration arbitrators generally have no *lex fori*, and the consequence among others is that they are not bound by particular or domestic rules of conflict of laws including concept of public policy of a given State. As one commentator aptly stated, "We are all familiar with the weaknesses of the conflict analysis. One of the ways to fight against these weaknesses is to allow room for the concept of transnational public policy."[343]

*Second*, certain prohibitions, such as of bribery or slavery, must be respected either in the application of public international law (e.g., particularly in investment arbitration) as the law governing the relations or as an exception to the application of any State or national law which would be the governing law particularly in a commercial contract context and which might tolerate bribery. In effect, the normally governing domestic law could be set aside or superseded. There is no basis to contend that a prohibition against bribery or slavery does not fit within the authoritative statement of international law in Article 38 (1) of the ICJ Statute, as will be discussed in detail below. If such transgressions indeed fit within this statement, then they are reflective of an international or transnational public policy and such policy may be considered to exist.

---

[342] G. B. Born, *supra* footnote 4, pp. 529, 539 *et seq.*; G. B. Born, *International Arbitration: Cases and Materials*, The Hague, Kluwer Law International, 2011, pp. 912 *et seq.*

[343] C. Kessedjian, "Transnational Public Policy", in A. J. van den Berg (ed.), *International Arbitration 2006: Back to Basics?*, ICCA Congress Series, Vol. XIII, Montreal, Kluwer Law International, 2007, p. 859.

*Third*, decisions of arbitral tribunals based on an international or transnational public policy, including in the context of case law and commentary already existing in the context of set aside or refusal of enforcement on public policy grounds, is hardly policy making or law making.

Rather, it is reflective of an effort already well under way to define what transcerning mandatory norms may exist which go beyond domestic public policy.

This does not mean that the concept of transnational public policy is superfluous, particularly with regard to matters of corruption which are not necessarily assumed already to be contained in all national governing laws.

The example of Swiss law respecting intermediary agreements [344] is a case in point of how a cross-border condemnation and prohibition of a kind of conduct can and should exist notwithstanding its toleration by one or more specific national legal systems, in this case a system coinciding with a leading locale of international commercial arbitration.

## 5. *Corruption and bribery in public and private international law*

Is there a transnational or international public policy prohibiting acts of corruption and if so what legal effect might or should it have? Does corruption offend customary international law and general principles of law respectively? It is submitted that the answer to both questions is yes.

As stated, the ICJ Statute contains an authoritative

---

[344] *Establishment of Middle East Country X* v. *South Asian Construction Company*, Interim Award, ICC Case No. 4145 (1983), *XII Yearbook Commercial* Arbitration, 1987, p. 107.

statement of the sources of customary law and general principles of law as part of the corpus of international law[345]. These include international conventions; international custom, as evidence of general practice accepted as law; general principles of law recognized by civilized nations; and judicial decisions and teachings[346].

The relevance to arbitration generally and to our topic specifically is apparent. In the case of commercial arbitration, one must consider public policy, including transnational public policy, to ensure enforceability at the seat and perhaps elsewhere. In the case of investment treaty arbitration, the arbitrator must consider public policy, particularly transnational public policy, as a component of the normally applicable public international law standard pursuant to the treaty, as well as to ensure enforceability (without a classical seat).

(a) *Prevailing opinion on bribery as a matter of customary law*

In the prevailing opinion, which I share, bribery indeed offends customary international law and general principles of law respectively. Customary law and general principles of law form part of the corpus of international law pursuant to Article 38 (1) of the ICJ Statute[347].

The foregoing is evidenced by a wide range of inter-

---

[345] Art. 38 of the Statute of the International Court of Justice, 26 June 1945, 59 Stat. 1055, 3 Bevans 1179, available at http://www.icj-cij.org/documents/index.php?p1=4&p2=2&p3=0#CHAPTER_V.

[346] See Art. 38 of the Statute of the International Court of Justice.

[347] Art. 38 of the Statute of the International Court of Justice.

national conventions, which condemn and interdict bribery, as well as the national laws of various States.

Thus, a number of instruments negotiated, signed and ratified under the aegis of the Organisation for Economic Co-operation and Development ("OECD") have the express aim and purpose of prohibiting acts constituting bribery[348].

As stated earlier, foremost here is the OECD Anti-Bribery Convention[349]. Further international conventions prohibiting bribery include the Inter-American Convention[350], European Union Convention[351], Council of Europe Criminal Law Convention[352], Council of

---

[348] See Organisation for Economic Co-operation and Development: Council Recommendation on Bribery in International Business Transactions, 27 May 1994, *International Legal Materials*, Vol. 33 (1994), p. 1389; Organisation for Economic Co-operation and Development: Council Recommendation C (96) 27/Final on the Tax Deductibility of Bribes to Foreign Public Officials of April 11, 1996, *International Legal Materials*, Vol. 35 (1996), p. 1311.

[349] Convention on Combating Bribery of Foreign Public Officials in International Business Transactions, 21 November 1997, *International Legal Materials*, Vol. 37 (1998), p. 4, available at http://www.oecd.org/dataoecd/4/18/38028044.pdf.

[350] Inter-American Convention against Corruption, 29 March 1996, *International Legal Materials*, Vol. 35 (1996), p. 727, available at http://www.oas.org/juridico/english/Treaties/b-58.html.

[351] European Union Convention on the Fight against Corruption Involving Officials of the European Communities or Officials of Member States, 1997 *Official Journal* (C 195), available at http://europa.eu/scadplus/leg/en/lvb/l33027.htm.

[352] Council of Europe Criminal Law Convention on Corruption, 27 January 1999, *International Legal Materials*, Vol. 38 (1999), p. 505, available at http://conventions.coe.int/Treaty/EN/Treaties/Html/173.htm.

Europe Convention[353], and African Union Convention[354].

The most recent and universal effort toward combating bribery within the international context is the UN Anti-Corruption Convention, which as of 24 December 2012 has 140 Signatories and 165 States parties[355].

In principle, such conventions and treaties are binding only on States parties. At the same time, as Brownlie has aptly stated:

> "the number of parties, the explicit acceptance of rules of law, and, in some cases, the declaratory nature of the provisions produce a strong law-creating effect at least as great as the general practice considered sufficient to support a customary rule"[356].

It is submitted that the prohibition against bribery is such a customary rule and bribery, whether committed

---

[353] Council of Europe Civil Law Convention on Corruption, 4 November 1999, 174 European Treaty Series No. 2, available at http://conventions.coe.int/treaty/en/treaties/html/174.htm.

[354] African Union Convention on Preventing and Combating Corruption, 11 July 2003, *International Legal Materials*, Vol. 43 (2004), p. 5, available at http://www.africa-union.org/Official_documents/Treaties_%20Conventions_%20Protocols/Convention%20on%20Combating%20Corruption.pdf.

[355] United Nations Convention against Corruption, 11 December 2003, *International Legal Materials*, Vol. 43 (2004), p. 37, available at http://www.unodc.org/documents/treaties/UNCAC/Publications/Convention/08-50026_E.pdf; for information on the number of States that have ratified the Convention, see United Nations Office on Drugs and Crime, United Nations Convention against Corruption — Ratification Status, 24 December 2012, available at http://www.unodc.org/unodc/en/treaties/CAC/signatories.html (last visited 13 February 2013).

[356] I. Brownlie, *Principles of Public International Law*, 7th ed., Oxford, Oxford University Press, 2008, p. 13.

by a State or non-State actor, offends public international law.

(b) *Widespread condemnation of bribery by tribunals*

Furthermore, the widespread international condemnation of bribery is evidenced by various decisions of international arbitral tribunals[357], including the two well-known ICC awards in *Westacre* v. *Jugoimport*[358] and *Hilmarton* v. *OTV*[359], holding that bribery contravenes international public policy. Even more recently and in the investment arbitration context, in *World Duty Free* v. *Kenya*, an arbitration under an investment contract providing for ICSID arbitration, the arbitral tribunal stated, in relevant part:

> "In light of domestic laws and international conventions relating to corruption, and in light of the decisions taken in this matter by courts and arbi-

---

[357] See, e.g., *Euro'n Gas Turbines SA* v. *Westman Int'l Ltd.*, 8 *International Arbitration Report*, pp. 8-13 (Paris Ct. App. 1993); ICC Case No. 1110, *supra* footnote 3; *Iranian Party* v. *Greek Party*, ICC Case No. 3916, 111 *Journal du droit international*, p. 930; *Establishment of Middle East Country X* v. *South Asian Construction Company*, Interim Award, ICC Case No. 4145, *XII Yearbook Commercial Arbitration*, 1987, p. 97; ICC Case No. 5943, Y. Derains *et al.*, *Collection of ICC Awards, Recueil des sentences arbitrales de la ICC : 1996-2000 (Collection of ICC Arbitral Awards Series Set)*, 1st ed., Kluwer Law International, 2003, pp. 431 *et seq.*; ICC Case No. 7047, Y. Derains *et al.*, *ibid.*, pp. 32, 45, 46; ICC Case No. 8891, Y. Derains *et al.*, *ibid.*, pp. 561 *et seq.*

[358] See ICC Case No. 7047 (1994), *supra* footnote 201, p. 332 (naming "provisions to fight corruption and bribery" as examples for provisions which are "part of the *ordre public international*").

[359] See *Hilmarton (Agent)* v. *Omnium/Algeria*, ICC Case No. 5622 (1988), *supra* footnote 196, p. 115.

tral tribunals, this Tribunal is convinced that *bribery is contrary to international public policy of most, if not all, States* or, to use another formula, to transnational public policy. Thus, *claims based on contracts of corruption or on contracts obtained by corruption cannot be upheld by this Arbitral Tribunal.*" [360]

Also in the investment arbitration context and in 2006, in *Inceysa* v. *El Salvador* the ICSID Tribunal, asked to consider the investor's violations of public policy by having obtained the underlying investment contract by fraud, stated:

"In light of the foregoing, not to exclude Inceysa's investment from the protection of the BIT would be a violation of international public policy, which this Tribunal cannot allow. Consequently, this Arbitral Tribunal decides that Inceysa's investment is not protected by the BIT because it is contrary to international public policy." [361]

*World Duty Free*, and the various other awards and decisions rightly condemning bribery which precede *World Duty Free* [362], do not establish as a matter of

---

[360] *World Duty Free* v. *Kenya*, *supra* footnote 44, para. 157 (emphasis added).

[361] See *Inceysa* v. *El Salvador*, *supra* footnote 174, para. 252. In interpreting the Spain-El Salvador BIT, the arbitral tribunal found that El Salvador's consent had been subject to the condition that the investment have been made in accordance with its domestic law. The arbitral tribunal denied jurisdiction on the grounds that the investment had not been made in accordance with El Salvador law since the underlying concession contract had been procured by fraud.

[362] For a discussion of various commercial arbitration awards and arbitration-related court decisions which effectively presage and echo the holding of *World Duty Free*, respecting the arbitral tribunal's condemnation of bribery,

dogma that the prohibition against bribery in international public policy forms part of international law. At the same time, the condemnation of bribery found in numerous international instruments and decisions as stated above can and should be classified as a general principle of public international law deriving from the *ordre public* concept well established in national legal orders, as I have written elsewhere[363]. Indeed, bribery is sanctioned by the criminal law of most countries[364].

Thus, the prohibition against bribery can and should be considered a general principle of law recognized by civilized nations in the sense of Article 38 (1) *(c)*, ICJ Statute[365]. As such, it has also been applied as a general principle in the context of investment arbitration awards.

(c) *Criticism of the existence of a transnational public policy prohibition against bribery*

It is not surprising that just as there has been criticism of the notion of transnational or international

---

see generally the discussion in R. Kreindler, *supra* footnote 41, p. 209.

[363] R. Kreindler, *supra* footnote 246, p. 437.

[364] See, e.g., Secs. 304, 307 Strafgesetzbuch [Austrian Penal Code] [StGB]; Art. 337, Código Penal [Brazilian Penal Code] [CP]; Arts. 301-307a, Bulgarian Criminal Code; Art. 250, Chilean Criminal Code; Secs. 160-62, Czech Criminal Code; Sec. 122, Danish Criminal Code; Secs. 331-336, Strafgesetzbuch [German Criminal Code] [StGB]; Korean Act on Preventing Bribery of Foreign Public Officials in International Business Transactions; Sec. 276a, Norwegian Penal Code; Art. 10, Japanese Unfair Competition Prevention Law — Supplementary Provisions; and Arts. 267, 268, Slovenian Penal Code.

[365] Statute of the International Court of Justice, 26 June 1945, 59 Stat. 1055, 3 Bevans 1179, available at http://www.icj-cij.org/documents/index.php?p1=4&p2=2&p3=0#CHAPTER_V.

public policy generally, so too there has been parallel criticism of the notion that there is such a public policy specifically against corruption.

*First*, the criticism has arisen that even accepting the premise of an international or transnational public policy, there is no such policy specifically against corruption. The argument is that the content of international law concerning bribery is not able to be derived from principles of customary international law and international public policy. It is further contended that State practice and *opinio juris* (the subjective obligation of being bound to law) are not established[366]. In this regard, it is reasoned, the wide range of international conventions condemning bribery[367] and national laws of various States[368] are not necessarily evidence of State practice or *opinio juris*. Decisions of international arbitral tribunals are seen the same way, as

---

[366] See generally R. Baker, "Customary International Law in the 21st Century: Old Challenges and New Debates", *European Journal of International Law*, Vol. 21 (2010), pp. 173 *et seq*., C. Tomuschat, "International Law: Ensuring the Survival of Mankind on the Eve of a New Century", *Recueil des cours*, Vol. 281 (1999), p. 86.

[367] The 1997 OECD Convention on Combating Bribery of Foreign Public Officials in International Business Transactions; the 1999 Conventions of the Council of Europe; the 2000 United Nations Convention against Transnational Organized Crime.

[368] Secs. 304, 307, Strafgesetzbuch [Austrian Penal Code] [StGB]; Art. 337, Código Penal [Brazilian Penal Code] [CP]; Arts. 301-307a, Bulgarian Criminal Code; Art. 250, Chilean Criminal Code; Secs. 160-162, Czech Criminal Code; Sec. 122, Danish Criminal Code; Secs. 331-336, Strafgesetzbuch [German Criminal Code] [StGB]; Korean Act on Preventing Bribery of Foreign Public Officials in International Business Transactions; Sec. 276a, Norwegian Penal Code; Art. 10, Japanese Unfair Competition Prevention Law — Supplementary Provisions; and Arts. 267, 268, Slovenian Penal Code.

not necessarily showing that bribery also offends international public policy as a general principle of law[369].

*Second*, international public policy is held not to be a broad concept which would permit arbitrators to override discipline of international law regarding corruption as a standard of decision-making, especially in the investment protection context.

*Third*, any so-called transnational public policy against corruption has at best an "amorphous" character and therefore arbitral tribunals should be circumspect in applying it to the extent it is an incoherent and inconsistent standard[370].

*Fourth*, decisions like *World Duty Free* v. *Kenya*, ICSID (2006)[371] do not in fact establish that bribery is contrary to transnational public policy, but rather reflect a cautionary approach to reliance on the existence of any concept of transnational public policy.

*Fifth*, even accepting the premise of international or transnational public policy and one specifically against corruption, there is no transnational consensus on the legal *consequences* of corruption as far as the invalidity of the main contract and/or the invalidity of the arbitration agreement and/or the invalidity of consent,

---

[369] *World Duty Free* v. *Kenya*, *supra* footnote 44, para. 157.

[370] C. B. Lamm, H. Pham *et al.*, "Fraud and Corruption in International Arbitration", M. Ángel Fernández-Ballesteros and D. Arias (eds.), *Liber Amicorum Bernardo Cremades* (La Ley, 2010), p. 708; M. A. Buchanan, "Public Policy and International Commercial Arbitration", *American Business Law Journal*, Vol. 26 (1988), pp. 513-514, A. Dickinson, "The Role of Public Policy and Mandatory Rules within the Proposed Hague Principles on the Law Applicable to International Commercial Contracts", *Sydney Law School Legal Studies Research Paper*, No. 12/81, p. 11.

[371] *World Duty Free* v. *Kenya*, *supra* footnote 44.

depending on whether in the context of commercial arbitration or an investment treaty.

The response to the criticisms of the view that transnational/international public policy prohibits corruption, it is submitted, is readily apparent and far more compelling than the criticism itself.

*First*, the prohibition against bribery can and should be considered a general principle of law recognized by civilized nations in the sense of Article 38 (1) *(c)* of the ICJ Statute inasmuch as that Article is an appropriate standard of measurement and its elements are fulfilled. Indeed this concept of a prohibition is widely and increasingly pervasively applied as a general principle in the context of both commercial and investment arbitration awards and commentary. On that basis alone, bribery offends customary international law and international public policy as a general principle of law.

*Second*, in the investment treaty context, for example BITs and MITs (such as the Energy Charter Treaty), international public policy in factor forms part of international law, which is the applicable legal standard (e.g., pursuant to Article 26, ECT)[372]. Thus, positing that bribery offends customary law and international public policy as a general principle of international law does not ignore the applicable legal standard at all. The applicable legal standard must be seen in terms of the traditional three sources: treaties, customary international law and general principles of law.

Indeed by establishing that bribery offends customary international law and general principles of law, one can rely on the same sources that, for example,

---

[372] C. B. Lamm, H. Pham, *et al.*, *supra* footnote 370, p. 711; *Plama Consortium Limited* v. *Republic of Bulgaria*, ICSID Case No. ARB/03/24, Award, 27 August 2008, paras. 141-143 (available at http://italaw.com/sites/default/files/case-documents/ita0671.pdf).

Professor Reisman had deemed an appropriate basis for the application of international public policy standards in international arbitration when he wrote, in 2006, as follows:

> "If international public policies are treaty-based and their application extends to parties before an international commercial arbitral tribunal, then they can be applied as part of the governing law. If the policies have been confirmed by customary international law, then their application may be appropriate insofar as the governing national law incorporates customary international law."[373]

While Professor Reisman referred to the applicability of international public policies in the context of commercial arbitration, they can and should *a fortiori* be applicable in the commercial and particularly investment arbitration context. International treaties sanctioning corruption as well as customary law and general principles of law prohibiting corruption are the legal standards applicable, including, for example, pursuant to Article 52, ICSID Convention[374], or Article 26 (6), ECT[375].

*Third*, it is submitted that there is no foundation to the concern that transnational public policy has an "amorphous" character and therefore arbitral tribunals should be circumspect in applying it as an incoherent and inconsistent standard. Support for this contention is occasionally sought in the ICSID award in *World Duty Free* v. *Kenya*:

> "[I]t has been rightly stressed that Tribunals must be very cautious in this respect and must carefully check the objective existence of a particular transna-

---

[373] W. M. Reisman, *supra* footnote 341, p. 856.
[374] Art. 52 of the ICSID Convention.
[375] Art. 26 (6) of the Energy Charter Treaty.

tional public policy rule in identifying it through international conventions, comparative law and arbitral awards."[376]

In fact, the approach adopted by the arbitral tribunal in *World Duty Free* conforms with the concept of the existence of an international or transnational public policy which prohibits corruption. The conclusion that bribery offends international law is based on the three sources that the ICJ Statute deems appropriate to show the "objective existence" of an international public policy (and as demanded by the arbitral tribunal in *World Duty Free*).

Furthermore, reference to *World Duty Free* with the goal of establishing that bribery is not or not necessarily contrary to transnational public policy is misguided. It is submitted that this ICSID award, to the extent reliance is placed on it and even if it were considered to reflect a cautionary approach to the concept of transnational public policy, is at the forefront of the fight against corruption in international investment law. Indeed the arbitral tribunal expressly concluded that bribery is contrary to transnational public policy and on that basis dismissed Claimants' claims[377].

In sum, it is submitted that acts of bribery, if and when proven or otherwise admitted, offend customary international law, general principles of law and public policy, which form part of the corpus of international law pursuant to Article 38 (1) of the ICJ Statute.

---

[376] *World Duty Free* v. *Kenya*, *supra* footnote 44, para. 141.

[377] *Ibid.*, para. 157.

CHAPTER IV

# THE QUESTION OF THE APPLICABLE LAW
## OR LAWS

In the face of suspected or manifest illegality of a contract or an investment in dispute, how can, should or must the arbitrator conduct itself in terms of the rule or rules of law which should or must be applied as to jurisdiction, separability, arbitrability and the merits?

Principles of competence-competence, separability, arbitrability and public policy may or must need to be applied and counter-balanced according to the relevant rule or rules of law. But which one(s)? And depending on the context, there is the additional question of the role of public international law, private international law and the otherwise chosen law in the context of the ability of arbitrator to adjudicate issues of corruption, depending on the law or laws applied.

In the context of commercial arbitration, there will be presumably a conventional choice of a national law, with an overlay of international public policy and transnational public policy. In the context of investment treaty arbitration, there will be a treaty-based choice of public international law and/or a mixture or hierarchy of national law and public international law, with an overlay of international public policy and transnational public policy. Each of these two contexts will be addressed in turn.

## A. *International Commercial Arbitration and the Applicable Law*

Generally, international commercial arbitration has various points of legal reference, including the (i) *lex contractus*, (ii) *lex arbitri*, (iii) *lex societatis* of the affected party, (iv) the law at the place of performance *(lex locus solutiones)* and (v) the law of the place or places of putative attempted enforcement of the arbitral award. The mere co-existence of these multiple sources of law already makes clear the possible tension and conflict of outcomes between two or more of these points of reference: what is "illegal" at the juridical seat may be "legal" under the choice of law and may be unregulated under the law at the place of performance. The decisions in the *Lebanese Traders Distributors* [378] and *Laburthe* v. *Sauveroche* [379] cases are examples of such a tension. Such tension can and will also exist where there is a claim or defence of illegality. Each of these reference points is now addressed in turn [380].

### 1. Lex contractus *as manifestation of party autonomy*

If the parties to the contract submitted to arbitration have agreed, by way of a customary choice-of-law clause, to apply the "laws of Germany" to their contract, must any alleged or manifest illegality, including bribery, be proven under that law?

Would it suffice to establish illegality under some other, "connected" body or rules of law (such as the substantive law of the seat)? Does the illegality under that other law, which is different from the one stipulated in the choice-of-law clause, mandatorily result in the illegality of the contract even under the stipulated governing law?

---

[378] Paris Court of Appeals, *Lebanese Traders Distributors & Consultants LTDC* v. *Reynolds*, 27 October 1994, 10 *International Arbitration Report* E7.

[379] *Laburthe* v. *Sauveroche*, 1961 *Bulletin des arrêts de la Cour de cassation* III, No. 125 (1961).

[380] See also generally R. Kreindler, *supra* footnote 41, pp. 249 *et seq*.

The substantive rights and duties of the parties (as opposed to the rights and duties of the arbitral tribunal) are governed first and foremost by the substantive law agreed, or otherwise determined, to be applicable to the contract.

Invariably, the separable agreement to arbitration in that contract is likewise considered to be construed and interpreted against the background of that same agreed body of law. Accordingly, the first, and perhaps only required, step in assessing an allegation or suspicion of illegality of the main contract, and the consequences for the parties' rights and duties, will normally be that applicable substantive law.

Rationally speaking, the parties will choose a *lex contractus* which does not result in unenforceability. Indeed under most substantive laws, when a contract term or contract as a whole is required to be interpreted, that interpretation which results in validity is favored over that which results in invalidity[381].

## 2. Lex contractus, lex arbitri *and the place of performance*

Let us suppose that the arbitral tribunal concludes that the main contract, for example providing for the promotion of the importation of counterfeit compact discs, offends public morals under the agreed German law. Let us also suppose that such contract does not — for the sake of argument — offend public morals under the substantive law reigning at either the non-German seat of arbitration or the non-German place of counterfeiting or importation, or both.

It is submitted that that fact would not prevent the

---

[381] *Texas Eastern Transmission Corp.* v. *Amerada Hess Corp.*, 145 F. 3d 737, 742 (1998) United States Court of Appeals, Fifth Circuit, 7 July 1998.

arbitral tribunal from making any and all rulings flowing from its finding of illegality under the applicable
*German lex contractus*. The rulings available to the
arbitral tribunal might include an order or award denying or upholding its jurisdiction and an award granting
or denying relief requested on one or both sides.

Any incompatibility of those rulings under German
law with a diverging law at the seat or the place of
"performance" would be irrelevant unless and to the
extent that the rulings violated a mandatory norm.
More specifically, in the case of the seat of arbitration
that mandatory norm would need to be such as to justify nullification of the award[382]. In the case of the
place of performance, that mandatory norm should be
wholly irrelevant unless enforcement of the award was
sought there, and the norm justified denial of enforcement under Article V of the New York Convention or
such other basis as might apply.

### 3. *The connectedness of the law of place of perfor-mance*

Would it suffice to establish illegality under some
other, "connected" body or rules of law? In our prior
example, there is no identity or overlap between the
State of the applicable substantive law, the State in
which the seat is located and the State in which the
"performance" occurs. One could assume, however, a

---

[382] Cf. also Arts. 9 (2), 21 of the Regulation (EC)
No. 593/2008 of the European Parliament and of the
Council of 17 June 2008 on the law applicable to contractual obligations (Rome I: "overriding mandatory provisions": "Nothing in this Regulation shall restrict the application of the overriding mandatory provisions of the law
of the forum." "The application of a provision of the law
of any country specified by this Regulation may be refused
only if such application is manifestly incompatible with
the public policy (*ordre public*) of the forum").

not unusual scenario in international arbitration, including in intermediary or lobbying agreements: namely, that both the agreed substantive law and the agreed law of arbitration resulting from the choice of a seat have nothing to do with the place of characteristic performance of the illegality — other than that the parties agreed to them.

Let us assume that the non-German and non-Swiss parties agreed, for example, to German substantive law and a Swiss seat in connection with an "intermediary contract" whose nexus is in neither Germany nor in Switzerland, but in Third Country X. Indeed the contract has everything to do with X, and nothing to do with Germany or Switzerland other than the "mere" party agreement. Let us also assume that the arbitral tribunal also suspects that the parties intentionally agreed to German law and a Swiss seat so as to distance the contract as much as possible from the reach of the law of X and X's prohibition against such contracts.

This scenario is in fact entirely realistic. Where the intermediary or brokerage contract is not illegal under German law or Swiss law, what happens if it is manifestly illegal under the law of Third Country X? To the extent X is closely connected to the contract, should its public policy be followed by the arbitral tribunal deciding under German substantive law in Switzerland?

It is submitted that the proper result is that unless the illegality under X's law rises to the level of a violation of notions of international public policy which *likewise* offend notions of international public policy in German and/or Swiss law, the illegality at X need not concern the tribunal, and cannot bind it[383]. This is not

---

[383] See, e.g., Award in ICC Case No. 1399 (1967), in which the arbitral tribunal refused to avoid a contract sub-

to say that the illegality of conduct in another country cannot easily render a contract immoral under the law of the seat or the law governing the contract. At the same time, the immorality resulting from the application of the foreign law should be of an egregious nature in order to supersede the agreed substantive law and contrary mandatory norms at the seat.

What of the role of conflict of laws rules and application of the national conflict rules of the seat? The fact that the law of X is, factually, closely connected to the contract — and that the laws of Germany and Switzerland respectively are not at all except for the contract terms — is, by itself, of no consequence. Even where such issues of connectivity might play a role in the national courts with their concept of a *lex fori*[384],

---

ject to French law although it was intended to circumvent Mexican customs law ("French law is not concerned with foreign customs laws")*; see also ICC Award dated 27 April 1992, upheld by Paris Court of Appeals, *Lebanese Traders Distributors & Consultants LTDC* v. *Reynolds*, 27 October 1994, 10 *International Arbitration Report* E7, *Revue de l'arbitrage* (1994), p. 709 (refusal to take account of Lebanese customs regulations in distributor termination dispute); and Award in ICC Case No. 6379 (1990), *Italian Principal* v. *Belgian Distributor*, XVII *Yearbook of Commercial Arbitration*, 1992, p. 212, *Revue de droit commercial belge*, 1993, p. 1146 (refusal to apply mandatory Belgian law respecting sales termination agreements in lieu of agreed Italian law); but cf. *Laburthe* v. *Sauveroche*, *1961 Bulletin des arrêts de la Cour de cassation III*, No. 125 (1961), in which the French Cour de cassation held void for illegality a contract intended to provide for bribery of a public official outside France, on the grounds that French public policy did not prohibit only bribery of French officials.

[384] Cf., e.g., in the European Union Art. 7 (1) of the 1980 Rome Convention on the Law Applicable to Contractual Obligations, enabling courts to factor in foreign mandatory rules; Germany, Luxembourg and the United Kingdom have taken the reservation pursuant to

such consideration has no binding effect in the arbitral sphere. Conflict of law rules which might bind the national courts will not bind the arbitral tribunal, for example, at our Swiss seat. Such issues are then governed by specific legislation on international arbitration (in this case, Article 187 (1) of the Swiss Act)[385], which supersedes any other conflicts principles.

Thus overall in international arbitration derogation from the *lex contractus* is appropriate solely in cases of *fraus legis*[386] or *fraude à la loi*[387]. Otherwise, foreign mandatory rules or laws — for example, which have different treatment of "intermediaries" — should not give rise to sufficiently legitimate and manifestly preponderant interests or be sufficiently closely connected so as to supersede the *lex contractus*. In any event, transnational public policy overrides national laws that may otherwise be applicable pursuant to whatever conflict of laws rules are considered to apply.

Thus the illegality at X does not mandatorily result in the illegality of the contract under the stipulated governing law or under the curial law — unless it fits into an egregious violation of public policy. Indeed notably in a country such as France which distinguishes between local public policy and international public policy offences, even a violation of *local* public policy at the seat as a result of the prohibition in

---

which their national courts may *not* take foreign mandatory rules into account.

[385] Art. 187 (1), Switzerland's Federal Code on Private International Law.

[386] M. Blessing, "Regulations in Arbitration Rules on Choice of Law", in A. J. van den Berg (ed.), *Planning Efficient Arbitration Proceedings, The Law Applicable in International Arbitration*, ICCA Congress Series, Vienna, Volume XII, Kluwer Law International, 1996, pp. 402 *et seq.*

[387] A. Sayed, *supra* footnote 2, pp. 169 *et seq.*

Country X should not mandate a finding of illegality where the parties and subject matter call for application of international, and not domestic, public policy standards[388].

In summary, the arbitral tribunal should declare the illegality of the act under the *lex arbitri* even if it is legal under the *lex contractus*. Even further, it should declare the illegality even if it legal under both the *lex arbitri* and *lex contractus* where it is illegal as a matter of the deemed "transnational" or "international" public policy.

### 4. *Violation of universal public policy versus local public policy*

Only a fundamental violation of transcending international public policy "in the German sense" under the substantive law and "in the Swiss sense" under the curial law would call for a finding of illegality based merely on the close connection to X and X's own mandatory norms:

> "If regard is to be had to mandatory provisions . . . of a law other than that of the forum or that chosen by the parties, then such provisions can only prevent the chosen law from being applied *if there is a close link between the contract and the country of that law and if they further such aims as are generally accepted by the international community*." (Emphasis added.)[389]

---

[388] R. Kreindler, *supra* footnote 41, p. 251.
[389] Art. 9 of the 1991 Resolution of the Institute of International Law concerning the autonomy of the parties in international contracts between private persons or entities, reprinted in Institut de droit international, "Tableau des résolutions adoptées" (1957-1991), at pp. 408, 413 (1992), *Revue critique de droit international privé*, 1992, p. 198.

Indeed the decision of the Swiss Federal Tribunal in *Beverly Overseas SA* v. *Privredna Banka Zagreb*, confirms this approach: if the facts which need to be analysed to determine the enforceability of the Swiss-based international award have no or only few links to Switzerland, then universal public policy considerations must be taken into account in addition to Swiss public policy[390]. Whether the Swiss award would have any prospect of successful enforcement in X is, of course, an entirely different matter. To what extent the tribunal should be concerned with that problem relates, again, to the discussion of, for example, Article 41 of the ICC Rules and the question of the extent of a duty to render an award which is "enforceable at law".

The tribunal's award respecting suspected or manifest illegality cannot make legal what would otherwise be illegal. At the same time, the arbitrator should not disregard the governing substantive law in favour of some other connected national law respecting illegality unless the application of the governing law (in disregard of the other connected law) would result in a violation of international public policy. This is no different from saying that the arbitrator need not apply the agreed or determined governing law if to do so would cause the arbitrator to violate international public policy. In such extreme cases, party autonomy is trumped by the "higher good" of international public policy.

In our scenario, the tribunal may disregard the mandatory public policy at X in favour of the agreed German law, even if German law has vastly less connection to the disputed contract than does X's law, unless such disregard would offend international public

---

[390] Tribunal Fédéral [Swiss Federal Tribunal], *Beverly Overseas SA* v. *Privnedna Banka Zagreb*, *supra* footnote 280, p. 807 (Swiss).

policy. And where disregard of the mandatory public policy at X would itself offend international public policy, the arbitrator has a right to apply the law of X over and above the agreed German law so as to avoid offending that transcending public policy:

> "The parties are to be enabled to subject their legal relations to the law they choose, and to exclude the national law which would otherwise apply. Therefore, provisions of the law which is excluded can only be recognized within the chosen law to the extent that they are part of the ordre public international." [391]

Once again, to the extent the arbitrator has a duty to render an award enforceable at law, it is submitted that it would then have a duty to apply the law of X in such case [392]. Where the provisions of foreign law are not considered to rise to the level of a transnational *loi de police*, then there should be no obligation *by the arbitrator* to apply them in lieu of the agreed substantive law:

> "although commercial corruption is deserving of strong judicial and governmental disapproval, few would consider that it stood in the scale of opprobrium quite at the level of drug-trafficking" [393].

---

[391] *Westacre* v. *Jugoimport*, ICC Case No. 7047, *supra* footnote 201, p. 332.

[392] Cf. E. Gaillard and J. Savage, *supra* footnote 1, para. 1533: "Accordingly, arbitrators have the right — *and even the obligation* — to themselves raise the issue of whether disputes contracts or legal provisions put before them satisfy the requirements of international public policy" (emphasis added), citing regarding European Community antitrust law ICC Awards No. 7315 (1992) and No. 7181 (1992).

[393] High Court, *Westacre* v. *Jugoimport*, *supra* footnote 319, p. 598.

Likewise, where the provisions of the foreign law are considered to be valid inasmuch as the parties *agreed* to them at arm's length, they may nevertheless not be applied *by the enforcing court* if the court considers that the mandate of party autonomy must yield to the mandate of forestalling absurd results which offend public policy. In the enforcement context, that public policy may in fact be local public policy, and not necessarily transnational public policy[394].

Practically speaking, in the area of corruption, bribery is likely to be contrary to public policy under *each* of the *lex contractus*, *lex arbitri* and the law of the place of performance, with certain possible exception. By way of example, bribing foreign persons (as opposed to foreign public officials) is prohibited under the UK Bribery Act, but it may be questioned whether "private-to-private" bribery falls within the rule of international or transnational public policy such as to override the *lex contractus* or even the *lex arbitri*. An indication of this doubt is the call in the context of Article 21 of the UN Convention against Corruption to prohibit private bribery. To the extent it is not yet expressly prohibited in such a convention, it may not necessarily be tantamount to an established norm of public policy.

All of the foregoing does not change the challenge confronting the arbitrator as to whether a *loi de police* or other prohibition should be regarded as local or transnational. Nor does it change the challenge of ascertaining whether in fact particular kinds of illegality which are *not* necessarily uniformly condemned

---

[394] *Soleimany, supra* footnote 302, where the Court of Appeal refused to enforce an award at the London seat under Jewish law in a dispute between two Iranian refugees where the award gave effect to a contract which violated Iranian customs regulations.

still give rise to a transnational norm justifying or requiring respect by the arbitrator. In cases where bribery or corruption are generally condemned throughout the world, what importance if any should the arbitrator attach to the fact that a particular corrupt practice is indeed widely practised and widely accepted in a single country, and it is that country which has the closest connection to the "performance" of the contract in dispute?

In cases where the illegal act relates to disrespect of a United Nations-sanctioned embargo against one or only a few States, what importance if any should be attached to the fact that respect of the embargo constitutes a *crime* in the target country, and that target country has the closest connection to the performance? In the case of a generally condemned corrupt practice which is nevertheless widely — perhaps even officially or statutorily — condoned in a single country, the arbitrator's task need not be complicated. The agreed substantive law should be applied except to the extent it violates generally accepted international norms. Alternatively, the tribunal may be entitled to conclude that even if the agreed substantive law is the law of that single country, it will *disregard* that governing law if applying it would contravene international public policy.

In such situations, the arbitrator cannot possibly be the servant to several different masters: it must observe generally accepted international norms, even if it is thereby likely that the award will have little prospect of cross-border enforcement in that single country. Inasmuch as Article V (2) *(b)* of the New York Convention should be seen as a mandatory guideline for the arbitrator[395], he must attempt to determine whether

---

[395] Neither fraud in the factum nor illegality is expressly mentioned as a basis for denial of enforcement under the New York Convention, although they may be

the broad consensus internationally is embodied in the application of the agreed substantive law or not. The same would apply to alleged illegality relating to embargo measures, where arguments could be made that the measures reflect the will of only a handful of States, and not necessarily global policy: "[i]n no case shall an arbitrator violate principles of international public policy as to which a broad consensus has emerged in the international community"[396].

At the same time, the existence of transnational conventions, resolutions and the like condemning a particular practice does not necessarily translate into a broad consensus which might be used by the arbitrator as justification for ascertaining the existence and violation of a principle of "international public policy":

> "Despite general lip-service one hesitates to believe in that there is an effectively practised worldwide consensus against corruption ('pots-de-vin') as long as under the fiscal law of many industrial countries bribes paid can be deducted as business expenses and corruption is endemic in many countries and rarely seriously fought."[397]

---

deemed to be encompassed within Arts. II (3), V (1), V (2) *(a)* or V (2) *(b)* depending upon the circumstances. Notably, while the UNCITRAL Model Law grounds for setting aside an award in Article 34 do not include corruption, the Singapore International Arbitration Act (Cap 143), entered into force on 27 January 1995 enacting the Model Law with minor modifications, adds two additional grounds for setting aside an award, one of which is fraud or corruption (the other is breach of natural justice).

[396] Art. 2 of the Resolution on Arbitration between States, State Enterprises or State Entities, and Foreign Enterprises, adopted by the Institute of International Law on 12 September 1989, *XVI Yearbook Commercial Arbitration*, 1991, p. 238.

[397] P. Karrer, "Commentary to Art. 187 of Swiss Private International Law Act", in H. Honsell *et al.* (eds.),

Among the many "industrialized" countries alluded to number or until recently numbered certain principle places of international arbitration in Western Europe, including Switzerland and Germany.

Furthermore, query how extensive and transparent such "broad consensus" in the international community really is on some of the issues of illegality which typically affect an international commercial arbitration proceeding:

> "even in particular areas of law one finds disappointingly few interventionist norms that are common to all or even just to the most *legal systems*: Even in the area of ordinary criminal law such common rules exist only in the narrow area of international substantive criminal law on the basis of international treaties (Genocide, drug trafficking, terrorism, slave trade, slavery, piracy)"[398].

In light of the foregoing, is an attempt to directly apply transnational *ordre public* simply too risky for an arbitrator, and therefore not his mandatory duty after all, but rather the duty of the reviewing or enforcing judge? Should the arbitrator avoid making a decision when international public policy may be such a moving target? Should the arbitrator simply resign his office where he believes that the illegality of the contract at issue is so distasteful as to prevent him from carrying out his role? The answer must be no, as set forth in greater detail below[399].

---

*International Arbitration in Switzerland — An Introduction and Commentary on Arts. 176-194 of the Swiss Private International Law Statute*, The Hague, Kluwer Law International, 2000, para. 160 at p. 520, also citing *a contrario* Tribunal Fédéral [Swiss Federal Tribunal], 30 December 2004, *ASA Bulletin*, Vol. 13 (1995), p. 224 consid. 2d.

[398] R. Kreindler, *supra* footnote 41, p. 254.

[399] See *infra* Chapter VIII.B.4.i.

## B. *International Investment Arbitration and the Applicable Law*

Now in the context of investment treaty arbitration, again given suspected or manifest illegality, principles of competence-competence, separability, arbitrability and public policy must be applied and counterbalanced according to relevant rule(s) of law. But which one(s)? Typically, a treaty-based arbitration will involve a choice of public international law and/or a mixture or hierarchy of national law and public international law, with an overlay of international and transnational public policy.

An investment arbitration is likely to have different points of legal reference which differ in some respects from an international commercial arbitration. In an ICSID Convention arbitration, there is typically no *lex contractus* rooted solely in national law, even if the arbitration does indeed arise out of an investment contract in parallel with the invocation of an investment treaty, such as in the case of *World Duty Free*. Moreover, there is typically no *lex arbitri*, unless the BIT or MIT provides for the option of choosing a national seat such as, not infrequently, The Hague or Stockholm and that option is exercised.

Furthermore, there is no *lex societatis* of the affected party, at least in the case of the host State party. And the law of the place of performance *(lex locus solutiones)* will invariably be that of the host State. In addition, there is no law of the place or places of putative attempted enforcement of the award in the ICSID scheme. Against this background, there may still be a possible and significant tension and conflict of outcomes, depending on the "seat" or the *lex contractus*/treaty: what is "illegal" under the *lex arbitri* may be "legal" under the *lex contractus*/treaty choice of law and may be unregulated under the law at the

place of performance/host State. The various issues
posed here are now discussed in turn.

## 1. *The autonomy of the parties to choose the law in international investment disputes*

In the investment treaty context, freedom to choose
the applicable law by agreement exists, but with
notable differences to international commercial arbitration.

*First*, there is the concept of an "offer" to submit to
arbitration and thereby to submit to an applicable body
or rules of substantive law, which "apply" only once
the offer is accepted[400]. This element of arbitration
without privity, as previously mentioned, permeates the
legal relationship between the investor and the host
State, including respecting the choice of law, and
thereby the choice of legal rules to apply to questions
of corruption. The investor and the State have not
agreed whatsoever on a choice of law in the classical
sense inasmuch as they have not agreed on anything in
the classical sense, particularly before the treaty-based
arbitration is invoked.

*Second*, there is the distinction to be drawn between
so-called "treaty claims" and "contract claims". While
this distinction has been the subject of some controversy and uniformity as to the distinction does not
exist[401], it is fair to say for present purposes that treaty

---

[400] R. Kreindler, "The Law Applicable to International
Investment Disputes", in N. Horn and S. Kröll (eds.),
*Arbitrating Foreign Investment Disputes*, Kluwer Law
International, 2004, p. 403.

[401] See, generally, M. Sasson, *Substantive Law in
Investment Treaty Arbitration : The Unsettled Relationship
between International Law and Municipal Law*, Kluwer
Law International, 2010, pp. 151 *et seq.*; G. Tawil, "The
Distinction between Contract Claims and Treaty Claims",
in A. J. van den Berg (ed.), *International Arbitration 2006 :*

claims: rest on (at least partially) treaty-based (e.g. BIT or MIT) causes of action to which the substantive law(s) apply which emerge from application of the treaty, and not of any contract.

In some respects, the situation is akin to the contingent nature of a choice-of-law clause in an agreement to which a non-signatory to commercial contract is sought to be bound: the putative defendant did not agree to the contractual choice of law, but may "accede" to it if jurisdiction is upheld over it. "Contract claims" encounter similar issues of applicable substantive law to those in commercial disputes, as addressed above, with the possible exception of substantive law issues raised particularly by the involvement of a State party.

*Third*, there is the issue of party autonomy and the law of the host State versus another State. In non-treaty-based investment arbitrations, the parties do not necessarily agree to the exclusive application of the host State law whereas in treaty-based investment arbitrations, they invariably are deemed to have agreed to

---

*Back to Basics?*, ICCA Congress Series, Vol. XIII, Montreal, Kluwer Law International, 2007, pp. 492 *et seq.*; M. Friedman, "Treaties as Agreements to Arbitrate — Related Dispute Resolution Regimes: Parallel Proceedings in BIT Arbitration", in A. J. van den Berg (ed.), *International Arbitration 2006: Back to Basics?*, ICCA Congress Series, Vol. XIII, Montreal, Kluwer Law International, 2007, p. 550; B. Stern, "Treaties as Agreements to Arbitrate: Comments", in A. J. van den Berg (ed.), *International Arbitration 2006: Back to Basics?*, ICCA Congress Series, Vol. XIII, Montreal, Kluwer Law International, 2007, pp. 578 *et seq.*; e.g. in *PSEG Global Inc.*, *The North American Coal Corporation and others* v. *Republic of Turkey*, ICSID Case No. ARB/02/5, Decision on Jurisdiction, 4 June 2004, para. 158, the tribunal pointed out that "recent cases" had established that "contract based disputes are different from treaty based disputes and arise out of separate causes of action".

principles of public international law, either alone or in symbiosis with a body or rules of national law. The choice of a "neutral" third-country law is potentially problematic, as the investor activities are linked to laws of the host State (e.g., taxation, customs, duties, permits, etc.) and may also be required by the respective treaty being invoked for protection to be in accordance with those local laws[402].

In the absence of any such choice of law, it will depend on the applicable arbitral rules as to whether the arbitral tribunal, in the most likely scenario, will apply the law "most closely related" (pursuant to general conflict principles)[403], which will likely not be a third-country law. Instead, the arbitrator may apply one or both of (i) the law of the host State party and (ii) the "applicable" international law, for example, under Article 42 (1), ICSID Convention[404]. This stands in

---

[402] R. Kreindler, *supra* footnote 400, p. 404; C. H. Schreuer, *The ICSID Convention: A Commentary*, 2nd ed., Cambridge, Cambridge University Press, 2009, Art. 42, para. 27. See also, for early views on these issues, B. Goldman, "Le droit applicable selon la Convention de la BIRD, du 18 mars 1965, pour le règlement des différends relatifs aux investissements entre États et ressortissants d'autres Etats", in *Investissements étrangers et arbitrage entre Etats et personnes privées — La Convention BIRD*, 1969, pp. 133 and 155; P. Kahn, "The Law Applicable to Foreign Investments: The Contribution of the World Bank Convention on the Settlement of Investment Disputes", *Indiana Law Journal*, Vol. 44 (1968), pp. 12-13.

[403] R. Kreindler, *supra* footnote 400, p. 404.

[404] Art. 42 (1), ICSID Convention, provides that

"the Tribunal shall decide a dispute in accordance with such rules of law as may be agreed by the parties. In the absence of such agreement, the Tribunal shall apply the law of the Contracting State party to the dispute (including its rules on the conflict of laws) and such rules of international law as may be applicable".

contrast to the Energy Charter Treaty and its Article 26, paragraph 4 (choice of ICSID, Additional Facility, UNCITRAL Rules or Stockholm Chamber of Commerce)[405]. Depending upon which of these options is chosen, it is possible that a slightly different choice of law provision will be triggered in the absence of a party agreement. In that regard, the investor may directly influence the law or rules of applied, in the absence of a choice of law, by selection of particular arbitral rules.

## 2. *Party autonomy and the law of the host State*

A straightforward reference to the domestic law of a host State is not infrequently encountered in commercial contracts and resulting arbitration disputes. Indeed in certain areas of commercial activity and in certain areas such as agency and distributorship agreements in particular Arabian Gulf countries, the "host" contractant may rely on local legislation to require the foreign principal to agree to the local substantive law (as well as to local arbitration rules and a local seat of arbitration).

In investment arbitration involving a "host State" or a host State instrumentality, it may therefore be somewhat surprising to conclude that such references to the domestic law of the host State are infrequent. However, in investment arbitrations which do not rest on a treaty basis, it is seldom the case that the parties have agreed to the exclusive application of the host law. And in investment arbitrations which do rest at least in part on a treaty basis, the treaty invariably refers in one or another manner to principles of public international law — either standing alone or in some stipulated or non-stipulated symbiosis with a body or rules of national law[406].

---

[405] See Art. 26 (4), Energy Charter Treaty.
[406] R. Kreindler, *supra* footnote 400, pp. 401 *et seq.*

### 3. The law of the investor or the law of a third State

In commercial arbitration involving a State entity, reference to the law of the investor or non-State entity is not unheard of, but also not frequently encountered. More frequent is an agreement to a "neutral" third-country law which is perceived to advantage or disadvantage all parties more or less equally, and is often coupled with a neutral seat meant to further "delocalize" the arbitration.

In investment arbitration, however, the choice of an ostensibly neutral third-country law can potentially create greater difficulties to the extent the investor's activities are closely linked to the laws and legislation of the host State (for example, respecting employment, taxation, etc.) [407].

In those investment arbitrations where the application of a law other than that of the host State is desirable, not impractical (e.g., as is sometimes the case for loan or licensing agreements [408]) and indeed reachable, such application must necessarily arise out of a party stipulation. Absent such a stipulation, depending upon the applicable arbitral rules respecting the choice of law, the tribunal may or may not apply the law "most closely related" to the relationship (as per general conflict of laws principles), which is likely not to be a neutral third-country law. Instead, the tribunal may apply one or both of (i) the law of the State party to the dispute and (ii) "applicable" international law, for example, in accordance with Article 42 (1) second sentence of the ICSID Convention [409].

---

[407] See *supra* footnote 402.

[408] G. R. Delaume, "ICSID and the Transnational Financial Community", *ICSID Review — Foreign Investment Law Journal*, Vol. 1 (1986), p. 243.

[409] See also C. H. Schreuer, *supra* footnote 402, Art. 42, para. 32.

## 4. The investment agreement as a self-contained legal system

One alternative to an agreement to the laws of the host State, the laws of the investor or the laws of a third country is the approach whereby the investment agreement is considered to be a self-contained legal system which is isolated from any extraneous body of law or rules. Indeed, many BITs contain choice of law clauses [410] which commonly refer to the BIT itself, the law of the Contracting State, the rules and principles of international law and, sometimes, the provisions of a particular investment agreement [411]. An interesting example of such a provision is the 1991/1992 Dutch-Czech BIT which figured in the partial and final awards in the UNCITRAL proceedings between CME Czech Republic BV and the Czech Republic. Specifically, Article 8 (6) of that BIT provides:

> "The arbitral tribunal shall decide *on the basis of the law*, taking into account *in particular though not exclusively:* the law in force of the Contracting Party concerned; the provisions of this Agreement, and other relevant Agreements between the Contracting Parties; the provisions of special agreements relating to the investment; the general principles of international law."

---

[410] A. R. Parra, "Provisions on the Settlement of Investment Disputes in Modern Investment Laws, Bilateral Investment Treaties and Multilateral Instruments on Investment", *ICSID Review — Foreign Investment Law Journal*, Vol. 12 (1997), p. 332; I. F. I. Shihata and A. R. Parra, "The Experience of the International Centre for Settlement of Investment Disputes", *ICSID Review — Foreign Investment Law Journal*, Vol. 14 (1999), p. 336.

[411] C. H. Schreuer, *supra* footnote 402, Art. 42, para. 81. See e.g. the US Model BIT of 2004, Art. 30 (available at http://www.state.gov/documents/organization/117601.pdf).

Article 3 (5) provides that the international law standard prevails in case of contradiction between international law and national law. In that context, the Respondent Czech State took the position that Czech national law should be given primacy in determining whether or not it had breached its obligations under the BIT and that international law would become applicable only if there was a "genuine gap" in Czech law and if Czech law needed to be corrected on the basis of inconsistency with international law[412].

BITs invariably also contain detailed provisions on obligations which normally serve as the focus for alleged breaches of duty, without any need for immediate reference to a national law or, for that matter, to principles of international law. By way of example, such BIT provisions frequently include (i) the obligation of fair and equitable treatment, (ii) the obligation not to impair investments by unreasonable or discriminatory measures, (iii) the obligation of full security and protection of the investment, (iv) the obligation not to deprive Claimant of its investment, and, notably, (v) the obligation to treat foreign investments in conformity with principles of international law. Thus enters international law by way of agreement to the BIT regime itself[413].

This approach is intellectually appealing in some respects. Arguably, it is just as legitimate as an agreement on a delocalized third-country law which is otherwise devoid of any connection to the parties or the agreement. At the same time, agreement to a self-contained, stand-alone legal system is fraught with poten-

---

[412] *CME Czech Republic B.V. (The Netherlands)* v. *The Czech Republic*, Final Award in UNCITRAL Arbitration Proceedings, 14 March 2003, paras. 398-399 (available at http://italaw.com/sites/default/files/case-documents/ita0180.pdf).
[413] See, generally, R. Kreindler, *supra* footnote 400.

tial problems. One likely consequence of such a choice is that in circumstances where the tribunal can find no guidance from the investment agreement on a particular issue, this may be treated by the tribunal as an "absence of agreement" on the applicable law concerning that particular question. Depending on the applicable regime, that outcome may in turn lead, whether by "default" or by active decision of the tribunal, to the application of the law of the host State (e.g., Article 42 (1), second sentence, of the ICSID Convention)[414].

One primary reason for the concern about *non liquet* situations in international investment arbitration is the perceived concern to be able to anticipate transnational or cross-border legal issues and to apply some form of legal regime to such issues where a domestic law does not necessarily dispositively address them. In fact, such a situation could just as easily arise in international commercial arbitration (or domestic commercial arbitration, for that matter) as in international investment arbitration.

Some national laws, by way of both codification and jurisprudence, have evolved rules for the judge or arbitrator to identify and then seek to fill gaps where either the contractual agreement or the applicable law or both do not squarely address the issue at hand. In most such cases, the judge or arbitrator does not necessarily determine that the parties have "not agreed on a choice of law", but rather that the agreement or law to which they did agree still applies, but with a gap which requires filling. Query whether the automatic resort to

---

[414] See also C. H. Schreuer, *supra* footnote 402, Art. 42, para. 38; G. Tawil, "International Centre for Settlement of Investment Disputes. Applicable Law" (UNCTAD, Course on Dispute Settlement, January 2003, Thailand, to be found at http://r0.unctad.org/dispsett/course.htm), pp. 7-8.

a conclusion of "absence of agreement", for example, in the ICSID regime, is the sole or even best solution for such circumstances.

The solution will depend on the particular case, and the particular BIT, if the arbitration is based upon a BIT. In the Czech Republic UNCITRAL case, for example, the tribunal concluded that the choice of law provision, discussed above, did not contain any ranking in the application of the national law of the host State versus the treaty provisions versus the general principles of international law, nor did it provide for any exclusivity of application of any one of these sources. The Dutch-Czech BIT to which the parties agreed compelled the tribunal to "take into account" (not apply) the four sources of law, "in particular though not exclusively"[415].

One related issue is the question of whether there is a strict interrelationship between domestic and international law which would require an arbitral tribunal to follow a certain prioritization or ranking when applying the law applicable to a BIT. This will depend on the wording of the BIT. Apart from the wording of the BIT there is the concept, for example, as set forth in the 1989 ICJ case concerning *Elettronica Sicula*, that "[w]here the determination of a question of municipal law *is essential* to the Court's decision in a case, the Court will have to weigh the jurisprudence of the municipal courts . . ."[416].

This obviously throws discretion back to the tribunal to decide what is essential. In this regard, one tribunal concluded that

---

[415] *CME* v. *The Czech Republic*, *supra* footnote 412, paras. 400-402.

[416] ICJ, case concerning *Elettronica Sicula S.p.A. (United States of America* v. *Italy)*, 20 July 1989, *ICJ Reports 1989*, p. 47, para. 62, available at http://www.icj-cij.org/docket/files/76/6707.pdf.

"[t]his does not mean that a tribunal is bound to research, find and apply national law which has not been argued or referred to by the parties and has not been identified by the parties or the Tribunal to be essential to the Tribunal's decision"[417].

## 5. *Rules of law versus bodies of law*

Various international investment contracts, and resulting disputes, involve agreements between the parties in which they did not — at least not originally in the contract — provide for any provision respecting the applicable law. This was the case, for example, in *Benvenuti* v. *Congo*[418], *SOABI* v. *Senegal*[419], *LETCO* v. *Liberia*[420] and *CDSE (Santa Elena)* v. *Costa Rica*[421]. Accordingly, a conflicts of law analysis in such cases becomes all the more relevant.

Despite the alleged convergence of many legal systems with respect to "conflicts of laws" analyses, it

---

[417] *CME* v. *The Czech Republic*, *supra* footnote 412, para. 411.

[418] *S.A.R.L. Benvenuti & Bonfant* v. *People's Republic of the Congo*, ICSID Case No. ARB/77/2, Award, 8 August 1980, *International Legal Materials*, Vol. 21 (1982), p. 740, with correction at *International Legal Materials*, Vol. 21 (1982), p. 1478.

[419] *Société ouest-africaine des bétons industriels* v. *Sénégal*, ICSID Case No. ARB/82/1, Award, 25 February 1988, *ICSID Review — Foreign Investment Law Journal*, Vol. 6 (1991), p. 125.

[420] *Liberian Eastern Timber Corporation* v. *Republic of Liberia*, ICSID Case No. ARB/83/2, Award, 31 March 1986, and Rectification of 17 June 1986, *International Legal Materials*, Vol. 26 (1987), p. 647.

[421] *Compañia del Desarrollo de Santa Elena S.A.* v. *Republic of Costa Rica*, ICSID Case No. ARB/96/1, Award, 17 February 2000, and rectified on 8 June 2000, *ICSID Review — Foreign Investment Law Journal*, Vol. 15 (2000), p. 169.

remains that numerous different approaches prevail: centre of gravity, locus of characteristic performance, presumed application of the law of the vendor to name just a few. Likewise, slightly different approaches have been taken even in recent years in such texts as the 1996 English Arbitration Act, the 1998 German Arbitration Act, which was in turn based on the UNCITRAL Model Law, and the UNCITRAL Model Law itself. It is therefore not surprising that in international investment arbitration more than one approach is possible and more than one is foreseen depending upon which regime applies.

By way of example, Article 42 (1) first sentence of the ICSID Convention refers to "rules of law", as opposed to systems of law or a body of national law. This is consistent with the generally accepted notion that the parties, whether in an investment context or otherwise, are not restricted to accepting an entire system of law, but rather are free to combine rules of diverse origin, including those which do not necessarily derive solely or at all from a national system of laws[422]. The same result may be achieved in certain BITs, depending upon their formulation, and their reference to the law of the host State and international law in a fashion similar to the "residual provision" of Article 42 (1), second sentence, of the ICSID Convention. To be contrasted is the ECT, whose Article 26 (4) allows the investor to choose between and among

---

[422] I. F. I. Shihata and A. R. Parra, "Applicable Substantive Law in Disputes between States and Private Foreign Parties: The Case of Arbitration under the ICSID Convention", *ICSID Review — Foreign Investment Law Journal*, Vol. 9 (1994), p. 189; G. R. Delaume, "The Proper Law of State Contracts Revisited", *ICSID Review — Foreign Investment Law Journal*, Vol. 12 (1997), pp. 1 *et seq*; C. H. Schreuer, *supra* footnote 402, Art. 42, para. 39.

four different modes of arbitration: ICSID, ICSID Additional Facility, UNCITRAL *ad hoc* or Stockholm Chamber[423].

Each one of these four regimes has a slightly different provision respecting choice of law and the manner in which the tribunal selects the law in the absence of party agreement; thus in the ECT scheme, the investor can directly influence the outcome of the law applied, in the absence of a prior agreement, by its selection of the arbitral regime. Going even further, if the investor were not happy with the progress of the arbitration path chosen and the law applied under its rules, under the ECT he could bring a local court action or contractual arbitration, and later bring an arbitration under Article 26, and this notwithstanding the provisions of Article II (3), New York Convention.

An extension of the mix-and-match approach, although not necessarily an advisable one in many cases, is the agreement to apply different systems of law to different parts of the contractual relationship, particularly where different aspects of the relationship are governed by separate agreements (so-called *"dépeçage"*)[424]. In international commercial arbitration, this circumstance is sometimes encountered particularly in the context of multi-tier, multi-party contracts[425].

In international investment arbitration, there is arguably no better and no worse reason to attempt the same cutting and pasting. At the same time, a reliance on this approach might actually increase the likelihood of a perceived "absence of agreement", and thereby

---

[423] Art. 26 (4), Energy Charter Treaty.

[424] T. Arnoldt, *Praxis des Weltbankübereinkommens (ICSID)*, Baden-Baden, Nomos Verlagsgesellschaft, 1997, pp. 43-45; G. Tawil, *supra* footnote 414, p. 8. See also C. H. Schreuer, *supra* footnote 402, Art. 42, para. 39.

[425] See also C. H. Schreuer, *ibid.*

result in a default reference to general principles of international law and/or to the law of the host State against the original intentions of the parties. Thus in *CDSE* v. *Costa Rica* the tribunal concluded that in any event, even where the investor and the host State enter into a direct agreement respecting the applicable law, their choice would have to be clear and unequivocal[426].

## 6. *The choice of "international law"*

From international commercial arbitration, one is familiar with the problems related to locating and defining "international law", notwithstanding the guidance provided by such instruments as the Vienna Convention on the Law of Treaties[427] and the Statute of the International Court of Justice (e.g., general principles of law, transnational law, international conventions, international custom, judicial decisions, the teachings of international law experts, quasi-international agreements, etc.)[428].

---

[426] "Art. 42 (1) of the ICSID Convention does not require that the parties' agreement as to the applicable law be in writing or even that it be stated expressly. However, for the Tribunal to find that such an agreement was implied it must first find that the substance of the agreement, irrespective of its form, is clear." (*Compañía del Desarrollo de Santa Elena, S.A. (CDSE)* v. *The Republic of Costa Rica*, ICSID Case No. ARB/96/1, Award, 17 February 2000, para. 63, available at http://italaw.com/documents/santaelena_award.pdf).

[427] The Vienna Convention on the Law of Treaties, done at Vienna on 23 May 1969, entered into force on 27 January 1980, *United Nations Treaty Series*, Vol. 1155, p. 331, available at http://untreaty.un.org/ilc/texts/instruments/english/conventions/1_1_1969.pdf.

[428] Statute of the International Court of Justice, 26 June 1945, 59 Stat. 1055, 3 Bevans 1179, available at http://

In some international commercial arbitration disputes, particularly those involving State instrumentalities or entities, the underlying choice of law may refer to "public international law", "international law principles consistent with the intentions of the parties", "the principles of international law common to and consistent with" the two different bodies of national law of the respective parties, etc. While oftentimes such agreements may lead to the application at least in part of *lex mercatoria* or something akin to it[429], the flexibility bestowed on the tribunal may be undone by the vagueness of the legal standard to be applied.

In international investment arbitration, particularly under regimes such as ICSID and NAFTA, the parties may be deemed to have directly agreed, by virtue of treaty, to the application of international law, at least in part. From the investor's standpoint, this result may be a way to shield it from an overbearing application of the host State's law. From the host State's standpoint, this result may be a way to avoid the application of a third-country law with no relation to the dispute.

Among the BITs containing clauses on applicable law referring exclusively to the BIT and applicable rules of international law are those which served as the foundation for the ICSID proceedings in *AAPL* v. *Sri Lanka*[430], *AMT* v. *Congo*[431] and *Fedax* v. *Venezuela*[432] as well as the NAFTA proceedings in *Azinian* v.

---

www.icj-cij.org/documents/index.php?p1=4&p2=2&p3=0#CHAPTER_V.

[429] R. Kreindler, *supra* footnote 400, p. 410.

[430] *AAPL* v. *Sri Lanka*, *supra* footnote 21.

[431] *American Manufacturing & Trading, Inc.* v. *Democratic Republic of the Congo*, ICSID Case No. ARB/93/1, Award, 21 February 1997, *International Legal Materials*, Vol. 36 (1997), p. 1534.

[432] *Fedax N.V.* v. *Republic of Venezuela*, ICSID Case No. ARB/96/3, Award, 9 March 1998; *International Legal Materials*, Vol. 37 (1998), p. 1391.

*Mexico*[433] and *Metalclad* v. *Mexico*[434]. Among the multilateral treaties providing for ICSID arbitration which contain clauses on applicable law referring exclusively to the relevant treaty and rules of international law are the following: NAFTA, Article 1131 (1): "A Tribunal established under this Section shall decide the issues in dispute in accordance with this Agreement and applicable rules of international law"; Energy Charter Treaty, Article 26 (6): "A Tribunal established under paragraph 4 shall decide the issues in dispute in accordance with this Treaty and applicable rules and principles of international law"; and Cartagena Free Trade Agreement between Mexico, Colombia and Venezuela[435], Article 17-20, which replicates Article 1131 of the NAFTA. It is worth mentioning the Colonia Investment Protocol of MERCOSUR[436], Article 9 (5), which provides as follows:

> "The Arbitration Agency will decide the controversies based on the terms of the present Protocol, the rights of the Contracting Party that is part of the controversy, including the rules related to Law con-

---

[433] *Robert Azinian and Others* v. *United Mexican States*, ICSID Case No. ARB(AF)/97/2, Award, 1 November 1999, *ICSID Review — Foreign Investment Law Journal*, Vol. 14 (1999), p. 538.

[434] *Metalclad Corporation* v. *United Mexican States*, ICSID Case No. ARB(AF)/97/1, Award, 30 August 2000; available at http://www.italaw.com/sites/default/files/case-documents/ita0510.pdf.

[435] The (Spanish) text of the FTA can be retrieved from www.sice.oas.org/Trade/go3/G3INDICE.ASP.

[436] Protocol of Colonia for the Promotion and Reciprocal Protection of Investments in Mercosur, made in the city of Colonia do Sacramento, in 17 January 1994. Original language available at http://www.sice.oas.org/Trade/MRCSR/colonia/pcoloniaText_s.asp#Art9, free translation available at http://www.cvm.gov.br/ingl/inter/mercosul/coloni-e.asp.

flicts, the terms of private agreements related to the investment that are concluded, as well as the principles of international law."

The interplay between the law applicable to the merits and the law applicable to jurisdiction is also of interest. For example, in ICSID arbitration matters relating to the tribunal's jurisdiction under Article 25 of the ICSID Convention are not governed by Article 42. Specifically, in *CSOB* v. *Slovakia* jurisdiction was based on an agreement between the parties and the tribunal there held that the question of "consent" was to be answered not by reference to national law, but was governed by international law as set out in Article 25 (1)[437].

One other issue here is the opportunity, under certain circumstances, to obtain interpretation or clarification of a treaty provision even during the pendency of a dispute, which may also relate to the issue of the appropriate applicable law. In this respect, two recent examples are noteworthy.

NAFTA Free Trade Commission Notes of Interpretation (2001) effectively interpreted or recast the NAFTA requirements so as to limit the liability of the host country in connection with several matters *sub judice* and limited the meaning of international law to "customary" minimum standards (Section B.1, 2), thereby preventing recourse to other sources of interna-

---

[437] "The question of whether the parties have effectively expressed their consent to ICSID jurisdiction is not to be answered by reference to national law. It is governed by international law as set out in Art. 25 (1) of the ICSID Convention." (*Ceskoslovenska Obchodni Banka, A.S. (CSOB)* v. *Slovakia*, ICSID Case No. ARB/97/4, Decision on Objections to Jurisdiction, 24 May 1999, *ICSID Review — Foreign Investment Law Journal*, Vol. 14 (1999), para. 35.)

tional law respecting restrictions on host State treatment of foreign investors[438]. In the Czech Republic UNCITRAL arbitration with a Stockholm seat, Article 9 of the relevant BIT provided that either State could call on the other at any time for "consultations" with a view to resolving any issue of interpretation and application of the treaty. In this case, the Czech State took advantage of such provision after issuance of a partial award and in the context of an announced intention to challenge the partial award. "Common positions" were then adopted in writing, including on the issue of the BIT applicable law provision, to the effect that "[t]o the extent that there is a conflict between national law and international law, the arbitral tribunal shall apply international law"[439].

There is also the well-established concept of contract interpretation and consideration of a convention or treaty as a whole, with constituent parts. The May 2001 decision by the Supreme Court of British Columbia in the challenge of the *Metalclad* NAFTA award that the award must be based solely upon Chapter 11 of NAFTA is therefore questionable[440]. An

---

[438] The full text of the Notes of Interpretation of Certain Chapter 11 Provisions (NAFTA Free Trade Commission) of 31 July 2001 available at http://webapps.dfait-maeci.gc.ca/minpub/Publication.asp?FileSpec=/Min_Pub_Docs/104441.htm.

[439] *CME* v. *The Czech Republic*, *supra* footnote 412, para. 91.

[440] In addition to specifically quoting from Art. 1802 in the section of the Award outlining the applicable law, the Tribunal incorrectly stated that transparency was one of the objectives of the NAFTA. In that regard, the Tribunal was referring to Art. 102 (1), which sets out the objectives of the NAFTA in clauses *(a)* through *(f)*. Transparency is mentioned in Art. 102 (1) but it is listed as one of the principles and rules contained in the NAFTA through which the objectives are elaborated. The other two principles and

additional question here is the extent to which choice of law provisions such as Article 26 (6) of the ECT[441] exclude the possible application of national law. The wording does not expressly exclude or prohibit such an application of national law, and there are indeed various scenarios whereby the interrelationship between international law and national law might arise.

*First*, a State expropriation: is there a conflict between the norms of the ECT and national law leading to, or ostensibly justifying, the expropriation? Not necessarily. The standard to be applied to the dispute is

---

rules mentioned in Art. 102, national treatment and most-favoured nation treatment, are contained in Chapter 11. The principle of transparency is implemented through the provisions of Chapter 18, not Chapter 11. Art. 102 (2) provides that the NAFTA is to be interpreted and applied in light of the objectives set out in Art. 102 (1), but it does not require that all of the provisions of the NAFTA are to be interpreted in light of the principles and rules mentioned in Art. 102 (1).

In its reasoning, the Tribunal discussed the concept of transparency after quoting Art. 1105 and making reference to Art. 102. It set out its understanding of transparency and it then reviewed the relevant facts. After discussing the facts and concluding that the Municipality's denial of the construction permit was improper, the Tribunal stated its conclusion which formed the basis of its finding of a breach of Art. 1105; namely, Mexico had failed to ensure a transparent and predictable framework for Metalclad's business planning and investment. Hence, the Tribunal made its decision on the basis of transparency. This was a matter beyond the scope of the submission to arbitration because there are no transparency obligations contained in Chapter 11. (*The United Mexican States* v. *Metalclad Corporation*, Decision, 2 May 2001, to be found at http://www.courts.gov.bc.ca/jdb-txt/sc/01/06/2001BCSC0664.htm.)

[441] Energy Charter Treaty, Art. 26 (6), provides as follows "A Tribunal established under para. 4 shall decide the issues in dispute in accordance with this Treaty and applicable rules and principles of international law."

not the national law, but rather the ECT provisions as they apply to the State measure of expropriation.

*Second*, what about the interplay with the chosen arbitration regime, for example, Stockholm Chamber Rules? The SCC Rules themselves contain a choice-of-law provision[442], which trumps any contrary or diverging choice-of-law provision in the Swedish Arbitration Act to the extent the ECT dispute is assigned a Swedish seat and Swedish *lex arbitri*. Here, a conflict between the application of the ECT and the application of a national law or rules of law would be avoided since there is no absence of a choice of law: the parties having chosen the ECT, the ECT provides for a choice of law, namely application of the ECT and applicable rules of international law as per Article 26 (6), ECT.

*Third*, what about when the investor and the State have actually entered into a private investment contract with the choice of a specific national substantive law? Here, it is conceivable to have the private contractual dispute subjected to private arbitration under ECT Article 26 (2) *(b)* or to ECT arbitration under ECT Article 26 (3) *(c)*[443]. The consequence would be that the choice of a national law in the private contract is not binding for the tribunal in the ECT arbitration. While this may appear odd and not entirely satisfactory depending on the perspective, again the basis for the trumping effect of international law over national law is to protect the investor from abusive application of the host State law to justify inappropriate acts of expropriation and the like which might be permissible

---

[442] Art. 22, Rules of the Arbitration Institute of the Stockholm Chamber of Commerce, adopted by the Stockholm Chamber of Commerce and in force as of 1 January 2010, available at http://www.sccinstitute.com/skiljedom-sregler-4.aspx

[443] See Art. 26 of the Energy Charter Treaty.

under the host State law but not under international law[444].

## 7. *International law as a component of domestic law*

The challenge, in both commercial arbitration and investment arbitration, of discerning and then applying "international law" is not necessarily as difficult or arcane as might first appear. Depending on the legal system involved, international law principles may frequently be deemed to be incorporated into, and even to supersede, domestic law as the "law of the land". Thus even where the parties have not agreed, directly or indirectly, to the application of international law "rules" or "principles", international law may already be internally applicable as part of the domestic law

---

[444] Cf. T. W. Wälde, "Investment Arbitration under the Energy Charter Treaty. From Dispute Settlement to Treaty Implementation", *Arbitration International*, Vol. 12 (1996), pp. 456 *et seq.*:

"It is, however, difficult to exclude national law from consideration by the tribunal when the arbitration deals with breaches of contractual and related obligations under Art. 10 (1) (last sentence). How can the arbitral tribunal exclude national law when, for example, the contract at issue specifically, in its choice of law article, makes national law applicable? Equally, two of the arbitration rules referred to by Art. 26 select, with priority, the law chosen by the parties and, in the absence of such choice, national law plus international rules applicable. . . . The Treaty, however, has primacy over national law when national law would be used to undermine the effectiveness of the Treaty's investment obligations, for example retroactive negation of the legal character of a contract/concession in order to escape the Treaty's obligation. While national law may have to be considered and used for some questions, it cannot provide an escape from the Treaty's obligations. In the main, it is controlled by the more specific Treaty obligations."

chosen by the parties (or deemed to apply by the tribunal, in the absence of express agreement) and may thus be relied upon by the tribunal as part of the local law[445].

Indeed, in the case of a BIT-based arbitration international law may enter into the calculation as a result of the lack of an agreement to a national law, in turn leading to a reference to international law while all the while the BIT itself is in fact incorporated into the national law of the host State. The challenge may remain, however, of determining whether the international law principle is part of domestic law, or rather is part of domestic law and supersedes conflicting domestic law. This relates to the parallel challenge of determining which international law principles are truly transnational and overarching in nature, and which are simply law merchant principles deserving of consideration as long as not inconsistent with specific domestic law principles.

At the same time, there is a risk in relying upon the incorporation of international law into the domestic law selected by the parties in so far as the status of international law varies according to the particular national constitution (particularly relevant in this context is the distinction between automatic application and specific legislative incorporation of international law). Furthermore, subsequent domestic legislative enactments may take precedence over international law. In this regard, where an investor seeking protection under international law is not able to procure a favourable choice of law clause that includes international law expressly, the next best thing may be to rely on a provision such as the second sentence of Article 42 (1) of the ICSID Convention.

---

[445] I. F. I. Shihata and A. R. Parra, *supra* footnote 422, p. 192.

Further, national investment laws providing for ICSID's jurisdiction may contain a clause on applicable law, though such an explicit provision will be rare.

However, the mere fact that jurisdiction is based on a provision of the host State's law cannot be taken as a choice of the law of the host State. Nor is a reference in an agreement between the parties to either a rule of domestic law or piece of legislation a reliable indication of a general choice of the relevant domestic law[446].

More often than not, BITs do not contain express stipulations respecting the law applicable to the merits of any dispute. In such case, the law applicable to the merits is often construed to be the "principles of international law" or "public international law" or sometimes *lex mercatoria*.

It may be asked why national law rules often play such a peripheral role in BIT-based arbitration disputes. While the protection of foreign investments is normally construed to be an emanation either of the BIT as *lex specialis* or of international law, is not sometimes the contract-based or even the treaty-based claim also rooted in conventional contract principles? Particularly in the case of the contract claim, need national obligations law be abandoned so precipitously in deference to international law principles which are oftentimes less well developed and less precise?

This raises two particularly interesting issues: *First*, the BIT itself, by virtue of its ratification, becomes national law which considering its international law character may overrule conflicting national law. In this respect, see ICSID case *Goetz* v. *Republic of Burundi*

---

[446] C. H. Schreuer, *supra* footnote 402, Art. 42, paras. 63 *et seq.*

to this effect[447]. *Second*, this overruling effect is not seen as an undermining of the principle of party autonomy, but rather as a consequence of the free entering into, and reliance upon, the BIT as the basis of the arbitration.

## 8. *International law in the "absence" of its choice by the parties*

Query whether "rules" or "principles" of international law are to be applied even where the parties have not expressly agreed to apply them in their choice-of-law provision. What about "transnational public policy" or "international public policy" principles? Already in international commercial contracts, we encounter the problem of international law, particularly in the form of public policy: What is it? Where does it come from and where does the arbitrator find it? What is the arbitrator's obligation to discern it? What is his or her obligation to apply it? By reference to which body of law or rules of law does the arbitrator purport to consider public policy? What is the relative importance of the governing law of the contract as opposed to the law at the place of primary performance? As opposed to the *ordre public* at the seat of the arbitration? As opposed to the mandatory norms at the putative place or places of enforcement, where not the same as the seat[448]?

What if, as in the case of certain investment arbitrations, there is no "seat" in the conventional sense, and

---

[447] *Antoine Goetz et consorts* v. *République du Burundi*, ICSID Case No. ARB/95/3, Award, 10 February 1999, *XXVI Yearbook Commercial Arbitration*, 2001, p. 24 (original decision in French available at http://italaw.com/sites/default/files/case-documents/ita0380.pdf).

[448] See also R. Kreindler, *supra* footnote 245, pp. 239 *et seq.*

indeed no opportunity for recourse against the award at the courts of any seat? Where there is an agreement on the choice of law which does not incorporate rules of international law, or does not incorporate a particular rule of international law which the tribunal considers "applying", what happens?

A first impulse would be to conclude that such rule should not be taken into account by the tribunal, and that its application would indeed be a mis-application or error of law, with the possible result of vitiating the enforceability of the award. Indeed such provisions as Article 42 (1), first sentence, of the ICSID Convention would indicate that such rules are not to be taken into account where there is an agreement on choice of law which does not incorporate rules of international law. However, the majority opinion of both tribunals and commentators is in fact that international law is nonetheless to be considered even in the "absence" of an agreement to apply it[449].

In *SPP* v. *Egypt*, for instance, a disagreement arose as to whether Egyptian law had been chosen by the parties (and consequently whether international law was applicable in accordance with Article 42 (1), second sentence, of the ICSID Convention). In fact, the tribunal held this disagreement to be irrelevant to the question of the applicability of international law. The reason provided by the tribunal was that international law was applicable in either case, as gaps in the chosen domestic law pointed towards absence of agreement and led to the application of international law under Article 42 (1), second sentence[450].

---

[449] See also C. H. Schreuer, *supra* footnote 402, at Art. 42, para. 105.

[450] "Finally, even accepting the Respondent's view that the Parties have implicitly agreed to apply Egyptian law, such an agreement cannot entirely exclude the

The tribunal applied international law to defeat the Egyptian argument that certain acts of its officials were invalid under Egyptian law and held that these acts created an expectation protected by a principle of international law, which established the international responsibility of States for unauthorized or *ultra vires* acts of its officials[451]. Thus, the tribunal went further than a

---

direct applicability of international law in certain situations. The law of the ARE, like all municipal legal systems, is not complete or exhaustive, and where a lacuna occurs it cannot be said that there is agreement as to the application of a rule of law which *ex hypothesi*, does not exist. In such case, it must be said that there is 'absence of agreement' and, consequently, the second sentence of Art. 42 (1) would come into play." (*Southern Pacific Properties (Middle East) Limited (SPP)* v. *The Arab Republic of Egypt*, ICSID Case No. ARB/84/3, Award, 20 May 1992, *ICSID Review — Foreign Investment Law Journal*, Vol. 8 (1993), p. 351 para. 80.)

[451] "Whether legal under Egyptian law or not, the acts in question were the acts of Egyptian authorities, including the highest executive authority of the Government. These acts, which are now alleged to have been in violation of the Egyptian municipal legal system, created expectations protected by established principles of international law. A determination that these acts are null and void under municipal law would not resolve the ultimate question of liability for damages suffered by the victim who relied on the acts. If the municipal law does not provide a remedy, the denial of any remedy whatsoever cannot be the final answer."

The tribunal also held that

"[w]hen municipal law contains a lacuna, or international law is violated by the exclusive application of municipal law, the Tribunal is bound in accordance with Art. 42 of the Washington Convention to apply directly the relevant principles and rules of international law". (*SPP* v. *Egypt*, *supra* footnote 450, p. 352, paras. 83 *et seq.*)

mere closing of lacunae in national law — it actually subjected the national law to the scrutiny and control of international law[452].

In this sense, *SPP* may be regarded as an example of a general reluctance to abandon international law in favour of the host State's domestic law. If international law were excluded completely in deference to the agreed national law or, depending on the applicable conflicts law, in deference to the host State's law, it is conceivable that discriminatory and arbitrary actions by the host State might have to be upheld as long as they accorded with applicable domestic law[453].

On the one hand, if this is what the parties agreed to, why not? Clearly, however, such a result is not compatible with the goals of the ICSID Convention[454] and indeed of efforts to develop a transnational public policy unfettered by parochial practices or laws of certain host States. Nor is it compatible with Article 27 of the 1980 Vienna Convention on the Law of Treaties, to the effect that a State party to a treaty may not invoke the provisions of its internal law as justification for its failure to perform the treaty[455].

These goals may or may not have anything to do with what the parties "intended" when entering into their relationship. Of course, intent is a relative concept in certain investment arbitrations, particularly those where the "relationship" is the outgrowth of a treaty or BIT application, and where particularly the investor had no particular "intent" respecting the applicable law in the conventional sense. Thus if, for

---

[452] C. H. Schreuer, *supra* footnote 402, Art. 42, para. 109.

[453] *Ibid*, para. 112.

[454] *Ibid*.

[455] See Art. 27 of the Vienna Convention on the Law of Treaties, *supra* footnote 427.

example, ICSID jurisdiction is based upon a provision in the host State's law or in a treaty, rather than by direct agreement between the parties, the parties will not have had the chance to choose the applicable law prior to the proceedings (normally, in such cases the first contact between the parties is at the time of the request for arbitration).

If the national legislation or treaty offering consent to, for example, ICSID jurisdiction contains its own clause on applicable law, the investor "accepts" that choice of law clause by taking up the offer of consent (e.g., by instituting proceedings) and the clause on applicable law thereby becomes a choice of law agreed by the parties[456]. The parties' freedom to choose the

---

[456] *Goetz* v. *Burundi*, *supra* footnote 447, p. 36. The tribunal concluded that

> "[u]ndoubtedly, the applicable law has not been deter-mined here, strictly speaking, by the parties to this arbi-tration (Burundi and the investors), but rather by the parties to the Bilateral Treaty (Burundi and Belgium). As was the case with the consent of the parties [to the arbitration], the Tribunal deems nevertheless that Burundi accepted the applicable law as determined in the above provision of the Bilateral Treaty by becoming a party to this Treaty, and that claimants did the same by filing their request for arbitration based on the Treaty. If this is not the first time, as it has been pointed out, that the jurisdiction of the Centre ensues directly from a bilateral treaty on investment protection rather than from a separate agreement between the host State and the investor, this is apparently one of the first instances in which an ICSID Tribunal has to apply the law directly determined by such a treaty." (Para. 39.)

See also I. F. I. Shihata, "Applicable Law in International Arbitration: Specific Aspects in Case of the Involvement of State Parties", in I. F. I. Shihata (ed.), *The World Bank in a Changing World*, Vol. II, The Hague, Kluwer Law International, 1995, p. 599; A. R. Parra, "Applicable Substantive Law in ICSID Arbitrations Initiated under Investment Treaties", *ICSID Review — Foreign Investment*

applicable rules of law is not limited in time[457]. If no choice of law has been made by direct agreement, by legislation or by treaty or by the time the arbitration is instituted, it is generally accepted that the parties can choose the law by subsequent agreement during the course of arbitration proceedings[458].

Indeed, where jurisdiction is based on national legislation or treaty and there is no provision on applicable law in such legislation or treaty, agreement on applicable law can only be reached after proceedings have been instituted[459]. In this regard, the investor may also not necessarily have had any discernible intent respecting the inclusion of international law. On the one hand, a foreign investor may be seen as having a "constructive intent" not to choose the total exclusion of international law, including, for example, international minimum standards for the protection of aliens and their property. By imputing such intent to the foreign investor, one may actually be giving it greater rights and protection than a domestic investor would have vis-à-vis the same host State. On the other hand, the domestic investor is not meant to enjoy international standards for protecting foreign investments

---

*Law Journal*, Vol. 16 (2001), p. 21; C. H. Schreuer, *supra* footnote 402, at Art. 42, paras. 23 and 80; W. Kühn, "Practical Problems Related to Bilateral Investment Treaties in International Arbitration", *ASA Special Series 2002*, No. 19, p. 56.

[457] G. R. Delaume, "How to Draft an ICSID Arbitration Clause", *ICSID Review — Foreign Investment Law Journal*, Vol. 7 (1992), p. 186; G. R. Delaume, *supra* footnote 422, pp. 19 *et seq.*; B. Goldman, *supra* footnote 402, p. 192; I. F. I. Shihata and A. R. Parra, *supra* footnote 422, p. 201; C. H. Schreuer, *supra* footnote 402, Art. 42, para. 56.

[458] C. H. Schreuer, *ibid.*

[459] P. Kahn, *supra* footnote 402, pp. 7 *et seq.*; C. H. Schreuer, *supra* footnote 402, at Art. 42, para. 60.

because he is not perceived to be disadvantaged vis-à-vis the host State by virtue of his mere status as an alien.

The view has also been expressed that the mandatory rules of international law which provide for minimum standards of protection for aliens exist independently of any choice of law made by the parties in so far as they constitute a framework of public order within which specific investment transactions operate and cannot be contracted out of by the parties. This is a bold view, to be sure, but not inconsistent with the original goals of, for example, the ICSID Convention[460].

When all else "fails", occasionally the parties' reliance on certain sources of law in their submissions is seized upon to support an implicit agreement on choice of law: in *AAPL* v. *Sri Lanka*[461] the tribunal found that the parties had not had an opportunity to choose the applicable law in advance of the proceedings since they had not concluded a directly negotiated arbitration agreement. Hence, the choice of law process would materialize during the course of the arbitration proceedings[462]. The tribunal found that the

---

[460] See, e.g., discussion at C. H. Schreuer, *supra* footnote 402, Art. 42, para. 115.

[461] *AAPL* v. *Sri Lanka*, *supra* footnote 21, para. 19.

[462] "the Parties in dispute have had no opportunity to exercise their right to choose in advance the applicable law determining the rules governing the various aspects of their eventual disputes. . . . In more concrete terms, the prior choice-of-law referred to in the first part of Art. 42 of the ICSID Convention could hardly be envisaged in the context of an arbitration case directly instituted in implementation of an international obligation undertaken between two States in favor of their respective nationals investing within the territory of the other Contracting State."

The tribunal further held that

parties acted in a manner which showed their mutual agreement to consider the provisions of the Sri Lanka/United Kingdom BIT as being the main source of the applicable legal rules[463]. The tribunal went on to determine, problematically, that the BIT had to be applied in the context of principles of State responsibility under general international law[464].

In other cases, the tribunal may reach a conclusion on choice of law independently, taking the parties submissions as confirmation of its own determination: *Amco* v. *Indonesia*[465]. There, the tribunal determined

---

"[u]nder these special circumstances, the choice-of-law process would normally materialize after the emergence of the dispute, by observing and construing the conduct of the Parties throughout the arbitration proceedings" (*AAPL* v. *Sri Lanka*, *supra* footnote 21, paras. 19 and 20).

[463] *AAPL* v. *Sri Lanka*, *supra* footnote 21, para. 38.

[464] "the *Bilateral* Investment Treaty is not a self-contained closed legal system limited to provide for substantive material rules of direct applicability, but it has to be envisaged within a wider juridical context in which rules from other sources are integrated through implied incorporation methods, or by direct reference to certain supplementary rules, whether of international law character or of domestic law nature . . .".

The tribunal further held that

"[i]n fact, the submissions of both Parties . . . clearly demonstrate that they are in agreement about admitting the supplementary role of the recourse — regarding certain issues — to general customary international law, other specific international rules rendered applicable in implementation of the most-favoured-nation clause, as well as to Sri Lankan domestic legal rules" (*AAPL* v. *Sri Lanka*, *supra* footnote 21, para. 21).

[465] *Amco Asia Corp. et al.* v. *Republic of Indonesia*, ICSID Case No. ARB/81/1, First Award, 20 November 1984, *ICSID Reports*, Vol. 1 (1993), p. 413.

that since the parties had not expressed agreement on the applicable rules of law, Indonesian law and rules which the tribunal determined were applicable were to be applied. The tribunal found support for this finding in the fact that both parties not only failed to deny the applicability of these two systems, but had also frequently referred to both of them[466].

## 9. *Consequences of non-application of proper law — nullity*

Ultimately, the consequence of a failure to apply the proper law may be the nullity of the award, depending upon the applicable law and regime. Thus, for example, under Article 52 (1) *(b)* (excess of powers) of the ICSID Convention while a mistake in applying the law will not be a valid ground for annulment, applying a different law from the one agreed to by the parties may lead to annulment[467]. In *Klöckner* v. *Cameroon* the *ad hoc* Committee applied the distinction between non-application of the governing law, which would generally constitute an excess of powers, and a mistaken application of such law, which would generally not constitute an excess of powers[468]. The *ad hoc*

---

[466] *Amco Asia Corp. et al.* v. *Republic of Indonesia*, *ibid.*, p. 452. See also C. H. Schreuer, *supra* footnote 402, Art. 42, para. 77.

[467] W. M. Reisman, "The Regime for *Lacunae* in the ICSID Choice of Law Provision and the Question of Its Threshold", *ICSID Review — Foreign Investment Law Journal*, Vol. 15 (2000), p. 380; C. M. Schreuer, *supra* footnote 402, Art. 52, para. 210.

[468] "While the complaint based on failure to observe Art. 42 is thus admissible in principle, it remains to be determined what exactly constitutes not deciding 'in accordance with such rules of law as may be agreed by the parties', or not 'applying the law of the Contracting

Committee held that the Tribunal, having identified the
law correctly, did not in fact apply it, but rather based
its decision on a broad equitable principle (i.e., a duty
of full disclosure to a partner in a contract) without
establishing its existence in positive law. In so doing,
the Tribunal had acted outside the scope of Article 42
(1) and thus exceeded its powers within the meaning of
Article 52 (1) *(b)*[469]. By not showing the existence of

---

State party to the dispute'. This raises the fine distinction between 'non-application' of the applicable law
and mistaken application of such law."

The tribunal further held that

"[i]t is clear that 'error in judicando' could not in itself
be accepted as a ground for annulment without indirectly reintroducing an appeal against the arbitral
award, and the *ad hoc* Committee under Art. 52 of
the Convention does not, any more than the Permanent Court of Arbitration in the Orinoco case, have
the 'duty . . . to say if the case has been well or ill
judged, but whether the award must be annulled'."
(*Klöckner Industrie-Anlagen GmbH and Others* v. *United
Republic of Cameroon and Société camerounaise
des engrais*, ICSID Case No. ARB/81/2, Decision on
Annulment, 3 May 1985, *ICSID Reports*, Vol. 2 (1994),
p. 119.)

[469] "It may immediately be noticed that here the
Tribunal does not claim to ascertain the existence (of a
rule or a principle) but asserts or postulates the existence of such a 'principle' which (after having postulated its existence) the Tribunal *assumes* or takes for
granted that it 'is a basic principle of French civil
law'." (*Klöckner* v. *Cameroon*, *ibid.*, p. 121).

The Tribunal concluded that

"it must be acknowledged that in its reasoning, limited
to postulating and not demonstrating the existence of a
principle or exploring the rules by which it can only
take concrete form, the Tribunal has not applied 'the
law of the Contracting State'" (*Klöckner* v. *Cameroon*,
*ibid.*, p. 125).

specific rules, the *ad hoc* Committee held that the Tribunal had not applied the proper law. This finding is to be distinguished from the position unsuccessfully taken by the Czech Republic in the UNCITRAL Stockholm proceedings to the effect that only a reference to a specific national law rule would prevent a tribunal decision from being characterized as *ex aequo et bono* [470].

In the unsuccessful petition for a declaration of invalidity and annulment of the award in *CME* v. *The Czech Republic* to the Swedish Svea Court of Appeal, the Court on 15 May 2003 held in this respect that "[t]he fact that each legal statement in the award is not directly derived citing a rule of law cannot be deemed to mean that the tribunal conducted a general

---

[470] "The basic mandate of the Treaty obligates the Tribunal to *'decide on the basis of law'*, which is a self-explanatory confirmation of the basic principle of law to be applied in international arbitration according to which the arbitral tribunal is not allowed to decide *ex aequo et bono* without authorization by the parties (*see* Art. 33 (2), UNCITRAL Arbitration Rules, and Art. 17 (3) ICC Arbitration Rules)."

According to the Tribunal, the application of the principles of international law must not be confused with *ex aequo et bono* decisions:

"gives the dubious impression that only a reference to specific national law rules would prevent a tribunal's decision from being characterized as a decision *ex aequo et bono*. This impression . . . would contrast with the principles of international law as applied by numerous international arbitral tribunals for decades."

The Tribunal held that

"an arbitral tribunal's decision is rendered 'on the basis of the law', if the award is based on well-recognized international law precedents as developed, e.g., by the International Court of Justice, or ICC or UNCITRAL tribunals . . ." (*CME* v. *The Czech Republic*, *supra* footnote 412, paras. 403-406).

assessment of reasonableness"[471], which might have constituted grounds for a declaration of invalidity and/or annulment under the Swedish Act. The Court also held under Section 43 (2) of the Act that its judgment may not be appealed to the Supreme Court of Sweden[472].

In *Amco* v. *Indonesia* the *ad hoc* Committee confirmed the distinction between non-application of the proper law and a mere error in law, and that only the first would constitute an excess of powers under Article 52 (1) *(b)*[473]. In this case, the Tribunal had not failed to select the proper law, but rather failed to apply an essential provision of the correctly chosen applicable law. In failing to do so, the *ad hoc* Committee

---

[471] *The Czech Republic* v. *CME Czech Republic B.V. (The Netherlands)*, Judgment of the Court of Appeal, Case No. T 8735-01, 15 May 2003, *World Trade & Arbitration Materials*, Vol. 15 (2003), p. 264.

[472] *Ibid.*, p. 276.

[473] "The law applied by the Tribunal will be examined by the *ad hoc* Committee, not for the purpose of scrutinizing whether the Tribunal committed errors in the interpretation of the requirements of applicable law or in the ascertainment or evaluation of the relevant facts to which such law has been applied. Such scrutiny is properly the task of a court of appeals, which the *ad hoc* Committee is not. The *ad hoc* Committee will limit itself to determining whether the Tribunal did in fact apply the law it was bound to apply to the dispute. Failure to apply such law, as distinguished from mere misconstruction of that law, would constitute a manifest excess of powers on the part of the Tribunal and a ground for nullity under Art. 52 (1) *(b)* of the Convention. The *ad hoc* Committee has approached this task with caution, distinguishing failure to apply the applicable law as a ground for annulment and misinterpretation of the applicable law as a ground for appeal." (*Amco Asia Corp. et al.* v. *Republic of Indonesia*, ICSID Case No. ARB/81/1, Decision on Annulment, 16 May 1986, *ICSID Reports*, Vol. 1 (1993), pp. 515 *et seq.*).

determined that the Tribunal had manifestly exceeded its powers, leading to the annulment of the relevant portion of the award.

In *MINE* v. *Guinea* the *ad hoc* Committee distinguished between disregard of the applicable law, being a ground for annulment and erroneous application of law, being no ground for annulment. The Tribunal in that case had applied a different law than that agreed by the parties[474].

In *Wena* v. *Egypt*, in the absence of a choice of law by the parties Article 42 of the ICSID Convention referred the Tribunal to the law of the host State, Egypt. The Tribunal nonetheless relied upon international law principles to grant a claim for interest. The *ad hoc* Committee held that in the absence of party agreement, as Egyptian law and policy and Egyptian State practice in investments widely incorporated international law, the Tribunal had not exceeded its powers, such as would justify annulment under Article 52 (1) *(b)*, ICSID Convention, by applying the rules of the

---

[474] However, in that case, the Committee refused to annul the award on the technical ground that the Tribunal had erroneously referred to French rather than the applicable Guinean law on a particular point in circumstances where the relevant provisions in the two pieces of legislation were identical:

"There is thus no basis for saying that the Tribunal failed to apply any law. Admittedly, the Tribunal erred in citing Art. 1134 of the French Civil Code. The Committee notes, however, that the relevant provisions of the applicable Guinean law is contained in the 'Code Civil de l'Union Française' with the same number and the same contents as Art. 1134 of the French Civil Code. For this reason, the Committee does not consider that this error warrants annulment." (*Maritime International Nominees Establishment* v. *Republic of Guinea*, ICSID Case No. ARB/84/4, Decision on Annulment, 22 December 1989, *ICSID Reports*, Vol. 4 (1997), p. 96).

United Kingdom-Egypt Treaty instead of Egyptian law to decide the dispute concerning a claim to interest.

Absent any provision on interest in the United Kingdom-Egypt Treaty, Egypt had argued that the Tribunal should have reverted to Egyptian law which, again according to Egypt, limited the Tribunal's ability to grant an interest component as part of Wena's compensation. The Tribunal had awarded Wena compound interest without referring to Egyptian law, in compliance with the general standards of compensation set out in the United Kingdom-Egypt Treaty and in accordance with international law standards. The *ad hoc* Committee concurred with this finding by concluding that "international law and ICSID practice, unlike the Egyptian Civil Code, offer a variety of alternatives" that are compatible with international law standards[475].

Another path to the same conclusion might have been that when a claim is permissible under international law, it cannot be rendered impermissible by an otherwise applicable national law as international law prevails, at least as a corrective. But ultimately, is the role of international law that of a corrective, or does it generally supersede? And if it generally supersedes, then when does national law apply at all?

On one level, in relation to Article 52 (1) *(b)*, ICSID Convention, the *Wena* annulment decision may put into question the meaning of the reference to the law of the Contracting State in Article 42 (1), second sentence, of the ICSID Convention. In any event, the annulment

---

[475] *Wena Hotels Limited* v. *Arab Republic of Egypt*, ICSID Case No. ARB/98/4, Decision on Annulment, 5 February 2002, *International Legal Materials*, Vol. 41 (2002), p. 943 para. 53. See also discussion in E. Gaillard, "Landmark in ICSID Arbitration: Committee Decision in 'Wena Hotels'", 3 *New York Law Journal* 4 (2002).

criteria in *Wena* may be seen as being narrower than
those applied in *Klöckner I* and *Amco I*, and consistent
with those in *MINE* and *Vivendi*.

## 10. Corruption and illegality in an investment treaty-based choice of law

When do breaches of domestic law affect protection
of a treaty-based investment under international law?
Here we must distinguish between breaches in the
presence of a "in accordance with host State law"
clause and breaches in the absence of an "in accordance with host State law" clause. Generally, claims of
rights of protection made under international law, for
example via ICSID Article 41 or ECT Article 26,
trigger international law as a frame of reference.

In terms of the relationship between the applicable
law and corruption or other illegality in the *presence* of
"in accordance with host State law" clauses, the question may be seen as whether and how claims of rights
of protection made under a treaty with such a clause
trigger international law as the frame of reference for
the test of illegality.

Here, there are two forms of link to compliance with
local law.

*First*, there is the link to the definition of the
"investment" protected. Where there is no compliance
with the domestic law including a law against bribery,
there may be no treaty protection: for example, *Salini*
v. *Morocco*, ICSID (2001)[476].

*Second*, there is the link to the provision on admission of new investments and the temporal limitation on
the scope of application of the treaty to existing complying investments. Where there is fraud and misrepresentation under the local law, then the investment may

---

[476] *Salini* v. *Morocco*, *supra* footnote 208, para. 46.

be deemed not have been legally acquired, with the result that no treaty protection for illegal investments is considered available: for example, *Inceysa* v. *El Salvador*, ICSID (2006)[477]. The determination of whether the alleged illegality was in accordance with domestic law is in turn based either on domestic law (e.g., *Fraport* v. *Philippines*, ICSID (2010)[478]) or on general principles of law: *Inceysa* v. *El Salvador*, ICSID (2006)[479]. It is submitted that the reference to domestic law is usually the preferable approach.

Three kinds of illegality under the host State law may be relevant to exclude investment treaty protection. *First*, there may be illegality *per se* of the obtaining of the investment or of the business activity and the use of assets. Here one must distinguish *de minimis* breaches of bureaucratic formalities (even if in violation of domestic law), such as discussed and found in *Tokios Tokelés* v. *Ukraine*[480], ICSID (2007), *Metalpar* v. *Argentina*, ICSID (2008)[481] and *Mytilineos* v. *Serbia*, ICSID (2006)[482]. Here one must also distinguish minor illegality unrelated to the nature and sphere of the investment regulation regime (even if in violation of

---

[477] *Inceysa* v. *El Salvador*, *supra* footnote 174, paras. 240 *et seq.*

[478] *Fraport AG* v. *The Republic of the Philippines*, *supra* footnote 176, para. 344.

[479] *Inceysa* v. *El Salvador*, *supra* footnote 174, para. 243.

[480] *Tokios Tokelés* v. *Ukraine*, *supra* footnote 213, para. 97.

[481] *Metalpar S.A. and Buen Aire S.A.* v. *The Argentine Republic*, ICSID Case No. ARB/03/5, Award, 6 June 2008 (available at http://italaw.com/sites/default/files/case-documents/ita0516.pdf).

[482] *Mytilineos Holdings SA* v. *The State Union of Serbia & Montenegro and Republic of Serbia*, Partial Award on Jurisdiction, 6 September 2006 (available at http://italaw.com/sites/default/files/case-documents/ita0549.pdf).

domestic law), such as discussed and found in *Saba Fakes* v. *Turkey*, ICSID (2010)[483]. But even if the *de minimis* illegality does not warrant complete withdrawal of protection, it might result in less generous application of the treaty standards, such as fair and equitable treatment: for example, *Champion* v. *Egypt*, ICSID (2006)[484].

*Second*, there may a legal investments obtained or maintained illegally under the host State law. One example might be a fraudulent misrepresentation which is deemed to be a breach of good faith, as found in *Inceysa* v. *El Salvador*, ICSID (2006)[485] or a Ponzi scheme found to exist irrespective of intentionality or knowledge, as in *Anderson* v. *Costa Rica*, ICSID (2010)[486].

*Third*, there may be restrictions on or a prohibition of ownership by foreign investors (e.g., "Anti-Dummy Laws"). In such cases, a question may arise as to the extent of the investor's awareness of the illegality, to be assessed either under a subjective or an objective test. An example of the subjective test can found in *Fraport* v. *Philippines*, ICSID

---

[483] *Saba Fakes* v. *Republic of Turkey*, ICSID Case No. ARB/07/20, Award, 14 July 2010, para. 119 (available at http://italaw.com/sites/default/files/case-documents/ita0314.pdf).

[484] *Champion Trading Company, Ameritrade International, Inc.* v. *Arab Republic of Egypt*, ICSID Case No. ARB/02/9 (formerly *Champion Trading Company, Ameritrade International, Inc., James T. Wahba, John B. Wahba, Timothy T. Wahba* v. *Arab Republic of Egypt*), Award, 27 October 2006 (available at http://italaw.com/sites/default/files/case-documents/ita0148.pdf).

[485] *Inceysa* v. *El Salvador*, *supra* footnote 174, paras. 53 and 202.

[486] *Alasdair Ross Anderson et al.* v. *Republic of Costa Rica*, ICSID Case No. ARB(AF)/07/3, Award, 19 May 2010, paras. 25 *et seq.* (available at http://italaw.com/sites/default/files/case-documents/ita0031.pdf).

(2010)[487] and in *Desert Line* v. *Yemen*, ICSID (2008)[488]. A finding of intentional bad-faith illegal ownership under local law was equated with illegal possession, which in turn led to a denial of protection. An example of the objective test, which it is submitted here is to be preferred, can be found in *Tokios Tokelés* v. *Ukraine*, ICSID (2007)[489].

Less frequently, in terms of the relationship between the applicable law and corruption or other illegality in the *absence* of "in accordance with host State law" clauses, can domestic law on corruption still play a role? Here the focus is whether and how claims of rights of protection made under a treaty without such clause trigger international law as a frame of reference for the test of illegality.

Usually there is an imputation of a general require-ment of lawfulness both generally and specifically under the host State law in order to enjoy treaty protec-tion, even in the absence of such a clause. This is the case under ICSID, which itself lacks such a clause: for example, *Yaung Chi* v. *Myanmar*, ICSID (2003)[490], *Kardassopoulos* v. *Georgia*, ICSID (2007)[491], and *Phoenix Action* v. *Czech Republic* (2009)[492].

---

[487] *Fraport AG* v. *The Republic of the Philippines*, *supra* footnote 176, paras. 290 *et seq.*

[488] *Desert Line* v. *Yemen*, *supra* footnote 214.

[489] *Tokios Tokelés* v. *Ukraine*, *supra* footnote 213.

[490] *Yaung Chi Oo Trading Pte. Ltd.* v. *Government of the Union of Myanmar*, ASEAN I.D. Case No. ARB/01/1, Award, 31 May 2003, para. 58 (available at http://italaw.com/sites/default/files/case-documents/ita0909.pdf).

[491] *Ioannis Kardassopoulos* v. *The Republic of Georgia*, ICSID Case No. ARB/05/18, Decision on Jurisdiction, 6 July 2007, para. 192 (available at http://italaw.com/sites/default/files/case-documents/ita0444.pdf).

[492] *Phoenix Action Ltd.* v. *The Czech Republic*, ICSID Case No. ARB/06/5, Award, 15 April 2009, para. 100 (available at http://italaw.com/sites/default/files/case-documents/ita0668.pdf).

To be contrasted, however, is *Saba Fakes* v. *Turkey*, ICSID (2010)[493], in which it was held that there was no implied requirement of compliance with domestic law for the purposes of ICSID Article 25 (1) jurisdiction ("any legal dispute arising directly out of an investment"). This is also the case under the ECT, which lacks such clause: for example, *Plama* v. *Bulgaria*, ICSID (2008)[494], in which Article 26 (6), ECT ("in accordance with this treaty and applicable rules and principles of international law") was construed to encompass a violation of the principle of good faith and *nemo auditur propriam turpitudinem allegans* (no one can benefit from his own wrongdoing), relying on *Inceysa*[495] and *World Duty Free*[496].

### C. Commercial versus Investment Arbitration: Reconciling Illegality and Applicable Law

The foregoing discussion of the applicable law in the context of international commercial and investment arbitration suggests the following comparisons and contrasts and opportunities for reconciliation, to the extent desirable.

*First*, a serious breach of the agreed or determined law should deprive the claimant of the benefits of his contract or the benefits of investment treaty protection.

*Second*, under the concepts of competence-competence and separability respectively, such breaches are not likely to deprive the arbitral tribunal of jurisdiction

---

[493] *Saba Fakes* v. *Republic of Turkey*, *supra* footnote 483, para. 91.

[494] *Plama Consortium Limited* v. *Republic of Bulgaria*, *supra* footnote 372, para. 140.

[495] *Inceysa* v. *El Salvador*, *supra* footnote 174, paras. 239 *et seq.*

[496] *World Duty Free* v. *Kenya*, *supra* footnote 44, paras. 52 *et seq.*

over the merits in the commercial context, but they may do in the investment context.

*Third*, illegality does not necessarily refer to every illicit act, particularly in terms of possibly triggering a violation of public policy nationally, internationally or transnationally.

*Fourth*, reference to the domestic law does not result in non-application of international law.

*Fifth*, corruption and bribery in the acquisition or performance of an — even otherwise legal — contract or investment are condemned under most domestic laws, under public international law principles, and under international or transnational public policy.

*Sixth*, corruption and bribery, irrespective of the agreed or determined law(s), will invariably deprive the contracting party or the investor of the benefits of the contract or treaty protection.

*Seventh*, when does an allegation or showing of corruption in the acquisition or performance of the contract or investment result in a denial of jurisdiction or admissibility, when in a dismissal on the merits? This last question is addressed further below.

CHAPTER V

CORRUPTION ALLEGATIONS,
SUSPICIONS, FINDINGS AND ADMISSIONS

A. *The Different Contexts in Which Corruption*
*Plays a Role*

*1. Overview of the problem of illegality in its different*
*forms*

Which kinds and forms of "illegality" concern us in
the present context, and which not? There are several
levels of differentiation and distinction which must be
made from the arbitrator's perspective.

There may be many forms and shades of illegal and
illicit contracts.

Not all of them necessarily enjoy generally uniform
condemnation and not all of them necessarily constitute "bribery" or "corruption", to which we will turn as
our main focus shortly. Not all of them should necessarily be seen as consequently causing the nullity of
the related agreement to arbitrate or otherwise undermining the authority of the arbitral tribunal to adjudicate the underlying claim. Here, it behooves us to
distinguish between and among competence-competence, arbitrability and separability, and to differentiate
between international commercial and investment-
treaty arbitration.

There are three primary scenarios in which illegality
or corruption may play a role in arbitration.

First is *fraude par l'arbitrage*, in which one or both
parties concludes an arbitration agreement which itself

is a fraud[497]. It is fair to say that this situation, where both parties are complicit, is both rare and exceedingly difficult to prove in most instances.

Second is *fraude dans l'arbitrage*, in which one or both parties engages in fraudulent conduct in the arbitration proceedings themselves, either separately or collusively[498]. This situation is less rare, for example in the form of reliance on and submission into evidence of fraudulent or forged evidence, and it seldom occurs collusively.

And third is *fraude, objet de l'arbitrage*, in which the tribunal is confronted with allegations or suspicions or findings of fraudulent conduct, including corruption, as part of the actual issues in dispute[499]. It is this third category which is most frequent and with which we concern ourselves here.

## 2. *Different kinds of illegality*

There are a range of factual circumstances affecting issues of jurisdiction, arbitrability, separability, and competence-competence, especially in the commercial context.

### (a) *Overtly illegal contracts*

*First*, one must distinguish between certain categories of "overtly illegal contracts" and other categories which may be less overtly illegal in nature. Contracts which are overtly illegal are those whose subject matter or purpose is generally considered to

---

[497] M. de Boisséson, "L'arbitrage et la fraude (A propos de l'arrêt Fougerolle, rendu par la Cour de cassation le 25 mai 1992)", *Revue de l'arbitrage* (1993), p. 3.

[498] *Ibid.*

[499] *Ibid.*

offend "public morality"[500]. The offence of public morality arises as a result of a consensus based upon, for example, (i) the vast majority of national legal systems, (ii) evolving notions of transnational or international public policy[501], (iii) emerging *lex mercatoria* considerations[502], or even (iv) local mandatory laws or *lois de police*[503]. We shall return to this concept of consensus which was discussed above in the narrower context of bribery *per se*[504].

Among such categories, particularly at the transnational level, are *(a)* facilitation or promotion of drug trafficking, *(b)* terrorism, *(c)* subversion, *(d)* prostitution, *(e)* child abuse, *(f)* slavery, and *(g)* other forms of human rights violations[505]. Generally, contracts relating to such subject matters may be considered to possess an overt illegality. That overt illegality or illicitness would render any contract null and void *ab initio* according to the vast majority of national laws and any other rules of law meant to withstand the scrutiny of national or international public policy[506].

Other categories of illicit contracts may be "less overtly illegal". Where the contract or associated conduct is less obviously contemptible, the challenge of the arbitrator to determine the extent of jurisdiction, arbitrability, severability, etc. in fact becomes potentially more difficult, and not less so. Such contracts include various forms of broker, sponsoring, agency, consultancy and intermediary agreements. Such agreements are invariably associated with the payment of a

---

[500] R. Kreindler, *supra* footnote 41, p. 212. *Supra* footnote 116.

[501] *Supra* footnote 509. *Supra* footnote 117.

[502] *Supra* footnote 509. *Supra* footnote 118.

[503] *Supra* footnote 509. *Supra* footnote 119.

[504] See *supra* Chapter III.B.3.

[505] *Supra* footnote 121.

[506] *Supra* footnote 122.

commission for some — often ill-defined or even non-existent — consideration or performance[507].

The reasons why the arbitrator's task here may be more difficult than in the case of an overtly illegal contract include the fact that such commission arrangements may be perfectly legal, or in any event not expressly proscribed, in some countries[508]. A further difficulty is the distinction, amongst such contracts, between those relating to the payment of a "commission" to a public official and those relating to the payment of a commission to a private entity. Particularly in the case of a bribe or other corrupt practice vis-à-vis a public official, the egregiousness of the conduct may be seen to rise dramatically. At the same time, a noticeable trend in recent years, as reflected in certain international conventions and national legislation, is the expanding of the focus to include not only private to public corruption, but also private to private. Bribing a public official remains the classic example of illegality here, but bribing a private person has been recognized as potentially being just as pernicious even if it lacks the element of a breach of the public trust[509].

### (b) *Illegality and lack of assent*

*Second*, one must consider illicit contracts which are manifestly illegal not necessarily because of their overtly offensive nature or purpose, but rather because they simply never came into effect as purported. A graphic example is a contract which the defendant claims, perhaps truthfully, never to have signed or otherwise assented to[510]. An even more graphic

---

[507] *Supra* footnote 123.
[508] *Supra* footnote 124.
[509] *Supra* footnote 125.
[510] *Supra* footnote 126.

example is a claim that the signature or other alleged manifestations of assent are in fact forgeries[511].

If such defence is true, the contract invariably becomes null and void *ab initio*[512]. This result of nullity is indeed not unlike the first category of overtly offensive contracts involving drug trafficking, prostitution, etc.[513] A principal difference between the two categories, of course, is that the drug smuggling contract is deemed null and void even where all contract-

---

[511] *Supra* footnote 127.

[512] *Supra* footnote 128.

[513] Cf. Redfern and Hunter, *supra* footnote 7, para. 2.97, holding that the validity of the arbitration agreement "must depend on the reason for which the contract is found to be null and void . . . [giving as an example 'that's not my signature']. No amount of insistence upon the autonomy of the arbitration clause can make it valid if the respondent was not a party to it", citing the so-called *Pyramids* case, Award in ICC Case No. 3493 (1983), *Southern Pacific Properties Ltd.* v. *Arab Republic of Egypt*, 22 *International Legal Materials* 767 (1983); *IX Yearbook Commercial Arbitration* 111 (1984); the Cour d'appel of Paris upheld a claim by the award debtor Egyptian Government that it was not a party to the underlying contract, with the result that the award made on the basis that it was in fact a party was set aside in France: CA Paris, 12 July 1984, *République arabe d'Egypte* v. *Southern Pacific Properties Ltd.*, 112 *Journal du droit international* 129 (1985), 23 *International Legal Materials* 1048 (1984). In fact, the *Pyramids* case did not stand so much for the proposition of "that's not my signature" in the sense of a forgery or falsification. Rather, its focus was whether the term "approval, agreement and ratification" of an arbitration clause implied an intention to become a party to that clause. Extension of the arbitration agreement signed by a State-owned entity to the State is a wholly different matter than the illegality of a contract containing an arbitration clause by virtue of forgery or falsification of an assent to that contract or arbitration clause. It is the latter, the forgery or falsification scenario, which concerns us here.

ing parties assented to it. The forged contract, on the other hand, is deemed null and void because of the lack of mutual assent, and not — or not solely — by reason of its underlying subject matter.

From the perspective of the arbitrator's (possible) jurisdiction, separability and arbitrability, should there be a difference between the illicit drug smuggling contract and the illicit forged contract[514]? In fact, it may be that in the case of both contracts unless the illicitness is manifest, it must still be proven, through submissions, to the satisfaction of the tribunal. The allegation of illegality based on smuggling or forgery is, at least initially, only a claim, or defence, and must be proven. In all such cases where proof is still to be adduced, the tribunal must normally have jurisdiction to establish the facts of the case and take evidence. In

---

[514] A relatively recent example of a prominent international arbitration dispute involving contentions of forgery, in this case forged documents submitted as evidence, was the territorial dispute between the State of Bahrain and the State of Qatar submitted to the International Court of Justice in The Hague: ICJ, case concerning *Maritime Delimitation and Territorial Questions between Qatar and Bahrain (Qatar v. Bahrain)*, Judgment of 16 March 2001, *International Legal Materials*, Vol. 40 (2001), p. 847. In that case, decided on the merits after a prolonged jurisdictional phase, claimant Qatar submitted, and then later retracted, various allegedly falsified historical documents respecting the 1939 award to Bahrain of the disputed Hawar islands lying between Bahrain and Qatar. The official judgment has been criticized for the fact that the ICJ judgment did not make any evaluation of the series of events related to the submission and later retraction of the allegedly forged documents: see, e.g., "Faking It: Eversheds, Freshfields and the ICJ Forgeries", *Legal Business*, Issue 114 (May 2001), pp. 66-71. This ICJ case may be seen as relating to illegality in the formation and performance of contract as well as in the conduct of the arbitration proceedings themselves, which is a separate subject altogether.

those cases where no proof is needed because the illegality is manifest, the question of whether the tribunal has jurisdiction to make any ruling over the dispute will normally depend on whether the illicitness, additionally, leads to the voidness of the separate arbitration agreement.

### (c) *Illicit contracts and public versus private parties*

*Third*, within the category of less overtly illegal contracts such as commission agreements, the arbitrator may need to distinguish between commission agreements providing for payment to a private party ("influence peddling") and those providing for payment to a public official ("bribery")[515]. In the latter case, the aim of the commission payment is customarily to secure a contract award or other advantage from an agent of a State by means of what is normally considered "bribery"[516]. In the former case, the commis-

---

[515] Cf. in German law, a decision of the German Supreme Court, 8 May 1985 — IV a ZR 138/83, 8 *Recht der International Wirtschaft* 653 *et seq.* (1985), holding that

"an agreement by which a foreign public official promises in criminal fashion to carry out a particular official act in exchange for payment of a bribe is void under Section 138 German Civil Code *[Sittenwidriges Geschäft]*. The same must apply for a contract between an interested party and an intermediary when its sole or main purpose consists of establishing an agreement to pay a bribe to the responsible public official and to forward this payment to him and when the bribe is included in the commission promised to the intermediary."

[516] Among the recent prominent cases of alleged bribery of public officials which became subject to arbitration included the sale of certain French naval frigates to the Republic of Taiwan by the French Thomson CSF via a Swiss "intermediary": *Frontier AG & Brunner Sociedad* v. *Thomson CSF*, ICC Case No. 7664 (1996).

sion payment may have somewhat the same nature and purpose, but not seek to corrupt an instrumentality of a Government. Should this distinction matter as to whether the arbitrator has jurisdiction over a dispute relating to such a commission agreement?

Depending upon the jurisdiction, "influence peddling" vis-à-vis public officials may be illegal, but not be sanctionable in the *private* domain as long as it does not implicate a public official. Whether influence peddling even in the private domain is sanctionable will depend upon the particular form of action taken and the applicable law[517].

### (d) *Illegality* ab initio *versus* ex post

*Fourth*, the arbitral tribunal may be called upon to make hairline distinctions between fraud in the inducement of the contract and so-called fraud in the factum. Fraud in the inducement may result in the illegality *ex post* of the contract[518]. Fraud in the factum may result in its illegality *ab initio*[519].

Should the arbitrator apply a different standard respecting arbitrability and separability when the contract is deemed to have become illegal "only later", as opposed to the case where there was never any contract at all? Does it not make a difference whether the alleged fraud is manifest, as opposed to requiring the parties first to be put to their proof?

## 3. *Different factual circumstances of illegality*

Wholly apart from the foregoing potential distinctions, the arbitrator may be confronted with a wide

---

[517] R. H. Kreindler, *supra* footnote 41, p. 214.
[518] *Supra* footnote 134.
[519] *Supra* footnote 135.

range of *factual* circumstances which could affect the issues of jurisdiction, arbitrability and separability.

### (a) *Initial awareness of the illegality by all parties*

*First*, whether the subject matter is overtly offensive or, rather, more of a "gray area" illegality, both parties were manifestly aware of the illegality *ab initio*. Both parties may have known of and intended the illicit nature and illicit purpose of the contract. Both parties may have known of and intended the inclusion of an agreement to arbitrate precisely to shield adjudication of any disputes from national courts which would strike down the contract as illegal.

The arbitrator must decide issues of arbitrability and separability in the context of an illegality going to the heart of both the underlying contract and the arbitration agreement. If the arbitrator does so, however, is he an "accomplice" to the illicit effort to shield adjudication from the national courts?

### (b) *Subsequent awareness of the illegality by all parties*

*Second*, both parties executed the contract on the assumption that it was licit in nature, and only subsequently became aware of the illegality in the course of performance. By extension, both parties included the agreement to arbitrate on the basis that it was a legitimate dispute resolution mechanism for a legitimate underlying contract.

The arbitrator must decide in the context of illegality of the main agreement. He must also decide in the context of whether the severity of the illegality should prevent him from affirming his jurisdiction on the basis of the arbitration agreement. How severe must the illegality be for the arbitrator no longer to be able to exercise jurisdiction on the basis of arbitrability and separability?

### (c) *Illicit intention and awareness by only one party*

*Third*, one party is aware of the illegality *ab initio*, working, for example, through a third-party "intermediary", while the other party is unaware of the illegality. The first party did not necessarily fraudulently induce the second party to enter into the contract, but it may have induced it to enter into the contract under false pretences. Is this not the same thing?

The arbitrator must assess the extent to which one party's good-faith reliance on the legality of the contract may influence his assessment of arbitrability and separability. Just because one of the two parties had an illicit intention, does this deprive the other party acting in good faith and in reliance on the licitness of the contract from having his day before the arbitrator? Normally, no.

### (d) *Reliance on the illegality as a claim or defence*

*Fourth*, the party seeking relief in the arbitration himself committed the illegality. He seeks the benefit of an arbitral award upholding the illegality. The defendant, who is being sued for manifest non-performance, seeks to use the illegality as a means to forestall judgment against it. The arbitral tribunal may be confronted with a situation where the illegality is sanctionable under only one of several potentially applicable bodies of law.

Should the tribunal condone the illegality in order to find against a clearly defaulting defendant, or should it deny its own jurisdiction due to the illegality even though the defendant will thereby be able to abscond despite its non-performance? What if the non-performance relates to a part of the contract which may be legal and severable from the remaining, illicit portions of the contract?

### (e) *Contracts of bribery versus contracts arising out of bribery*

*Fifth*, the underlying contract is not alleged to represent an agreement to pay a bribe, but rather is a contract which is alleged to have arisen and been made possible as a result of an antecedent payment of an illegal bribe involving the same parties.

The tribunal must distinguish between the two contracts and decide whether its jurisdiction is in any way undermined by the circumstances which gave rise to the contract.

### 4. *Suspicion of illegality versus knowledge or obviousness of the same*

Each of the above possible permutations may be affected by the extent to which the arbitral tribunal has a "mere" suspicion that illegality obtains, as opposed to a firm knowledge based on the obviousness or manifest nature of the same.

Particularly in such cases, how far should arbitrators go to determine whether the contract submitted to them has been procured or performed by illegal means, or otherwise suffers from some illicitness which may render (i) it null and void, (ii) perhaps the arbitration agreement null and void, and (iii) the arbitrator defunct?

In the case of "mere" suspicion, the conviction with which the tribunal decides whether it is in a position to assert jurisdiction and render an award may be influenced by the "degree" of suspicion involved. In particular, the following issues may arise for the tribunal in the case of a suspicion falling short of concrete knowledge or admission of the illegality.

### (a) *Maintaining impartiality and equal treatment*

*First*, arguably the existence of a "mere" suspicion will place special challenges on the tribunal to maintain the requisite level of impartiality and/or independence and to ensure equal treatment. This may be the case particularly where the suspicion of illegality attaches to only one party, and not to all parties jointly. As a matter of the applicable arbitral rules, the *lex arbitri* and any other potentially relevant standards, the arbitrators have a duty, for example, to maintain such impartiality and to treat the parties equally[520].

To the extent the tribunal suspects illegality on the part of one party but not of all, it must ensure that it does not allow unsubstantiated or even half-substantiated indicia of impropriety on one side to influence its even-handedness in conducting the arbitration. This is a matter of impartiality and independence. It is also an issue of equal treatment, due process and a balanced affording to both sides of an opportunity to present the respective case. The extent of such "opportunity" will depend upon the applicable arbitral rules and *lex arbitri*[521].

### (b) *Dilatory tactics and allegations of illegality*

*Second*, where the suspicion is based primarily or solely on a "mere" allegation of illegality by the *defen-*

---

[520] See, e.g., UNCITRAL Model Law on International Commercial Arbitration, Arts. 12 and 18.

[521] UNCITRAL Model Law, Art. 18, provides for "a full opportunity of presenting his case" whereas ICC Rules, Art. 22 (4), speaks, in the context of *clôture de la procédure*, of "a reasonable opportunity to present their cases".

*dant*, the tribunal may see fit to be marginally more rigorous and circumspect in its readiness to conclude that such an illegality exists. Quite apart from the not infrequent occurrence of a dilatory defendant espousing arguments primarily for the purpose of postponing or derailing completely the day of judgment, a mere allegation of illegality by the defendant should not immediately make non-arbitrable a contract which is otherwise on its face arbitrable.

The marginally greater rigour brought to bear on the defendant may not in any way offend the arbitrator's duty of equal treatment and due process under the relevant rules and curial law. In the case of a counterclaim, it may well be that it is the claimant who then relies on a partial illegality as its defence to any liability under the counterclaim.

### (c) *Mutual denial of illegality*

*Third*, it may be that *both* parties deny that the underlying contract is illegal and at least the claimant insists on its arbitrability. Should the tribunal's "mere" suspicion of a true illegality be more readily put to rest by the fact that both parties "agree" that the contract is not illegal? Or should the tribunal enquire nevertheless into the grounds for its continuing suspicion?

The fact that both parties deny an underlying illegality does not necessarily make any less compelling the grounds for the tribunal's suspicion to the contrary; indeed the fact or manner of mutual denial may actually fire the tribunal's suspicions all the more. The mutual denial may be a concerted effort to shield the illegality from the tribunal.

Alternatively, it may be an attempt to seek resolution of the dispute from a private tribunal in circumstances where a national court would not be receptive.

## B. *Illegality and Jurisdictional Limitations*

Even in the context of Judge Lagergren's perceived pathbreaking — and subsequently largely criticized — analysis of the arbitration of illegality issues[522], the focus has initially and substantially been on (i) arbitrability in the sense of competence-competence and (ii) separability of the arbitration agreement from the allegedly or manifestly illegal main contract. This is ultimately a question of whose province it is, the arbitral tribunal's or the national court's? The analysis applies well to commercial arbitration, less well to investment treaty-based arbitration.

### 1. *Competence-competence*

What is the extent to which an arbitrator has jurisdiction to decide whether it has jurisdiction — jurisdiction to issue an award upholding or denying its jurisdiction and jurisdiction to issue an award adjudicating the merits once it has upheld its overall jurisdiction[523]?

### (a) *Commercial arbitration*

The question is central to the issue of illegality. Insofar as the allegedly or manifestly illegal contract may be null and void even *ab initio*, the tribunal must query whether it may still make any rulings on disputes arising out of the contract and the arbitration agreement within it? Even if the tribunal derives a jurisdictional power from the now widely accepted doctrine of competence-competence, does it retain jurisdiction where as a result of the illegality the contract — and

---

[522] Award in ICC Case No. 1110, *supra* footnote 3.
[523] See generally R. Kreindler, *supra* footnote 41, pp. 226 *et seq.*

perhaps the arbitration agreement — is deemed never to have come into existence?

In the past, this analysis has often been couched in terms of the allocation of power between the arbitrator on the one hand and the national courts on the other to decide challenges to the legality of the underlying contract. In recent years, with the partial exception of England and notably the United States, national legislation and uniform model legislation have largely sought to allocate such power to the arbitrator.

Thus, for example, Article 178 (3) of Chapter 12 of the 1987 Swiss Private International Law Act provides succinctly: "The validity of an arbitration agreement cannot be contested on the ground that the main contract may not be valid." This formulation, particularly the wording "may not", accurately reflects the predicament of the arbitrator who has only an initial suspicion of illegality and has not yet made a full determination. The formulation also fits the arbitrator who, even upon manifest proof of legality, may not yet have determined, without further party submissions, the consequences of such illegality for the contract and possibly for the arbitration agreement itself.

Likewise, the far-reaching acceptance of the principle is reflected in most other leading national legislation and rules and in the UNCITRAL Model Law Article 16 (1): "The arbitral tribunal may rule on its own jurisdiction, including any objections with respect to the existence or validity of the arbitration agreement." In short, corruption and illegality issues generally do not undermine residual competence. This generally entitles the commercial arbitration to render a "negative" decision against further competence where the nature of the illegality renders the arbitration agreement void *ab initio*.

Institutional arbitration rules likewise address issues of competence-competence in a manner relevant to illegality. In the context of the ICC Rules of Arbitration, these issues have in part been seen in the context of a "prima facie" analysis of agreement to ICC arbitration. Upon a "finding" by the ICC Court of such a basis for agreement to ICC arbitration, any further jurisdictional questions related to illegality or otherwise have historically been referred summarily to the tribunal to-be, once it is seised with the file.

By virtue of this institutional sequence, the arbitral tribunal essentially receives its competence-competence *immediately* to hear allegations of illegality (or if not immediately, arguably subject to the signature or approval of the Terms of Reference document). Also by virtue of this sequence, the tribunal thereupon normally understands itself to have "instant" jurisdiction to render an award arising out of such illegality. This would include an award denying its jurisdiction on the basis of illegality. The jurisdiction being denied would be the tribunal's remaining jurisdiction, since it would already have exercised "residual" jurisdiction to issue an award against jurisdiction in the first place.

In fact, the approach under the ICC Rules has not always been entirely conducive to clarity on the issue of how and when the arbitration may proceed in the face of allegations of corruption, bribery and the like. Under Article 7 of the former, 1988 ICC Rules, the arbitration was not to proceed where, objectively, there was "no *prima facie* agreement between the parties to arbitrate". This placed the initial burden upon the ICC Court to determine whether there were some minimal indicia of the existence of an ICC arbitration agreement between the named parties. Such determination would normally take place upon receipt of the Request for Arbitration and *before* any submissions by the named defendant.

Thus the analysis was not likely to extend to issues of illegality, even most manifest forms. Even where the defendant answered and called upon the ICC Court to dismiss the arbitration on the grounds of nullity, former Article 8 (3) permitted the arbitration to proceed where the ICC Court was, subjectively, "*satisfied of the prima facie existence* of such an agreement [to arbitrate]" (emphasis added). Here again, even a well-founded defence of illegality, going to the root of the arbitration agreement and fundamental public morals, would not be likely to lead to subjective "dissatisfaction" on the part of the ICC Court.

The landscape under the 1998 ICC Rules is slightly different. Article 6 (2) of the 1998 Rules respecting competence-competence provides that the "Court may decide . . . that the arbitration shall proceed if it is *prima facie satisfied* that an arbitration agreement under the Rules of Arbitration of the ICC *may exist . . .*". It is the "satisfaction" of the ICC Court which is now prima facie, and not the existence of the agreement which is subject to the prima facie test. Moreover, the satisfaction is linked to the possible existence of an ICC arbitration agreement, and not its definitive existence[524]. Article 6 (4) of the 2012 ICC

---

[524] Cf. also Y. Derains and E. Schwartz, *A Guide to the New ICC Rules of Arbitration*, 2nd ed., The Hague, Kluwer Law International, 2005, p. 80: "it is the Court's determination that is of a *prima facie* nature and . . . it is not to be inferred from the Court's decision that it has concluded that there is, in fact, an agreement".
See also R. Kreindler, "Impending Revision of the ICC Arbitration Rules — Opportunities and Hazards for Experienced and Inexperienced Users Alike", *Journal of International Arbitration*, Vol. 13 (1996), p. 79:

"The Defendant is obliged to respond to the Request, in the manner provided for in the Rules, only to the extent it has entered into, or somehow later become bound by, an agreement with the Claimant to submit to ICC arbitration";

see also R. Kreindler, "Pitfalls and Pratfalls in the

Rules is essentially to the same effect[525]. This temporizing of the ICC standard may be seen as being more in tune with the fairly far-reaching competence-competence powers of the arbitral tribunal vis-à-vis the powers of the ICC Court. It also more accurately reflects the difficulties which an arbitral institution may have at the early stage of the proceedings: on what basis can or should the tribunal responsibly seek to make any conclusory determination of illegality when it often has only perfunctory submissions of the parties to work with?

In this regard, the affirmation of competence-competence and separability contained in the ICC Rules is, on its face, actually more far-reaching than those contained in the UNCITRAL Rules and the UNCITRAL Model Law. Article 21 (2) of the UNCITRAL Rules of Arbitration and Article 16 (1) of the UNCITRAL Model Law provide: "A decision by the arbitral tribunal that the contract is null and void shall not entail *ipso jure* the invalidity of the arbitration clause." On their face, the UNCITRAL provisions address solely the effects of a ruling that the underlying contract is *void*, as opposed to the not necessarily identical problem of the contract's *non-existence*.

The distinction between voidness on the one hand and non-existence on the other may arise particularly in the context of allegations of "fraud in the factum", as opposed to fraud in the inducement, and has loomed large in United States jurisprudence[526]. Fraud in the

---

Launching of an ICC Arbitration: Practical Guidelines and Substantive Solutions", *Arbitration & Dispute Resolution Law Journal*, 1993, pp. 154 *et seq.*

[525] Art. 6 (4) of the 2012 ICC Rules: "The arbitration shall proceed if and to the extent that the Court is prima facie satisfied that an arbitration agreement under the Rules may exist . . ."

[526] In the case of "fraud in the factum", there is "ineffective assent to the contract . . . misrepresentation of the

factum may encompass situations of forged signatures
or other falsified documents going to the root of assent
to the contract. In such cases, the ICC Rules may be
seen as empowering the ICC Court in the first instance
and the tribunal to-be in the second instance to *proceed*
with the arbitration, leading to either an award on jurisdiction or an award on the merits or both.

Whether such empowerment will always be in harmony with the law at the seat of arbitration is another
question and another layer of analysis. See, for
example, in the United States, *Kyung In Lee* v. *Pacific
Bullion (New York) Inc.*, 788 F. Supp. 155 (EDNY
1992): "if a party's signature were forged on a contract, it would be absurd to require arbitration". Such
an approach may lead to the conclusion that it is for
the State courts to adjudicate disputes as to whether
alleged fraud in the factum imperils the existence and
validity of the arbitration agreement itself, as opposed
to that of the main contract. Yet such conclusion would
not appear to be in harmony with the broad powers
provided for in the ICC Rules. Indeed under those provisions, even an allegation that fraud in the factum
went to the forgery of the arbitration agreement *alone*
— separately from any forgery of the main contract —
might not suffice to oust the ICC tribunal of its competence-competence. By contrast, under the UNCITRAL
Rules or the UNCITRAL Model Law, the tribunal is
not assured of continuing to have jurisdiction even in
such cases[527].

---

character or essential terms of a proposed contract [in such
a way that] assent to the contract is impossible [and] there
is no contract at all": *Cancanon* v. *Smith Barney, Harris,
Upham & Co.*, 805 F. 2d 998 (11th Cir. 1986).

[527] Derains and Schwartz, *supra* footnote 524, p. 112:

"[The UNCITRAL Rules and the UNCITRAL
Model Law] only deal with the effects of a decision
that the contract is null and void. Moreover, even in

In any event, a mere allegation that the commercial contract is, or may be, invalid even to the point of being offensive to public morals should not, without more, result in the invalidity of the arbitration agreement which the contract contains. Otherwise, any and all such allegations, including those made in bad faith and those which are well intentioned but without basis, could lead to the disenfranchisement of the arbitrator.

### (b) *Investment treaty arbitration*

Here, we have essentially a comparable overarching competence, which is also reflected in MITS, BITs and applicable rules. Thus pursuant to ICSID Convention Article 42 (1) and (2), the Tribunal "shall be the judge of its own competence" and any objection by a party to the dispute that that dispute is not within the jurisdiction of the Centre, or for other reasons is not within the competence of the Tribunal "shall be considered by the Tribunal which shall determine whether to deal with it as a preliminary question or to join it to the merits of the dispute" [528].

Indeed "jurisdictional" or "admissibility" objections, by the host State, are pervasive. At the same time, corruption and illegality issues generally do not undermine residual treaty-based competence. Where in the treaty context an agreement to arbitrate is deemed based on an MIT and/or BIT "consent", the arbitral tribunal is entitled to render a "negative" decision against further competence if the nature of the illegality renders such "consent" void *ab initio*.

---

such case, they do not, unlike Art. 6 (4) [of the ICC Rules], affirm that the tribunal 'shall continue to have jurisdiction', but state rather that, in the event of such a decision, the arbitration clause shall not *ipso jure* be regarded as invalid."

[528] Art. 42 (1) and (2), ICSID Convention.

2. *Illegality and separability of the arbitration agreement*

(a) *Commercial arbitration*

The separateness of the commercial arbitration agreement from the validity of invalidity of the underlying contract is a far-reaching principle in most jurisdictions, and is reflected in the UNCITRAL Model Law Article 16 (1): "A decision by the arbitral tribunal that the contract is null and void shall not entail ipso jure the invalidity of the arbitration clause." This principle entitles the arbitrator to adjudicate classical issues of validity and termination of contract.

An exception may occur where voidness *ab initio* of the contract infects the arbitration agreement *ab initio*[529]. At the same time, generally corruption and illegality issues do not undermine separability: *Fiona Trust*, UK House of Lords (2007)[530]; *National Power* v. *Westinghouse*, Swiss Federal Tribunal (1993)[531]. There are exceptional cases where the illegality renders

---

[529] R. Kreindler, *supra* footnote 41, p. 241; P. Leboulanger, "The Arbitration Agreement: Still Autonomous?", in A. J. van den Berg (ed.), *International Arbitration 2006: Back to Basics?*, ICCA Congress Series, Vol. XIII, Montreal, Kluwer Law International, 2007, pp. 11 *et seq.*

[530] *Premium Nafta Products Limited (20th Defendant) and Others (Respondents)* v. *Fili Shipping Company Limited (14th Claimant) and Others*, House of Lords, 17 October 2007, [2007] UKHL 40 (available at http:// www.publications.parliament.uk/pa/ld200607/ldjudgmt/jd0 71017/ship.pdf). This judgment upheld the decision of the England and Wales Court of Appeal (Civil Division), *Fiona Trust & Holding Corporation and Others* v. *Yuri Privalov and Others*, [2007] EWCA Civ 20, 24 January 2007. The Court of Appeal's decision is available at http:// www.bailii.org/ew/cases/EWCA/Civ/2007/20.html.

[531] Tribunal Fédéral [Swiss Federal Tribunal], *National Power Corporation* v. *Westinghouse*, *supra* footnote 75.

separate arbitration agreement void *ab initio*, including in certain cases of (i) *non est factum*[532], (ii) forgery[533], (iii) threat[534], (iv) mistake of identity[535], and (iv) signature absent authority[536]. Bribery is not an exception: see, for example, *Premium Nafta* v. *Fili*, UK House of Lords (2007)[537]. The competence-competence principle would normally entitle a (negative) decision on separability in such situation.

Interestingly, while the UNCITRAL Model Law (Article 16 (1)) addresses the situation where the arbitrator has already decided, in exercise of competence-competence, that the contract is — and not merely "may be" — invalid, this provision is lacking from the Swiss Private International Law Act and indeed is also missing from Article 1040 (1) of the 10th Book of the German Civil Procedure Code, which was revised as of 1 January 1998 to implement substantially the UNCITRAL Model Law in Germany. Article 1040 (1)

---

[532] *Harbour Assurance Co. Ltd.* v. *Kansa General International Insurance Co. Ltd., Tapiola International Insurance Co. Ltd. and Others*, Court of Appeal, 28 January 1993, *XX Yearbook Commercial Arbitration*, 1995, pp. 787 *et seq.*

[533] ICJ, case concerning *Maritime Delimitation and Territorial Questions between Qatar and Bahrain (Qatar v. Bahrain)*, *supra* footnote 130.

[534] *Westinghouse and Bruns & Roe (USA)* v. *National Power Company and the Republic of the Philippines*, ICC Case No. 6401, *supra* footnote 271: ("There may be instances where a defect going to the root of an agreement between parties affects both the main contract and the arbitration clause. An obvious example is a contract obtained by threat").

[535] *TTMI Sarl* v. *Statoil ASA* [2011] EWHC 1150 (Comm).

[536] See, e.g., P. V. Tytell, "The Detection of Forgery and Fraud", in A. J. van den Berg, *supra* footnote 41, p. 315.

[537] *Supra* footnote 530.

follows the first two sentences of corresponding Article 16 (1) of the Model Law, but does not include the foregoing reference to nullity and voidness.

Does this make the Swiss and German legislation less supportive of competence-competence and the separability of the arbitration agreement in the face of the nullity of the main contract? The answer must be no. Rather, the Swiss and German approaches to the survival and independence of the arbitration agreement, even in the face of illegality, are so firm that there was no need to confuse or dilute the approach by adding the final sentence from the Model Law. The arbitration agreement does not *ipso jure* share the fate of the main agreement and vice versa, full stop[538].

Having exercised its jurisdiction and conclusively found that the contract is illegal, the arbitrator must not necessarily then conclude that the arbitration agreement is likewise null and void. Where the tribunal con-

---

[538] In the case of German arbitration law, this is a major development as compared with the pre-1998 regime at least with respect to competence-competence (but not with respect to separability, which was already well entrenched). Prior to 1998, under former Section 1025 I of the German Civil Procedure Code disputes were required to be capable of "settlement" in order to be subject to arbitration. Thus the same grounds which could nullify the main agreement could also prevent the valid conclusion of a settlement and thereby render the agreement itself invalid. Examples included gambling and betting demands (Section 762, Civil Code (Unvollkommene Verbindlichkeit)) illegal contracts (Section 134, Civil Code (Gesetzliches Verbot)), offensive or usurious contracts (Section 138, Civil Code (Sittenwidriges Rechtsgeschäft; Wucher)), etc. The ability to "settle" is no longer a prerequisite under German law for valid conclusion of an arbitration agreement apart from non-economic claims. Therefore, those cases where previously the arbitration agreement was deemed to share the fate of nullity of the main contract must be revisited. This might even include cases of voidability on the grounds of *fraud or threat*.

cludes that the arbitration agreement shares the illegal fate of the underlying contract, it would then have to conclude that it had no basis to exercise competence-competence to make such conclusion in the first place.

While this may appear to potentially tie the arbitrator up in knots, the predicament is not as complicated as it may appear. Normally, competence-competence will obtain unless the nature and circumstances of the main contract's voidness inextricably also apply to the arbitration agreement so as to make it void as well.

A reason why competence-competence may still obtain is that, pursuant to prevailing trends, the arbitrator's decision on its own jurisdiction will, absent an effective waiver, be subject to judicial control in set aside proceedings at the seat and in enforcement proceedings at the seat or elsewhere. For this reason alone, allocation of the power to decide challenges to legality to the tribunal is not seen as a usurpation of the State courts' prerogatives. Article V (3) of the 1961 European Convention on International Commercial Arbitration makes this point clear:

> "*Subject to any subsequent judicial control provided for under the lex fori*, the arbitrator whose jurisdiction is called into question shall be entitled to proceed with the arbitration, to rule on his own jurisdiction, and to decide upon the existence or validity of the arbitration agreement or of the contract of which the agreement forms part." (Emphasis added.)[539]

---

[539] Art. V (3), European Convention on International Commercial Arbitration of 1961, done at Geneva, 21 April 1961, United Nations, *Treaty Series*, Vol. 484, p. 364, No. 7041 (1963-1964), available at http://www.jus.uio.no/lm/europe.international.commercial.arbitration.convention.geneva.1961/portrait.pdf.

## (b)  *Investment treaty arbitration*

In the investment treaty context, there is no issue of the separateness of the arbitration agreement from underlying main contract unless we also have an investment contract with the investor, as was the case in *World Duty Free* v. *Kenya*[540]. Instead, normally the issue revolves around the separateness of the treaty-based "consent" to arbitration and its validity from the (in)validity of the underlying investment and even the existence of "investment" if it deemed to be illegal.

In this context, the arbitrator is entitled to adjudicate classical issues of existence and validity of the investment either as a preliminary issue of jurisdiction and/or admissibility or as a merits issue: see, for example, ICSID Convention Articles 42 (1) and (2). Thus, corruption and illegality issues generally do not undermine separability, as defined here.

Where in a treaty context the agreement to arbitrate is based on an MIT and/or BIT "consent", competence-competence normally does not call for a decision on separability, as above. As in the case of commercial arbitration, the situations in which illegality renders the separate "consent" void *ab initio* include (i) *non est factum*[541], (ii) forgery[542], (iii) threat[543], (iv) mistake of identity[544], and (iv) signature absent authority[545]. But in contrast to commercial arbitration, *proven bribery* can also be added to this enumerative list: see, for example, *World Duty Free*[546], *Inceysa*[547] and *Plama*[548].

---

[540]  *World Duty Free* v. *Kenya*, *supra* footnote 44.
[541]  *Supra* footnote 542.
[542]  *Supra* footnote 543.
[543]  *Supra* footnote 544.
[544]  *Supra* footnote 545.
[545]  *Supra* footnote 546.
[546]  *World Duty Free* v. *Kenya*, *supra* footnote 44.
[547]  *Inceysa* v. *El Salvador*, *supra* footnote 174.
[548]  *Plama* v. *Bulgaria*, *supra* footnote 372.

## 3. *Arbitrability*

### (a) *Commercial arbitration*

In the commercial context, there is a principal ability to submit almost any subject matter of dispute to arbitration, and to oust the jurisdiction of the national courts, including as a matter of enforceability, especially under the *lex arbitri*. There has been a farreaching expansion of arbitrability in national laws and international practice. Thus the German Arbitration Act Section 1030 (1) (Model Law-based) provides: "Any claim involving an economic interest ('vermögensrechtlicher Anspruch') can be the subject of an arbitration agreement." Some exceptions remain, in Germany and other countries, inasmuch as arbitrability is linked to public policy and in turn to diverging national approaches.

This far-reaching concept of arbitrability entitles the arbitrator to adjudicate most "money-related" issues in contract or tort/delict. Corruption and illegality issues generally are deemed to be arbitrable under the *lex arbitri*, but with a civil law remedy. There are exceptional cases where the nature of the act is deemed to be the province of the criminal law or of prosecutorial authorities.

In this regard, there have also been certain few idiosyncratic court decisions which have attempted to narrow the scope of arbitrability of illegality issues: see, for example, *Hubco* v. *WAPDA*, Supreme Court of Pakistan (2000)[549]. The predominant trend, however, is rightly that competence-competence entitles the arbitrator to render a "negative" decision against arbitrability and that a finding of non-arbitrability will be a

---

[549] *Hubco* v. *WAPDA*, Supreme Court of Pakistan, 11 August 1999, *Arbitration International*, Vol. 16 (2000), p. 439.

bar to further competence notwithstanding the principle of separability. In short, non-arbitrability in the commercial context will trump separability.

### (b) *Investment treaty arbitration*

There is no issue of arbitrability of the subject matter and competing jurisdiction of national courts in the investment treaty context unless there is, rarely, a dispute as to whether the underlying claims are "treaty claims" or "contract claims": see, for example, *SGS* v. *Philippines*[550]. "Arbitrability" *per se* is framed as a jurisdictional or admissibility requirement of "nationality", "investor", "investment" under the respective treaty and/or as a merits issue of a "protectible investment".

Again, this context entitles the arbitrator to adjudicate classical issues of the existence and validity of the investment either as a preliminary issue of jurisdiction and/or admissibility or as a merits issue: see, for example, ICSID Convention Articles 42 (1) and (2). Corruption and illegality issues can certainly undermine the "arbitrability" in the context of treaty requirements as a preliminary issue or can be deferred to be decided as a merits issue.

Where in a treaty context arbitration is based on an MIT or BIT "consent", competence-competence entitles and requires a "negative" decision against arbitrability as so defined. And again cases where illegality renders a separate "consent" void *ab initio* and/or denies the status of "protective investment" include (i) *non est factum*, (ii) forgery, (iii) threat,

---

[550] *SGS Société Générale de Surveillance* v. *Republic of the Philippines*, ICSID Case No. ARB/02/6, Decision on Objections to Jurisdiction, 29 January 2004 (available at http://italaw.com/sites/default/files/case-documents/ita0782.pdf).

(iv) mistake of identity, (iv) signature absent authority *and indeed proven bribery*.

## 4. Corruption issues and competence, separability and arbitrability

Ultimately, the foregoing issues are a question of ousting or not ousting the jurisdiction of the national courts, including for corruption issues.

In the case of competence-competence, corruption will generally not affect competence-competence, and will allow a "negative" decision against further competence where illegality renders the arbitration agreement or the "consent" void *ab initio*.

In the case of separability, corruption will also generally not affect separability, even where the arbitration agreement might be rendered void *ab initio* in cases of *non est factum*, forgery, threat, etc., but again competence-competence normally entitles a (negative) decision on separability. In the investment treaty context, corruption can render the separate "consent" void *ab initio*.

In the case of arbitrability, corruption and illegality generally are deemed to be arbitrable under the *lex arbitri*, and non-arbitrability will be a bar to further competence notwithstanding separability. In the investment treaty context, corruption and illegality can undermine "arbitrability" in the context of treaty requirements as a preliminary issue or be decided on the merits, and can render separate "consent" void *ab initio* and/or cause denial "worthiness" of protection.

# CHAPTER VI

# THE BURDEN OF PROOF AND THE STANDARD OF PROOF OF ILLEGALITY

What needs to be shown, to be proved in order to establish illegality and draw consequences from such a finding for the powers of the arbitral tribunal?

## A. Introduction

Whether in litigation or arbitration, there are conceptual challenges to burden of proof generally, of which the following can be mentioned here.

*First*, there is no single theory, rule, or measure of burden of proof or thresholds of evidence which applies from case to case, let alone cross-border[551].

*Second*, there is not even a unitary approach to the fundamental purpose of evidence: is it to ascertain the truth or simply to resolve the dispute, or something in between?

*Third*, there is no single approach to allocation the burden of proof, reversing it or alleviating it, even if one might identify an international "best practice" for allocating burden of proof[552].

---

[551] A. Redfern, "The Practical Distinction between the Burden of Proof and the Taking of Evidence — An English Perspective", in A. Redfern, C. Reymond *et al.*, "The Standards and Burden of Proof in International Arbitration", *Arbitration International*, Vol. 10 (1994), pp. 321 *et seq.*; G. M. von Mehren and C. Salomon, "Submitting Evidence in an International Arbitration: The Common Lawyer's Guide", *Journal of International Arbitration*, Vol. 20 (2003), pp. 290 *et seq.*

[552] A. Reiner, "Burden and General Standards of Proof", in A. Redfern, C. Reymond *et al.*, "The Standards

*Fourth*, there is no single applicable standard of proof, since different legal systems have different approaches running from preponderance of the evidence to clear and convincing evidence to proof beyond a reasonable doubt[553].

*Fifth*, both the admissibility of the evidence and the proper weight to be given to admitted evidence are subject to various approaches, and different weight may be assigned to different kinds of evidence.

*Sixth*, uniformity is lacking as to the proper role of adverse inferences and whether such inferences can or should be drawn by the arbitrator expressly or impliedly[554].

---

and Burden of Proof in International Arbitration", *Arbitration International*, Vol. 10 (1994), pp. 340 *et seq.*

[553] A. Redfern, *supra* footnote 551, pp. 326 *et seq.*; G. M. von Mehren and C. Salomon, *supra* footnote 551, p. 291; S. Wilske and T. J. Fox, "Corruption in International Arbitration and Problems with Standard of Proof: Baseless Allegations or Prima Facie Evidence?", in S. Kröll, L. Mistelis, *et al.* (eds.), *International Arbitration and International Commercial Law: Synergy, Convergence and Evolution*, The Hague, Kluwer Law International, 2011, pp. 496 *et seq.*

[554] Art. 9 of the 2010 IBA Rules on Taking of Evidence attempt to address several of these issues in the context of disclosure or discovery of witnesses and documents:

"1. The Arbitral Tribunal shall determine the admissibility, relevance, materiality and weight of evidence."

"2. The Arbitral Tribunal shall . . . exclude from evidence or production any Document, statement, oral testimony or inspection for any of the following reasons: *(a)* lack of sufficient relevance to the case or materiality to its outcome; *(b)* legal impediment or privilege under the legal or ethical rules determined by the Arbitral Tribunal to be applicable; . . . *(f)* grounds of special political or institutional sensitivity (including evidence that has been classified as secret by a government or a public international institution) that the Arbitral Tribunal determines to be compelling; or

Against the foregoing background, it is therefore no surprise that there are special challenges and burdens in the case of corruption issues and burdens of proof, and that these challenges are magnified by any attempt to reconcile similarities and differences between commercial and investment disputes.

## B. Burden of Proof Generally

### 1. Commercial context

The far-reaching concept of party autonomy extends to the selection of the substantive and procedural framework for the resolution of the dispute. This begs the question in turn of whether questions of burden of proof are to be seen as procedural or rather substantive.

Procedural freedom is reflected, for example, in the UNCITRAL Model Law Article 19, which provides that "[s]ubject to the provisions of this Law, the parties are free to agree on the procedure to be followed by the arbitral tribunal in conducting the proceedings"[555] and that

> "[f]ailing such agreement, the arbitral tribunal may, subject to the provisions of this Law, conduct the arbitration in such manner as it considers appropriate. The power conferred upon the arbitral tribunal includes the power to determine the admissi-

---

*(g)* considerations of procedural economy, proportionality, fairness or equality of the Parties that the Arbitral Tribunal determines to be compelling. . . ."

"5. If a Party fails without satisfactory explanation to produce any Document . . . ordered to be produced by the Arbitral Tribunal, the Arbitral Tribunal may infer that such document would be adverse to the interests of that Party."

[555] Art. 19, UNCITRAL Model Law.

bility, relevance, materiality and weight of any evidence."[556]

The substantive freedom is reflected, for example, in UNCITRAL Model Law Article 28:

> "(1) The arbitral tribunal shall decide the dispute in accordance with such rules of law as are chosen by the parties as applicable to the substance of the dispute. Any designation of the law or legal system of a given State shall be construed, unless otherwise expressed, as directly referring to the substantive law of that State and not to its conflict of laws rules."

These provisions, or analogous provisions in national laws including non-Model Law jurisdictions, relate directly to the question of the rights and duties of the arbitrator and the extent of the tribunal's power to adjudicate disputes, including evidentiary issues related to corruption allegations.

## 2. *Investment treaty context*

Party autonomy in the investment treaty context can likewise be divided into a substantive and procedural framework, but in a manner slightly different than for commercial arbitration.

As stated earlier, here there is also the interesting potential difference that depending upon the BIT or MIT at issue the claimant investor may have the option of choosing which rules to apply, which in turn may result in slightly different outcomes for the framework of burden of proof.

Procedural freedom is reflected, for example, in ICSID Arbitration Rules 34 (1): "The Tribunal shall be

---

[556] Art. 19, UNCITRAL Model Law.

the judge of the admissibility of any evidence adduced and of its probative value", as also discussed in, for example, *Tradex* v. *Albania*, ICSID (1999)[557] and *Asian Agric.* v. *Sri Lanka*, ICSID (1990)[558]. Substantive freedom is reflected, for example, in ICSID Convention Article 42 (1):

> "The Tribunal shall decide a dispute in accordance with such rules of law as may be agreed by the parties. In the absence of such agreement, the Tribunal shall apply the law of the Contracting State party to the dispute (including its rules on the conflict of laws) and such rules of international law as may be applicable."

Interestingly, in terms of the sources of the standard of proof applied by investment tribunals in the absence of a direct reference to a national procedure, three approaches can be identified broadly speaking.

*First*, some tribunals have offered no specification of a standard of proof, as opposed to a burden of proof: see, for example, *World Duty Free* v. *Kenya*, ICSID (2006)[559]; *TSA* v. *Argentina*, ICSID (2008)[560]; *Inceysa* v. *El Salvador*, ICSID (2006)[561]; and *Wena Hotels* v. *Egypt*, ICSID (2000)[562].

---

[557] *Tradex Hellas S.A.* v. *Republic of Albania*, ICSID Case No. ARB/94/2, Award, 29 April 1999, para. 77 (available at http://italaw.com/sites/default/files/case-documents/ita0871.pdf).
[558] *AAPL* v. *Sri Lanka*, *supra* footnote 21, paras. 55 *et seq.*
[559] *World Duty Free* v. *Kenya*, *supra* footnote 44, para. 166.
[560] *TSA Spectrum de Argentina, S.A.* v. *Argentine Republic*, ICSID Case No. ARB/05/5, Award, 19 December 2008, para. 175 (available at http://italaw.com/documents/TSAAwardEng.pdf).
[561] *Inceysa* v. *El Salvador*, *supra* footnote 174.
[562] *Wena* v. *Egypt*, *supra* footnote 475, paras. 59 *et seq.*

*Second*, some tribunals have applied effectively a domestic standard under the host State law: see, for example, *SGS* v. *Pakistan*, ICSID (2003)[563]; and *Fraport* v. *Philippines*, ICSID (2007)[564].

*Third*, occasionally a generalized standard has been applied in the abstract: see, for example, *EDF* v. *Romania*, ICSID (2009)[565].

It is submitted that the first approach is clearly the easiest to apply, but also with the least amount of helpfulness to the parties or for that matter to future parties, the second approach is probably the most rooted in a specific legal system, and the third is probably close to the first but marginally more helpful.

## 3. *General approaches to burden of proof and its allocation*

The general approaches to the burden of proof and the allocation of the burden in arbitration are not necessarily the same as or similar to civil litigation approaches.

UNCITRAL Rules Article 27 is generally axiomatic in this context: "(1) Each party shall have the burden of proving the facts relied on to support its claim or defence" and "(4) The arbitral tribunal shall determine the admissibility, relevance, materiality and weight of the evidence offered." This is to be compared with

---

[563] *SGS Société Générale de Surveillance S.A.* v. *Islamic Republic of Pakistan*, ICSID Case No. ARB/01/13, Decision on Objections to Jurisdiction, 6 August 2003 (available at http://www.italaw.com/sites/default/files/case documents/ita0779.pdf).

[564] *Fraport AG* v. *The Republic of the Philippines*, *supra* footnote 176, para. 399.

[565] *EDF (Services) Limited* v. *Romania*, ICSID Case No. ARB/05/13, Award, 8 October 2009, para. 221 (available at http://www.italaw.com/sites/default/files/case-doc-uments/ita0267.pdf).

the approach, for example, in the Swiss Civil Code Article 8 applicable to civil litigation, which provides: "Unless the law provides otherwise, the burden of proving the existence of an alleged fact shall rest on the person who derives rights from that fact." This is generally consistent with the concept of *"Ei qui affirmat non ei qui negat incumbit probatio"* or *"onus probandi actori incumbit"*.

The burden of proof is to be distinguished from the standard of proof. The standard of proof is often assumed to be the "balance of probabilities"[566] or "more likely than not"[567] or "preponderance"[568], but it can also sometimes be the somewhat different standard of "clear and convincing"[569]. Whatever the standard is, in arbitration it will apply in the context of the more limited powers of the arbitrator as compared with the State judge respecting the powers of investigation, notwithstanding the broadly worded prerogatives in

---

[566] A. Reiner, *supra* footnote 552, p. 335: "it is something 'more likely true than not true' . . ." See also, Denning J in *Miller v. Minister of Pensions*, [1947] 2 All ER 372 stated

"It must carry a reasonable degree of probability, but not so high as is required in a criminal case. If the evidence is such that the tribunal can say: 'we think it more probable than not', the burden is discharged, but if the probabilities are equal it is not."

[567] A. Reiner, *supra* footnote 552, p. 357.
[568] *Ibid.*, p. 335; G. M. von Mehren and C. Salomon, *supra* footnote 551, p. 291; S. Wilske and T. Fox, *supra* footnote 553, pp. 496 *et seq.*
[569] A. Sayed, *supra* footnote 2, pp. 103 *et seq.*; A. Reiner, *supra* footnote 552, pp. 327 and 336. See also, *Himpurna California Energy Ltd.* v. *Perusahaan Listruik Negara*, Award, 4 May 1999, *XXV Yearbook Commercial Arbitration*, 2000, p. 43 para. 116: "a finding of illegality or other invalidity must not be made lightly, but must be supported by clear and convincing proof".

laws and rules bestowing discretion to investigate the facts with all appropriate means[570], and the powers of compulsion such as subpoena and enforcement[571].

## C. *Burden of Proof and Corruption*

### *1. General challenges*

Attempting to assess the admissibility and weight of evidence in the context of corruption in arbitration poses serious challenges.

*First*, corruption and bribery are typically specifically masked, obscured, concealed, destroyed or altered. Corruption may therefore be difficult to find, may be poorly documented or not documented at all, may be dependent solely or primarily on witness testimony, and thus may be question of one person's word against another[572].

*Second*, corruption will most often involve public officials or individuals who pretend or are alleged to have acted in a public capacity. As will be discussed below, this raises potentially complex issues of attribution and *ultra vires*, which in turn may depend on proof[573].

*Third*, often issues of bribery are dependent upon sufficiency of proof in the context of an "interme-

---

[570] Art. 25 (1) of the ICC Rules reads as follows: "The arbitral tribunal shall proceed within as short a time as possible to establish the facts of the case by all appropriate means."

[571] A. Reiner, *supra* footnote 552, p. 345.

[572] M. Hwang and K. Lim, *supra* footnote 8, pp. 14 *et seq.*

[573] *SPP* v. *Egypt*, *supra* footnote 450, p. 352 paras. 83 *et seq.* See more recently in *Kardassopoulos* v. *Georgia*, Decision on Jurisdiction, *supra* footnote 491, paras. 190-194.

diary", "agency" or "consultancy" relationship[574]. These relationships in turn pose difficulties in terms of the nature or scope of the "services" foreseen (e.g., legitimate "lobbying" versus illegal "influence peddling"), the extent of actual performance of services or "concrete deliverables", how to document "influence", and the proportionality of the services to the remuneration foreseen or paid including in the form of success fee percentages.

Furthermore, there may be questions of proof relating to payment structures, documentation and use of third parties, subcontractors, etc., the degree of causation between services performed and the alleged unjust enrichment or influence, and finally the extent of a party's knowledge of the intermediary's actions including so-called "wilful blindness"[575].

## 2. Parallel litigation, arbitration or investigations

Parallel proceedings, including "forum shopping", are normally considered to be a litigation phenomenon, but it is by no means confined to litigation. In the context of corruption, it may involve not only arbitration proceedings but also notably simultaneous or antecedent civil or criminal proceedings or investigations[576].

---

[574] M. Hwang and K. Lim, *supra* footnote 8, pp. 16, 54 and 59; H. Raeschke-Kessler and D. Gottwald, *supra* footnote 60, pp. 612 *et seq.*; ICC Case No. 6497 (1994), *XXIV Yearbook Commercial Arbitration*, 1999, p. 71.

[575] See M. Hwang and K. Lim, *supra* footnote 8, p. 33.

[576] *Malicorp Limited* v. *The Arab Republic of Egypt*, ICSID Case No. ARB/08/18, Award, 7 February 2011, para. 71 (available at http://italaw.com/sites/default/files/case-documents/ita0499.pdf), R. Mirzayev, "International Investment Protection Regime and Criminal Investigations", *Journal of International Arbitration*, Vol. 29 (2012), pp. 71 *et seq.*

In the litigation sphere, forum shopping substantially relates to the search for one or more court venues (and their corresponding local rules) where multiple options exist based on privity or other grounds, where the parties have not specified a single forum, where a basis for assertion of jurisdiction by another forum may be present, or where a basis for assertion of jurisdiction notwithstanding an agreement to arbitration may exist.

In the arbitration sphere, parallel proceedings and forum shopping can relate to the search for one or more seats and/or rules of arbitration (and their corresponding curial law) where multiple arbitration options exist based on privity or other grounds, where the parties have not specified a single seat and/or rules, where a basis for assertion of arbitral jurisdiction at another seat or under other rules may be present, or where a basis for assertion of arbitral jurisdiction notwithstanding a choice of forum may exist.

When corruption or bribery allegations are considered, then not only can one or more of the foregoing permutations apply, but also civil or criminal proceedings in the country of one of the parties, in the country of the seat of arbitration if there is a seat, or elsewhere[577].

Parallel proceedings can occur with contractual privity or in the absence of contractual privity, including in the context of corruption.

---

[577] See, generally, R. Kreindler, "Arbitral Forum Shopping", in B. M. Cremades and J. Lew (eds.), *Parallel State and Arbitral Procedures in International Arbitration*, Dossiers – ICC Institute of World Business Law, Paris, ICC Publishing, 2005, pp. 153 *et seq.* and R. Kreindler, "Parallel Proceedings: A Practitioner's Perspective", in M. Waibel *et al.* (eds.), *The Backlash against Investment Arbitration*, Kluwer Law International, 2010, pp. 127 *et seq.*

(a) *Absence of contractual privity*

The following broad areas of arbitral forum shopping may be identified and briefly outlined where no contractual privity exists.

*First*, a commercial arbitration may be brought against another party without any basis in contract and without any basis for a specific agreement to arbitration. In fact, these are two different hurdles. The absence of a contract *per se* does not necessarily constitute an absolute bar to the successful assertion of arbitral jurisdiction over a would-be defendant.

While the absence of a document memorializing the rights and duties of the parties may pose a significant obstacle to the proof of a contractual relationship, the existence of such a relationship *per se* is not a requirement for the assertion of an arbitration claim any more than for the assertion of a claim in litigation without contractual privity. Neither such barometers as the New York Convention nor the UNCITRAL Model Law, nor for that matter institutional arbitral rules such as those of the International Chamber of Commerce, serve to bar the assertion of arbitral jurisdiction over claims in which a written or even oral contract cannot be shown.

*Second*, in recent arbitral legislation, as also reflected in Article 7 (1) of the UNCITRAL Model Law, "arbitrable" claims are not defined as those which are necessarily contractual in nature. Thus, under Article 7 (1) an "arbitration agreement" is defined as an agreement by the parties to submit to arbitration all or certain disputes which have arisen or which may arise between them in respect of a defined legal relationship, "whether contractual or not".

Accordingly, forum shopping may take place to assert arbitral jurisdiction on the basis of a relationship which is not necessarily memorialized in a contract and whose nexus may be definable not by virtue of specific agreements between the parties, but as a function of the domicile of a party, the location of characteristic performance, etc.

*Third*, the more common example is a dispute between parties who do not have contractual privity, but based on a relationship which is subject to a contract, and perhaps also to an arbitration agreement contained therein. Thus case law and commentary too numerous to mention here stand for the proposition that under certain circumstances, arbitral jurisdiction may be asserted by one party which is a signatory to a contract against another entity which is not an original signatory to that same contract containing an arbitration agreement, where the non-signatory may be deemed to have stepped into the shoes of a signatory, become a third-party beneficiary, be the real party in interest, be a member of a group of companies encompassed by the assent to the contract by the signatory, etc.

*Fourth*, arbitral jurisdiction may be asserted on the basis of an investment treaty between the State of which an investor is a national and the State in which the investor has invested and claims to have suffered damages. Here, there is no issue whatsoever of a contract having arisen between the claimant investor and defendant State on the basis of a private transaction or relationship, but rather by virtue of a public international law commitment entered into between the defendant State and the State of which the investor is a national. Such bilateral investment treaty may have been entered into before the activity at issue in the host State, or afterwards, and such timing may conceivably play a role in the question of whether such assertion of jurisdiction via a BIT should be upheld.

*Fifth*, jurisdiction without contractual privity may be asserted on the basis of a bilateral investment treaty which itself in turn provides the investor with options to choose from when bringing an investment-related claim against the signatory State. Such options may be contained in a so-called "fork-in-the-road" clause whereby the investor may choose as its forum domestic courts, previously agreed dispute settlement procedures or international arbitration, with such choice then being considered binding[578].

### (b) *Existence of contractual privity*

The following broad areas of arbitral forum shopping may be identified and briefly outlined where contractual privity does exist.

*First*, arbitration may be commenced against another party without any basis for a specific agreement to arbitration. In such case, the party seeking arbitration may shop around for an advantageous set of rules and/or seat of arbitration, and the named respondent may consent to the assertion of jurisdiction, thereby giving rise to an agreement to arbitrate. As long as the respondent consents to the assertion of arbitration despite the absence of a prior arbitration agreement, it is not likely that the particular rules or seat invoked by the claimant will have a material impact on whether an arbitration agreement is deemed to have arisen after the fact.

*Second*, in the investor-State area the investor may have entered into a contract with a specific dispute resolution mechanism with a State entity, but seeks to commence arbitration not against such entity, but against the host State itself on the basis of, for example, a bilateral investment treaty. It thereby effectively seeks to bypass a prior contractually agreed

---

[578] R. Kreindler, "Parallel Proceedings: A Practitioner's Perspective", *loc. cit.* p. 427.

dispute resolution mechanism with the State entity with which it did have a contract.

In such case, the forum shopping which may occur is between the dispute resolution mechanism which could be invoked against the State entity and the dispute resolution options contained in the BIT. Depending upon the provisions in the BIT, reliance on it may in turn provide the investor with "fork-in-the-road" options to pursue, at its choice, the domestic courts, any previously agreed dispute settlement procedures or international arbitration invoked against the State itself. Also depending upon the precise provisions of the BIT, the international arbitration option may itself be broken down into more than one further option, such as UNCITRAL arbitration with a specific seat, ICC arbitration with a specific seat or ICSID arbitration.

*Third*, the investor may have entered into a contract with a specific dispute resolution mechanism not with a State entity, but with the State itself, and seeks to commence arbitration against the State, but again on the basis of, for example, a BIT, seeking to bypass the previously agreed dispute resolution agreement with that same State. Again depending upon the exact provisions of the BIT, the investor may have the option to pursue various kinds of dispute resolution against the State, including ICSID arbitration.

*Fourth*, the investor may have agreed to a dispute resolution mechanism in a contract directly with the State, and seeks to bring in ICSID arbitration not only treaty-based claims against the State on the basis of a BIT, but also contract-based claims, seeking to bypass the agreed dispute resolution agreement respecting contract claims with the State. In such a case, a core question will be whether an individually negotiated investor-State arbitration agreement, providing for a particular seat and a particular national law, takes precedence over a competing agreement to ICSID arbitration resulting from application of an investment treaty for the purposes of adjudicating contract claims between the investor and that State.

*Fifth*, an additional potential source of arbitral forum shopping, particularly in the investment area, is the possibility and the assertion of multiple arbitrations (and also local court proceedings) in parallel, with different seats, different institutional or *ad hoc* rules, different substantive and procedural laws, and identical or not wholly identical parties. In such cases, a proverbial "race to judgment" may ensue, multiple inconsistent awards may be rendered, and multiple inconsistent annulment and enforcement proceedings may ensue. The complications in the context of *lis pendens, res judicata*, issue and action estoppel are numerous.

*Sixth*, a single, multicontract arbitration may involve a complicated horizontal or vertical consortium or joint venture structure in which one or more claimants invoke the arbitration agreement from one contract to assert arbitration against parties from other, interrelated contracts. Such other, interrelated contracts may well have their own arbitration agreements which provide for a different seat, different arbitral rules, different substantive law and even different language than the arbitration agreement relied upon by the originating parties.

The forum shopping effectively consists of the choice exercised by the claimants to invoke the arbitration agreement in the one contract in order to settle the disputes also arising out of the other, related contracts, even though they were meant to be subject to different, conflicting arbitral and legal regimes. Depending upon how narrow or broad the arbitration agreement invoked is and whether it does encompass claims arising in relation to the other contracts, the claimants may in fact succeed in imposing a different regime of arbitral rules, curial law and even substantive law on the rights and obligations arising under the related contracts.

## (c) *Issues related to the seat and/or applicable arbitral rules*

To the extent that the burden and standard of proof may be seen as deriving from the applicable procedural law or the applicable substantive law, depending upon the approach and circumstances, the following additional areas of arbitral forum shopping and parallel proceedings may be identified in both the commercial and the investor-State area in relation to the seat and the applicable rules.

*First*, a contract with or without State involvement in which non-ICSID arbitration is provided for, or asserted, a specific seat is stipulated, and the claimant seeks to commence the arbitration on the basis of an entirely *different* seat. As in other cases, should the named respondent consent to the unilateral change of seat, then a new, binding agreement shall have arisen displacing the old seat. Otherwise, depending upon which institutional or *ad hoc* rules apply to the arbitration, it shall be for the institution, the arbitral tribunal and/or the courts at the seat (either the agreed seat or the newly asserted seat) to confirm that the arbitration may continue only on the basis of the one or the other of the seats.

Where the seat was indeed validly agreed to previously, then the attempt to assert a wholly different seat should normally fail. However, where no arbitral institution or tribunal is able or willing to declare that the previously agreed seat remains the official seat, it is possible that ambiguity on the issue may persist. And indeed even if an arbitral institution or the tribunal should fix the seat at the agreed location, it cannot be ruled out that the claimant (or defendant) seeking to

have the seat of arbitration be considered to be elsewhere will not succeed in either maintaining a parallel
arbitration at that other seat or obtaining a declaration
from the local courts at that other seat that the previous
agreement is invalid[579] or even "annulling" or refusing
enforcement of any award rendered at the previously
agreed seat on the basis that holding the arbitration at
that venue was a violation of the parties' procedural or
other agreements[580].

---

[579] See, e.g., *Four Seasons Hotel and Resorts* v.
*Consorcio Barr,* 267 F. Supp. 2d 1335 (SD Fla. 2003), in
which an AAA award in a contract between a US and a
Venezuelan party subject to Venezuelan law and with a
Miami seat was enforced as a "non-domestic" award under
the New York Convention by the Florida court despite a
ruling by a Venezuelan court purporting to annul the award
on the basis that the underlying arbitration agreements
were invalid under Venezuelan law; the US court ruled
that the "competent authority" in the context of Art. V (1)
*(e)* of the New York Convention was "a court of the country
that supplied the procedural law used in the arbitration".

[580] See, e.g., *Gulf Petro Trading Company, Inc*. v.
*Nigerian National Petroleum Corporation* (ND Tex.,
23 October 2003, Civil Action No 3:03-CV-0406-G). A
US court, applying the ground for refusal of enforcement
under Art. V (1) *(e)* of the New York Convention ("the
award . . . has been set aside . . . by a competent authority
of the country in which, or under the law of which, that
award was made"), held that as it was not the agreed seat
of arbitration (which was Switzerland), it was without
"primary jurisdiction" (i.e., a court under whose law the
arbitration was conducted), and had no subject matter
jurisdiction under the New York Convention to set aside or
modify such arbitral award. In *Karaha Bodas Co., LLC* v.
*Perusahaan Pertambangan Minyak Dan Gas Bumi
Negara*, 364 F. 3d 274 (5th Cir. 2004), a US court rejected
a challenge to enforcement of an award made in Switzerland on the grounds that subsequent "annulment" by the
Indonesian courts did not preclude enforcement and that
the Indonesian courts had only "secondary jurisdiction"
over the Swiss award and therefore, pursuant to the New
York Convention, could not annul it.

*Second*, a contract with or without State involvement in which non-ICSID arbitration is provided for, or asserted, a specific seat is stipulated, and the claimant seeks to commence the arbitration on the basis of an entirely *different* set of institutional or *ad hoc* rules than stipulated. As in the foregoing case, the named respondent is free to consent to such new basis for arbitration. While no ambiguity exists with respect to the seat of the arbitration, depending upon which institutional or *ad hoc* rules apply or are asserted to apply to the arbitration, the institution, the arbitral tribunal and/or the courts at the seat will be called upon to confirm or order that the arbitration may continue only on the basis of one set of rules.

Again, it can also not be ruled out that the claimant (or defendant) seeking to have different rules of arbitration apply might not succeed in maintaining a parallel arbitration under those other set of rules or obtaining a declaration from the courts at the seat that the previously agreement to arbitral rules is invalid or "annulling" or refusing enforcement on the basis that holding the arbitration under those rules was a violation of the parties' procedural or other agreements.

*Third*, parties may agree to a so-called "home and home" arbitral agreement, whereby the seat of the arbitration is not fixed until the arbitration is commenced and the seat becomes that of the named respondent. Such sanctioned forum shopping is meant to discourage either party from commencing an arbitration by creating the disincentive of having to accept the home jurisdiction of the named defendant as the official seat, for all purposes. While this kind of forum shopping mechanism is clear-cut, it obviously contains an inherent uncertainty with respect to the applicable curial law, standard of annulment and other consequences which flow from the fixing of a seat of arbitration.

### (d)  *Degree of relatedness and relevance*

In light of the foregoing, what are the specific challenges for the arbitrator confronted with issues of corruption in which parallel litigation, arbitration or State proceedings or investigations are pending or have already taken place?

*First*, the arbitrator will need to assess the degree or relatedness and relevance of parallel proceedings, also depending on the applicable law and standard. The arbitrator may conclude that the parallel proceedings relating to corruption or overlapping factual circumstances are closely linked or are not linked at all, or that even if they are linked they have no legal relevance to the arbitration itself.

*Second*, the arbitrator must assess the degree of deference to be accorded to evidence obtained in parallel proceedings, particularly in the country of the alleged corrupt act. Where document or witness evidence has already been obtained, including evidence which the arbitral tribunal itself would not necessarily have been able to procure, query to what extent the arbitrator should consider that evidence or the outcome attributed to that evidence by the parallel court, arbitration or investigative authority.

*Third*, a key issue will be the balancing of the public policy of *res judicata* versus the public policy against corruption, a question to which I turn below in greater detail in the context of enforceability: see, for example, *Westacre* v. *Jugoimport*, English Court of Appeal (1999)[581]. What is more important for the arbitrator and for what reason: following a prior result of exoneration, acquittal or dismissal in the name of precedent or comity or both, or rather coming to a dif-

---

[581] Court of Appeal, *Westacre* v. *Jugoimport*, *supra* footnote 206.

ferent decision in the name of condemning and prohibiting corruption?

*Fourth*, the arbitrator may also be confronted with parallel proceedings which are already completed and which applied, either expressly or impliedly, a different standard or burden of proof, perhaps resulting in exoneration, acquittal or dismissal, than the arbitrator considers it should or even must apply in the arbitration.

By way of example, different fora in different jurisdictions may have different approaches to the concept of *in dubio pro reo*, whereby doubtful facts which may incriminate the accused may not be considered while doubtful facts which are favourable to the accused must be considered[582].

Alternatively, parallel criminal, civil or other investigative proceedings may be pending, particularly in the country of the alleged corrupt act, but have not yet come to a result. Query whether the fact that those proceedings have yet resulted in an outcome — for or against a finding of corruption — speaks more in favour of the arbitrator giving the benefit of the doubt to the accused party or rather concluding that the suspicion of illegality must be well founded, since otherwise the investigative proceedings would have been terminated earlier on.

*Fifth*, the arbitrator has the special challenge in the face of corruption issues of what standard of proof to apply. Should he apply a *lower standard* of proof, for example to facilitate proving the illegality in view of the challenges and impediments, already discussed, such as the concealment, obscuring and destruction of

---

[582] R. Kreindler, "Applications for 'Revision' in Investment Arbitration: Selected Current Issues", in M. Á. Fernández-Ballesteros and D. Arias (eds.), *Liber Amicorum Bernardo Cremades*, La Ley, 2010, p. 694.

evidence of the illegality? Or should he *heighten the standard* of proof, for example, in view of the seriousness of allegations of corruption attached to public officials and the disinclination to condemn a public official absent a manifest demonstration of the illegality? Indeed it has been commented that even with a legally valid admission of corruption, the opposing party may still be obligated to prove corruption — Amerasinghe (2005), citing *Corfu Channel*, ICJ (1947)[583].

Alternatively, the arbitrator could even *reverse the burden* of proof onto the impugned party upon a prima facie showing of a bribe. It could do after fulfilment of an initial threshold of showing indications of corruption, especially assuming that the accused party has the ability to produce countervailing evidence of legitimacy.

Finally, the arbitrator, also in view of the challenges of fully meeting the standard of probability or certainty, could *continue to apply the "balance of probabilities"* standard.

He could do so on the rationale that the foregoing other approaches are not warranted and threaten to encourage baseless assertions of illegality and that these approaches are a slippery slope which threaten the rule of natural justice and due process. In so doing, he could still consider such factors as the seriousness of the allegation, the legal consequences, the inherent likelihood of corruption under the specific circumstances, circumstantial evidence, and adverse inferences.

---

[583] See generally C. F. Amerasinghe, *Evidence in International Litigation*, Leiden/Boston, Martinus Nijhoff Publishers, 2005, p. 188 citing to ICJ, *Corfu Channel (United Kingdom* v. *Albania)*, Judgment of 9 April 1949, *ICJ Reports 1949*, p. 84 (dissenting opinion of Judge Azevedo).

## 3. *Approaches to proof in commercial and public law arbitration*

It is interesting to examine how the foregoing approaches have in fact been applied in commercial and public law arbitrations other than investment treaty-based matters.

With regard to a *lower standard* of proof, which is to be distinguished from the drawing of the adverse inference discussed further below, this is in fact a rare approach. While there are examples of a "relaxation" of the standard of proof when the facts are difficult to prove and obscured due to fraud or corruption [584], most of the examples are from highly specific circumstances or tribunals which are not easily transposed to international commercial arbitration. Thus, for example, a lower standard of proof has been applied in the case of admissions as statements against interest — *Nicaragua* v. *United States*, ICJ (1986) [585].

Furthermore, the Rules of the International Criminal Court foresee no application of the "beyond reasonable doubt" standard to victim reparations [586]. And the "reasonable minimum" of evidence standard has been applied for some categories by the United Nations Compensation Commission for reparations related to the 1990-1991 Iraqi invasion and occupation of

---

[584] D. V. Sandifer, "Evidence before International Tribunals", Charlottesville, University Press of Virginia, 1975, p. 130.

[585] Case concerning *Military and Paramilitary Activities in and against Nicaragua (Nicaragua* v. *United States of America)*, 27 June 1986, *ICJ Reports 1986*, p. 14 (available at http://www.icjcij.org/docket/files/70/6503.pdf).

[586] See Arts. 94-98 of the International Criminal Court Rules of Procedure and Evidence, ICC-ASP/1/3 (Part.II-A), available at http://www2.icc-cpi.int/NR/rdonlyres/F1E0AC1C-A3F3-4A3C-B9A7-B3E8B115E886/284955/RPE4thENG08Feb1200.pdf.

Kuwait, which was occupied by massive destruction of evidence relating to loss of property, natural resources, damage to public health and environmental damage[587]. Finally, the standard of "plausibility in light of all circumstances" was applied by the Claims Resolution Tribunal for Dormant Accounts[588].

With regard to a *heightened standard* of proof, various tribunals have seen fit to apply the standard of "clear and convincing", "very high probability" or "beyond doubt". *Corfu Channel*, ICJ (1949)[589]; *Westinghouse* v. *Philippines*, ICC (1991)[590]; *Oil Field of Texas* v. *Iran*, Iran-US CT (1986)[591]; *Westacre* v. *Jugoimport*, ICC (1994)[592]. A middle ground between

---

[587] *Decision concerning Explanatory Statements by Claimants in Categories "D", "E", and "F"*, UN Compensation Commission, UN doc. S/AC. 26/Dec. 46 (3 February 1998), available at http://www.uncc.ch/decision/dec_46.pdf.

[588] See Art. 22 of the Rules of Procedure for the Claims Resolution Process, adopted on 15 October 1997 by the Board of Trustees of the Independent Claims Resolution Foundation (available at http://www.crt-ii.org/_crt-i/frame.html).

[589] ICJ, *Corfu Channel (United Kingdom* v. *Albania)*, *supra* footnote 583, p. 18 ("The proof may be drawn from inferences of fact, provided that they leave *no room* for reasonable doubt").

[590] ICC Case No. 6401, *Westinghouse and Burns & Roe (USA)* v. *National Power Company and the Republic of the Philippines*, *supra* footnote 271.

[591] *Oil Field of Texas, Inc.* v. *The Government of the Islamic Republic of Iran, The National Iranian Oil Company (NIOC) and Others*, Award, IUSCT Case No. 43 (258-43-1), 8 October 1986, *XII Yearbook Commercial Arbitration*, 1987, p. 288 para. 25 ("The burden is on [defendant] to establish its defence of alleged bribery in connection with the Lease Agreement. If *reasonable doubts* remain, such an allegation cannot be deemed to be established" (emphasis added)).

[592] *Westacre* v. *Jugoimport*, ICC Case No. 7047 (1994), *supra* footnote 201, p. 343 ("The statement of facts and

"balance of probabilities" and "beyond reasonable doubt", applying generalized international principles, may be seen to have been applied in *Hilmarton* v. *OTV*, ICC (1988)[593]. On balance, however, according to a 2003 study carried out by Professor Crivellaro, there has been no discernible clearly prevailing standard, with only 5 of 25 awards regarding bribery requiring "clear and convincing" evidence to void the underlying agreement[594].

With regard to a *reversal of the burden* of proof, this appears to have occurred rarely, and only in "in special circumstances and for very good reasons . . . to show 'counter-evidence'" — ICC Case No. 6497 (1994)[595].

Finally, there is the trend of continuing to *apply the "balance of probabilities" standard*: for example, ICC Case No. 8891 (1998)[596]. This includes a willing to draw adverse inferences, including in the context of the IBA Rules as addressed above[597]. Common requirements for the drawing of adverse inferences include that the party asking for the inference must produce evidence corroborating the inference, that the evidence must be accessible, and that the inference must be

---

the burden of proof are therefore upon the defendant. The word 'bribery' is clear and unmistakable").

[593] *Hilmarton (Agent)* v. *Omnium/Algeria*, ICC Case 5622, *supra* footnote 196, p. 105.

[594] See A. Crivellaro, *supra* footnote 6, pp. 109 *et seq.*

[595] ICC Case No. 6497, *supra* footnote 574, p. 73 ("The 'alleging Party' may bring some relevant evidence for its allegations, without these elements being really conclusive. In such case, the arbitral tribunal may exceptionally request the other party to bring some counter-evidence, if such task is possible and not too burdensome. If the other party does not bring such counter-evidence, the arbitral tribunal may conclude that the facts alleged are proven [Art. 8 Swiss Civil Code]").

[596] ICC Case No. 8891 (1998), *supra* footnote 357.

[597] *Supra* footnote 554.

reasonable, consistent with facts and related to the evidence. Furthermore, the party seeking the inference must have first produced prima facie evidence and the adverse party must or should know of its duty to produce evidence rebutting the inference. See, for example, *Rockwell* v. *Iran*, Iran-US CT (1989)[598].

## 4. *Approaches to proof in investment treaty arbitration*

It is rare for a *lower standard* of proof to be applied. A "relaxation" was found to be appropriate where the facts were difficult to prove and were considered obscured due to fraud or corruption: *AAPL* v. *Sri Lanka*, ICSID (1990)[599]; *Middle East Cement* v. *Egypt*, ICSID (2002)[600]. Prima facie evidence may be deemed to suffice in such circumstances.

By contrast, a *heightened standard* of proof of "clear and convincing", "certainty", "conclusive", etc. even moving in the direction of the criminal standard of "beyond a reasonable doubt"[601] has been applied in certain cases, such as *Siag* v. *Egypt*, ICSID (2009)[602];

---

[598] *Rockwell International Systems, Inc.* v. *The Government of the Islamic Republic of Iran (The Ministry of National Defence)*, Iran-United States Claims Tribunal — Case No. 430 Chamber One — Award No. 438-430-1, 5 September 1989, *XV Yearbook Commercial Arbitration*, 1990, p. 239.

[599] *AAPL* v. *Sri Lanka*, *supra* footnote 21, paras. 55 *et seq.*

[600] *Middle East Cement Shipping and Handling Co. S.A.* v. *Arab Republic of Egypt*, ICSID Case No. ARB/99/6, Award, 12 April 2002, paras. 89-91 citing to *AAPL* v. *Sri Lanka*. The Award is available at http:// italaw.com/sites/default/files/case-documents/ita0531.pdf.

[601] A. Reiner, *supra* footnote 552, p. 327; R. H. Kreindler, *supra* footnote 582, pp. 690 *et seq.*

[602] *Waguih Elie George Siag and Clorinda Vecchi* v. *The Arab Republic of Egypt*, ICSID Case No. ARB/05/15, 1 June 2009, paras. 325-326 (available at http://italaw. com/sites/default/files/case-documents/ita0786_0.pdf).

*F-W Oil* v. *Trinidad*, ICSID (2006)[603]; and *Int'l Thunderbird* v. *Mexico*, UNCITRAL (NAFTA) (2006)[604]. In the case of *EDF* v. *Romania*, ICSID (2009), the approach taken was in fact closer to a criminal standard. Indeed State-related arbitrations have been seen to justify more stringent scrutiny of allegations, including allegations of corruption by the State: see, for example, *African Holdings* v. *Congo*, ICSID (2009): "irrefutable evidence . . . such as evidence which results from criminal investigations in countries in which corruption is a crime"[605].

It is not entirely clear what the legally defensible justification for this heightened standard is, and indeed whether it can fairly be met in many cases where corruption nonetheless is strongly suspected. If a conviction or similar result is required in each case, in particular by State authorities investigating the same

---

[603] *F-W Oil Interests, Inc.* v. *The Republic of Trinidad and Tobago*, ICSID Case No. ARB/01/14, 3 March 2006, para. 212 (available at http://italaw.com/sites/default/files/case-documents/ita0350.pdf).

[604] *International Thunderbird Gaming Corporation* v. *The United Mexican States*, UNCITRAL, Award, 26 January 2006, para. 106 ("In the absence of legal control however, the Tribunal is of the opinion that de facto control must be established beyond any reasonable doubt"); available at http://italaw.com/sites/default/files/case-documents/ita0431.pdf.

[605] Trans. from *African Holding Company of America, Inc. and Société Africaine de Construction au Congo S.A.R.L.* v. *La République démocratique du Congo*, ICSID Case No. ARB/05/21, Sentence sur les déclinatoires de compétence et la recevabilité, 29 July 2008, para. 52 ("Le Tribunal est disposé à considérer toute pratique de corruption comme une affaire très grave, mais exigerait une preuve irréfutable de cette pratique, telle que celles qui résulteraient de poursuites criminelles dans les pays où la corruption constitue une infraction pénale"). Available at http://italaw.com/sites/default/files/case-documents/ita0016.pdf.

State, then it is submitted that it is naive to apply such standard automatically in any case.

Yet a requirement of conviction of bribery was precisely what was required in *TSA* v. *Argentina*, ICSID (2008)[606], and in *African Holding* v. *Congo*, ICSID (2009)[607]. Of course, a conviction is to be distinguished from such other outcomes as a formal accusation, an arraignment, an indictment, a guilty plea, a plea bargain, a settlement without judgment or an acceptance of alleged facts of corruption. The question is what suffices and what does not, especially where some of these vehicles do not even exist in most countries. It also raises the question of whether such an outcome should result in a preclusion from litigating the same corruption issue in other fora, including in an arbitration.

Ultimately, it is submitted that only proven corruption could or should have an impact on the protection of investment under international law, and that normally the pendency of an investigation, an accusation, an arraignment, etc. should not be equated with a formal finding of culpability, at least not yet. Indeed even prior convictions should have no evidentiary weight if they are unrelated to the alleged corruption in the new case: *Methanex* v. *US*, UNCITRAL (NAFTA) (2005)[608].

Finally, more often than not what is applied is the *"balance of probabilities" standard*. Thus adverse inferences are frequently taken, without necessarily calling them as such. Indeed under ICSID Arbitration

---

[606] *TSA* v. *Argentina*, *supra* footnote 560.

[607] *African Holding* v. *Congo*, *supra* footnote 605.

[608] *Methanex Corporation* v. *United States of America*, UNCITRAL, Final Award of the Tribunal on Jurisdiction and Merits, 3 August 2005, Part III, Chapter B, p. 7, paras. 13 *et seq.* (available at http://italaw.com/sites/default/files/case-documents/ita0529.pdf).

Rules Article 34 (3) (Evidence: General Principles), "[t]he Tribunal shall take formal note of the failure of a party to comply with its obligations under this paragraph and of any reasons given for such failure". In *Europe Cement* v. *Turkey*, ICSID (2009), an adverse inference was drawn from a failure of the investor to rebut the presumption that he did not own any shares of the case-relevant companies on the critical date[609].

## 5. *Similarities and differences in commercial and investment approaches to proof*

It is difficult to attempt a reconciliation of the commercial and investment treaty approaches to the burden and standard of proof and specifically in the context of corruption. It suffices to say that corruption allegations in investment disputes may be argued to be subject to a higher standard, due to the function and credibility of investment protection, but that any automatic heightening of the standard to the benefit of the accused State official would be both unjustified and dangerous.

Furthermore, just as the pendency or completion of a criminal investigation by the State in which the corruption is alleged to have occurred may be relevant, so too the failure or refusal of the State to prosecute bribery under its own domestic law may be relevant. This can of course go in both directions: the failure to

---

[609] *Europe Cement Investment & Trade S.A.* v. *Republic of Turkey*, ICSID Case No. ARB(AF)/07/2, Award, 13 August 2009, paras. 150-164 ("This contributes to the inference that the originals of the documents copied in its Memorial and on which its claim was based either were never in the Claimant's possession or would not stand forensic analysis, in which case the claim that Europe Cement had shares in CEAS and Kepez at the relevant time was fraudulent"); available at http://italaw.com/sites/default/files/case-documents/ita0311.pdf.

prosecute or the failure to punish may be seen as an indication of the absence of illegality under that law, or it may be seen as a further sign of collusion by State organs in the illegality or of lack of rigour and seriousness.

Finally, illegality alleged as a matter of the host State civil or criminal law should be subject to the relevant local standards of proof, unless the actions accused of are also illegal under an applicable international standard. At the same time, the failure to prove illegality under the local standard should not be an automatic bar to treaty protections arising out of that same factual conduct.

Nor should an investment tribunal necessarily be bound to prior determinations on evidence by host State criminal or civil authorities, especially if the tribunal does not agree with the standard or methods applied by those authorities. Furthermore, corruption proven "in relation to an investment" may be different than corruption "of the investment", and may have different legal consequences depending on the contract or the treaty basis of the claim.

CHAPTER VII

# ATTRIBUTION OF ILLEGAL ACTIONS
# AND KNOWLEDGE OF THE STATE

Particularly in investment-treaty arbitrations, but not only, when is illegality to be attributed to the State party itself? If it is not attributable, then the State is not legally responsible for the consequences of such illegality.

## A. Introduction

Both commercial and investment disputes involving States parties may raise questions of attribution. Particularly in investment disputes, the State is invariably the respondent but occasionally attribution will also play a role for the claimant. An example was the case of *CSOB* v. *Slovak Republic*, ICSID (1999), concerning the legal status of the claimant as a private party in dispute[610].

There are significant conceptual challenges to attribution generally.

*First*, there is the question of the attribution of an action or knowledge of an organ, province or municipality to the State itself.

*Second*, there is the issue of attribution of the State entity to the State itself.

*Third*, in the commercial context, for example, involving an investment contract with a State or State entity, there may be the question of attribution to a

---

[610] *CSOB* v. *The Slovak Republic*, *supra* footnote 437, para. 32.

State signatory, to a State non-signatory, which may in turn be governed by the *lex contractus* as well as customary international principles on attribution[611].

*Fourth*, in the investment context, for example, involving a treaty-based dispute, there may be the question of attribution to a State signatory, governed by the rules of law pursuant to the treaty, including international law[612]. There may be responsibility of the State for even the "lowest-level" organs in relation to foreign direct investment.

## B. *Attribution Generally in International Arbitration Involving States*

Under customary international law, a State has responsibility for all of its organs, including territorial units such as provinces and municipalities[613]. This is the case regardless of the level of organ and regardless of the position within the State apparatus[614]. It extends to all branches of government, including the executive, legislature and judiciary. Thus the International Law Commission Articles on State Responsibility at Article 4 provide:

> "1. The conduct of any State organ shall be considered an act of that State under international law,

---

[611] K. Hobér, "State Responsibility and Investment Arbitration", *Journal of International Arbitration*, Vol. 25 (2008), pp. 545 *et seq.*, K. Hobér, "State Responsibility and Attribution", in R. Muchlinski *et al.* (eds.), *The Oxford Handbook of International Investment Law*, New York, Oxford University Press, 2008, p. 551.

[612] K. Hobér, "State Responsibility and Investment Arbitration", *Journal of International Arbitration*, Vol. 25 (2008), pp. 545 *et seq.*

[613] R. Dolzer and C. H. Schreuer, *supra* footnote 165, p. 195.

[614] *Ibid.*

whether the organ exercises legislative, executive, judicial or any other functions, whatever position it holds in the organization of the State, and whatever its character as an organ of the central Government or of a territorial unit of the State.

2. An organ includes any person or entity which has that status in accordance with the internal law of the State."

The practice of commercial and investment tribunals follows Article 4, as exemplified by the decisions in *CMS* v. *Argentina*, ICSID (2003)[615]; *Loewen* v. *US*, NAFTA (2001)[616]; *Eureko* v. *Poland*, *Ad Hoc* (2005)[617]; and *Jan de Nul* v. *Egypt*, ICSID (2008)[618]. Thus there will be attribution of ministers, armed forces, police, treasury, legislature, courts, but *not* of private persons in their private capacity — for example, *Tradex* v. *Albania*, ICSID (1999)[619].

Attribution of State organs to the State can and will take place even if contrary to the law and even if in

---

[615] *CMS Gas Transmission Company* v. *The Republic of Argentina*, ICSID Case No. ARB/01/8, Decision on Objections to Jurisdiction, 17 July 2003, para. 108 (available at http://italaw.com/sites/default/files/case-documents/ita0183.pdf).

[616] *Loewen Group, Inc. and Raymond L. Loewen* v. *United States of America*, ICSID Case No. ARB(AF)/98/3, Decision on Hearing of Respondent's Objection to Competence and Jurisdiction, 5 January 2001, paras. 47, 70 (available at http://italaw.com/sites/default/files/case-documents/ita0469.pdf).

[617] *Eureko B.V.* v. *Republic of Poland*, Partial Award, 19 August 2005, para. 128 (available at http://italaw.com/sites/default/files/case-documents/ita0308_0.pdf).

[618] *Jan de Nul N.V. and Dredging International N.V.* v. *Arab Republic of Egypt*, ICSID Case No. ARB/04/13, Award, 6 November 2008, paras. 158 *et seq.* Available at http://italaw.com/sites/default/files/case-documents/ita0440.pdf.

[619] *Tradex* v. *Albania*, *supra* footnote 557, para. 165.

violation of instructions, so that the State cannot plead
a defence of *ultra vires* — ILC, Article 7:

> "The conduct of an organ of a State or of a
> person or entity empowered to exercise elements
> of the governmental authority shall be considered
> an act of the State under international law if the
> organ, person or entity acts in that capacity, even
> if it exceeds its authority or contravenes instruc-
> tions."

This approach has been accepted in arbitral practice:
for example, *SPP* v. *Egypt*, ICSID (1992), such that an
investor may rely on official representations of the
Government, whether legal or not. These expectations
are deemed protected by international law[620]. The same
principles apply to territorial units such as provinces
and municipa-lities, and indeed certain treaties specifically extend the application to political subdivisions —
ECT, Article 23 (1)[621].

This too has been accepted in international arbitral
practice: for example, *Vivendi* v. *Argentina (I)*, ICSID
(2000)[622]; *Enron* v. *Argentina*, ICSID (2004)[623];

---

[620] *SPP* v. *Egypt*, *supra* footnote 450, para. 85.

[621] Art. 32 (1) of the The Energy Charter Treaty.

[622] *Compañiá de Aguas del Aconquija S.A. and Vivendi
Universal S.A.* v. *Argentine Republic*, ICSID Case
No. ARB/97/3 (formerly *Compañía de Aguas del Aconquija, S.A. and Compagnie Générale des Eaux* v. *Argentine Republic*), Award, 21 November 2000, p. 3 (available
at    http://italaw.com/sites/default/files/case-documents/ita
0206.pdf).

[623] *Enron Corporation and Ponderosa Assets, L.P.* v.
*Argentine Republic*, ICSID Case No. ARB/01/3 (also
known as: *Enron Creditors Recovery Corp. and Ponderosa Assets, L.P.* v. *The Argentine Republic*), Decision on
Jurisdiction, 14 January 2004, para. 32 (available at http://
italaw.com/sites/default/files/case-documents/ita0290.
pdf).

*Mondev* v. *US*, NAFTA (2002)[624]; *Metalclad* v. *Mexico*, NAFTA (2000)[625].

Furthermore, attribution may also occur to other entities, in particular two categories.

*First*, entities which are empowered with the structure and function of "governmental authority" — ILC, Article 5:

> "The conduct of a person or entity which is not an organ of the State under article 4 but which is empowered by the law of that State to exercise elements of the governmental authority shall be considered an act of the State under international law, provided the person or entity is acting in that capacity in the particular instance."

*Second*, entities which are directed or controlled by the State — ILC, Article 8:

> "The conduct of a person or group of persons shall be considered an act of a State under international law if the person or group of persons is in fact acting on the instructions of, or under the direction or control of, that State in carrying out the conduct."

The foregoing is likewise largely accepted in international arbitral practice: for example, *Maffezini* v. *Spain*, ICSID (2000)[626]; *Salini* v. *Morocco*, ICSID (2001)[627], and governmental and commercial conduct

---

[624] *Mondev International Ltd.* v. *United States of America*, ICSID Case No. ARB(AF)/99/2, Award, 11 October 2002, para. 67 (available at http://italaw.com/sites/default/files/case-documents/ita1076.pdf).

[625] *Metalclad* v. *Mexico*, *supra* footnote 434.

[626] *Emilio Agustín Maffezini* v. *The Kingdom of Spain*, ICSID Case No. ARB/97/7, Award, 13 November 2000, para. 83 (available at http://italaw.com/sites/default/files/case-documents/ita0481.pdf).

[627] *Salini* v. *Morocco*, *supra* footnote 208, para. 18.

is generally not distinguished in this regard. There are partial exceptions, such as in *Noble Ventures* v. *Romania*, ICSID (2005), in which the tribunal states that the distinction between commercial and governmental conduct plays an important role in the field of sovereign immunity when one comes to the question of whether a State can claim immunity before the courts of another State[628].

## C. The Intersection between Corruption and Attribution

Bribery may or may not raise issues of attribution. And the question of the tainting of a contract or investment may or may not require an analysis applying the ILA Draft Articles. Manifest corruption may be equally manifestly "attributable".

On the State side, it may be attributable to the State respondent, or not — this is the more frequent issue. Alternatively, corruption may be manifest but difficult to attribute or difficult to prove but, if and when proven, manifestly easy to attribute.

On the investor side, it may be attributable to the investor claimant, or not — this is the *less* frequent issue. Here, there is in fact the accepted principle of attribution of an agent's acts and knowledge to the principal employing him, including under national law, for example: the US Restatement (Third) — Agency, § 2.04 *(respondeat superior)*: the employer is liable for torts committed by employees while acting within their employment[629]. And German Civil Code Sec. 31,

---

[628] *Noble Ventures, Inc.* v. *Romania*, ICSID Case No. ARB/01/11, Award, 12 October 2005, para. 82 (available at http://italaw.com/sites/default/files/case-documents/ita0565.pdf).

[629] See § 2.04 "Respondeat Superior " of Restatement of the Law — Agency (Third) (available at http://users.

German Supreme Court (1991): knowledge and subjective intent of an agent to commit acts against public policy can be attributed to the legal entity[630].

The special challenge here is however the attributability of the conduct of individual public officials accepting or receiving bribes. There is a general principle that such conduct is attributable to the corrupting party, for example, to the investor offering the bribe, and *not* to the State of which the individual is an official[631]. Two particular cases in recent years illustrate the challenge of attribution in the area of corruption allegations. In both such cases, the corrupt activity, admitted in the one case and not admitted or proven in the other case, resulted in a decision of non-attribution of illegality to the State party.

In *World Duty Free* v. *Kenya*, ICSID (2006)[632], the relevant facts may be summarized in brief as follows: in 1989, Kenya concluded an agreement with a company called the "House of Perfume" (as from 1990: "World Duty Free Company Ltd." — incorporated under the laws of the Isle of Man (UK)) for the construction, maintenance and operation of duty-free complexes at Mombasa and Nairobi airports. In order to obtain the agreement, the representative of World Duty Free made a "personal donation" to the then President of Kenya in the amount of US$2,000,000. Later, World Duty Free was purportedly implicated in a scandal resulting from an illegal reelection financing of the Kenyan President.

Subsequently, according to World Duty Free, Kenya took over the control of World Duty Free's assets in

---

wfu.edu/palmitar/ICBCorporations-Companion/Additional Readings/Restatement(third)Agency.pdf).

[630] See Sec. 31, German Civil Code.

[631] C. B. Lamm, H. Pham *et al.*, *supra* footnote 370, p. 726.

[632] *World Duty Free* v. *Kenya*, *supra* footnote 44.

Kenya in order to ensure the destruction of essential evidence for any successful prosecution of the fraud. World Duty Free was placed in receivership and its representative was forced to leave Kenyan territory. In 2000, World Duty Free filed an ICSID request for arbitration seeking restitution of its assets, alternatively, compensation for their value.

The investor claimant side admitted that it had engaged in and offered a bribe in connection with the investment at issue. The claim for damages against the host State was based on an actual investment contract providing for ICSID arbitration, which was subject to English and Kenyan law, and not in the first instance on public international law principles. The decision has been interpreted as standing for a variety of propositions, including that bribery contravenes international public policy. In this regard, the arbitral tribunal stated in relevant part:

> "In light of domestic laws and international conventions relating to corruption, and in light of the decisions taken in this matter by courts and arbitral tribunals, this Tribunal is convinced that *bribery is contrary to international public policy of most, if not all, States* or, to use another formula, to transnational public policy. Thus, claims based on contracts of corruption or on contracts obtained by corruption cannot be upheld by this Arbitral Tribunal." [633]

In this regard, *World Duty Free*, and the various other awards and decisions condemning bribery which precede *World Duty Free* [634], do not establish as a

---

[633] *Supra* footnote 632, para. 157 (emphasis added).

[634] For a discussion of various commercial arbitration awards and arbitration-related court decisions which effectively presage and echo the holding of *World Duty Free*, respecting the arbitral tribunal's condemnation of bribery, see generally the discussion in R. Kreindler, *supra* footnote 41, p. 209.

matter of dogma that the prohibition against bribery in international public policy forms part of international law. At the same time, the condemnation of bribery found in numerous international instruments and decisions as stated above can and should, in my opinion, be classified as a general principle of public international law deriving from the *ordre public* concept well established in national legal orders, as I have written elsewhere[635].

The *World Duty Free* decision is noteworthy for a variety of reasons, including in the areas of justification, excuses and defences discussed further below[636]. For present purposes, its importance relates to the decision of the arbitral tribunal that the essentially uncontroverted evidence that the head of State of Kenya had taken receipt of a cash bribe from the investor, while done "covertly", was also done "privately" and "is not legally to be imputed to [the State] itself"[637].

On the one hand, the public official implicated in an admitted effectuated bribery was the highest official in the land; on the other hand, his action was deemed to be private and not done, directly or indirectly, in a manner attributable legally to the State itself. While the circumstances of each case of a bribe of the head of State directly may differ, query whether it is both factually naive and legally untenable to make such an exculpatory distinction in every case. A head of State has a right to engage in private activity which is not attributable to the State itself; not every private activity, including an illegal one, is done in the capacity as head of State just as not every activity of a low-level official is to be deemed public in nature.

---

[635] R. Kreindler, *supra* footnote 245, pp. 429, 437.

[636] See *infra* Chapter X.D.6.

[637] *World Duty Free* v. *Kenya*, *supra* footnote 44, para. 167.

On the other hand, depending on the facts such activity by the highest representative of the State may well sooner be deemed to be related to his public capacity, to the investment in question and thereby to the State's role in such investment. In the case at hand, it is submitted that on its face it is not apparent what the factual and legal justification was for deeming the head of State's receipt of a cash bribe from a foreign investor in Kenya for a foreign investment purpose to be solely or even predominantly "private" in nature.

In *EDF* v. *Romania*, ICSID (2009)[638], the arbitral tribunal held that an alleged demand made by officials on behalf of the Romanian Prime Minister that the investor pay them a bribe was not attributable to the State unless the officials in question were acting *not* in their personal interest, but rather on behalf of and for the account of the Government of Romania. The approach in principle was not dissimilar to that of *World Duty Free* and for that matter of the ILC Draft Articles[639]. The bribe was not admitted and was held not to have been proven.

Query to what extent one or both of the foregoing cases, and also the ILC Draft Articles, are satisfactory in their conception and application of the concept of attribution. ILC Draft Article 7 states,

> "The conduct . . . shall be considered an act of the State under international law if the organ, person or entity acts *in that capacity*, even if it exceeds its authority or contravenes instructions." (Emphasis added.)

---

[638] *EDF* v. *Romania*, *supra* footnote 565.

[639] Draft Articles on Responsibility of States for Internationally Wrongful Acts, with commentaries 2001 (available at http://untreaty.un.org/ilc/texts/instruments/english/commentaries/9_6_2001.pdf).

The Commentary to Article 7 states, in relevant part, that Article 7

> "comprises only the actions and omissions of organs *purportedly or apparently carrying out their official functions*, and not the private actions or omissions of individuals *who happen to be* organs or agents of the State.
>
> In short, the question is whether they were acting with apparent authority" (Emphasis added.)

And a footnote to the Commentary states,

> "One form of ultra vires conduct covered by article 7 would be for a State official to accept a bribe to perform some act or conclude some transaction . . . Where one State bribes an organ of another to perform some official act, the corrupting State would be responsible either under article 8 or article 17. The question of the responsibility of the State whose official had been bribed towards the corrupting State in such a case could hardly arise . . ."[640]

There are problematic areas in the application of Article 7, which begin with the "official function" — where does it begin and end, and under what standards? While this will be a matter of proof, it is submitted that it is an imprecise science at best as to how and on what basis to conclude that a government official, whether of the lowest level or as the head of State, is or is not acting in his or her official function when demanding or accepting a bribe.

If the measure of "official function" is whether the bribe money is meant to benefit that official directly or,

---

[640] See commentary to Art. 7 of the Draft Articles on Responsibility of States for Internationally Wrongful Acts, footnote 150.

in the unlikely event, is intended to be deposited in the public coffers, then the public official will almost never be acting in his "official function" for attribution purposes. And yet this may be a short-sighted and counter-intuitive measure, since from the perspective of the investor, of the official or indeed both, the reason for participating in the bribe is precisely to achieve an advantage vis-à-vis the State which the public official purports to be able to effectuate, and not simply to achieve a private advantage. Indeed even if the bribe is destined for the private pockets of the public official, the official may be demanding it or the investor may be offering it in a hoped-for exchange for a promise of official preferential treatment. This presumably was also the motivation behind the bribe to the Kenyan head of State in connection with the investor's plans to establish a duty free shop network in Kenya.

On the other hand, as apparently concluded in both *World Duty Free* and *EDF*, one could just as well conclude that the public officials in both cases "happened to be organs or agents of the State", that therefore their public function was not of characteristic or central relevance to the illegality, and that they engaged in such activity without "apparent authority" so that attribution should not lie. Again, it will depend on the circumstances, but it is submitted that in both of the above-referenced cases, at least based on the available record, the conclusion of non-attribution was problematic and tenuous at best.

Particularly in the case of *World Duty Free*, it strains credulity to conclude after the admission of the bribery and the underlying circumstances that the Kenyan head of State was not acting in his official capacity. It seems curious to conclude that he was not acting with apparent authority. And it seems strained to decide that he was not acting manifestly, and not just by "happenstance", as an organ or agent of the State. Indeed he was the State.

For these reasons, the question of attribution in the case of bribery and corruption will occupy us for many years to come in both the commercial and investment arenas as a result of the interplay between the case law, the ILC Articles and the otherwise developed commentary on attribution.

CHAPTER VIII

## THE RIGHTS AND DUTIES
## OF THE ARBITRATOR

### A. Introduction

What can, should or must the arbitral tribunal do in the face of suspected illegality of a contract or investment in relation to which it is meant to adjudicate a dispute? How should a tribunal behave in the face of illegality which is admitted or otherwise manifest?

The focus here is on the rights and duties of the international arbitrator in the context of corruption allegations, suspicions and findings. It relates to the conceptual challenges and issues respecting the rights and duties generally and in the specific context of corruption and bribery. It also relates to the arbitrator's procedural and investigative rights and duties generally and in the specific context of corruption and bribery.

### B. Conceptual Challenges and Issues Related to Rights and Duties Generally

#### 1. Rights of the international arbitrator

The limits of party autonomy reside not only in public policy as manifested by constraints on arbitrability or a prohibition against corruption, but also in the rights of the arbitrator himself or herself, particularly — but not only — where the parties are simply *not* in agreement. That the parties are often unable or unwilling to agree on even the simplest procedural or substantive aspects of their dispute, obliging the arbitral tribunal to step into the breach, is obvious, but in its frequency often underestimated.

Thus under UNCITRAL Model Law Article 19, "(1) Subject to the provisions of this Law, *the parties are free to agree on the procedure* to be followed by the arbitral tribunal in conducting the proceedings", whereas "(2) Failing such agreement, the arbitral tribunal may, subject to the provisions of this Law, conduct the arbitration *in such manner as it considers appropriate*" which also "includes the power to determine the admissibility, relevance, materiality and weight of any evidence[641].

Similarly, the recently revised 2012 ICC Rules of Arbitration provide at Article 22 (2),

> "In order to ensure effective case management, the arbitral tribunal, after consulting the parties, may adopt *such procedural measures as it considers appropriate*, provided that they are not contrary to any agreement of the parties."

In the investment treaty context, ICSID Convention Article 43 provides:

> "Except as the parties otherwise agree, the Tribunal may, *if it deems it necessary at any stage of the proceedings*, *(a)* call upon the parties to produce documents or other evidence, and *(b)* visit the scene connected with the dispute, and conduct such inquiries there as it may deem appropriate."

On the one hand, the parties are substantially free to agree on the conduct of the proceedings. On the other hand, that freedom has its limits, and can and may result in a collision with the freedom of the arbitral tribunal to conduct the proceedings as it deems appropriate.

---

[641] Art. 19 (2), sent. 2, UNCITRAL Model Law.

## 2. *Duties of the international arbitrator*

### (a) *Duties of the arbitrator and party autonomy*

The international arbitrator, both generally and in the specific context of illegality, has not only rights, but also duties, and constraints. He must heed and cede to party autonomy, particularly — but not only — where the parties are indeed in agreement and that agreement is both permissible and acceptable. And just because the parties are not in agreement does not mean that they do not respectively have individual party autonomy which must likewise be considered and may constrain the rights of the arbitrator.

Thus again UNCITRAL Model Law Article 19 (1) provices that "Subject to the provisions of this Law, the *parties are free to agree on the procedure* to be followed by the arbitral tribunal in conducting the proceedings", so that a permissible agreement can indeed bind the arbitral tribunal and thereby impose a duty on it to proceed pursuant to that agreement.

Not every agreement will have such result, but a legal and permissible agreement in many if not most instances can and should do so, subject to narrow exceptions. The 2012 ICC Rules at Article 25 (1) provide that the arbitral tribunal "*shall proceed within as short a time as possible* to establish the facts of the case by all appropriate means". Its Article 22 (1) provides: "The arbitral tribunal and the parties *shall make every effort to conduct the arbitration in an expeditious and cost-effective manner*, having regard to the complexity and value of the dispute."

These recitals reflect both rights and duties on the part of the arbitral tribunal. On the one hand, the tribunal has the discretion and option to pursue "all appropriate means", on the other hand it must do so in an expeditious and cost-effective manner. This interplay between rights and duties can apply to such regularly occurring questions as the number of pleadings to be received, the number of written witness statements accepted, how many witnesses shall be heard orally, how many hearings days shall be scheduled, what extent of document requests shall be permitted, will site visits be allowed, etc. Particularly the question of how many witnesses may be heard orally, in what level of detail, with what degree of questioning by counsel, etc. can play directly into the possible tension between party rights and expectations and tribunal prerogatives.

### (b) *Duties of the arbitrator and public policy*

Yet the duties of the international arbitrator, both in the commercial and the investment context, in fact reach far further, as they are controlled by the parties' rights and by public policy, and those rights can often assume the level of a procedural public policy guarantee.

Thus UNCITRAL Model Law Article 18 states: "The parties *shall be treated with equality* and each party *shall be given a full opportunity* of presenting his case." Similarly but not identically, the 2012 ICC Rules at Article 22 (4) provide: "In all cases, the arbitral tribunal shall act fairly and impartially and ensure that each party has a *reasonable opportunity* to present its case."

"Reasonable opportunity" might be seen as a different standard than "full opportunity", which in turn might be seen as a different threshold than "equal opportunity", and query where the parties in their arbitration agreement have provided for the one standard by virtue of their selection of a *lex arbitri* and for another standard by virtue of their more specific selection, as permitted by the *lex arbitri*, of certain institutional rules. "Full opportunity" might suggest that the parties have full rights of presentation and control and that the tribunal must in all cases accommodate those rights. "Reasonable opportunity" might suggest that they decidedly do not have such a "full" opportunity unless it is deemed to be "reasonable". And treatment "with equality" might suggest that whether "reasonable" or "full", the opportunity or in any event the treatment must be "equal", which could leave open the conclusion that "equally bad treatment" is also "equal treatment" and thereby not a denial or infringement of the "opportunity" in the sense of a right to present one's case.

Such situations can and do come to the fore where, for example, one party insists on the right to present in writing and in person dozens of witnesses, the other party likewise insists on the right to present numerous witnesses, and the one party makes the arithmetically inspired argument that its right to be heard and to equal treatment would be violated if it were not allowed exactly the same number of witnesses at the hearing, even if both of the originally offered numbers are first winnowed down by the tribunal.

As awkward and even childish as this might seem at first blush, it is a situation which arises and which poses the question of how to balance the rights of the parties and the rights of the tribunal to conduct the proceedings. The situation may be complicated where the parties in fact "agree" each out of self-interest that they will respectively reduce the number of witnesses which they wish to present, but the total number remains high and from the perspective of the tribunal exorbitant, inflated, unnecessary and inappropriate. Furthermore, illegality can play a role, for example, in the case of collusive illegal conduct by the parties toward the tribunal on a procedural level. In that specific case, the parties' right to "agree on the procedure" (UNCITRAL

Model Law Article 19, ICSID Conv. Article 43) will normally *not* bind the arbitrator to the agreed procedure[642].

(c) *Standards of procedural international public policy*

The foregoing possible tension between rights of the parties and rights of the tribunal particularly respecting the procedure leads to the question of standards of "procedural public policy". Can procedure be a question of public policy and can it thereby rise to a separate and even higher level than "due process" or "equal treatment" such as to affect the analysis of this tension. And if there is a notion of procedural public policy, in international commercial and particularly investment cases can there be a notion of international or transnational procedural public policy which informs the tribunal's decision as to this tension[643]?

Generally, to make out a standard of "transnational substantive public policy," the modern trend favours relying upon a consensus as to its content. The presence of a consensus is, in turn, demonstrated especially by the body of international convention law, and also by whether there is a convergence between and among various elements. These include national laws, national case law, arbitral case law, public international law, the general principles of law, and customs and usages. On that basis, transnational substantive public policy has indeed found a place in international arbitration. It is referred to and relied upon as such, whether by arbitrators or by judges. For example, the consensus that

---

[642] G. B. Born, *supra* footnote 4, pp. 1636 *et seq.*, and 1757.

[643] See, generally, F. Mantilla-Serrano, "Towards a Transnational Procedural Public Policy", *Arbitration International*, Vol. 20 (2004), pp. 333 *et seq.*

corruption and bribery offend transnational substantive public policy, as addressed above[644].

Is it the same for transnational procedural public policy? In many respects, yes: reference, for example, to such sources as the UNCITRAL Model Law[645], the New York Convention[646], the ILA Report on Public Policy as Bar to Enforcement of International Arbitral Awards, national arbitration laws[647], and national case

---

[644] See *supra* Chapter III.B.5.

[645] Cf., e.g., Art. 34 (2) *(a)* (ii) of the UNCITRAL Model Law and Part B, Sec. 7 *(b)*, para. 46, Explanatory Note by the UNCITRAL Secretariat on the Model Law on International Commercial Arbitration: "[Public policy] is to be understood as serious departures from fundamental notions of procedural justice."

[646] Cf., e.g., Arts. V (1) *(b)* and V (1) *(d)*, New York Convention.

[647] For example, the English Arbitration Act explicitly provides that an arbitral award may be vacated if "the award *or the way in which it was procured* [are] being contrary to public policy". English Arbitration Act, Art. 68 (2) *(g)* (emphasis added). See also, e.g., Art. 1065 (1) *(e)* Netherlands Code of Civil Procedure ("the award, or the manner in which it was made, violates public policy or morals"). For a definition of procedural public policy under Swiss law, see Tribunal Fédéral [Swiss Federal Tribunal], *X Inc.* v. *Z. Corp.*, *supra* footnote 281, p. 365 ("L'ordre public procédural garantit aux parties le droit à un jugement indépendant sur les conclusions et l'état de fait soumis au Tribunal arbitral d'une manière conforme au droit de procédure applicable; il y a violation de l'ordre public procédural lorsque des principes fondamentaux et généralement reconnus ont été violés, ce qui conduit à une contradiction insupportable avec le sentiment de la justice, de telle sorte que la décision apparaît incompatible avec des valeurs reconnues dans un Etat de droit") ("Procedural public policy guarantees to the parties the right to an independent judgment respecting the conclusions and the nature of the facts submitted to the arbitral tribunal in a manner conforming to the applicable procedural law; public policy is being violated when fundamental and generally recognized principles were violated, leading to an

law as well as arbitral awards give ready support to a consensus of three kinds.

*First*, that the right to a reasonable opportunity to be heard and the right to equal treatment (respecting both the constitution of the tribunal and the later proceedings) are fundamental procedural rights that may not be violated.

*Second*, however, that violation of these rights does not necessarily automatically give rise to grounds for denial of enforceability to the award. In addition, some jurisdictions require the argument (and in some cases evidence) provided for by the appealing party that the violation has had (respectively could have had or that it cannot be excluded to have had) an impact on the outcome of the arbitral award.

*Third*, that even where violation does lead to annulment or refusal of enforcement because the violation affected the outcome of the award, that is not the whole story. Namely, violation does not necessarily trigger the separate ground of violation of public policy, in this case procedural public policy and more specifically transnational procedural public policy. In order to constitute grounds for non-enforcement, the violation of procedural laws or rules must be severe and deprive a party of fundamental rights[648]. In this regard, transnational procedural public policy is arguably more problematic and elusive than transnational substantive public policy.

Especially with regard to commercial arbitration

---

unbearable contradiction to the sense of justice such that the relevant decision appears to be incompatible with the accepted values in a state governed by the rule of law" (author's translation)). See also R. Kreindler and T. J. Kautz, *supra* footnote 281, pp. 576 *et seq.*

[648] R. Kreindler and A. Tevini, *supra* footnote 233, p. 461; D. Otto and O. Elwan, *supra* footnote 240, p. 389 (with further references).

public policy is an accepted and legitimate limitation to international arbitration, but it is also recognized that public policy must be interpreted and applied restrictively, since a more lenient interpretation would jeopardize the effectiveness of international commercial arbitration overall[649]. Moreover, the public policy exception must arguably also be applied more restrictively in arbitration than in litigation since, by choosing arbitration, parties voluntarily waive the protection of their own national courts[650]. It should be only in extreme cases that party autonomy is trumped by the "higher good" of international public policy[651]. However, overall there is no general international consensus with regard to the permissible or desirable extent of a court's public policy control[652].

Thus, there is a ready assumption that opportunity to be heard and equal treatment are universally pro-

---

[649]  See J. G. de Enterría, "The Role of Public Policy in International Commercial Arbitration", *Law and Policy in International Business*, Vol. 21 (1989-1990), p. 391.

[650]  *Ibid.*, p. 394.

[651]  R. Kreindler and A. Tevini, *supra* footnote 233, p. 457; R. Kreindler, *supra* footnote 245, p. 244 ("[T]he arbitrator need not apply the agreed or determined governing law if doing so would cause him or her to violate international public policy. In such extreme cases, party autonomy is trumped by the 'higher good' of international public policy . . . Where disregard of the mandatory public policy at [a third] Country X would itself offend international public policy, moreover, the arbitrator has a right to apply the law of Country X over and above the agreed . . . law so as to avoid offending that transcending public policy"). See also R. Kreindler *supra* footnote 246, p. 435. On the question whether the arbitrator is to be primarily the servant of the parties or that of truth see *ibid.*, pp. 439 *et seq.* See extensively on duties of the arbitrator when faced with issues of potential public policy violations and illegality, R. Kreindler, *supra* footnote 41, pp. 225 *et seq.*

[652]  For additional discussion, see B. Hanotiau and O. Caprasse, *supra* footnote 234, pp. 804 *et seq.*

tected. Yet both statutory and case law approaches show that some jurisdictions will uphold an award where one of these rights was even manifestly violated *unless* the violated party can demonstrate that the violation affected the outcome of the award. Thus some jurisdictions, such as Switzerland[653] by case law and Germany[654] by both case law and statute, require an outcome-determinative test.

The result is that not every violation of these rights will be fatal. And not every violation of New York Convention Article V (1) *(b)* or V (1) *(d)* would also be a violation of Article V (2) (b)[655]. Furthermore, even

---

[653] M. Scherer, "Introduction to the Case Law Section", *ASA Bulletin*, Vol. 30 (2012), p. 771.

[654] Bundesgerichtshof [German Federal Court of Justice], BGHZ 3, 215; P. Schlosser, Anhang § 1061, *Stein/ Jonas Kommentar zur Zivilprozessordnung*, 22nd ed., Tübingen, Mohr Siebeck, 2002, para. 82.

[655] See Art. V (1) *(b)*, New York Convention:

"Recognition and enforcement of the award may be refused, at the request of the party against whom it is invoked, only if that party furnishes to the competent authority where the recognition and enforcement is sought, proof that: . . . The party against whom the award is invoked was not given proper notice of the appointment of the arbitrator or of the arbitration proceedings or was otherwise unable to present his case";

Art. V (1) *(d)*, New York Convention:

"*(d)* The composition of the arbitral authority or the arbitral procedure was not in accordance with the agreement of the parties, or, failing such agreement, was not in accordance with the law of the country where the arbitration took place";

Art. V (2) *(b)*, New York Convention:

"Recognition and enforcement of an arbitral award may also be refused if the competent authority in the country where recognition and enforcement is sought finds that: . . . *(b)* The recognition or enforcement of the award would be contrary to the public policy of that country."

where the violation is fatal because the violated party succeeds in showing that the violation affected the outcome, the violation will not necessarily also be a violation of public policy, in this case procedural public policy.

Thus not every denial of equal treatment is fatal. And not every fatal denial of equal treatment is also proscribed by procedural public policy. In fact, vacatur or non-enforcement of an arbitral award on grounds of procedural public policy violations, however, is rare[656]. By way of example, in the oft-commented upon Swiss Federal Tribunal decision in *Egemetal* v. *Fuchs*[657] a wrong or arbitrary application of the agreed arbitration rules was not egregious enough to constitute a violation of public policy, in this case procedural public policy, under Section 190 (2) of the Swiss Federal Private International Law Act.

This disjuncture between a violation of equal treatment or due process on the one hand and a lack of violation of procedural due process on the other is noteworthy for at least two reasons.

*First*, under the New York Convention and the UNCITRAL Model Law we experience a duality of petition-driven objections and *ex officio* objections. That is, enforceability can be denied by the State court, *sua sponte*, on the ground of violation of procedural public policy, even if the debtor does not plead or does not prove violation of due process or equal treatment, including where the outcome-determinative test is applied by the State court.

*Second*, in investment arbitrations under the ICSID

---

[656] R. Kreindler and A. Tevini, *supra* footnote 233, p. 460; P. Pinsolle and R. Kreindler, *supra* footnote 285, p. 60.

[657] Tribunal Fédéral [Swiss Federal Tribunal], *Egemetal Demir Celik Sanayi ve Ticaret A.S.* v. *Fuchs Systemtechnik GmbH*, 28 April 2000, BGE 126 III 249.

Convention, the enforcement regime does not include a public policy ground for annulment at all, so that any alleged or even manifest violation of procedural public policy would need to be subsumed under — for example, manifest excess of powers.

With regard to treaty-based investment arbitration generally, of course the lack of specific reference to public policy as an annulment ground in the ICSID Convention has not led to the irrelevance of transnational *substantive* public policy in such arbitrations — quite the contrary — for example, the decision in *World Duty Free* on the prohibition against corruption. So why should that lack ofreference to public policy any more lead to the irrelevance of transnational *procedural* public policy in treaty-based investment arbitrations?

This should be the case even though the choice of law provisions in a bilateral investment treaty, the Energy Charter Treaty, or the ICSID Convention typically do not expressly refer to a governing international procedural law. The fact that a dispute is subject to principles of international law, coupled with the fact that the arbitration proceedings do not have a *lex arbitri* in the classic commercial arbitration sense, would suggest all the more need or even obligation to seek to ascertain and apply a transnational procedural public policy. Why?

Because, in such cases, an arbitrator's competence is based on an international treaty which contains a clear choice of law leading to application of international law principles, for example, pursuant to Article 44 ICSID Convention[658].

---

[658] G. C. Moss, "Tribunal's Powers versus Party Autonomy", in R. Muchlinski *et al.* (eds.), *The Oxford Handbook of International Investment Law*, New York, Oxford University Press, 2008, p. 1229.

And, in such cases, the arbitrator does not even have a national seat of arbitration. In such cases, surely the arbitrator can and must heed transnational substantive public policy. Therefore, in such cases, there is also no reason why he can and must not heed transnational procedural public policy.

What are those procedural principles, if "opportunity to be heard" and "equal treatment" do not fully capture the standard? To answer this question, there would appear to be no alternative to reviewing case law of leading jurisdictions, in the annulment and enforcement context. And examples from Germany, Switzerland, France and the United States are instructive here.

*First*, we come across some examples of actions which were held to be violations of procedural public policy, although not always in an international or transnational context, in recent years:

(a) disregard of the *res judicata* effect of an interim arbitral award in the same matter between the same parties [659];

---

[659] For Swiss courts' decisions see Tribunal Fédéral [Swiss Federal Tribunal], 13 April 2010, BGE 136 III 345 E 2, see also Tribunal Fédéral [Swiss Federal Tribunal], 19 February 1990, *ASA Bulletin*, Vol. 8 (1990), pp. 171 *et seq*. French courts do not handle *res judicata* concerns uniformly: for a case vacating an arbitral award for failure to apply *res judicata* rules, see Cour d'appel [CA] [regional court of appeal] Paris, 28 September 1979, *Revue de l'arbitrage* (1980), p. 506 (Fr.); for a judgment rejecting a public policy violation based on the tribunal's failure to apply *res judicata* rules, see Cour de cassation [Cass.] [supreme court for judicial matters] 1ᵉ civ., 5 February 1991, *Revue de l'arbitrage* (1991), p. 625 (Fr.); see also Cour d'appel [CA] [regional court of appeal] Paris, 9 June 1983, *Revue de l'arbitrage* (1983), p. 497 (Fr.); for an example of a US court decision see *Aircraft Braking Sys. Corp.* v. *Local 856, Int'l Union et al.*, 97 F. 3d 155, 159

*(b)* failure to include reasons for an arbitral award;

*(c)* violation of the right to impartial access to justice *(Gebot der überparteilichen Rechtspflege)*;

*(d)* violation of equal treatment in appointing the arbitral tribunal[660];

*(e)* unilateral communication by one party with the arbitral tribunal, which did not subsequently share the communication with the other party; the OLG Hamburg (1977) held that it was unable to exclude the possibility that a more favourable outcome might have been reached had the communication been shared;

*(f)* failure by the arbitral tribunal to comply with the parties' agreement to a time limit for the rendering of the award (Court of Appeals of Paris, 1995), since the time limit was inherent to the contractual character of arbitration; and

*(g)* a procedure which prevents a party from submitting any evidence whatsoever, even if the aggrieved party waived its right to object or even if that party expressly agreed to such procedure.

*Second*, we also have some examples of actions in violation of the agreed rules, equal treatment, and/or due process which were held not to be violations of procedural public policy, in recent years:

*(a)* refusal of the arbitral tribunal to stay its own proceedings in favour of an expected verdict in a pending criminal proceeding;

---

(6th Cir. 1996) ("Arbitrators are not free to ignore the preclusive effect of prior judgments under the doctrines of res judicata and collateral estoppel, . . .").

   [660] *Siemens* v. *Dutco*, French Cour de Cassation, 1992, NCCP §1520(2) and (5); but see Bundesgerichtshof [German Federal Court of Justice], 1 February 2001, *XXIX Yearbook Commercial Arbitration*, 2004, p. 708 (respecting procedures for the selection of arbitrators).

*(b)* denial of the right to introduce or comment on certain evidence where the arbitral tribunal did not base its award on such evidence[661];

*(c)* denial of the right to introduce or comment on certain evidence where the arbitral tribunal based its award on multiple sources of evidence, and not solely on the one source of evidence as to which due process was denied;

*(d)* denial of the right of further argument on points which the arbitral tribunal considered or would have considered to be irrelevant to its award;

*(e)* allowing the claimant to modify the legal basis for its claim in its final brief, on the grounds that a new legal clarification to the facts did not constitute *ultra petita*[662];

*(f)* allowing a sole arbitrator to be appointed by only one party, where there was no showing of any actual partiality on the part of the arbitrator and where the failure to participate in the appointment was the fault of the complaining party[663];

*(g)* regarding alleged conflicts of interests of a party's counsel[664];

---

[661] Bundesgerichtshof [German Federal Court of Justice], BGHZ 31, 43, 48.

[662] Tribunal Fédéral [Swiss Federal Tribunal], 30 December 1994, *XXI Yearbook Commercial Arbitration*, 1996, p. 172 (original in French, *ASA Bulletin*, Vol. 13 (1995), p. 217).

[663] Bundesgerichtshof [German Federal Court of Justice], 15 May 1986, *XII Yearbook Commercial Arbitration*, 1987, pp. 489 *et seq*; cf. Bundesgerichtshof [German Federal Court of Justice], 1 February 2001, *XXIX Yearbook Commercial Arbitration*, 2004, p. 708 (respecting procedures for the selection of arbitrators).

[664] *Fitzroy Eng'g* v. *Flame Eng'g, Inc.*, 1994 US Dist. LEXIS 17781 (ND Ill. 1994).

*(h)* respecting the lack of presence of an allegedly necessary party to the proceedings[665];

*(i)* respecting the submission of fraudulent evidence in the proceedings[666];

*(j)* allowing an allegedly biased expert, where no clear partiality was shown and the complaining party did not make timely objection[667]; and

*(k)* refusal of arbitral tribunal to permit further cross-examination, where no effect on the outcome was shown and arbitral tribunal was held not to have taken into account the objectionable contents of the prior witness testimony in rendering its award[668].

Interestingly, the yardstick for the outcome-determinative test is the perspective of the arbitral tribunal, and not of the reviewing court or of the allegedly aggrieved party. This is potentially problematic, however, since it means that no violation will be found as long as the arbitrators establish the "fact" of there being no effect of their own violation on the outcome of the award.

The question remains which violations can be considered to be part of what a transnational procedural public policy condemns and forbids. Likely candidates include *(a)* disregard of the *res judicata* effect of an award in the same matter between the same parties, *(b)* violation of the right to impartial access to justice *(Gebot der überparteilichen Rechtspflege)*, *(c)* violation of equal treatment in appointing the arbitral tribu-

---

[665] *Nicor Int'l Corp.* v. *El Paso Corp.*, 292 F. Supp. 2d 1357 (SD Fla. 2003).

[666] Oberster Gerichtshof [Austrian Supreme Court of Justice], 26 January 2005, *XXX Yearbook Commercial Arbitration*, 2005, p. 421.

[667] Tribunal Fédéral [Swiss Federal Tribunal], BGE 126 III 249.

[668] *Generica, Ltd.* v. *Pharmaceutical Basics, Inc.*, 125 F. 3d 1123 (7th Cir. 1997).

nal, *(d)* unilateral substantive communication by one party with the arbitral tribunal, which did not subsequently share the communication with the other party, and *(e)* a procedure which prevents a party from submitting any evidence whatsoever, even if the aggrieved party waived its right to object or even if that party expressly agreed to such procedure.

One obstacle in the way of positing a truly transnational procedural public policy on a wide front is that, largely speaking, the Anglo-American and Continental European conceptions of procedural public policy differ: The former relates somewhat narrowly to public morals and health and safety, the latter more widely to "breaches of procedural justice"[669]. On the other hand, almost to disprove the point, the US Federal Arbitration Act (FAA) annulment grounds respecting procedure[670] are arguably more expansive or in any event more explicit than those in the UNCITRAL Model Law[671], German law[672] or Swiss law[673].

They include within "arbitrator misconduct" acts such as

"refusal to postpone the hearing, upon sufficient cause shown, refusal to hear evidence pertinent and material to the controversy, or of any other misbehavior by which the rights of any party have been prejudiced"[674].

Similarly, the English Arbitration Act 1996, Sections 68 (1) and (2), speak to "serious irregularity", includ-

---

[669] Cf., ILA Interim Report on Public Policy as Bar to Enforcement of International Arbitral Awards, 2000, at 10.

[670] See § 10 *(a)*, FAA.

[671] See Art. 34 (2) *(b)* (ii), UNCITRAL Model Law.

[672] See Sec. 1059 ZPO (German Code of Civil Procedure).

[673] See Art. 190 (2) *(e)*, PILA.

[674] FAA § 10 *(a)* (3).

ing "the award or the way in which it was procured being contrary to public policy"[675].

Here the test is not solely outcome-determinative in contrast to Germany: if the procedure used in order to reach the award was seriously irregular, it may offend public policy irrespective of whether it impacted on the outcome of the award[676]. Query whether US case law is actually converging more with Continental European concepts of procedural public policy. While the ILA Final Report states that "It is widely accepted that procedural public policy should not include manifest disregard of the law or of the facts", case law in the United States has allowed for such an annulment ground, arguably within the context of procedural public policy. However, the recent US Supreme Court decision in *Hall Street Associates, LLC*. v. *Mattel, Inc.*[677] betokens a possible retreat, and thereby a possible falling in line with transnational procedural public policy.

The UNCITRAL Model Law Commission Report states that public policy, as used in the New York Convention Article V (2) *(b)* encompasses both procedural and substantive elements. This is helpful as far as it goes: a violation of procedure can be a violation of public policy. The ILA Final Report on Public Policy as Bar to Enforcement of International Arbitral Awards, 2002, Rec. 1 *(c)*, is to the same effect. But it no more provides a content or meaning to procedural public policy than it does to substantive public policy.

If we go back to the public international law notion

---

[675] See Sec. 68 (2) *(g)*, English Arbitration Act.

[676] See Sec. 68 (1), English Arbitration Act, which explicitly provides for the possibility to challenge the arbitral award "on the ground of serious irregularity affecting the tribunal, the proceedings *or* the award" (emphasis added).

[677] 128 S. Ct. 1396 (2008).

of "consensus" and the accepted way of ascertaining such consensus, procedural public policy seems to prove trickier than substantive public policy: notwithstanding the Model Law Article 18, the ILA, the New York Convention and for that matter the IBA Rules on Taking of Evidence, conventions and statutes (with the partial exception of the US FAA) do not readily provide a basis for determining whether there is a consensus. Essentially, only case law is reliable here. And in view of the modern trend to de-emphasize the law of the seat, including its procedure, except for mandatory norms, the law of the seat is generally quite unobtrusive.

Ultimately, an identification of an international procedural public policy or a transnational procedural public policy is not easy, and is a function largely of case law. On the premise that increasing cross-pollination of best practices in international arbitration may accelerate the establishment of cross-border procedural norms, the next ten years or so may see a clearer consensus on a procedural level emerging. And the further acceptance of the best practices in the IBA Rules of Evidence, revised in 2010, could conceivably accelerate that process all the more, including in the area of investment arbitration without a seat.

### (d) *Policy-related concerns, including enforceability*

In view of the foregoing, the question remains of whether the duties of the arbitrator include an obligation to render an enforceable award, including in the context of procedural public policy. Is the enforceability of the ultimate award a duty or does it inform the duties of the arbitral tribunal, or is it rather a "mere" goal? The question is relevant generally in commercial and investment arbitration, but also specifically in the context of illegality and corruption issues which may affect the enforceability of the award, including in the context of competence-competence, arbitrability and other controls.

The question is put into focus by the 2012 ICC Rules and their Article 41 (formerly Article 35 in the 1998 Rules), which provides:

> "In all matters not expressly provided for in the Rules, the Court and the arbitral tribunal *shall act in the spirit of the Rule*s and *shall make every effort to make sure that the award is enforceable at law*."

This is to be compared with the 1998 LCIA Rules Article 32 (2), which provides:

> "In all matters not expressly provided for in these Rules, the LCIA Court, the Arbitral Tribunal and the parties *shall act in the spirit of these Rules* and *shall make every reasonable effort* to ensure that an award is legally enforceable."

If one sought a comparable provision in the ICSID context, the closest might be ICSID Arbitration Rules Article 20 (2):

> "In the conduct of the proceeding the Tribunal shall apply any agreement between the parties on procedural matters, except as otherwise provided in the Convention or the Administrative and Financial Regulations."

The ICC recital contains the strongest reflection of a hortatory, not precatory provision approaching the concept of a duty: the arbitral tribunal "shall make every effort to make sure that the award is enforceable at law". The LCIA equivalent speaks, somewhat more mildly, of "shall make every reasonable effort". Both provisions foresee governance by this rule in "all matters not expressly provided for in" the respective rules, which of course is a vast array of situations. Both provisions abstain from specifying under what law and where the "enforceability at law" is to be sought.

It can be readily agreed that "enforceability at law" in international commercial arbitration and also in international investment arbitrations which have a juridical seat must include enforceability under the one law which is beyond question: the law of the seat of arbitration which has either been agreed or, in the absence of agreement, been fixed by the institution, the tribunal or a court depending on the circumstances. The *lex arbitri* is the one clear port of call for enforceability, insofar as under the prevailing theory of territoriality in international commercial arbitration the award can be annulled solely at the seat, and not elsewhere[678]. While this principle has had its competitors in prior decades[679], and while certain courts even to the present day have purported to annul awards not rendered in their jurisdiction[680], the territoriality principle governs far and wide[681].

In that regard, query whether an arbitrator with a known seat has a duty to make every effort to make sure that the award is enforceable at law under the *lex arbitri*. It is submitted that the answer should be yes, as long as it is understood that this is a mandatory aspirational duty, and not a duty to guarantee a result. As for

---

[678] See Art. V (1) *(e)* of the New York Convention. See also G. B. Born, *supra* footnote 4, pp. 1260, 1287.

[679] *Oil & Natural Gas Commission* v. *Western Company of North America* (1987), All Indian Reports SC 674; *National Thermal Power Corporation* v. *The Singer Corp. et al.* 1992 (3) 7 Judgments Today SC 198.

[680] *Venture Global Engineering* v. *Satyam Computer Services Ltd. & Anr*, Supreme Court of India, Civil Appeal No. 309 of 2008.

[681] See, e.g., G. B. Born, *supra* footnote 4, p. 2412.

enforceability under the law of another jurisdiction award from the seat, including a country in which indisputably all enforceable assets are uniquely located and the parties have announced they will confine any compulsory enforcement efforts, query whether the duty still holds.

It is submitted that the duty can still not be as great in such circumstances as under the law at the seat, but that the duty still exists. Indeed how could it not be so in cases where the seat of arbitration was chosen, as is often the case, precisely because of its complete lack of connectedness to all of the parties and their assets whereas another jurisdiction is agreed by the parties to be the sole place of potential useful recognition and enforcement? A tribunal's manifest disregard of the law at that other place would not seem to be consistent with the "every effort" or even "every reasonable effort" command, but again the duty certainly cannot be transformed into a guarantee of results.

The analysis is of course even more complex in the case of investment treaty-based arbitrations, notably ICSID, without a juridical seat, where the ICSID Convention and ICSID Arbitration Rules do not contain such a hortatory provision, where there is no *lex arbitri per se*, and where annulment proceedings are conducted pursuant to the ICSID annulment mechanism by annulment committees and not in the national courts.

In commercial arbitrations with a classical seat, the grounds for annulment which may be relevant to the existence and content of a duty of the arbitrator to render an enforceable award, including in the context of illegality, are well encapsulated in UNCITRAL Model Law Article 34 (2) and its grounds for "recourse against the award": (i) incapacity, invalidity of arbitration agreement, (ii) lack of proper notice or of due process, (iii) lack of jurisdiction or an excess of authority, (iv) improper procedure, (v) lack of arbitrability, and (vi) *against public policy*. These are to be compared with the grounds in ICSID Convention Article 52 for "annulment": *(a)* improper constitution, *(b) manifest excess of powers*, *(c)* corruption by arbitrator, *(d)* serious departure from fundamental rule of procedure, or *(e)* failure of award to state reasons.

The ICSID grounds, notably, do not mention the arbitration agreement, do not mention due process, do not mention lack of jurisdiction, do not mention arbitrability, and do not mention public policy. Any or all of these grounds may be subsumed under "manifest excess of powers", as discussed above[682].

## 3. The arbitrator's investigative rights and duties in the context of corruption

In the context of illegality and corruption allegations, suspicions and findings, the arbitrator is confronted with a challenge of investigation of facts, difficulties of proof and concealment or denial of actions. Even assuming the far-ranging prerogatives accorded the arbitral tribunal under, for example, the ICC Rules, are there no *limits* to the tribunal's ability to investigate illegality, especially when the legality is not manifest or not even expressly alleged? The tribunal may fear that in the event of an underlying illegality and the rendering of an award on the merits, it would be acting as an accomplice to an illegal enterprise, or contributing to a violation of local or transnational public policy. Under such circumstances and given the imperative of avoiding such "complicity", is "mere" suspicion of illegality enough justification for the tribunal to investigate, *sua sponte*, the possible illegality?

---

[682] See *supra* Chapter II.G.3, Chapter III.A.2 and Chapter III.B.3.c.

## 4. *Should or must an arbitrator always decide illegality when alleged?*

Both in commercial and in investment treaty-based arbitration, the answer should normally be yes, assuming the respective prerequisites have been fulfilled: competence, arbitrability, admissibility, jurisdiction, relatedness, etc.

It is submitted that where the claim or defense is *expressly* premised on another party's corruption, or on joint corruption, then the arbitrator must investigate and rule on the existence and consequences of the alleged illegality. Furthermore, neither in commercial nor investment arbitration should most admitted illegality undo the residual competence of the arbitrator, as part of the competence-competence, to negatively declare a lack of jurisdiction or inadmissibility.

In this regard, there may be certain particularities of investment-treaty arbitration. In the investment context, the application of international instruments leads to the application of international rules of law against corruption, which it is submitted should lead to a duty on that basis to investigate corruption. However, there has in fact been an inconsistency in ICSID investment approaches, partly depending on the evidentiary standard applied.

On the one hand, there has been what may be called the "eyes shut" approach, reflected by such decisions as *SPP* v. *Egypt* (1992)[683], *Azurix* v. *Argentina* (2006)[684], *African Holdings* v. *Congo* (2008)[685] and *EDF* v. *Romania* (2009)[686]. On the other hand, there is the "zero tolerance" approach, reflected by *World*

---

[683] *SPP* v. *Egypt*, *supra* footnote 450.

[684] *Azurix Corp.* v. *Argentine Republic*, ICSID Case No. ARB/01/12, Award of 14 July 2006.

[685] *African Holding* v. *Congo*, *supra* footnote 605.

[686] *EDF* v. *Romania*, *supra* footnote 565.

*Duty Free* v. *Kenya* (2006)[687] and *Plama* v. *Bulgaria* (2008)[688].

In the former approach, the arbitral tribunal does not necessarily investigate, in the latter case it does. The additional wrinkle here in ICSID cases is the increased likelihood of third-party allegations due to the greater transparency of the proceedings and even the possibility in some cases of *amicus curiae* participation in the arbitration under ICSID Arbitration Rules Article 37: ". . .; submissions of non-disputing parties"[689].

What could be the justification for turning a blind eye to the illegality[690]? One school of thought would be that the tribunal is primarily a servant of the parties in their private adjudicatory process, even if the tribunal's conduct is likewise subject to concurrent review by the courts (but only if there indeed is any such review). Accordingly, the tribunal should limit its analysis to the contractual rights and obligations of the parties, in a civil law and not penal law context. If, for example, a "commission" was not paid, then presumably the reason for the non-payment was that the bargain was not kept. This would be simply a matter of proof, and would be confined to what the contract required the parties to do — as opposed to a value judgment as to the legality of the contract.

To be sure, the arbitrator is an instrument brought to life by the parties and first and foremost an adjudicator of their internal relations. It is also true that he is charged with applying the legal standard agreed by the

---

[687] *World Duty Free* v. *Kenya*, *supra* footnote 44.

[688] *Plama* v. *Bulgaria*, *supra* footnote 372.

[689] Art. 37 of the ICSID Arbitration Rules, available at https://icsid.worldbank.org/ICSID/StaticFiles/basicdoc/CRR_English-final.pdf.

[690] See generally R. Kreindler, *supra* footnote 41, pp. 253 *et seq.*

parties or, in the absence of agreement, as determined according to the applicable procedural and substantive rules. Indeed he is also "bound" by a valid waiver in advance of the parties' rights to challenge an award by set aside proceedings, to the extent such a waiver can validly be made and has been validly made under the applicable law including notably that of the seat[691]. Particularly in those countries such as Switzerland, where such a waiver of possible grounds for nullification is possible based on, for example, the underlying illegality of the contract, why should the arbitrator be concerned about such illegality?

The answer is that there are a number of reasons why the determination of the illegality, and the drawing of the consequences therefrom, remain the business and the duty of the arbitrator. Flowing from the various duties of the arbitrator discussed above is a duty to adjudicate the dispute in its various facets. This includes the determination of the illegality, also in those situations where the tribunal may need to initiate an inquiry into the illegality itself. The fact that the parties may, in rare instances, have validly waived their right of recourse in no way softens the existence or reach of the tribunal's duties.

(a) *Degree or lack of reviewability of the award*

Knowledge that the award will not be subject to review by the courts at the seat even on public policy

---

[691] See, e.g., Art. 192 of the Swiss Private International Law Act:

"Provided that neither of the parties has its domicile, habitual residence or place of business in Switzerland, they can agree, in express terms either in the arbitration agreement or in a subsequent agreement, to waive the right to file an appeal; they can also exclude some of the grounds set out in Art. 190 para. 2."

grounds should not embolden the arbitrator to be lax in consideration of illegality. Rather, the finality of the award and the impossibility of nullification of the findings on illegality should doubly motivate the tribunal to determine the illegality and rule on it.

Of course, even a commercial award as to which annulment has been validly ruled out may still be subject to denial of enforcement either at the seat[692] or elsewhere. Therefore, all of the duties which may flow from Article V of the New York Convention, and equivalent or parallel national legislation on cross-border enforcement, will enable the award debtor, or the enforcing court *ex officio*, to review the tribunal's award to a certain degree respecting illegality.

(b) *The limited extent and quality of review of the award*

Where the award is normally subject to review by the courts at the seat (and elsewhere), the tribunal should still not turn a blind eye to suspected, admitted or manifest illegality of the contract and the parties. The fact that the courts at the seat and/or at a place of attempted enforcement abroad might have an opportunity to review and assess the illegality themselves does not make it any less imperative for the award already to have done so.

The award is meant, to the greatest extent possible, to be final and binding. It is meant to be based on the arbitrators' conscientious establishment of the facts

---

[692] Art. 192 (2) of the Swiss Private International Law Act provides:

"Have the parties agreed on a total waiver of their rights to file an appeal and shall the award be enforced in Switzerland, the New York Convention of June 10, 1958 on the Recognition and Enforcement of Foreign Awards applies accordingly."

and, where necessary, the law of the case on the basis of often copious and extensive taking of evidence. The reviewing or enforcing court, even if it were entitled to review certain elements of the illegality essentially *de novo*, cannot possibly have the same access to the evidence as did the tribunal. In most cases, the reviewing court is not allowed to conduct such an enquiry in any event. Therefore, the tribunal must not forsake the opportunities provided by the unique access which it has to the facts during the arbitration.

(c) *The unlikelihood of review or annulment of the award*

The prospect of review by a court at the seat or elsewhere should not be seen as a Sword of Damocles. The award is meant to be final and binding and to be carried out voluntarily by the parties, without attack at the courts of the seat and without compulsory enforcement there or abroad. The strength of a well-reasoned and judiciously penned award lies in large part in the hope that it will be complied with by the parties without further ado.

For this reason, the duty of the tribunal to address the illegality issue may be seen as all the more compelling. The parties may determine from the award that the tribunal has carefully considered the existence and ramifications of the illegality, and that the award stands up to scrutiny in this and all other respects which might affect its enforceability. Moreover, it is conceivable that the award will never be attacked in the first place, for whatever reason.

(d) *The quality of the award and its subsequent scrutiny*

Precisely because of the unique position of the tribunal to assess the illegality, it should carry out its taking of the evidence respecting the illegality with a depth and transparency that any effective reviewing court can readily appreciate. The greater the doubts of the reviewing court as to the precision of the tribunal's analysis of the illegality, the greater the likelihood that the reviewing court may take it upon itself to revisit the evidence respecting the illegality. In those jurisdictions, such as England and the United States, where the tribunal may have a statutory basis for reviewing manifest errors respecting the illegality finding, the likelihood of second-guessing by the court could rise.

### (e) *The precedential value or use of the award*

It is not the primary duty of the tribunal to be concerned with the precedential value of its award, whether as a result of an official reporting of its findings via subsequent court proceedings or by its entering into the bloodstream of arbitral practice and jurisprudence through unseen channels. On the other hand, in view of the importance of combating illegality and the difficulties of defining any "consensus" as to which kinds of illegality offend public policy transnationally, it is all the more important to ensure transparency and uniformity on this issue, where possible.

The award should not be rendered primarily on the basis of "how it might read" if and when published. At the same time, the fact that it is a private adjudication process does not mean that the award is rendered in a vacuum. The background of public policy concerns at the seat and elsewhere is particularly important where standards of illegality are still emerging and in need of further embellishment.

### (f) *Social engineering within the constraints of the arbitral mandate*

There is no uniform code of ethics regarding illegality and corruption. Arbitrators cannot pretend to impose one of their own making. At the same time, the fact that there is no single transnational public policy even as to certain kinds of corruption and illegality does not make the goal of striving toward such uniformity any less important. Certain issues of illegality remains regional, cultural, religion-based, etc., and depend on arguably parochial needs which may make the ends justify the means in one region but not another. These parochial standards are a product of socio-political conditions and cannot always be prejudged by an outsider.

However, this should not prevent an arbitrator from endeavouring to establish and civilly sanction the illegality. He may do so based on the standards agreed by the parties or as otherwise determined by the arbitrators, and subject to public policy as the tribunal perceives it.

The arbitrator has no mandate to engage in social engineering, but it would be a mistake to assume that his office did not give him a legitimate platform from which to investigate and combat illegality, within the constraints of his mission.

### (g) *Toleration of illegality as a discouragement for future conduct*

A failure or refusal to address the illegality issue head-on in arbitral proceedings could be seen as a toleration, or indeed perpetuation of nefarious practices. While those practices might be tolerated and widespread in a particular country, the arbitrator should not condone or support hindrances to the elimination of those practices.

Seen less in the context of a private adjudication as in the context of transnational goals, ignoring or tolerating illegality in such situations can be seen as contributing to distortion and suppression of competitive forces as well as discouragement of future investment. The arbitrator's primary duty is not one of righting the world's wrongs. On the other hand, to the extent arbitration has become a method of choice for transnational, East-West and North-South dispute resolution, the larger implications of ignoring illegality in contracts, particularly at the State level, cannot be smoothed over.

(h) *Pressure and moral suasion on the reviewing instance*

In those cases where the arbitrator's findings respecting illegality are attacked either at the seat or elsewhere, the State judiciary will of course be implicated in the decision on illegality. To the extent the arbitrators have made a conscientious and unobjectionable ruling as to the existence and consequences of the illegality under the applicable standards, the reviewing or enforcing court may be obliged to decide whether to condone or reward the illegality.

This is a useful pressure and moral suasion to place on the courts, particularly in the context of their transnational obligations under Article V (2) *(b)* of the New York Convention, where applicable.

(i) *The undesirable option of resignation*

Resignation from office in the face of a distasteful or otherwise troublesome illegality should not be countenanced, except insofar as the reasons relate to an inability to guarantee continuing impartiality or other incapacity in carrying out the arbitrator role. Otherwise, throwing in the towel could be seen as aiding and abetting the underlying illegality and abdicating the powers and duties which the arbitrator has to civilly sanction the illegality.

Indeed resignation might be seen as a form of

complicity in the original illegality where the arbitrator surrendered his opportunity to actively condemn. Depending upon the applicable rules, resignation without rendering any ruling or award at least confirming the illegality might allow the parties to seek another tribunal which could take a softer approach to the issue. Where the tribunal concludes that it must resign on the grounds of lack of jurisdiction due to the voidness of the contract and the arbitration agreement, the tribunal should strive for a legitimate basis to do so by enforceable award with *res judicata* effect, within the confines of relevant law on competence-competence and arbitrability. For the arbitrator has just as much a duty to ensure that illegal contracts referred to him are not allowed to flourish, by rendering a corresponding award, as to ensure that legal contracts referred to him are allowed to stand, also by rendering an award[693].

(j) *The arbitrator and the appointing authority*

To what extent should the arbitrator who has suspected or established serious illegality inform the

---

[693] Cf. Y. Derains, "'Observations' following Award in ICC Case No. 4145", *Journal du droit international*, Vol. 112, pp. 987-990, discussing Lagergren decision, *supra* footnote 3:

"Les parties s'étant engagées dans une activité réprouvée par le droit, elles ne sauraient faire appel à lui. Si cette optique procédurale est conceptuellement fort éloignée de celle qui voudrait que le caractère illicite du contrat conduise à son annulation, le résultat est pratiquement le même puisque dans les deux cas la demande d'exécution du contrat est rejetée."

See also *Hilmarton (Agent)* v. *Omnium/Algeria*, ICC Case No. 5622 (1988), *supra* footnote 196, in which the tribunal decided to proceed to the merits of the dispute and said this approach was to be preferred "since it makes it possible to declare null and void all contracts which are illicit or contrary to morality".

appointing authority or other arbitral supervisory institution to which the parties are deemed to have agreed by their arbitration clause or by operation of, for example, a bilateral investment treaty? Invariably, it may be contended that the arbitral institution shares with the arbitrators the duty of acting in the spirit of the applicable rules, including efforts to render an award enforceable at law. In the case of the ICC, this duty will arise more apparently than with certain other institutions, in view of its involvement, albeit of a largely administrative nature, in the scrutiny of the award.

Where the institution has the power, and perhaps the duty, to ascertain whether a manifest or apparent illegality exists such as to call into question the existence of the related ICC arbitration agreement, the institution may also have a right to be informed of an illegality later on, after its prima facie inspection of the basis for arbitration. There would appear to be no reason not to entitle and even obligate the arbitrator to inform the tribunal of such illegality, particularly in those cases where the circumstances give rise to penal sanctions which go beyond the arbitrator's review of the civil obligations between the contracting parties.

Ultimately, in extreme cases of illicitness, the institution might have no obligation to participate as appointing or administering authority if such participation constituted abetting a manifestly illegal enterprise. The appointing authority to which the parties agreed or are deemed to have agreed can no more validly derogate from mandatory public policy constraints than can the arbitrator.

Indeed Article 41 of the ICC Rules expressly imposes a duty not only on the tribunal, but also on the ICC Court, and thereby on the entire ICC arbitral institution. On the basis of the wording of the provision ("In all matters not expressly provided for in these Rules . . . shall act in the spirit of these Rules . . ."), the argument is most often made that Article 41, and its former equivalent Article 25, does not impose any supplemental duty on the tribunal or the ICC Court which is not already set forth in the Rules. Article 6 gives express prerogatives to the ICC Court particularly at the opening stage of the arbitration. Any tribunal-initiated enquiry into suspected illegality would, it might be reasoned, be possible only in the context of Article 6. The tribunal is bestowed with competence-competence under Article 6 only after the ICC Court is "*prima facie* satisfied" under Article 6 (4). In this sense, it is reasoned, the *institution* has the power, and indeed perhaps the duty, to ascertain whether a manifest or apparent illegality exists such as to call into question the existence of the related ICC arbitration agreement[694].

Such power would appear to emerge from the wording of Article 6 (4). Such duty would appear to emerge from Article 41 as applied to the institution, unless by circular reasoning Article 41 was deemed not to apply since Article 6 provides that the Court "may decide" and not "shall decide". That reasoning would indeed be circular and counterproductive, since Article 6 (4) itself provides that the Court may decide, *or may not decide*, that an ICC arbitration agreement may exist.

In the extreme case, where a would-be claimant

---

[694] But cf., e.g., Arts. 1 (3) and 36 of the 1998 AAA International Arbitration Rules, which do not provide the same framework for analysis: Art. 1 (3) provides: "These rules specify the duties and responsibilities of the administrator, the American Arbitration Association." Art. 36 provides: "The tribunal shall interpret and apply these rules insofar as they relate to its powers and duties. The administrator shall interpret and apply all other rules." Absent provisions and mechanisms comparable to Art. 6 of the ICC Rules, the AAA administrator would not appear to have the same rights, or duties, respecting initial illegality as may redound to the ICC Court.

files a Request for Arbitration relating to an illicit contract promoting or facilitating prostitution and containing a standard ICC arbitration clause, can or must the ICC Court exercise Article 6 (4) to decline to entertain the arbitration? The answer would appear to be affirmative, and based at least in part on Article 41[695]. When this power and duty of the institution will apply in less clear-cut cases of illegality is a greater problem. In any event, the opportunity to decline to entertain the arbitration firmly exists. In the case of a pure *ad hoc* arbitration, such opportunity will not arise with an institution. Instead, the national courts of appropriate jurisdiction, normally at the seat of arbitration, may be the best or only alternative for stay or dismissal of the arbitration in such overt cases of illegality[696].

---

[695] Cf. also Art. 1.1 of Appendix I (Statutes of the International Court of Arbitration of the ICC): "The function of the International Court of Arbitration . . . is to ensure the application of the [ICC Rules], and it has all the necessary powers for that purpose."

[696] For example, Chapter 12 of the Swiss Private International Law Act, which of course may also apply in non-institutional arbitrations with a Swiss seat and at least one non-Swiss party, presumably gives the tribunal a similar power, and even duty. Art. 186 (1) provides succinctly: "The arbitral tribunal shall decide on its own jurisdiction." This provision may be construed to entitle the tribunal to decide on its jurisdiction, and deny it, even when not raised or attacked by any party. That decision is subject to the control of the reviewing court, the Federal Tribunal, under Art. 190 (2) *(b)*: "Proceedings for setting aside the award may only be initiated: . . . Where the arbitral tribunal has wrongly declared itself to have or not to have jurisdiction." Cf. Lalive Poudret Reymond, *Le droit de l'arbitrage interne et international en Suisse* (1989), Art. 186 n. 11, reasoning that the tribunal should not necessarily always verify its own jurisdiction except, in international arbitrations, where Swiss international public policy may otherwise be violated:

"[L]'arbitre qui constate qu'il est saisi d'une

The case of a semi-administered *ad hoc* arbitration such as under the UNCITRAL *ad hoc* rules is somewhat different. There, any appointing institution stipulated in the arbitration agreement (or by default the Secretary-General of the Permanent Court of Arbitration at The Hague) will presumably be limited to functions related to appointment, as opposed to prima facie acceptance of the Request for Arbitration. To that extent, the appointing institution would appear to have no express power, or duty, to decline to entertain the arbitration in the sense of its appointment functions.

On the other hand, coming back again to the extreme case of an illicit contract relating to prostitution, the institution would arguably likewise have no obligation to participate as appointing authority if such participation constituted abetting a manifestly illegal enterprise. Support for an institutional refusal to offer

---

demande non arbitrable au sens de l'art. 177 doit-il se déclarer d'office incompétent? Cela paraît être le cas en arbitrage interne . . ., mais la loi fédérale ne contient pas de disposition semblable en matière d'arbitrage international . . . A notre avis et contrairement à celui de Marc Blessing (p. 53), l'art. 177 al. 1$^{er}$ n'est pas, comme tel, d'ordre public. S'il *convient aux parties de soumettre une contestation non pécuniaire à l'arbitrage, l'arbitre ne peut pas, de ce seul fait, se déclarer d'office incompétent. En revanche il peut le faire, nous semble-t-il, s'il estime que l'ordre public international de la Suisse s'oppose à ce que la contestation dont il est saisi soit portée devant un arbitre.*" (Emphasis added.)

In international arbitrations in Switzerland, the standard of public policy under Art. 190 (2) *(e)* (setting aside "where the award is incompatible with public policy") may be equated with Swiss notions of international public policy as opposed to local Swiss *lois de police*. In that context, the Act may be seen as authorizing self-enquiry by the tribunal into its jurisdiction *vel non* in the face of a suspected or manifest illegality.

its appointing services might be found directly in Article 1 (2) of the UNCITRAL Rules:

> "These Rules shall govern the arbitration except that where any of these Rules is in conflict with a provision of the law applicable to the arbitration from which the parties cannot derogate, that provision shall prevail."

The appointing authority is bound by the Rules. At the same time, the Rules calling for its assistance in constitution of a tribunal (whose basis is an illegal contract and also a void arbitration agreement) cannot supersede mandatory public policy. This is clear from the Rules themselves: "except that where any of these Rules is in conflict with a provision of the law applicable to the arbitration from which the parties cannot derogate". Such public policy must be deemed to encompass the nullity of manifestly offensive contracts. Neither the parties nor the appointing authority can validly derogate from such public policy.

Defining *which* national or transnational public policy should apply is, again, a potential challenge. In the case of prostitution, child abuse, torture, slavery, drug trafficking and the like, there will presumably be little or no room to contend that international public policy does not offer a global proscription — even if there were somehow room to contend that some *local* public policy does not expressly proscribe such conduct.

In the context of the foregoing, the arbitrator should inform the institution of circumstances which might cause the institution unwittingly to engage in such derogation from mandatory public policy. Providing such information to the institution should not be seen as in any way comprising the confidentiality of the relationship which may be deemed to exist between and among the parties and the tribunal. Indeed this fits in precisely with those confidentiality obligations

which are expressly included in arbitration rules, which
contain exceptions as in the LCIA Rules Article 30.1
and 30.2, as applied to the arbitrator:

> "save and to the extent that disclosure may be
> required of a party by legal duty, to protect or
> pursue a legal right or to enforce or challenge an
> award in bona fide legal proceedings before a state
> court or other judicial authority".

While this wording admittedly speaks of "a party"
and not of the arbitrator, it is submitted that it equally
allows for an exception to confidentiality on the part of
the arbitrator. The right or even duty on the part of the
arbitrator is no less compelling in the case of the vast
majority of arbitration rules, legislation and jurisprudence, which do not contain an express confidentiality
obligation. There too the arbitrator may be seen as
having a "legal duty" to inform the institution or
the authorities of the corruption, including, as in the
Australian and New Zealand approach, in the context
of the "public interest"[697].

In any event, any implied or even express confidentiality duty may be a red herring to the extent that the
duty or right to disclose may be seen as overriding the
confidentiality duty or establishing an exception to it,
also as a matter of public policy.

*First*, a failure to report a suspicion, admission or
finding of a crime itself to the authorities may be seen
as a crime by the arbitrator under the national law at
the seat, if any, under the national law at the locus of
the crime, or under mutual legal assistance and
enforcement provisions of international anti-corruption
treaties, to the extent applicable not only to judicial
authorities but also to tribunals[698].

---

[697] R. Kreindler, *supra* footnote 246, p. 447.
[698] M. Hwang and K. Lim, *supra* footnote 8, p. 48.

*Second*, a failure to report to the institution may be seen as a malfeasance by the arbitrator under the rules of arbitration or internal rules of the arbitral appointing institution, if any, or as a matter of a perceived contract between and among the arbitrator, the parties and the arbitral institution, for example, in the German sense of a *Schiedsrichtervertrag*[699].

*Third*, there may be the possibility of attribution to the arbitrator of a quasi-judicial function with public competence under the national law at the seat, if any, under the national law at the locus of the crime, or again under mutual legal assistance and enforcement provisions of international anti-corruption treaties[700].

*Fourth*, there may be relevant national legislation to which the arbitrator is subject, at the seat, for example respecting money-laundering. Australian law provides a case in point: Secs. 23D (1) and 23D (8)-(9), International Arbitration Act 1974 as revised through 2010[701]. Even more vividly, in Singapore, Sec. 39 (1) of the Corruption, Drug Trafficking and Other Serious Crimes Act stipulates a specific duty of the arbitrator with a seat in Singapore:

> "knows or has reasonable grounds to suspect . . . shall disclose . . . to a Suspicious Transaction Reporting Officer . . . the disclosure shall not be

---

[699] P. Schlosser, Vorbemerkungen vor § 1025, *Stein/Jonas Kommentar zur Zivilprozessordnung*, 22nd ed., Tübingen, Mohr Siebeck, 2002, paras. 7 *et seq.*; see also *supra* footnote 53.

[700] Regarding the status of the arbitrators and the governing rules, see E. Gaillard and J. Savage (eds.), *supra* footnote 1, paras. 1010 *et seq.*; ICC (ed.), "Final Report on the Status of the Arbitrator", *ICC Bulletin*, Vol. 7 (1996), pp. 37 *et seq.*

[701] Cf. R. Garnett and L. Nottage, "The 2010 Amendments to the International Arbitration Act: A New Dawn for Australia?", *Asian International Arbitration Journal*, Vol. 7 (2011), p. 29 *et seq.*

treated as a breach of any restriction upon the disclosure imposed by the law, contract or rules of professional conduct . . .".

Query whether this duty applies regarding illegality having its locus away from a Singapore seat.

*Fifth*, there may be national legislation to which the arbitrator is subject, away from the seat. The Singapore SIAC Rules 2010 provide that the arbitrator may disclose matters relating to arbitration "in compliance with the provisions of the laws of any State which are binding on the party making the disclosure", which could be a law away from seat[702].

*Sixth*, investment-treaty arbitrations under a BIT or MIT without a juridical seat may also result in a right or even duty on the party of the arbitrator to disclose. National legislation of the locus of illegality could still apply, including notably host State laws. Furthermore, a national court order of disclosure "in the public interest" could still apply, for example, in the Australian model[703]. Moreover, national legislative exceptions for "public interest" or "interests of justice" could still apply, in the Australian or New Zealand conception.

*Seventh*, the right of the arbitrator to enlist a State court's assistance in taking of evidence as effective disclosure should not be forgotten, even if admittedly it is made use of fairly infrequently. Thus, for example, UNCITRAL Model Law Article 27 provides:

> "The arbitral tribunal or a party with the approval of the arbitral tribunal may request from a competent court of this State assistance in taking evidence. The court may execute the request within its competence and according to its rules on taking evidence."

---

[702] Art. 35 (2) *(d)*, SIAC Rules 2010.
[703] Sec. 23F (1) *(a)* and 23G (1) *(a)* of the Australian International Arbitration Act.

The provision does not contain any *per se* limitation of "competent court" to civil authorities.

### (k) *Informing the penal authorities of the illegality*

To what extent does the tribunal have a duty to inform the police or judicial authorities of a suspected or established illegality? In the case of illegality which carries no penal sanctions, there is presumably no risk that the tribunal may be deemed to have aided and abetted a criminal act. Of course, this begs the question of which standard to use when trying to define whether the act is criminal. It also does not answer the question of whether the tribunal has a moral duty, as opposed to a duty under threat of penal sanctions, to inform the authorities.

In such cases, it would appear difficult to construct a moral duty to inform the authorities based on anything within the specific mission of the tribunal. The powers and duties of the arbitrator to condemn illegality through its role as private adjudicator would not necessarily extend to a duty to inform the penal authorities of a criminal act.

Likewise, the powers and duties of the arbitrator to take into consideration mandatory norms and public policy when rendering its award respecting the parties' civil obligations would not necessarily translate into a duty to tell all. In an extreme case, the tribunal could obtain unique knowledge, through its appointment, of heinous acts associated with the contract containing the agreement to arbitrate. The desire and duty to inform the authorities of the suspicion or existence of such acts, and their perpetrators, would be great, but not necessarily flow from the mission as arbitrator.

The foregoing is separate and apart from the question of the danger of infringing upon or appearing to usurp competent State civil or criminal authorities, whether at the seat (if any), at the place or places of putative enforcement or at some other "centre of gravity". We have already addressed the general challenge of parallel proceedings and *lis pendens* above, including State court proceedings versus arbitration proceedings versus civil or criminal investigations and prior pending or subsequently commenced versus still pending or completed proceedings[704].

Three particular questions are posed here.

*First*, there may be the question of the approach of judicial authorities at the seat (if any). In the strictest of cases, there may be a strict definition of corruption as "criminal" and thus as not referable to arbitration: for example, *Pakistan — Hubco* v. *WAPDA*, Supreme Court Pakistan (2000): corruption is "not referable to arbitration"[705]. Also in the Pakistani context, *SGS* v. *Pakistan*, a ruling of the Supreme Court of Pakistan (2002): corruption is not "relatable" to the contract[706]. This approach is generally exceptional and does not reflect the general international trend nor, it is submitted here, is it usually the correct approach to take[707].

---

[704] See *supra* Chapter VI.C.2.

[705] *Hubco* v. *WAPDA*, *supra* footnote 549, pp. 458 *et seq.*

[706] *Société Générale de Surbveillance S.A.* v. *Pakistan*, Supreme Court of Pakistan (Appellate Jurisdiction), 3 July 2002, *Arbitration International*, Vol. 19 (2003), pp. 179-212.

[707] See also S. Sattar, "National Courts and International Arbitration: A Double-edged Sword?", *Journal of International Arbitration*, Vol. 27 (2010), p. 59

"This decision [*Hubco* v. *WAPDA*] of the Pakistani Supreme Court, which was based on spurious grounds of public policy and arbitrability, has raised serious concerns in the international community and has dealt a severe blow to the Pakistani arbitration regime. It demonstrates a clear abuse of the national court's supervisory powers."

*Second*, there may be the question of the extent of a duty to render an enforceable award at least at the seat, if any, as discussed above. In this context, there may be a need to balance the *Hubco*-like approach with the mandate of upholding the public policy prohibition against corruption, and in most cases that public policy should prevail.

*Third*, there may be the question of balancing the policy of *res judicata* against the mandate of public policy, as also already addressed above[708].

This in turn may raise the issue of the degree of deference to be afforded to evidence obtained in parallel proceedings, particularly in the country of the alleged corrupt act. Where those parallel proceedings are either not yet concluded or have resulted in acquittal, the arbitral tribunal will need to assess whether it can find corruption where the related proceedings at the alleged locus of corruption have not resulted in conviction. The arbitrator will also need to be wary of interfering with or contradicting the course or result of the local proceedings, including where the local proceedings are not concluded. See, for example, *African Holding Co. of America, Société Africaine de Construction au Congo* v. *Congo*, ICSID Case No. ARB/05/21:

> "Le Tribunal est disposé à considérer toute pratique de corruption comme une affaire très grave, mais exigerait *une preuve irréfutable de cette pratique, telle que celles qui résulteraient de poursuites criminelles dans les pays où la corruption constitue une infraction pénale.*"

> "The Tribunal considers every act of corruption to be a very serious matter, but requires *irrefutable evidence of such act, such as evidence which results from criminal investigations in countries in which*

---

[708] See *supra* Chapter III.B.3.c.

*corruption is a crime*." (Translation of convenience; emphasis added.) [709]

See also *TSA Spectrum de Argentina S.A.* v. *Argentina*, ICSID Case No. ARB/05/5:

> "The Arbitral Tribunal notes that investigations about criminal offences in connection with the Concession granted to TSA have been initiated in Argentina. These proceedings are being pursued but have not been terminated. There is an indictment against two persons connected with TSA . . . for complicity in misuse of public office, but *no judgment has been rendered, and the issue of bribery is still being investigated*." [710] (Emphasis added.)

Nor was it sufficient evidence that the authorities had investigated allegations of corruption or that certain individuals had been indicted for complicity in misuse of public office as long as no judgment had been rendered [711]. Where, by contrast, the local proceedings have resulted in conviction, the arbitrator should not feel bound by such outcome, even assuming that the conviction is the result of proceedings conducted in good faith and in observance of due process and equal treatment rights.

## 5. *How should or must the arbitrator treat illegality* when admitted?

As discussed previously, in some cases the illegality is concealed and likely occurred but cannot be confirmed under the applicable burden and standard of

---

[709] *African Holding* v. *Congo*, *supra* footnote 605, para. 52.
[710] *TSA* v. *Argentina*, *supra* footnote 560, paras. 174-175.
[711] *Ibid*.

proof. In other cases, the illegality is admitted, as was the case in *World Duty Free*[712] and *Azpetrol*[713].

In the case of admitted corruption, the arbitral tribunal should declare the illegality and ascertain the consequences, if any, for its jurisdiction and admissibility of the claims. It is submitted that a failure or refusal to do so could be considered instrumentalizing of the arbitrator by the illicit party. Indeed it would be contrary to international public policy for the arbitrator to fail to consider a commercial party or investor's acknowledged illegality as an offence of international law and public policy: see, for example, *Inceysa* v. *El Salvador*, ICSID (2006), where the underlying concession was procured by fraud. Indeed if the illegality is against public policy, then the refusal to address it as part of the verification of jurisdiction is also a violation of public policy.

Moreover, taking cognizance of the legal consequences of illegality is vital in ICSID Convention cases. The grounds for annulment under Article 52 do not expressly include a breach of international public policy. If the arbitrator fails to consider whether the acts at issue were contrary to international law and public policy and the consequences for justiciability and admissibility, this issue would never be examined by the trier of fact who had enjoyed first-hand access to the admission of illegality. Again, neither in commercial nor treaty context should most admitted illegality undermine residual procedural competence to negatively declare lack of jurisdiction and/or inadmissibility.

---

[712] *World Duty Free* v. *Kenya*, *supra* footnote 44.

[713] *Azpetrol International Holdings B.V. et al.* v. *The Republic of Azerbaijan*, ICSID Case No. ARB/06/15, Award, 8 September 2009. Available at http://italaw.com/documents/Azpetrolaward.pdf.

## 6. *Should or must the arbitrator,* sua sponte*, decide illegality when* not *alleged?*

More often than not, the answer should be yes. As the primary "trier of fact", the arbitrator is in a unique position, not shared by the reviewing court or reviewing instance, to ascertain the facts. It is submitted that the arbitrator should "err" on the side of initiating investigation, and thereby preempt any need or temptation of the reviewing court to reopen the case. The *Westacre* scenario, as addressed above, is a case in point[714].

But are there tensions here between the mandate of *ultra petita* and the mandate of conforming with public policy? Perhaps yes, but they can and should be resolved where possible in favour of public policy. Where suspected or manifest illegality is arguably "relevant", it is also relevant to the duty, if any, to render an enforceable award, especially at the seat, if any:

> "[The position] that an arbitral tribunal has no duty to investigate bribery unless one of the parties explicitly raises the issue is *incompatible* with the modern significance of bribery in international public policy."[715]

This correct view is to be contrasted with the prior, classical view in ICC Case No. 1110, decided by Lagergren, where both parties acknowledged bribery but they remained of the view that their agreement was valid and binding and sought an arbitral ruling without reference to the corrupt purpose.

Of course, the arbitrator can take a certain "com-

---

[714] ICC Case No. 7047 (1994), *supra* footnote 201, p. 301. See *supra* Chapter II.G.3.
[715] B. M. Cremades and D. Cairns, "Corruption, International Public Policy and the Duties of Arbitrators", *Dispute Resolution Journal*, 1 November (2003).

fort" from the fact that adjudication of illegality, like other justiciable issues, is subject to control of Article V (1) *(c)*, New York Convention, UNCITRAL ML, Articles 34 (2) *(a)* (iii) and 36 (1) *(a)* (iii) and Article 52 (1) *(b)*, ICSID Convention: *ultra petita* is narrowly construed by the courts as long as the issue is deemed "relevant": Swiss Federal Tribunal (19 December 2001)[716]; Paris Court of Appeal (10 March 1988)[717]; *Minmetals Germany* v. *Ferco Steel*, UK Commercial Court (1999)[718]. In short, under most circumstances allegations of corruption and its consequences fall well within the mandate or mission of the tribunal. At the same time, there are outliers, such as ICC Case No. 6497 (1994), in which the tribunal ruled that it had no *sua sponte* power to enquire into bribery[719], and ICC Case No. 7047 (1994): "The word 'bribery' is clear and unmistakeable. If the defendant does not use it in his presentation of facts, an arbitral tribunal does not have to investigate."[720]

---

[716] Tribunal Fédéral [Swiss Federal Tribunal], *N.V. Belgische Scheepvaartmaatschappij-Compagnie Maritime Belge, Anvers (Belgique)* v. *N.V. Distrigas, Bruxelles (Belgique)*, 19 December 2001, *ASA Bulletin*, Vol. 20 (2002), p. 493.

[717] P. Fouchard, "Note — Cour d'appel de Paris (1$^{re}$ Ch. suppl.) 10 mars 1988 — *Société Crocodile Tourist Project Company (Egypte)* v. *Aubert, ès qual. et autres*", *Revue de l'arbitrage* (1989), p. 269.

[718] UK No. 53, *Minmetals Germany GmbH* v. *Ferco Steel Ltd.*, High Court of Justice, Queen's Bench Division (Commercial Court), 20 January 1999, in A. J. van den Berg (ed), *XXIV Yearbook Commercial Arbitration*, 1999, pp. 739-752.

[719] ICC Case No. 6497, *supra* footnote 574, p. 73 ("A civil court, and in particular an arbitral tribunal, has not the power to make an official inquiry and has not the duty to search independently the truth").

[720] *Westacre* v. *Jugoimport*, ICC Case No. 7047 (1994), *supra* footnote 201, p. 343.

It is submitted that in most cases this approach is naive and culturally obtuse, even while each case will depend on its particular facts. That having been said, the challenge to the tribunal in assessing when such independent investigation is appropriate and permissible is considerable:

> "It appears however, that it is for one or other of the parties to the arbitration to make and prove the allegation. That is to say, it is not the duty of an arbitral tribunal to make and prove the allegation. That is to say, *it is not the duty of an arbitral tribunal to assume an inquisitorial role and to search officiously for evidence of corruption where none is alleged.* At the same time — and this may be a difficult balance to strike — *the arbitral tribunal should not allow itself to be used by the parties to sanction conduct which is illegal.*"[721] (Emphasis added.)

How can the tribunal weigh these risks to its proper execution of its own mission against the possible risk of ruling *ultra petita* on a matter which the parties did not expressly or impliedly submit to it for decision? Admittedly, the major sets of arbitration rules and model legislation do not expressly state that the arbitral tribunal may or shall decide upon its own jurisdiction even where the parties have *not* made a plea in this regard. Neither the ICC Rules[722] nor the UNCITRAL

---

[721] R. Kreindler, *supra* footnote 41, pp. 226 *et seq.*; A. Redfern and M. Hunter, *Law and Practice of International Commercial Arbitration*, 3rd ed., London, Sweet & Maxwell, 1999, Sec. 3-28; F. Knoepfler, "Corruption et arbitrage international", *Publication CEDIDAC*, Lausanne 1998, p. 365.

[722] In the case of the ICC Rules, Y. Derains and E. A. Schwartz, *supra* footnote 524, p. 104: "Art. 6 (2) does not provide, however, that the Arbitral Tribunal shall otherwise decide upon its jurisdiction in the absence of a plea of one of the parties . . ."

Rules or UNCITRAL Model Law so state. Indeed in the case of Article 21 of the UNCITRAL Rules, the tribunal has the power "to rule on *objections* that it has no jurisdiction" and in the case of Article 16 (1) of the UNCITRAL Model Law, the arbitral tribunal "may rule on its own jurisdiction, including any objections with respect to the existence or validity of the arbitration agreement".

Yet what if no "objection" has been made but the tribunal still suspects an illegality potentially resulting in the nullity of the main contract and/or the agreement to arbitrate? While the powers of the tribunal in such cases do not flow expressly from such bodies of rule, the better argument must be that the tribunal may, indeed perhaps must, properly make such enquiry. The right and duty to do so may be seen as deriving from a general mandate to ensure that the tribunal's conduct and any award rendered are "enforceable at law". Such right and duty may also be linked to the overlapping mandate to ensure that the relevant public policy (whether national, transnational or otherwise) is not violated by the tribunal's acts of *omission or commission*.

Using the ICC Rules as an example, none of its provisions expressly prohibits the tribunal from engaging in a *self-initiated investigation* of potential illegality on the basis not of overt party pleas to this effect, but solely the tribunal's own suspicions or reasoned beliefs.

There is good reason to contend that in any event Article 41 of the ICC Rules, providing that

> "In all matters not expressly provided for in these Rules, the Court and the Arbitral Tribunal shall act in the spirit of these Rules and shall make every effort to make sure that the Award is enforceable at law"

empowers the tribunal[723] to make such investigation particularly where the purpose of the enquiry is to avoid arbitral conduct and/or an arbitral award which might violate the relevant public policy. The restrictive or inconsequential interpretation which is often accorded Article 41, to the effect that it has no particular stature or standing on its own but is largely a catch-all "throw-away", cannot be supported. Article 41 is fully consistent with the mandate of the tribunal not to violate the relevant public policy or policies; what that policy or policies requires is of course another question, as addressed further below.

The absence of Article 41 or its equivalent from the agreed arbitral rules would in no way diminish the duty of the tribunal to make every effort to ensure that any award is "enforceable at law". Arguments to the effect that Article 41 cannot possibly require the tribunal to verify the enforceability of its actions and rulings under any and all conceivable bodies of law at multiple far-flung places of possible enforcement[724] are not on all fours with the current context.

For the question here is not the extent of due diligence which the tribunal can or should conduct under multiple bodies of public policy across the globe. The question, rather, is the extent to which the tribunal may, should or must engage in self-enquiry as to pos-

---

[723] G. B. Born, *supra* footnote 4, p. 2183.

[724] Cf., e.g., Y. Derains and E. A. Schwartz , *A Guide to the ICC Rules of Arbitration*, 2nd ed., Kluwer Law International, 1998 , p. 351-52:

"[Former Art. 35] is not intended, however, to have any influence on the Arbitral Tribunal's resolution of substantive issues in the arbitration. Nor does it require the Arbitral Tribunal to ensure that the Award would be subject to execution in any particular country, provided that it has been rendered in accordance with the formal requirements of the place where made."

sible illegality when no party has pleaded or otherwise relied upon an illegality objection. The question also extends to the scope of due diligence when the parties have been given a reasonable opportunity to develop their competing views on a possible illegality and its consequences, but the tribunal considers the feedback insufficient to make proper determination of the illegality question.

Such situation cannot simply be compared with the frequently encountered case where the tribunal is dissatisfied and ill-served by inept feedback from the parties on typical questions of jurisdiction or the merits unrelated to a possible illegality. In such cases, barring the limited circumstances in jurisdictions where lack of further self-enquiry could trigger a charge of manifest disregard of the law or error of law, the tribunal appropriately confines its enquiry and decision to the parties' pleas. However, in the case of possible corruption or bribery which may offend public morals, the tribunal may fear that lack of further self-enquiry could trigger a violation of public policy. For that reason, the tribunal may see fit not to confine its enquiry to what the parties have "fed" it.

In short, is the arbitrator caught between a rock and a hard place by initiating his own verification of suspected illegality despite the parties' failure to plea illegality[725]? Failure to engage in such self-enquiry might cause the arbitrator to be an "accomplice" to a contract against public morals or to issue an award which violates public policy[726]. Initiating its own investigation,

---

[725] See, generally, R. Kreindler, *supra* footnote 41, pp. 254 *et seq.*

[726] The arbitrator might do so if he believes that he would otherwise become involved in a breach of public policy. See, e.g., P. Mayer, *supra* footnote 76, p. 379. Such a resignation could be justified under, e.g., Art. 12 (1) of the ICC Rules: "An arbitrator shall also be replaced . . .

on the other hand, and in particular drawing its own conclusions as to such illegality in its award might constitute an impermissible foray into a dispute "not contemplated by or not falling within the terms of the submission to arbitration, or contain[ing] decisions on matters beyond the scope of the submission to arbitration" in the sense of Article 34 (2) *(a)* (iii) of the Model Law or, in virtually the same wording, Article V (1) *(c)* of the New York Convention. Inviting the parties to make submissions on the suspected illegality might assuage concerns about each party's ability to "present his case" in the sense of Article V (1) *(b)* of the New York Convention, but compliance with the due process commandment would not necessarily also guarantee compliance with the *ultra petita* commandment.

If it were correct that the arbitrator's choice resided between violating public policy and violating *ultra petita*, an instinctual reaction might be that in the hierarchy of mandatory norms avoiding an offence to public policy supersedes avoiding an offence to *ultra petita*. Whether this is in fact a correct analysis, or even an analysis which can possibly be conducted, needs not be answered. The reason is that the tribunal's self-enquiry into possible illegality, whether considered a right or a duty, should normally not be a violation of *ultra petita* in the first place, even where no party plea of illegality has been raised.

A second "instinctual reaction" in many such cases of illegality, which can be addressed briefly, would be that the arbitrator literally throws up his hands and

---

upon the acceptance by the Court of the arbitrator's resignation . . ." Art. 14 (1) of the UNCITRAL Model Law is somewhat more responsive in this regard: "If an arbitrator becomes *de jure* or *de facto* unable to perform his functions . . . his mandate terminates if he withdraws from his office . . ."

decides not to proceed, but instead to *resign* from office[727]. It is submitted that abstention and resignation under most circumstances of illegality is neither desirable nor necessary, but rather the tribunal is entitled to proceed with the matter. The arbitrator may not have a duty to remain in office at all costs[728] in the face of a thoroughly distasteful illicit dispute[729]. However, it is submitted that his original declaration of ability to take on the case and see it through to the end[730] should be

---

[727] See, e.g. Lagergren in ICC Case No. 1110, *supra* footnote 3.

[728] The distinction between French domestic arbitration law and French international arbitration law is interesting in this regard. Under Art. 1457 of the French New Code of Civil Procedure applying to domestic arbitration, "[e]ach arbitrator shall carry out his or her mission until it is completed" while under Art. 1463 "[a]n arbitrator may refuse to act or be challenged only on a ground which is revealed or arises after his or her appointment". Query what happens when, absent a more specific party agreement, in an international arbitration with a French seat the arbitrator resigns due to a distaste for an illegality of contract which existed and was known to him at the time of his consent to serve as arbitrator. Cf. E. Gaillard and J. Savage (eds.), *supra* footnote 1, para. 882, citing to TGI Paris, réf., 15 February 1995, *Industrialexport* v. *K.*, *Revue de l'arbitrage* (1996), p. 503, holding that "[the judge] cannot attempt, by issuing an injunction against the defaulting arbitrator, to compel the latter to resume and pursue *a task as personal as that of judging*" (emphasis added).

[729] Cf. also other arbitration legislation providing that in principle once the arbitrator has accepted office, he cannot resign without proper grounds — which begs the question of whether a thoroughgoing illegality and distastefulness for the same would constitute such grounds: e.g., Art. 1029 (2) of the Dutch Code of Civil Procedure, Art. 1689 of the Belgian Judicial Code, and Art. 813 of the Italian Code of Civil Procedure.

[730] Cf. Art. 11 (5) of the 2012 ICC Rules, providing that "[b]y accepting to serve, arbitrators undertake to carry out their responsibilities in accordance with the Rules".

overcome only in extreme circumstances. A distaste for the illegality of the case or a frustration with a difficulty of choice between competing mandatory norms should not normally justify resignation.

In fact, certain arbitration regulations are so strict in their provisions meant to reduce the impact of an arbitrator's dilatory conduct that an arbitrator acting conscientiously under such regulations might find it exceedingly difficult to resign even where his reason related to a fear of his "complicity" in illegality, as opposed to dilatoriness[731]. Article 13, paragraph 5, of the rules of the Iran-United States Claims Tribunal are an interesting case in point, providing that arbitrators must continue to serve in all cases where they have already participated in a hearing on the substance of the dispute. In all such cases, however, presumably an arbitrator may resign without any external approval where the illegality-related grounds are properly set forth and/or affect his independence toward the parties in a manner which he did not cause[732].

In any event, the difficulty of choice between *ultra petita* and due process does not arise here in a way which should cause the arbitrator to throw up his hands: *ultra petita* is a cardinal principle of international

---

[731] For example, Art. 15 (1) of the 2012 ICC Rules provides that an arbitrator's resignation must be accepted by the ICC International Court, while Art. 8 (2) of the ICSID Arbitration Rules allows the tribunal to accept or reject the resignation of a party-appointed arbitrator.

[732] See also E. Gaillard and J. Savage (eds.), *supra* footnote 1, para. 1131:

"Arbitrators can of course resign, with or without the approval of the arbitral institution or their colleagues, if there are proper grounds to justify their resignation. For example, it may become impossible for them to pursue their functions, or a circumstance may arise, through no fault of their own, which affects their independence vis-à-vis the parties."

arbitration with direct relevance to standards of review and enforcement. At the same time, this commandment must be seen in the proper and realistic context. For example, the notion that the scope of the tribunal's mission can best, or even only, be monitored in an ICC or ICC-like arbitration which benefits from Terms of Reference seems to be a potential overstatement[733].

Whether the "list of issues to be determined" is in fact a reliable and exclusive roadmap to the *petita* of the parties can in fact be seriously questioned. This is all the more so in the case of such "lists" which delineate the issues in intentionally generic and vague, and therefore somewhat unhelpful, terms[734]. It may also be doubted whether vague and generic "summaries" of the parties' claims and prayers for relief in the sense of the ICC Rules, often with no specific quanta, are particularly helpful in the sense of *infra* or *ultra petita*. There are of course many cases where Terms of Reference — or comparable documents such as "constitutional orders" in non-ICC proceedings — are formulated in such a way as to provide a genuinely accurate roadmap to the claims and prayers for relief. But even in such

---

[733] There is little doubt that a Terms of Reference agreement in the sense of the ICC Rules, including a "list of issues to be determined", may serve a number of salutary and even indispensable purposes in an arbitration. The summary of the parties' respective claims and prayers for relief as well as the "list of issues to be determined" have generally been regarded as a useful basis for monitoring *infra* and *ultra petita* issues leading up to and after the rendering of the award. Indeed the Working Party charged with drafting what became the 1998 ICC Rules itself noted that Terms of Reference could be helpful in *ultra petita* control: see, generally, R. Kreindler, *supra* footnote 524, p. 99.

[734] For example, "Is the Claimant entitled to any or all of the relief sought as set out in Section X above? If so, to which relief and in what monetary amount, if any, is the Claimant entitled?"

cases, it is by no means guaranteed that there will be a hand-in-glove overlap between such document and the "differences contemplated by or . . . falling within the terms of the submission to arbitration" in the sense of Article V (1) *(c)* of the New York Convention.

Arguments or differences not originally contemplated by the parties at the time of their ICC Terms of Reference — or at the time of the "constitutional order" or the like where there is no Terms of Reference *per se* — may well arise in the course of the later proceedings. Such arguments may even consume more attention than the originally trumpeted differences. These arguments will normally become part of the "mission" of the tribunal, and may figure as part of the final award. The same would hold true for illegality contentions going to the nullity of the main contract and/or the agreement to arbitrate.

Arguments or differences relating to illegality, even if initiated by the tribunal itself, should normally be deemed to "fall within the terms of the submission to arbitration". While an illegality analysis may not be a "difference contemplated by" the terms of the submission, it has a core relevance to arbitrability and public policy. For that reason among others, it should be seen as necessarily falling within the terms of virtually any submission to arbitration.

Moreover, there can be little doubt that a tribunal-initiated investigation of illegality is not tantamount to *ultra petita*. The tribunal comes to a legal conclusion as to the validity of the main contract, the claims under that contract and/or the arbitration agreement, or the unmeritoriousness of the claims due to the invalidity of the contract. Even when it does so without being expressly asked, its action should not vitiate the enforceability of an award made on this basis as long as the parties are given a reasonable opportunity to react to the tribunal's conclusion first.

The tribunal's decision following on such self-initiated investigation can "fit" into the claims and, perhaps less so, defences already made. Alternatively, without being asked to do so the tribunal can conclude that as a result of a fundamental illegality it has no competence and render an award denying its jurisdiction on such basis as part of a duty to self-police its jurisdiction where public policy concerns apply[735]. In this regard, Wetter, writing in 1994 respecting the 1963 Lagergren award, wrote:

> "the question whether or not a dispute is arbitrable is one which must be examined by an international arbitral tribunal of its own motion, *ex officio*, because a tribunal must satisfy itself that it does have jurisdiction legally conferred upon it by the parties . . ."[736].

One need not necessarily go as far as to advocate a duty *ex officio* even in the absence of any allegation or indication of illegality which might affect issues of arbitrability or public policy. But in the presence of such an allegation or even a suspicion on the part of the tribunal, the validity of the arbitration agreement may be at stake.

Analysis of the validity of the arbitration agreement is part and parcel of an analysis of the validity of the underlying contract. The tribunal must undertake such an analysis in the presence of a party plea of corruption or other illicit conduct which may permeate both the main contract and the arbitration agreement. Likewise, the tribunal should and perhaps must undertake this

---

[735] For an interesting case in this regard, see Tribunal Fédéral [Swiss Federal Tribunal], *Bank Saint Petersburg PLC* v. *ATA Insaat Sanayi ve Ticaret Ltd.*, 2 March 2001, *ASA Bulletin*, Vol. 19 (2001), p. 531.

[736] J. G. Wetter, *supra* footnote 74, pp. 280 *et seq.*

analysis on its own initiative when it suspects such a thoroughgoing illegality. A similar approach was adopted in the *Westinghouse* matter[737], and may also be applied to cases of tribunal-initiated investigation of illegality.

In conclusion, the rights of the arbitrator in the face of corruption are considerable, and although less frequently and coherently considered thus far, the duties of the arbitrator are likewise significant. While there may be certain potential tensions between due process and public policy or between *ultra petita* and competence-competence, they can be resolved in favour of the right and duty to investigate in most instances. Where the suspected or manifest illegality is arguably "relevant", it is also relevant to an affirmation or denial of competence, jurisdiction, arbitrability, admissibility, and even the merits.

Accordingly, in some circumstances even a self-initiated enquiry by the arbitrator may not be *ultra petita* insofar as the *petita* are to be deemed to encompass the right to ascertain precisely competence, jurisdiction, arbitrability, and admissibility. In that regard, it may be that the arbitrator should in some situations also "err" on the side of proactively conducting an inquiry and assessing the consequences for his own power and authority.

---

[737] *Westinghouse*, ICC Case No. 6401, *supra* footnote 271, Preliminary Award, 19 December 1991, *International Arbitration Report*, Vol. 7 (1992), p. 48.

## CHAPTER IX

## LEGAL CONSEQUENCES OF A FINDING OR ADMISSION OF CORRUPTION

### A. Introduction

From the prior discussion, it is apparent and can be reprised that we can distinguish between and among at least four kinds of arbitration which may give rise to issues of legal consequences from a finding of illegality and specifically corruption: (i) commercial arbitration based on privity of contract with an agreement to arbitrate, (ii) investment arbitration having the same basis, (iii) investment arbitration based on an investment contract and providing for treaty-based arbitration, and (iv) investment arbitration based on a non-contractual investment and providing for treaty-based arbitration.

Furthermore, certain general conclusions may be drawn on the basis of the foregoing distinctions and indeed transcending them.

*First*, serious breach of the agreed or determined law can and should deprive the party responsible for such breach of the benefits of the underlying contract or of the benefits of treaty protection.

*Second*, under the generally accepted principles of competence-competence and separability, such breaches are not likely to deprive and should not deprive the arbitrator of jurisdiction in the *commercial* context, but depending on the circumstances they may do so in the *investment* context.

*Third*, illegality does not necessarily refer to every illicit act, particularly in order to trigger a violation of public policy nationally, internationally or transnationally, but rather the act must reach a certain level of egregiousness which is not always easily defined.

*Fourth*, a reference to domestic law as governing or forming the rights and duties under the contract or the investment-treaty based claim does not normally result in a non-application of international law where international law would otherwise apply.

*Fifth*, corruption and bribery in the acquisition or performance of an — even otherwise legal — contract or investment is condemned under most domestic laws, under public international law, and under international or transnational public policy.

*Sixth*, corruption and bribery, irrespective of the agreed or determined law(s), will invariably deprive the contracting party or investor of the benefits of the contract and/or of treaty protection.

In light of these conclusions, the following questions arise from the perspective of both the parties and the arbitral tribunal: when should an allegation, admission or finding of corruption in the acquisition or performance of a contract or investment trigger dismissal of the claim on the level of jurisdiction or admissibility or both, when on the level of the merits? And when might corruption or illegality be legally excused or justified?

The arbitral tribunal will be called upon to decide whether it lacks jurisdiction because acts which may be attributable to the claimant or the respondent may render the contract or investment illegal and estop it from invoking protections under, for example, the applicable law, the ECT and the ICSID Convention. Independently, the arbitral tribunal may need to decide whether it lacks jurisdiction due to a lack of consent to arbitration on the basis of fraud or illegality and, in the case of investment treaty arbitration, by the respondent host State to submit the dispute to jurisdiction.

Furthermore, the arbitral tribunal may need to determine whether it lacks jurisdiction due to any estoppel on the part of the claimant from invoking the agreement to arbitration or, in the case of investment treaty arbitration, from accepting the respondent's offer to submit to jurisdiction, according to the one or other principle which may trigger estoppel, such as the Unclean Hands Doctrine. The Unclean Hands Doctrine stands for the principle that "He who comes to equity for relief must come with clean hands"[738] and "He who seeks equity must do equity."[739] In such case, and again depending upon the specific circumstances, the arbitral tribunal may need to assess whether, for example, under the Unclean Hands Doctrine, any acts of bribery could render the claims inadmissible.

## B. *Jurisdiction and Admissibility versus the Merits:*
## *General Conceptual Challenges*

Exploration of these questions, which go to the heart of the requests for relief of the parties and the decision-making conduct of the tribunal, calls for a distinction between the issues common to the commercial and investment treaty context and the issues which differ.

---

[738] In the context of the Unclean Hands Doctrine, see G. Fitzmaurice, *supra* footnote 172, p. 119; see also *Cathcart* v. *Robinson*, 5 Pet. 264, 276 (US Supreme Court 1831) (USA) (citing, among others, *Thompson* v. *Smith*, 1 Madd. Ch. 405, 56 Eng. Reprint, 149 (1815) (England).

[739] G. Fitzmaurice, *ibid.*, PCIJ, *Diversion of Water from the Meuse (Netherlands* v. *Belgium)*, 28 June 1937, *1937 PCIJ, Series A/B*, No. 70, p. 77, para. 323 (opinion of Judge Hudson) (concerning allegations that Belgium's construction of canals and the diversion of a river violated treaty obligations between Belgium and the Netherlands). Available at http://www.worldcourts.com/pcij/eng/decisions/1937.06.28_meuse.htm.

*1. Issues common to commercial and investment treaty context*

(a) *Time and cost of adjudication*

There is the issue of the time and cost of adjudication from the perspective of the respective party and of the tribunal. The parties and the tribunal must focus on the question of addressing liability and quantum at an early stage versus at a later stage of the proceedings, and together with jurisdictional and other preliminary objections or separately, if at all, if and when jurisdiction is upheld.

Whether a "bifurcation" of preliminary issues and merits issues or a trifurcation of preliminary, liability and damages issues will make sense will surely depend on the facts and circumstances. The notion that bifurcation is *per se* more time- and cost-efficient particularly where jurisdiction may well be denied has been examined somewhat more circumspectly in recent years, in part in relation to the recent amendment to the ICSID Arbitration Rules in this respect[740]. To the extent bifurcation is, statistically considered[741], less

---

[740] L. Greenwood, "Does Bifurcation Really Promote Efficiency?", *Journal of International Arbitration*, Vol. 28 (2011), pp. 105 *et seq.*; see Art. 41 (3) of the ICSID Arbitration Rules.

[741] L. Greenwood, *ibid.*, p. 106 and footnote 6:

"The author contacted the International Chamber of Commerce (ICC), the London Court of International Arbitration (LCIA), the Stockholm Chamber of Commerce and the International Centre for Dispute Resolution (ICDR) to establish whether they maintained statistics in relation to the bifurcation of arbitration proceedings. None of the institutions maintained statistics on the use of bifurcation in international arbitrations. The ICC maintains statistics on partial awards, but it is not possible to extrapolate from this the number of ICC proceedings that are bifurcated."

prevalent in very recent years than previously in ICSID arbitration, the challenges to the arbitrator will be all the greater when faced with the question of whether an illegality or corruption allegation which may affect the tribunal's adjudicatory authority should be examined up front and separately, or rather in combination with the overall merits.

(b) *Assessment of the issue at an early, uninformed stage*

In this regard, commercial and investment treaty-based arbitration share the challenge of whether to expend effort on the questions of liability and damages if jurisdiction and admissibility are unclear and/or are questioned and the degree of overlap factually between preliminary and merits issues is unclear, at least at an early stage. Separation of matters in dispute, particularly at an early, uninformed stage.

As part of the discretion enjoyed by the tribunal to decide whether to bifurcate or to postpone the decision to bifurcate, a main consideration will be the degree of such overlap. If the assessment of the degree of such overlap necessarily is to be made at a relatively early stage of the arbitration, before the taking of document and witness evidence on any issues including the merits issues, it may be correspondingly difficult for the tribunal to have an adequate appreciation of the issue.

Particularly in common-law inspired, notice-pleading arbitrations in which one or more of the parties have intentionally plead their claims or defences leanly on the assumption of benefiting from later evidentiary disclosure, the record on which the tribunal must make this discretionary decision may too be lean. This challenge may be exacerbated by the question of which law applies to which issues and whether legal issues are relevant to the preliminary objections or to the merits issues or to both. To the extent the parties are in dispute as to the applicable substantive law, a decision on that question could decisively impact a decision on whether there is sufficient overlap between preliminary and merits issues to decline bifurcation.

(c) *The right of the arbitrator to confirm his authority*

While there are differences respecting competence, jurisdiction, arbitrability, separability and admissibility requirements between commercial and investment treaty arbitration, in both cases the arbitral tribunal should be seen as having an *ex officio* right or duty of verification under the applicable rules, the *lex arbitri* (if any) or both.

Simply, even if a party does not raise a jurisdictional objection which would deprive the tribunal of authority, the tribunal cannot proceed unless it has jurisdiction and should deny jurisdiction of its own accord if it is aware of that objection, has given the parties an opportunity to address the issue, and then concludes that it indeed lacks jurisdiction on that basis. As long as the tribunal handles this issue carefully and with a view toward due process and equal treatment, its conduct should not run afoul of these mandates or of the mandates of *ultra petita* and of impermissibly assisting a party[742]. The issue is a delicate one, related to the right or duty of the arbitrator to verify his jurisdiction[743], to investigate the matter with all appropriate

---

[742] N. Blackaby and C. Partasides with A. Redfern and M. Hunter, *supra* footnote 7, paras. 5.14 *et seq.*, 5.67 and 5.99 *et seq.*

[743] N. Blackaby and C. Partasides with A. Redfern and M. Hunter, *supra* footnote 7, paras. 5.99 *et seq*; E. Gaillard and J. Savage (eds.), *supra* footnote 1, paras. 650 *et seq.*

means[744], and to ensure that the parties state their prayers for relief effectively[745]. The alternative would be that the tribunal would ignore a manifest objection to jurisdiction, proceed to the merits phase and then render an award which proved to be unenforceable at either the annulment or enforcement stage on precisely the basis of lack of jurisdiction.

### (d) *Waiver of objections by the party*

To be clear, in most cases this will not be a danger to the extent that the party which could have raised the jurisdictional objection but did not so will be deemed to have *waived* the jurisdictional objection at some stage of the arbitration as well as the right to invoke it in order to oppose the award. However, waiver will not and should not deprive an award from being denied enforceability in certain narrow cases respecting, for example, illegality, where enforcement of the award on the basis of a non-challenged jurisdiction might offend public policy.

That is, public policy may and should be a higher and superseding control over the presence or lack of jurisdiction even in those cases where jurisdiction has been waived. This is not as astonishing as it may sound at first blush and is indeed reflected in the New York Convention Article V (2): irrespective of whether a party raises the public policy objection to oppose

---

[744] Art. 25 (1) of the 2012 ICC Rules: "The arbitral tribunal shall proceed within as short a time as possible to establish the facts of the case by all appropriate means."

[745] M. Wirth, "Rechtsbegehren in internationalen Schiedsverfahren — Wie bestimmt müssen sie sein?", in M. Jametti Greiner *et al.* (eds.), *Festschrift für Franz Kellerhals zum 65. Geburtstag*, Bern, Stämpfli Verlag, 2005, p. 158.

enforcement of an award to which the Convention applies, the enforcing court may refuse enforcement on that basis *sua sponte*, including where arbitrability and/or jurisdiction was not challenged. Of course, the affirmation of arbitrability or jurisdiction itself must rise to the level of a violation of public policy in such cases.

### (e) *Characterization of the objection or defence*

In both commercial and investment treaty cases there may be the question of whether the objection or defence should be characterized as a preliminary issue or rather as a defence on the merits. This is not only a question of the degree of overlap of the factual circumstances, but also of whether the objection *per se* is one of procedure or of a preliminary nature which does not or should not relate to the question of principle.

The demarcation line will not always be clear, quite apart from the fact that the parties, as stated above, may often be in disagreement as to which national law or principles of law apply to the characterization itself. Furthermore, the parties may be in disagreement, depending on the applicable law, as to what prerequisites apply to the admission of a claim on the merits.

### (f) *Tribunal considerations in making the characterization*

Here too, as in the case of almost any preliminary objection, the respondent party will normally be intent upon a characterization which allows and even obliges the tribunal to decide the issue as a gateway preliminary matter, without the need to spend time and money on exploration of the principle, let alone quantum. The claimant party will normally wish the opposite, consistent with its position that a proper analysis requires a composite consideration of the facts and law and particularly the evidence. In particular, the claimant will normally desire to avoid an early unfavourable outcome or, even in the case of an affirmation of jurisdiction, a delay in the merits phase as a result of a challenge to the interim award affirming jurisdiction.

By the same token, a tribunal may factor into its discretionary decision whether to bifurcate the very fact that its decision on jurisdiction has been requested in the form of an award, either partial or final depending on the result. As part of that decision, the tribunal may consider the extent to which its decision affirming or denying jurisdiction would enjoy more robust enforceability based on a composite adjudication of all preliminary and merits issues together, or rather can be made solidly and completely on the basis of a strict bifurcation. Even in the case of a strict bifurcation, the preliminary issue of jurisdiction can and often of course is also made only after a phase of taking documentary and witness evidence, on the issue of jurisdiction itself.

(g) *Bifurcation and the further arbitral proceedings*

The tribunal may and often does consider whether to bifurcate based on the ability, under the applicable law and rules, to pursue the arbitration on the merits further even pending a petition to annul its prior partial award upholding jurisdiction. Increasingly, as a reflection of the trend toward greater autonomy of the arbitral process and lesser ability of the national courts to intervene in the process particularly in the commercial context, the arbitrator may have greater comfort that he can decide not to suspend the merits proceedings pending the outcome of a challenge of his interim affirmation of jurisdiction, and that this decision not to suspend will itself survive any attempt to enjoin entering into the merits proceedings.

While the rules and legislation differ from jurisdiction to jurisdiction, and opportunities to enjoin will continue to exist even in pro-arbitration locales[746], the trend reflected by the amendments to the French arbitration law is noteworthy, and may betoken a continuing immunization of the arbitral process from interference or intervention by the State courts including even at the seat[747].

Whether this trend will prove to be a popular one with the ultimate users of arbitration or in fact backfire remains to be seen.

It is submitted that at least from the perspective of many common-law and particularly US and UK parties who are used to the still surviving remedies of State court supervision of arbitration, this further emboldening of the arbitrator versus the courts at the seat may in fact be counter-productive to increasing the popularity of such seats as France.

---

[746] See generally, J. L. Gorskie, "US Courts and the Anti-Arbitration Injunction", *Arbitration International*, Vol. 28 (2012), pp. 295 *et seq.;* R. Das and A. Keyal, "Judicial Intervention in International Arbitration", *National University of Juridical Sciences Law Review*, Vol. 2 (2009), pp. 585 *et seq.*

[747] See R. Das and A. Keyal, *ibid.*, citing Art. 1458, Nouveau Code de Procédure Civile (New Code of Civil Procedure) which provides that "if a dispute pending before an arbitral tribunal on the basis of an arbitration agreement is brought before a state court, it shall declare itself incompetent unless the arbitration agreement is manifestly null and void"; *Republic of Equatorial Guinea* v. *Fitzpatrick Equatorial Guinea, de Ly, Owen and Leboulanger*, Tribunal de grande instance de Paris (réf.), 10/52825, 29 March 2010 (available at http://arbitration.practicallaw.com/cs/Satellite ?blobcol=urldata&blobheader=application%2Fpdf&blobkey=id&blobtable=MungoBlobs&blobwhere=1247502191056&ssbinary=true).

## 2. *Differences between commercial and investment treaty context*

Notable differences in this context may be high-lighted, which exist side by side with the far-reaching similarities identified above.

### (a) *Perspectives on time and cost of adjudication*

There is the question of the time and cost of adjudi-cation from the perspective of the respective party and of the tribunal. In the case of commercial arbitration, empirical observations or even generalizations about the frequency of bifurcation petitions and bifurcation itself are difficult if not impossible to make.

At the same time, it is submitted based on my own experience and observation as counsel and arbitrator that at least as many commercial arbitrations proceed without a jurisdictional objection as with one, and that many such commercial arbitrations are not bifurcated. By comparison, at least until very recent years and the amendment to the ICSID Arbitration Rules addressed above [748], in the investment treaty context including ICSID and non-ICSID objections to jurisdiction or admissibility by the State respondent were so frequent as almost to be a *de rigueur* step.

### (b) *Trends in requesting and granting requests for bifurcation*

While a certain decrease in frequency and popular-ity of both bifurcation requests and bifurcation deci-sions has been identified [749], my own experience and observation indicates that it is a decrease in decisions

---

[748] *Supra* footnote 740.
[749] L. Greenwood, *supra* footnote 740.

but not necessarily a loss of appetite for the underlying request for bifurcation. There are many reasons why such requests and granting of bifurcation will likely remain more frequent in the investment treaty sphere than in commercial arbitration.

These include the transparency with which such requests have been made and partially succeeded in the past, the fact that the respondent is invariably a State which has the means and determination to pursue all procedure options, and the fact that the jurisdictional and other preliminary prerequisites for the exercise of treaty-based jurisdiction are in their own way more numerous and more complex than in the conventional commercial sphere.

Furthermore, invariably a decision to bifurcate results in an award on the bifurcated issue which more often than not is attacked in annulment proceedings which in turn indeed delay or suspend the prosecution of the merits. Finally, in the investment treaty realm the State respondent almost never has counterclaim or for that matter even a defence by way of set-off, and so has less motivation than in many commercial cases involving claims and counterclaims to ensure a speedy prosecution of the dispute on a composite basis.

### (c) *The applicable law or laws*

Competence, jurisdiction, arbitrability, separability and admissibility requirements often operate somewhat differently than in a conventional commercial matter. In the investment treaty realm, absent a *lex arbitri* the verification of the fulfilment of the prerequisites for jurisdiction — such as nationality, "investor", "investment" and "accordance with local law" — will take place largely or even exclusively as a matter of the applicable investment treaty, the applicable convention and the applicable public international law principles, separately and in tandem one with the other. The absence of a *lex arbitri* can and often does make it more difficult, and not less so, to narrow down the universe of applicable legal principles to be considered in making these decisions, and in turn in deciding whether they can be considered strictly of a preliminary nature.

### (d) *Privity of contract versus "consent"*

These challenges are augmented by the absence of conventional contractual privity and the presence of the factor of "consent" to the arbitration, in particular by the respondent State party, through the antecedent State-to-State treaty accession. On some levels, this lack of privity and this construed consent make decisions respecting bifurcation easier, in some respects harder, depending on the perspective. Jurisdiction is essentially not based on conventional commercial arbitration privity issues of capacity, signature, third-party accession or benefit, or the scope of the arbitration agreement — not to minimize how difficult even these straightforward issues can be in the commercial realm.

Instead, jurisdiction will be based to the greatest extent on fulfilment of nationality, investor, investment, local law, and exhaustion of remedies requirements, as well as many others. In addition, in investment treaty arbitration a distinction may be made between a kind of personal jurisdiction *(ratione voluntatis)* and a kind of subject matter jurisdiction *(ratione materiae)* not experienced in quite the same way in conventional commercial arbitration[750].

---

[750] See, e.g., *Inceysa* v. *El Salvador*, *supra* footnote 174, paras. 63 and 134-161; *Phoenix Action* v. *The Czech Republic*, *supra* footnote 492, paras. 54-80.

(e) *Distinguishing jurisdiction and admissibility*

Competence, jurisdiction, arbitrability, separability and admissibility requirements can and will trigger the *ex officio* right or duty on the part of the arbitrator, addressed above[751], to verify to what extent the corruption allegations affect the threshold authority of the tribunal. In this regard, jurisdiction and admissibility may need to be distinguished.

In commercial disputes, certain legal systems, such as that of Germany, make a careful delineation between jurisdiction and admissibility or lack thereof, with admissibility being a typical requirement alleged to have been fulfilled or not fulfilled even where jurisdiction is present, while certain other jurisdictions essentially elide admissibility with jurisdiction[752]. In commercial and investment arbitrations in which corruption allegations are present, the distinction may be quite significant, also insofar as a characterization as an objection of admissibility, particularly in the investment sphere, could be invoked to justify adjudication together with, and not bifurcated from, the merits.

Generally, an arbitral tribunal is prevented from hearing and determining the merits of a case if it either lacks jurisdiction, or it declares the claims before it to be inadmissible or both[753]. An objection to jurisdiction has been described as "a plea that the tribunal itself is incompetent to give any ruling at all", while an objec-

---

[751] See *supra* Chapter VIII.B.4.

[752] Cf. J. Paulsson, "Jurisdiction and Admissibility", in *Global Reflections on International Law, Commerce and Dispute Resolution — Liber Amicorum in Honour of Robert Briner*, ICC Publishing, 2005, pp. 601 *et seq.*; C. Brown, "Comment: Jurisdiction and Admissibility in International Arbitration", *TDM*, Vol. 2 (2005).

[753] J. Collier and V. Lowe, *The Settlement of Disputes in International Law: Institutions and Procedures*, Oxford, Oxford University Press, 1999, pp. 155-166.

tion to the substantive admissibility of the claim has been described as "a plea that the tribunal should rule the claim inadmissible on some ground other than its ultimate merits"[754].

Such distinction between jurisdiction and admissibility can and in my opinion should also be usefully drawn in the context of treaty-based investment arbitration. Thus, Keith Highet, in his Dissenting Opinion in *Waste Management Inc.* v. *United Mexican States*, distinguished jurisdiction and admissibility usefully as follows: "Jurisdiction is the power of the tribunal to hear the case; admissibility is whether the case itself is defective — whether it is appropriate for the tribunal to hear it."[755] In short, usefully the arbitral tribunal may consider itself to have jurisdiction to hear the case, but it may also determine peremptorily that the claims *cannot possibly be maintained* as a matter of law, even assuming the claimant's version of the facts.

Thus a distinction can be meaningfully drawn between matters of jurisdiction and those of admissibility. At the same time, investment arbitration tribunals appear not to have eagerly sought to establish what makes a claim inadmissible as opposed to devoid of jurisdiction.

My scrutiny of the jurisprudence indicates that arbitral practice has nonetheless developed essentially two basic approaches to admissibility. On the one hand,

---

[754] G. Fitzmaurice, *The Law and Procedure of the International Court of Justice*, Cambridge, Grotius Publications, 1986, p. 438. A similar distinction is made, *inter alia*, by I. Brownlie, *supra* footnote 356, pp. 475 *et seq.* (discussing State-State disputes).

[755] *Waste Management, Inc.* v. *United Mexican States*, ICSID Case No. ARB(AF)/98/2, dissenting opinion of Keith Highet on Jurisdiction, 8 May 2002, para. 58. Available at http://italaw.com/sites/default/files/case-documents/ita0894.pdf.

according to Rosenne, as also cited by the arbitral tribunal in *Methanex* v. *United States* [756],

> "As a rough rule-of-thumb, it is probable that when the facts and arguments in support of the objection are substantially the same as the facts and arguments on which the merits of the case depend, or when to decide the objection would require decision on what, in the concrete case, are substantive aspects of the merits, the plea is not an objection but a defence to the merits." [757]

On the other hand, the arbitral tribunal in *Occidental Exploration and Production* v. *Ecuador* dismissed a claim by the investor on grounds of inadmissibility based on an evident lack of merit:

> "A claim of expropriation should normally be considered in the context of the merits of a case. However, it is so evident that there is no expropriation in this case that the Tribunal will deal with this claim as a question of admissibility." [758]

---

[756] *Methanex Corporation* v. *United States of America*, First Partial Award, 7 August 2002, para. 125 (available at. http://italaw.com/sites/default/files/case-documents/ita 0518.pdf). For a related analysis, see I. A. Laird, "A Distinction without a Difference? An Examination of the Concepts of Admissibility and Jurisdiction in Salini v. Jordan and Methanex v. USA", in T. Weiler (ed.), *International Investment Law and Arbitration: Leading Cases from the ICSID, NAFTA, Bilateral Treaties and Customary International Law*, London, Cameron May, 2005, pp. 201 *et seq.*

[757] S. Rosenne, *Law and Practice of the International Court, 1920-1996*, Vol. 2, 3rd ed., M. Nijhoff, 1997, pp. 88, 915.

[758] *Occidental Exploration and Production Company* v. *The Republic of Ecuador*, LCIA Case No. UN3467, Award, 1 July 2004, para. 80 (concerning violations of United States-Ecuador BIT) (available at http://italaw. com/sites/default/files/case-documents/ita0571.pdf).

In short, while jurisdiction and admissibility are not always distinguished or for that matter plead separately, there should clearly be a basis for doing so and for determining dismissal expressly on the basis of inadmissibility even where declining to dismiss on the basis of lack of jurisdiction.

As for the authority to rule on inadmissibility in investment arbitration, neither the ICSID Convention nor the ECT mentions the concept of admissibility expressly. Accordingly, it can be asked whether an arbitral tribunal constituted thereunder is authorized to dismiss claims on the basis of inadmissibility. It is submitted that the lack of an express authority to do so under the ICSID Convention need not and should not prevent arbitral tribunals from considering such issues. At the same time, in order to derive such authority, certain arbitral tribunals have held that the classical distinction between jurisdiction, on the one hand, and admissibility, on the other, is not relevant in the context of ICSID arbitration. For example, the arbitral tribunal in *CMS Gas Transmission Company* v. *Republic of Argentina* stated the following:

> "The distinction between admissibility and jurisdiction does not appear quite appropriate in the context of ICSID as the Convention deals only with jurisdiction and competence." [759]

The Tribunal then decided the challenge brought to the admissibility of one of the claims in referring to both admissibility and jurisdiction.

A similar approach was adopted by the arbitral tribunal in *LG&E* v. *Argentina* [760]. Other arbitral tribunals

---

[759] *CMS* v. *Argentina*, *supra* footnote 615, para. 41.

[760] *LG&E Energy Corp., LG&E Capital Corp., and LG&E International, Inc.* v. *Argentine Republic*, ICSID Case No. ARB/02/1, Decision on Obejections to Juris-

in investment proceedings have, at times, decided issues of jurisdiction that might sooner have been categorized as issues of admissibility. Thus, in *Salini v. Jordan*, the arbitral tribunal regarded the following question to be an issue of jurisdiction:

> "[T]he Tribunal will . . . seek to determine whether the facts alleged by the Claimants in this case, if established, are capable of coming within those provisions of the BIT which have been invoked." [761]

On the basis of the foregoing, the preliminary question of whether an investment claimant has an arguable legal case (or whether it is necessary to definitively decide on the legal meaning of the relevant substantive provisions) can ultimately be decided by the arbitral tribunal in the context of either jurisdiction or admissibility.

At the same time, the virtue of maintaining a distinction between the two — particularly when a defence is raised *expressis verbis* as an inadmissibility defence — is that the focus of the arbitral tribunal's enquiry can thereby be sharpened. A respondent may not necessarily contest the competency of the arbitral tribunal to adjudicate the claims, for example, based on lack of consent under the ECT. Rather, a respondent may contest the existence of any arguable legal case

---

diction, 30 April 2004, para. 68 (available at http://italaw.com/sites/default/files/case-documents/ita0458.pdf).

[761] *Salini Costruttori S.p.A. and Italstrade S.p.A.* v. *The Hashemite Kingdom of Jordan*, ICSID Case No. ARB/02/13, Decision on Jurisdiction, 9 November 2004, paras. 139, 151 (available at http://ita.law.uvic.ca/documents/salini-decision_000.pdf). The *Salini* tribunal cited, *inter alia*, to ICJ, *Oil Platforms (Islamic Republic of Iran* v. *United States of America)*, Judgment on Preliminary Objections, 12 December 1996, *ICJ Reports 1996*, p. 810, para. 16.

even assuming, or particularly assuming, the facts as
alleged by the claimant.

### C. Jurisdiction and Admissibility versus the Merits: The Illegality and Corruption Context

In light of the foregoing, we now turn to the issues
common to the commercial and investment treaty
context and the issues which differ specifically in the
context of illegality and corruption.

### 1. Issues common to the commercial and investment treaty context

#### (a) Jurisdiction and admissibility as early-stage problems

Issues of illegality and corruption are normally
alleged at the commencement stage or in any event
early on in any arbitration, whether commercial or
investment. To the extent the issues relate or are
alleged to relate to gateway questions of jurisdiction,
admissibility and the like, there will be a heavy
presumption and indeed burden of doing so, not least
because of the spectre of waiver of the objection
addressed above[762]. Moreover, unless the circumstances of the alleged illegality arise only later on in the
arbitration as a result of further due diligence or indeed
taking of evidence, more often than not the role of
corruption will likely already be at the fore at an early
stage.

From the perspective of claimant, it will likely have
considered the issue of corruption on the part of the

---

[762] See generally C. A. Miles, "Corruption, Jurisdiction
and Admissibility in International Investment Claims",
*Journal of International Dispute Settlement*, Vol. 3 (2012),
pp. 1 *et seq.* See also *supra* Chapter IX.B.1.d.

respondent as part and parcel of its own claims, and factored the issue into its decision whether to sue in the first place.

From the perspective of the respondent, even a respondent who is caught unawares by the bringing of the arbitration, it too will likely have considered whether corruption on the part of the claimant can be asserted as grounds to negate jurisdiction or entitlement to the claim, and will need to consider its defences to an allegation that its own corruption is at the heart of the claim brought against it.

### (b) *The form of decision and the further merits proceedings*

As a corollary of the foregoing observations the enforceability of any adjudication of a preliminary issue will depend on the form of the decision.

In investment treaty arbitrations and particularly ICSID, which to a large extent enjoys a certain transparency of results, a petition for annulment of a preliminary award affirming jurisdiction or a final award denying jurisdiction is almost a *de rigueur* step.

While it is difficult to know the percentage of ICSID awards on jurisdiction which have been challenged in annulment proceedings before, if at all, proceedings to a merits phase, experience suggests that the percentage is relatively high, and in any event likely higher than in commercial arbitration.

Again, there are many reasons for this difference, one being the particularity of the ICSID annulment mechanism, another being the likelihood that such annulment proceedings will indeed result in a delay or suspension of the merits proceedings, and another being that the grounds for ICSID annulment may be seen as being more flexible and open than the typical grounds for annulment under, for example, UNCITRAL Model Law Article 34[763]. Indeed the very fact that the grounds for annulment under ICSID Convention Article 52 do not include an express ground related to violation of public policy, a typical catch-all ground in commercial arbitration annulment proceedings, must be seen as encouraging and not discouraging annulment efforts in ICSID.

This encouragement must also be seen as being fostered further by the absence of a strict *res judicata* or *stare decisis* precedent mechanism from one ICSID decision to the next.

While a body of law continues to develop in the direction of a soft underbelly of ICSID precedent[764], the fact remains that each case is to a certain extent *sui generis* in a way and to an extent that simply does not exist in most national jurisdictions, even those which

---

[763] See generally B. M. Aronson, "A New Framework for ICSID Annulment Jurisprudence: Rethinking the 'Three Generations'", *ICL Journal*, Vol. 6 (2012), p. 1.

[764] See generally C. H. Schreuer and M. Weiniger, "A Doctrine of Precedent?", R. Muchlinski *et al.* (eds.), *The Oxford Handbook of International Investment Law*, New York, Oxford University Press, 2008, pp. 1191 *et seq.*; *Liberian Eastern Timber Corporation* v. *Republic of Liberia*, ICSID Case No. ARB/83/2, Award, 31 March 1986, *ICSID Reports*, Vol. 2 (1994), p. 352: "Though the tribunal is not bound by the precedents established by other ICSID Tribunals, it is nonetheless instructive to consider their interpretations . . ."; *World Duty Free* v. *Kenya*, *supra* footnote 44, para. 16; *ADC Affiliate Limited and ADC & ADMC Management Limited* v. *The Republic of Hungary*, ICSID Case No. ARB/03/16, Award, 2 October 2006, para. 293: "However, cautious reliance on certain principles developed in a number of those cases, as persuasive authority, may advance the body of law, which in turn may serve predictability in the interest of both investors and host States." Available at http://italaw.com/sites/default/files/case-documents/ita0006.pdf.

themselves do not have an express concept of binding precedent [765].

## (c) *Proof and law*

Corruption allegations often pose problems of the appropriate burden and standard of proof and of the relative weight of documents versus witnesses, as discussed earlier [766]. The legal consequences if any to be drawn from such allegations may differ in some cases between commercial and investment treaty arbitration, but the general challenges of proof are often the same if not quite similar.

Furthermore, corruption allegations often pose problems of the applicable law or laws, as addressed above [767]. Just as an act may be legal or illegal depending on the law applied, especially to the extent national law is applied, so too the legal consequences for the arbitrator's authority may depend on this analysis in both commercial and investment disputes.

## 2. *Differences between the commercial and investment treaty context*

### (a) *Reciprocal allegations of corruption*

Reciprocal allegations of corruption are made with increasing frequency in investment arbitration and would appear to play a disproportionate role in such disputes. This is not surprising to the extent that investment disputes involve issues and actors which typically

---

[765] See generally R. H. Kreindler, "Perspectives on State Party Arbitration: The Future of BITs — The Practitioner's Perspective", *Arbitration International*, Vol. 23 (2007), pp. 43 *et seq.*

[766] See *supra* Chapter VI.C.1.

[767] See *supra* Chapter IV.

give rise to corruption issues more than some areas of commercial life: participation of public officials, highly competitive bidding processes, complex infrastructure projects involving significant monetary stakes, efforts of investors large and small to obtain favourable legal and financial consideration and treatment, State control or monopoly over commercial sectors relevant to foreign investment, political instability and immature or transparent legal structures.

In investment arbitration typically the investor may make an allegation of corruption on the part of the host State as a basis for its claim of breach of a treaty or international obligation, while the respondent State may make an allegation of corruption on the part of the investor as a basis for its objection to jurisdiction or admissibility, its defence on the merits or its excuse of its own conduct. This is one of the most important and fascinating areas of illegality in arbitration, and will be addressed further below [768].

In this regard, competence, jurisdiction, arbitrability, separability and admissibility requirements may operate differently. An allegation of corruption, particularly against the claimant, will rarely be relevant in commercial arbitration to jurisdictional or admissibility requirements and rarely defeat them, while such an allegation in investment treaty-based arbitration is frequent and could be fatal to fulfilment of the requirements for jurisdiction and admissibility already at a preliminary bifurcated stage.

(b) *Legality of the investment as a gateway issue*

Investment treaties, including ICSID and the ECT, do not expressly address the legal effects of illegality

---

[768] See *infra* Chapter IX.D.1, Chapter X.C and Chapter X.D.

or corruption. This to be compared with the UN Corruption Convention Article 34, which provides: "State Parties may consider a relevant factor in legal proceedings to annul or rescind a contract, withdraw a concession or other similar instrument or take any other remedial action". This provision could in fact serve as a possible basis for invoking corruption on the part of the *investor* as a defence to possible liability for breach of treaty by the host State, as will be addressed below[769].

At the same time, legality of the investment may be seen already as a prerequisite of investment-treaty based jurisdiction. Both the ECT and the ICSID Convention provide as a prerequisite for ICSID jurisdiction that the dispute must relate to an investment[770] or arise out of an investment[771]. "Investment" is defined in Article 1 (6), ECT, as "every kind of asset, owned or controlled directly or indirectly by an Investor". The ICSID Convention is silent on the definition of "investment".

It should follow from the context, object and purpose of the ECT and the ICSID Convention that only legal investments shall enjoy protection under these treaties. The purpose of the ECT presumably does not include the promotion of illegal investments, including those that are illegal by reason of corruption. This follows not only because corruption is against good morals, but also because it hinders the aims of economic growth and development that the ECT strives to achieve[772]. Moreover, the international consensus that

---

[769] See *infra* Chapter X.D.4.
[770] Art. 26 (1), Energy Charter Treaty.
[771] Art. 25 (1), ICSID Convention.
[772] On the growing international consensus that corruption hinders economic growth and seriously undermines the credibility of public institutions, se*e* E. de Laurentiis, *supra* footnote 177, p. 244.

corruption offends international law and public policy should be considered. Thus, in order to interpret the term "investment" under the ECT in conformity with international law and public policy[773], it must normally be concluded that only legal, non-corrupt investments enjoy its protections.

The same principles can and should also be applied when construing the term "investment" under the ICSID Convention. The Preamble of the ICSID Convention likewise foresees sustainable economic development through investment protection as a main objective: "Considering the need for international cooperation for economic development, and the role of private international investment therein . . ."[774] Additionally, the ICSID Convention provides that disputes under the Convention shall be decided by reference to international law[775].

Finally, the ICSID Convention must be interpreted in accordance with international law[776].

The view that only legal investments, not tainted by illegal investor behaviour, are protected under international investment protection instruments has also been confirmed in various ICSID awards.

In *Inceysa* v. *El Salvador*, the arbitral tribunal declined jurisdiction and thus denied protection under the Spain–El Salvador BIT to an investment tainted by fraud, holding that the investment was thereby contrary

---

[773] Such interpretation would have to be done in conjunction with the Vienna Convention on the Law of Treaties (hereinafter "VCLT"), 27 January 1980, 1155 *UNTS* 331, UN doc. A/CONF.39/27 (1969), available at http://untreaty.un.org/ilc/texts/instruments/english/conventions/1_1_1969.pdf, Art. 31 (3) *(c)*.

[774] ICSID Convention Preamble.

[775] Art. 42 (1), ICSID Convention.

[776] Art. 31 (3) *(c)*, Vienna Convention on the Law of Treaties.

to public policy[777]. In *Ionannis Kardassopoulos* v. *Georgia*, in assessing whether the investment enjoyed protection under the ECT and the relevant BIT, the arbitral tribunal stated that

> "[t]his Tribunal must decide the issues in dispute between the parties in accordance with the applicable rules and principles of international law"[778].

---

[777] *Inceysa* v. *El Salvador*, *supra* footnote 174, paras. 248-252:

> "If this Tribunal declares itself competent to hear the disputes between the parties, it would completely ignore the fact that, above any claim of an investor, there is a meta-positive provision that prohibits attributing effects to an act done illegally . . . It is not possible to recognize the existence of rights arising from illegal acts, because it would violate the respect for the law which, as already indicated, is a principle of international public policy . . . In light of the foregoing, not to exclude Inceysa's investment from the protection of the BIT would be a violation of international public policy, which this Tribunal cannot allow. Consequently, this Arbitral Tribunal decides that Inceysa's investment is not protected by the BIT because it is contrary to international public policy."

[778] *Kardassopoulos* v. *Georgia*, Decision on Jurisdiction, *supra* footnote 491, paras. 144, 182 (rejecting Georgia's objection to jurisdiction under the Georgia-Greece BIT based on alleged illegality of concession and joint venture agreement). It then proceeded to apply the following general interpretative principles in order to assess whether the investment complied with the host State law:

> " 'Protection of investments' under a BIT is obviously not without some limits. It does not extend, for instance, to an investor making an investment in breach of the local laws of the host Sate. A State thus retains a degree of control over foreign investments by denying BIT protection to those investments that do not comply with its laws . . . This control, however, relates to the investor's actions in making the investment."

Furthermore, in the original award in *Fraport* v. *Philippines*, the arbitral tribunal held by majority that an investment not made in accordance with the host State law would not necessarily lose protection under the applicable BIT if the investor had rendered the investment illegal by mistake in good faith. Applying the facts, the majority held that "the comportment of the foreign investor was egregious . . . and cannot benefit from the presumptions which might ordinarily operate in favour of the investor"[779]. The arbitral tribunal in *Fraport* elaborated upon this principle as follows:

> "As for policy, BITs oblige governments to conduct their relations with foreign investors in a transparent fashion. Some reciprocal if not identical obligations lie on the foreign investor. One of those obligations is the obligation to make the investment in accordance with the host state's law. It is arguable that even an investment which is not made in accordance with host state law may import economic value to the host state. But that is not the only goal of this sector of international law. Respect for the integrity of the law of the host state is also a critical part of development and a concern of international investment law."[780]

And indeed in his dissenting opinion to the *Fraport* v. *Philippines* decision Professor Cremades wrote as follows:

> "Of course, any illegal behaviour by an investor

---

[779] *Fraport AG* v. *The Republic of the Philippines*, *supra* footnote 176, para. 397 (considering whether Fraport's investment fell under the protection of the German-Philippine BIT in light of Fraport's alleged violations of Philippine law).

[780] *Ibid.*, para. 402.

is likely to have consequences. Criminal conduct can and should be punished within the domestic criminal justice system. Illegal conduct by the investor might well excuse or limit any liability of the State Party in an arbitration pursuant to the BIT, depending on the circumstances. It is also possible for the Contracting Parties to a BIT to exclude the jurisdiction of an arbitral tribunal for illegalities committed by the investor. Investor illegality is serious, and there are many means to address it."[781]

### (c) *Enforceability of the award and corruption*

The enforceability of a commercial arbitration award on jurisdiction may operate fundamentally differently than of a comparable investment award, even when based on essentially the same facts and legal issues. Typically, the commercial award will be based on a national substantive law and its review will be based on the annulment grounds under the *lex arbitri* and the enforcement standards under the New York Convention, including its public policy ground. The ICSID investment award will likely be based on public international law principles with an overlay or underlay of local law of the host State and its review will be based on the annulment grounds of the ICSID Convention, without an express public policy control, and without any application of the New York Convention.

### D. *Legal Consequences and Effects of a Positive Finding of Illegality or Corruption*

We turn to the legal consequences and effects of a positive finding of illegality or corruption, first in the

---

[781] *Supra* footnote 779, dissenting opinion, § 14, at p. 10.

investment treaty context and then in the commercial context.

## 1. *The investment treaty context and claimant investor illegality*

Particular consequences and effects can be identified in the context of investment treaty arbitrations and illegality on the part of the claimant investor[782].

### (a) *Legality as a prerequisite for jurisdiction and consent*

Apart from determining whether acts of bribery have occurred, whether they are attributable to the claimant party, and whether they render the investment illegal and result in a lack of jurisdiction under the specific circumstances, a further question may arise, namely whether jurisdiction independently is lacking for a failure of *consent* as required under, for example, the ICSID Convention. That is, apart from whether jurisdiction may be lacking by reason of the illegality of the investment, jurisdiction could be lacking by reason of the failure to consent, depending upon the circumstances.

It is submitted that an arbitral tribunal lacks jurisdiction *ratione materiae* where a claimant investor's acts of bribery render its investment illegal. As a result, the illegal investment enjoys protection neither under, for example, the ECT nor the ICSID Convention. In this regard, the jurisdictional requirements of Article 26, ECT, and of Article 25 (1), ICSID Convention,

---

[782] See generally R. Kreindler, "Corruption in International Investment Arbitration: Jurisdiction and the Unclean Hands Doctrine", K. Hobér *et al.* (eds.), *Between East and West: Essays in Honour of Ulf Franke*, Huntington, Juris, 2010, pp. 309 *et seq.*

must be met. Again, both the ECT and the ICSID
Convention provide as a prerequisite for ICSID jurisdiction that the dispute must relate to an investment[783]
or arise out of an investment[784]. "Investment" is
defined in Article 1 (6), ECT, as "every kind of asset,
owned or controlled directly or indirectly by an
Investor". The ICSID Convention is silent on the definition of "investment".

The requirement that only legal investments enjoy
protection under these treaties and thus give rise to
ICSID jurisdiction is not explicitly stated in the provisions cited above. At the same time, it can and should
be derived from the objective and purpose of both the
ECT and the ICSID Convention, as well as from
general principles of international law.

*First*, the term "investment" must be interpreted,
pursuant to Article 31 (1) of the Vienna Convention on
the Law of Treaties (hereinafter "VCLT")[785], in "good
faith in accordance with the ordinary meaning to be
given to the terms of the treaty in their context and in
the light of its object and purpose". Furthermore,
Article 31 (3), VCLT, provides: "There shall be taken
into account, together with the context: any relevant
rules of international law applicable in the relations
between the parties."

It should follow from the context, object and purpose of the ECT and the ICSID Convention that only
*legal* investments shall enjoy protection under these
treaties. The purpose of the ECT presumably does not
include the promotion of *illegal* investments, including
those that are illegal by reason of corruption. This fol-

---

[783] Art. 26 (1), Energy Charter Treaty.
[784] Art. 25 (1), ICSID Convention.
[785] Vienna Convention on the Law of Treaties,
27 January 1980, 1155 *UNTS* 331, UN doc. A/CONF.39/27
(1969).

lows not only because corruption is against good morals, but also because it hinders the aims of economic growth and development that the ECT strives to achieve[786]. Moreover, as set forth earlier, the international consensus that corruption offends international law and public policy should be considered[787]. Thus, in order to interpret the term "investment" under the ECT in conformity with international law and public policy[788], it must normally be concluded that only legal, *non-corrupt* investments enjoy its protections.

*Second*, the same principles can and should also be applied when construing the term "investment" under the ICSID Convention. The Preamble of the ICSID Convention likewise foresees sustainable economic development through investment protection as a main objective: "Considering the need for international cooperation for economic development, and the role of private international investment therein . . ."[789] Additionally, the ICSID Convention provides that disputes under the Convention shall be decided by reference to international law[790]. Finally, the ICSID Convention must be interpreted in accordance with international law[791]. Therefore, it is submitted that for the exercise of jurisdiction pursuant to its Article 25 (1) the ICSID Convention likewise requires that the

---

[786] On the growing international consensus that corruption hinders economic growth and seriously undermines the credibility of public institutions, see E. de Laurentiis, *supra* footnote 177, p. 244.

[787] See *supra* Chapter III.

[788] Such interpretation would have to be done in conjunction with Art. 31 (3) *(c)*, Vienna Convention on the Law of Treaties.

[789] ICSID Convention Preamble.

[790] Art. 42 (1), ICSID Convention.

[791] Art. 31 (3) *(c)*, Vienna Convention on the Law of Treaties.

investment be in accordance with international law, and not be tainted by illegality.

*Third*, the view that only legal investments, not tainted by illegal investor behaviour, are protected under international investment protection instruments has also been confirmed in various ICSID awards.

In *Inceysa* v. *El Salvador*, the arbitral tribunal declined jurisdiction and thus denied protection under the Spain-El Salvador BIT to an investment tainted by fraud, holding that the investment was thereby contrary to public policy:

> "If this Tribunal declares itself competent to hear the disputes between the parties, it would completely ignore the fact that, above any claim of an investor, there is a meta-positive provision that prohibits attributing effects to an act done illegally . . . *It is not possible to recognize the existence of rights arising from illegal acts, because it would violate the respect for the law which, as already indicated, is a principle of international public policy . . . In light of the foregoing, not to exclude Inceysa's investment from the protection of the BIT would be a violation of international public policy, which this Tribunal cannot allow.* Consequently, this Arbitral Tribunal decides that Inceysa's investment is not protected by the BIT because it is contrary to international public policy."[792]

In *Ionannis Kardassopoulos* v. *Georgia*, in assessing whether the investment enjoyed protection under the ECT and the relevant BIT, the arbitral tribunal stated that "[t]his Tribunal must decide the issues in dispute between the parties in accordance with the applicable

---

[792] *Inceysa* v. *El Salvador*, *supra* footnote 174, paras. 248-252 (emphasis added).

rules and principles of international law"[793]. It then proceeded to apply the following general interpretative principles in order to assess whether the investment complied with the host State law:

> " 'Protection of investments' under a BIT is obviously not without some limits. It does not extend, for instance, to an investor making an investment in breach of the local laws of the host Sate. A State thus retains a degree of control over foreign investments by *denying BIT protection to those investments that do not comply with its laws* . . . This control, however, relates to the investor's actions in making the investment."[794]

The arbitral tribunal then held that the claimant's investment did fall under the protections of the BIT because "Respondent does not allege that Claimant committed any act in violation of Georgian law"[795]. From this may be derived the conclusion that if an illegal act committed by the investor itself had rendered the investment illegal, the arbitral tribunal would have held that the claimant's investment no longer enjoyed protection under the BIT.

Finally, in the original award in *Fraport* v. *Philippines*, the arbitral tribunal held by majority that an investment not made in accordance with the host State law would not necessarily lose protection under the applicable BIT if the investor had rendered the investment illegal by mistake in good faith[796].

---

[793] *Kardassopoulos* v. *Georgia*, Decision on Jurisdiction, *supra* footnote 491, para. 144 (rejecting Georgia's objection to jurisdiction under the Georgia-Greece BIT based on alleged illegality of concession and joint venture agreement).

[794] *Ibid.*, para. 182 (emphasis added).

[795] *Ibid.*, para. 183.

[796] *Ibid.*, para. 402.

The tribunal then continued in citing *Lucchetti* v. *Peru*[797]:

> "Lucchetti may therefore consider it a harsh result that its effort at obtaining an international remedy is brought to a halt before the merits of its contentions are even examined. Such a conclusion, however, would not be warranted in the light of the fact that *Lucchetti did not have an* a priori *entitlement to this international forum.*"[798]

In view of the foregoing, it is submitted that it is established that investments which are contrary to international law and illegal due to the investor's own illegal conduct do not enjoy any protection under the relevant investment protection treaty. An illegal investment that offends international law does not enjoy protection specifically under the ECT, nor does it meet the requirements to establish ICSID jurisdiction under Article 26, ECT, or under Article 25 (1), ICSID. Consequently, an arbitral tribunal confronted with such a case should consider that it lacks jurisdiction *ratione materiae* over the investor's claim.

The relevant point in time at which the investor must still have conducted itself legally in order to maintain the investment's legality and not compromise jurisdiction is the date of the institution of the arbitral proceedings. Both the ECT and the ICSID Convention are silent regarding the date on which the requirements for the existence and exercise of jurisdiction must be

---

[797] *Empresas Lucchetti, S.A. and Lucchetti Peru, S.A.* v. *The Republic of Peru*, ICSID Case No. ARB/03/4 (also known as: *Industria Nacional de Alimentos, A.S. and Indalsa Perú S.A.* v. *The Republic of Peru*), Award, 7 February 2005, para. 61 (available at http://italaw.com/sites/default/files/case-documents/ita0275.pdf).

[798] *Fraport AG* v. *The Republic of the Philippines*, *supra* footnote 176, para. 403 (emphasis added).

met. However, the requirement that the date in question is the date of the institution of arbitral proceedings can and should be derived from accepted principles of international adjudication. As stated by Professors Dolzer and Schreuer, for example,

"[i]t is an accepted principle of international adjudication that, in the absence of treaty provisions to the contrary, the relevant date for purposes of jurisdiction is the date of the institution of proceedings"[799].

This general principle has also been affirmed in *Vivendi II* in the context of an investment arbitration:

"It is [a] generally recognized [principle] that the determination of whether a party has standing in an international judicial forum, for purposes of jurisdiction to institute proceedings, is made by reference to the date on which such proceedings are deemed to have been instituted. ICSID Tribunals have consistently applied this Rule."[800]

This principle has been cited or applied approvingly by various other ICSID arbitral tribunals in different

---

[799] R. Dolzer and C. H. Schreuer, *supra* footnote 165, p. 41 (citing the following cases for this principle: *Questions of Interpretation and Application of the 1971 Montreal Convention arising from the Aerial Incident at Lockerbie (Libyan Arab Jamahiriya* v. *United States of America)*, Preliminary Objections, 27 February 1998, *ICJ Reports 1998*, p. 130, available at http://www.icj-cij.org/docket/files/89/7249.pdf; *Arrest Warrant of 11 April 2000 (Democratic Republic of the Congo* v. *Belgium)*, 14 February 2002, *ICJ Reports 2002*, p. 13, available at http://www.icj-cij.org/docket/files/121/8126.pdf).

[800] *Compania de Aguas del Aconquija, P.A. & Vivendi Universal P.A.* v. *Argentina (Vivendi II)*, *supra* footnote 166, para. 60 (dismissing Argentina's objections to Claimant's *jus standi*).

contexts[801]. Thus, it can and should be viewed as an established principle that the investment must have been maintained in accordance with international law and thus not tainted by a concomitant or subsequent illegal act at the time the arbitral proceedings related to such investment are instituted. Here, a claimant would have had to maintain its investment in accordance with international law, without any concomitant or subsequent acts of bribery, up until the date it initiated the arbitration.

The foregoing principle respecting the timing of the legality of the investor's original investment and the commencement of proceedings should be considered to be firm. At the same time, it leads to the related question of whether the investor must *maintain* the legality of its original investment as of the date of commencing proceedings. In my opinion, the answer is yes. Accordingly, failure or refusal to do so can and should result in the lack of jurisdiction over claims under that investment by reason of non-compliance with the applicable international law.

Only an investor who is in compliance with international law at the time of the institution of the proceeding should be entitled to enjoy protection under, for example, the ECT.

*First*, while international law is generally applicable only between States, it is a well-established principle in investment arbitration law that the investor's investment itself must also comply with international public policy, which forms part of international law[802]. The investor is making and maintaining the investment subject to protections under either an investment contract

---

[801] See R. Dolzer and C. H. Schreuer, *supra* footnote 165, p. 41, for further references.

[802] See, e.g., the general reasoning in *Inceysa* v. *El Salvador*, *supra* footnote 174, para. 252; *World Duty Free* v. *Kenya*, *supra* footnote 44, para. 157.

or a bilateral investment and/or a multilateral investment treaty, which in turn trigger the application of international law. It can be derived therefrom that the investor must comply with international law and public policy while making and maintaining the investment. This also derives from the concept that if the investor is granted subjective rights under international law, it also has a subjective *duty* to comply with the general principles and legal standards of the ECT, as the ECT is in turn governed by international law[803].

*Second*, on the basis of this principle as well as the previously discussed objectives of the ECT and international law, the investor's obligation to comply with international law is *ongoing*. That ongoing obligation relates not only to the making of the investment, but also to the maintenance of the investment. The ongoing compliance with international law is a reciprocal obligation that can and should be derived from the objective and purpose of the ECT and from international law, as explained above. In accord with this principle of an obligation of legality of conduct on the part of the investor, the majority in *Fraport* v. *Philippines* stated, in a somewhat different factual context, in relevant part:

> "As for policy, BITs oblige governments to conduct their relations with foreign investors in a transparent fashion. *Some reciprocal if not identical obligations lie on the foreign investor.*"[804]

---

[803] For the position that the investor is granted subjective rights under international law in the context of investment arbitration, see Muchlinski, *supra* footnote 175, pp. 535, 547, 557 ("a duty to conduct the investment, once it has been undertaken, in a reasonable manner"). See also R. Happ, *supra* footnote 175, p. 138; O. Spiermann, *supra* footnote 175.

[804] *Fraport AG* v. *The Republic of the Philippines*, *supra* footnote 176, para. 402 (emphasis added).

Whether the investment is *made* illegally or *maintained* illegally should not be viewed as an outcome-determinative distinction. The general purpose of an investment protection treaty such as the ECT is to give protection only to legal investments not tainted by corruption. If protection were denied only for investments that were made illegally and not to those that were maintained illegally, investors could be incentivized to maintain protection by forming the investment legally and committing criminal acts at a later stage.

Accordingly, it would be inconsistent for international law to sanction corruption but still protect a corrupt investment if the corruption were committed in order to maintain the investment instead of initially in order to procure it. With respect to the deleterious effects of corruption, it makes no difference whether the corruption occurs at the time of procurement or while maintaining or seeking to maintain the investment at a later time. Furthermore, only investors complying with basic principles of international law promote growth that would be sustainable *without* ongoing bribery[805].

Thus, it would be contrary to international law and public policy if investors were permitted to commit illegal acts such as corruption in order to maintain their investment and still take advantage of either contract-based or particularly treaty-based protections for their investments in conformity with applicable standards of international law. Indeed, a failure to maintain the investment legally should normally result in a failure to remain in conformity with those standards.

Consequently, it can and should be concluded that

---

[805] On the growing international consensus that corruption hinders economic growth and seriously undermines the credibility of public institutions, see E. de Laurentiis, *supra* footnote 177, p. 244.

an investor who does not maintain the investment in
compliance with international law thereby loses protections under the applicable investment protection treaty
which it might otherwise enjoy.

(b) *Jurisdiction and estoppel based on "unclean
hands"*

What about jurisdiction and estoppel from accepting
the offer to submit the dispute to jurisdiction, on the
basis of the Unclean Hands Doctrine? Could it be that
apart from whether jurisdiction may be lacking by
reason of the illegality of the investment and/or the
failure of consent by the respondent, the claimant
investor could be estopped from accepting the respondent's offer to submit to jurisdiction because of its own
unclean hands? Under the Unclean Hands Doctrine, a
tribunal can and should deny relief to a claimant
"whose conduct in regard to the subject-matter of the
litigation has been improper"[806]. Likewise, a tribunal
"will refuse to aid a complainant in protecting any
right acquired or *retained* by inequitable conduct"[807].
Thus, international tribunals have dismissed claims
tainted by illegal behaviour by applying the Unclean
Hands Doctrine as a general principle of public international law.

---

[806] PCIJ, *Diversion of Water from the Meuse (Netherlands* v. *Belgium), supra* footnote 739, p. 77, para. 323
(individual opinion of Judge Hudson); *S&E Contractors,
Inc.* v. *United States*, 92 S. Ct. 1411, 1419 (US Supreme
Court 1972) (USA) ("Patents obtained with unclean hands
and contracts that are based on those patents are similarly
tainted and will not be enforced").

[807] *International News Service* v. *The Associated Press*,
248 US 215 (US Supreme Court 1918) (stating in dictum
that the doctrine of unclean hands did not apply where the
plaintiff newspaper relied on news stories first published
by the defendant news service) (emphasis added).

General principles of law are principles that are encountered in the domestic legal orders of the individual members of the international community and which are applied in order to fill gaps in the law of nations[808]. As the Unclean Hands Doctrine is encountered in the domestic legal orders of many States, it should generally qualify as a general principle of law, and thus as a source of international law pursuant to Article 38 (1) *(c)* of the ICJ Statute.

The doctrine was originally developed at common law, but today can be found in the laws of many jurisdictions, civil- and common-law alike[809].

It derives from more general principles of good faith and is also rooted in principles of Roman Law, which are the basis of the laws of most civil-law countries[810].

---

[808] C. Tomuschat, *supra* footnote 366, p. 335; I. Brownlie, *supra* footnote 356, p. 16.

[809] For example, Sec. 817 (2), Bürgerliches Gesetzbuch [German Civil Code] [BGB]; Sec. 242, Bürgerliches Gesetzbuch [German Civil Code] [BGB], which corresponds to the Unclean Hands Doctrine and encompasses the principle "Die Rechtsausübung kann unzulässig sein, wenn dem Berechtigten eine Verletzung eigener Pflichten zur Last fällt"; "Dieser Grundsatz hat sich aus der exceptio doli specialis=praeteriti des röm. und gemeinen Rechts entwickelt. Er entspricht im anglo-amerikanischen Rechtskreis dem Einwand der 'unclean hands'" ("This principle developed from the principle exceptio doli specialis=praeteriti of Roman and Common law. It corresponds to the 'unclean hands' defence known in Anglo-American law" (my translation)); C. Grüneberg, Palandt Bürgerliches Gesetzbuch, 72nd ed., Munich, Verlag C.H. Beck, 2013, Sec. 242, BGB, paras. 43, 46.

[810] L. Garcia-Arias, "La Doctrine des 'Clean Hands' en Droit International Public", *Yearbook, Association of Attenders of Alumni of the Hague Academy of International Law*, Vol. 30 (1960), pp. 14, 16 (referring to fragments in the *Codex* and the *Digest* establishing the "clean hands" doctrine).

The Unclean Hands Doctrine is closely related to several similar Latin maxims[811]: *ex delicto non oritor actio* ("an unlawful act cannot serve as the basis of an action in law")[812]; *nemo ex suo delicto meliorem suam conditionem facit* ("no one can put himself in a better legal position by means of a delict")[813]; *ex turpi causa non oritur actio* ("an action cannot arise from a dishonourable cause")[814]; *inadimplenti non est adimplendum* ("one has no need to respect his obligation if the counter-party has not respected its own")[815]; and *nullus commodum capere potest de injuria sua propria*

---

[811] P. Wendel, *State Responsibility for Interferences with the Freedom of Navigation in Public International Law*, London, Springer, 2007, p. 157 ; International Law Commission, Sixth Report on Diplomatic Protection, UN doc. A/CN.4/546 (5 August 2005) (prepared by John Dugard), http://daccessdds.un.org/doc/UNDOC/GEN/N04/457/55/PDF/N0445755.pdf?OpenElement, at 2.

[812] B. Cheng, *General Principles of Law as Applied by International Courts and Tribunals*, Cambridge, Cambridge University Press, 2006, p. 155 (citing to PCIJ, *Legal Status of Eastern Greenland (Denmark v. Norway)*, 5 September 1933, *1933 PCIJ Series A/B*, No. 55.

[813] B. Cheng, *ibid.*, p. 156 (citing to Ecuadorian-United States Claims Commission in 1862, 3 *International Arbitration*, pp. 2738-2739).

[814] Discussed in *British Columbia* v. *Zastowny*, 2008 SCC 4 (Supreme Court 2008) (Canada) (holding that the victim of a sexual assault by a prison guard could not recover the loss of income resulting from his injuries, as he was himself the perpetrator of several crimes).

[815] Discussed in *Klöckner Industrie-Anlagen GmbH and Others* v. *United Republic of Cameroon and Société camerounaise des engrais*, ICSID Case No. ARB/81/2, Award, October 21, 1983, English translations of French original at J. Paulsson, "The ICSID Klöckner v. Cameroon Award: The Duties of Partners in North-South Economic Development Agreements", *Journal of International Arbitration*, Vol. 1 (1984), p. 160 (defining the maxim *inadimplenti non est adimplendum* as a general principle of international law).

("no one can be allowed to take advantage of his own wrong")[816].

The wide adoption of the Unclean Hands Doctrine and similar principles could justify treating it as a "general principle of law recognized by civilized nations" as cited in Article 38 (1) *(c)*, ICJ Statute. Moreover, the Unclean Hands Doctrine not only can qualify as a general principle of law, but it also has been applied with some frequency and alacrity by international tribunals. The doctrine was first cited by the Permanent Court of International Justice in the *Diversion of Water from the Meuse* case[817]. In a dissenting opinion, Judge Azilotti stated that "[t]he principle . . . *(adimplenti non est adimplendum)* is so just, so equitable, so universally recognized that it must be applied in international relations . . ."[818].

The Unclean Hands Doctrine has also been raised in other ICJ cases, for example in the advisory proceedings on *Legal Consequences of the Construction of a Wall in the Occupied Palestinian Territory*[819], the *Oil Platforms* case[820] and in the *Arrest Warrant* case[821].

---

[816] B. Cheng, *supra* footnote 812, p. 149 (citing the *Montijo* case, 2 *International Arbitration*, pp. 1437 (1875)).

[817] PCIJ, *Diversion of Water from the Meuse (Netherlands* v. *Belgium)*, *supra* footnote 739.

[818] PCIJ, *Diversion of Water from the Meuse (Netherlands* v. *Belgium)*, *supra* footnote 739, p. 50, para. 211 (dissenting opinion of Judge Anzilotti).

[819] ICJ, *Legal Consequences of the Construction of a Wall in the Occupied Palestinian Territory*, Advisory Opinion, 9 July 2004, *ICJ Reports 2004*, p. 163, available at http://www.icj-cij.org/docket/index.php?p1=3&p2=4&code=mwp&case=131&k=5a.

[820] ICJ, *Oil Platforms (Islamic Republic of Iran* v. *United States of America)*, 6 November 2003, separate opinion of Judge Simma, at pp. 176-178, available at http://www.icj-cij.org/docket/files/90/9735.pdf.

[821] *Arrest Warrant of 11 April 2000 (Democratic Republic of the Congo* v. *Belgium)*, *supra* footnote 799,

While the ICJ has not explicitly upheld the Unclean Hands Doctrine by any majority opinion, it has not dismissed or sought to discredit it either in those cases in which it figured. Thus, on the foregoing basis one could conclude that the Unclean Hands Doctrine is a general principle of public international law[822]. Furthermore, the Unclean Hands Doctrine has been applied in various commercial arbitration proceedings, specifically in the corruption context[823]. Likewise, it has been so applied in State court proceedings involving issues of transnational commerce and corruption. In *Adler* v. *Republic of Nigeria*, for example, the US Court of Appeals held that the individual claimant was barred from relief because of his own "unclean hands", reasoning that he had voluntarily participated in a money laundering and corruption scheme involving Nigerian public officials[824].

The Unclean Hands Doctrine has also been affirmed as a general principle in investment arbitration regard-

---

at p. 160 (dissenting opinion of Chris Van den Wyngaert).

[822] International Law Commission, Report of the International Law Commission, Fifty-seventh session, 2 May-3 June and 11 July-5 August 2005, General Assembly, *Official Records*, Sixtieth Session, Supplement No. 10 (A/60/10), 114, para. 236, http://untreaty.un.org/ilc/reports/2005/2005report.htm; C. Amerasinghe, *Diplomatic Protection*, Oxford, Oxford University Press, 2008, p. 212.

[823] See ICC Case No. 2730, Collection of ICC Arbitral Awards 1974-1985, at 497, 498 (1982) (citing to ICC Case No.1110); ICC Case No. 6248, *XIX Yearbook Commercial Arbitration*, 139 (1994); ICC Case No. 1110, *supra* footnote 3, at p. 6; ICC Case No. 8891, *supra* footnote 357, at pp. 561, 567.

[824] *Adler* v. *Federal Republic of Nigeria*, Case Number 98-55456 (9th Cir. 1999), available at 15 *Mealey's International Arbitration Report* A-1 (2000) (USA) (concerning claim to payments made to Nigerian government officials ).

ing claims tainted by corruption. In a prominent relatively recent example, an ICSID tribunal chaired by Judge Guillaume, former President of the ICJ, dismissed the investor's claim in *World Duty Free* because it had been tainted by corruption. It essentially applied the Unclean Hands Doctrine by specifically referring to the grounds for the dismissal on the basis of *ex turpi causa non oritur actio*[825]. The reliance on the maxim *ex turpi causa non oritur actio* can and should be considered as another application of the Unclean Hands Doctrine. The arbitral tribunal held that the acts of bribery committed by the investor were contrary to international public policy. In so doing, it cited the opinion of Kerr LJ in *Euro-Diam*:

> "It would be an 'affront to public conscience' to grant to the Claimant relief which it seeks because this Tribunal 'would thereby assist and encourage the plaintiff in his illegal conduct'. . . . Accordingly, the Tribunal rejects the Claimant's submissions."[826]

The question now arises apart from whether juris-

---

[825] *World Duty Free* v. *Kenya*, *supra* footnote 44, para. 179.

[826] *Ibid.*, para. 178. See generally R. Kreindler, "Aspects of Illegality in the Formation and Performance of Contracts", *supra* footnote 634, at 258 ("While certain practices might be tolerated and widespread in a particular country, the Arbitral Tribunal should not condone or support hindrance to the elimination of those practices") and R. Kreindler, *Strafrechtsrelevante und andere anstößige Verträge als Gegenstand von Schiedsverfahren: Zum Vorgehen von Schiedsgerichten bei Rechtsverletzungen von Vertragsparteien — ein rechtsvergleichender Beitrag zur nationalen und internationalen Schiedsgerichtsbarkeit [Illegal and Other Objectionable Contracts as the Subject of Arbitration: A Comparative Law Contribution to National and International Arbitration]*, Schriftenreihe Abhandlungen zum Recht der Internationalen Wirtschaft, Band 71, Verlag Recht und Wirtschaft, 2005.

diction may be lacking by reason of the illegality of the investment or by reason of the failure of consent, whether jurisdiction could be considered to be independently lacking because a claimant is estopped by reason of "unclean hands" from accepting respondent's offer? In this context, the arbitral tribunal in *World Duty Free* held,

> "If, from the plaintiff's own stating or otherwise, the cause of actions appears to arise *ex turpi causa*, or the transgression of a positive law of this country, there the court says he has no right to be assisted."[827]

One question will be whether there is any evidential ambiguity as to the fact that acts of bribery attributable to a claimant were indeed committed: is the bribery admitted or otherwise proven? Another question will be whether the investment and the causes of action arise *ex turpi causa* and specifically whether the investment was maintained in violation of national criminal law and in offence of international law. Under such circumstances, a claimant should not be "assisted" in enforcing the claims arising out of its investment tainted by the illegal conduct.

The question also arises in the case of bribery, for example, of government officials, whether a claimant investor could raise the defence that the respondent host State was equally at fault. This would assume, *arguendo*, that the acts of bribery of its government officials could be legally attributed to the respondent. Is there any evidence or even specific allegation that any government officials who received bribes were acting on the specific instructions of or under the direction or control of the respondent in receiving the

---

[827] *World Duty Free* v. *Kenya*, *supra* footnote 44, para. 181.

bribes? Can one assume "equality of fault"? Such defence, if raised, could well fail depending on the circumstances: "where both are equally at fault, *potior est conditio defendentis*".

In such a scenario, it may be that the balancing would not favour the claimant investor and would thereby not unfairly advantage the respondent host State. Rather, the beneficiary of such balancing would be the respondent State itself. As noted, the law does not protect "the litigating parties but the public — or in this case, the mass of tax-payers and other citizens making up one of the poorest countries in the world"[828] — a characterization which may also be apt to the respondent State. This argument was also indirectly discussed in *World Duty Free* v. *Kenya*. While the arbitral tribunal did not make the balance of interests part of its reasoning, it stated that it was a highly disturbing feature that the corrupt recipient of the Claimant's bribe was more than an officer of State but its most senior officer and that no attempt had been made by Kenya to prosecute him for corruption or to recover the bribe in civil proceedings. However, the arbitral tribunal then resolved this conflict of interest by holding that the balance should tip in favour of the public interest, i.e., the people of Kenya.

In summary, the legal effects of a positive finding of illegality or corruption in investment treaty arbitration are manifold, but can be reduced to a few variations.

*First*, a possible denial of benefits of the arbitration agreement and estoppel from the accepting State "consent" in the treaty, resulting in a lack of *jurisdiction*. The focus here is on a kind of personal jurisdiction *(ratione voluntatis)*, in terms of the respondent's consent to arbitration, and not on subject matter jurisdic-

---

[828] *World Duty Free* v. *Kenya*, *supra* footnote 44, para. 181.

tion *(ratione materiae)*: see, for example, *Inceysa* v. *El Salvador*, ICSID (2006)[829]. The State "consent" is governed by, *inter alia*, transnational public policy via the 1969 Vienna Convention on the Law of Treaties, Article 31 (3) *(c)*, whereby the arbitrator must consider "any relevant rules of international law applicable in the relations between the parties", which in turn includes transnational public policy. The investor who illegally made or illegally maintained an investment is estopped from availing itself of the open invitation in the treaty if it did not have a "legal and bona fide investment" — *Phoenix Action* v. *Czech Republic*, ICSID (2009)[830]. At the same time, there is "no open invitation" if corruption is deemed to have rendered the consent void: "Nobody can benefit from his own wrong" *(nemo auditor propriam turpitudinem allegans)* — *Inceysa* v. *El Salvador*, ICSID (2006)[831]. The right to arbitrate as a substantive treaty right is to be denied on the basis of estoppel, so that no agreement has been concluded *ab initio*, as opposed to an "open" arbitration agreement being deemed invalidated.

*Second*, where treaty protection is limited to investments made "in accordance with the law", the treaty does not cover disputes relating to investments "made" illegally (procured, also possibly maintained), resulting in a lack of *jurisdiction*. The legality of the investment is an express treaty prerequisite to protectable investment. Again, the focus here is on a kind of personal jurisdiction *(ratione voluntatis)*, in terms of the respondent's consent to arbitration only of investments made in accordance with local law, and not on ubject matter

---

[829] *Inceysa* v. *El Salvador*, *supra* footnote 174, para. 144.

[830] *Phoenix Action* v. *The Czech Republic*, *supra* footnote 492, paras. 100 *et seq.*

[831] *Inceysa* v. *El Salvador*, *supra* footnote 174, para. 240.

jurisdiction *(ratione materiae)*, which is connected to the question whether there is an investment dispute, not whether the dispute arises out of an investment in accordance with local law: *Saba Fakes* v. *Turkey*, ICSID (2010)[832]; *Inceysa* v. *El Salvador*, ICSID (2006)[833].

Accordingly, if illegality affects the consent to arbitration, then it is a matter of *jurisdiction*; if illegality does not affect the consent to arbitration, then it is a matter of *merits* affecting substantive protections. Fraud or misrepresentation in a bidding process does not meet the treaty requirement of legality: *Inceysa* v. *El Salvador*, ICSID (2006)[834]. Dissimulation of true ownership and circumvention of law equates to a lack of jurisdiction *ratione materiae*: *Fraport* v. *Philippines*, ICSID (2007)[835]. And investments in breach of basic principles of host law, which normally outlaw fraud and corruption, will likewise result in a lack of jurisdiction: *Desert Line* v. *Yemen*, ICSID (2008)[836].

*Third*, where treaty protection is *not* limited to investments made "in accordance with the law" (e.g., ECT) or where jurisdiction upheld and investor committed illegality in relation to investment, treaty substantive protections may be denied, resulting in a lack of *admissibility*, including on the basis of "unclean hands". Legality may not be an express treaty jurisdictional prerequisite, but it is still an *implied* admissi-

---

[832] *Saba Fakes* v. *Republic of Turkey*, *supra* footnote 483, paras. 119 *et seq*.
[833] *Inceysa* v. *El Salvador*, *supra* footnote 174, paras. 183 *et seq*.
[834] *Inceysa* v. *El Salvador*, *supra* footnote 174, paras. 201 *et seq*.
[835] *Fraport AG* v. *The Republic of the Philippines*, *supra* footnote 176, para. 401.
[836] *Desert Line* v. *Yemen*, *supra* footnote 214, para. 104.

bility prerequisite: *Saluka* v. *Czech Republic*, ICSID (2006)[837]; *Plama* v. *Bulgaria*, ICSID (2008)[838]; *Phoenix Action* v. *Czech Republic*, ICSID (2009)[839]; but cf. *Saba Fakes* v. *Turkey*, ICSID (2010)[840].

Here a distinction between issues of jurisdiction and admissibility and merits may need to be made.

> "Objections to admissibility . . . even if the Court has jurisdiction and the facts stated by the applicant State are assumed to be correct, nonetheless there are reasons why the Court should not proceed to an examination of the merits."[841]

Jurisdiction and admissibility are not always distinguished or pleaded separately, but there may be ample basis for determining dismissal on inadmissibility even where upholding jurisdiction: *Methanex* v. *US*, NAFTA (2002)[842]; *Occidental Exploration* v. *Ecuador*, LCIA (2004)[843]. The investor is estopped from seeking redress through protection of substantive rights in the treaty if it has "unclean hands", independent of whether the acts are (also) a breach of transnational

---

[837] *Saluka Investments B.V.* v. *The Czech Republic*, UNCITRAL, Partial Award, 17 March 2006 (available at http://italaw.com/sites/default/files/case-documents/ita 0740.pdf).

[838] *Plama* v. *Bulgaria*, *supra* footnote 372.

[839] *Phoenix Action Ltd.* v. *The Czech Republic*, *supra* footnote 492.

[840] *Saba Fakes* v. *Republic of Turkey*, *supra* footnote 483.

[841] ICJ, *Oil Platforms (Islamic Republic of Iran* v. *United States of America)*, Judgment, 6 November 2003, para. 29 (available at http://www.icj-cij.org/docket/files/90/9715.pdf).

[842] *Methanex Corporation* v. *United States of America*, *supra* footnote 772, paras. 122 *et seq.*

[843] *Occidental Exploration and Production Company* v. *The Republic of Ecuador*, *supra* footnote 758.

public policy, as a result of the absence of necessary *locus standi in judicio*[844].

The respondent's own illegality should have no influence on the (in)admissibility of the corrupt investor's claims. The Unclean Hands Doctrine should be applied to dismiss claim tainted by corruption even if the host State was manifestly or admittedly equally corrupt: *World Duty Free* v. *Kenya*, ICSID (2006)[845]; *Kardassopoulos* v. *Georgia*, ICSID (2007)[846]. Where *both* are blameworthy, then the defendant is in the stronger position: *in pari delicto potior est conditio possidentis*. In receiving a bribe, the individual government official should be held to be acting *ultra vires*, so that any alleged illegality of the respondent State, even if attributable to the State, should not be considered to be "equal" with that of the illegality by the investor claimant.

Should a "balancing test" of degrees of egregiousness be applied? The tribunal in *World Duty Free* found that even assuming such a balancing, the result would still tip in favour of the respondent State representing the interests of the public, namely the people of Kenya — "the law protects not the litigating parties but

---

[844] B. Cheng, *supra* footnote 812, pp. 155 *et seq.*; J. Bassett Moore, *History and Digest of the International Arbitrations to Which the United States Has Been a Party*, Vol. III, 1898, pp. 2738 *et seq.*; I. Brownlie, *Principles of Public International Law*, *supra* footnote 362, p. 503; G. Fitzmaurice, *supra* footnote 172, p. 119. See also *Pelletier* case, 2 *Moore International Arbitration Reports* p. 1749; *Medea & Good Return* case, 3 *Moore International Arbitration Reports*, p. 2739; ICJ, *Military and Paramilitary Activities in and against Nicaragua (Nicaragua* v. *United States of America)*, *supra* footnote 585, Judge Schwebel dissenting opinion, p. 394.

[845] *World Duty Free* v. *Kenya*, *supra* footnote 44.

[846] *Kardassopoulos* v. *Georgia*, Decision on Jurisdiction, *supra* footnote 491.

the public; or in this case, the mass of taxpayers and other citizens making up one of the poorest countries in the world"[847]. And Muchlinki has opined in this regard,

> "[W]hile the conduct of the investor may be weighed against the conduct of the host country authorities in determining whether the latter had indeed acted wrongly, . . . that conduct must meet a threshold level of unconscionability to negate the improper conduct of the host authorities."[848]

This could in fact imply a balancing or proportionality test after all, in which case the criteria to apply would need to be articulated, and the question of whether it becomes a merits issue after all would need to be answered.

*Fourth*, where jurisdiction has been upheld and the investor committed illegality in relation to the investment, the investor's claims may be deemed to breach transnational public policy, resulting in a lack of *admissibility*. In most treaty-based disputes, principles of international law, including transnational public policy, govern the substance. "[I]t is not possible to recognize the existence of rights arising from illegal acts . . . Would violate . . . international public policy."[849]

This relates to the fundamental maxim that illegality cannot become a source of legal right to a wrongdoer *(ex injuria jus non oritur)*[850]. This is to be distinguished from a refusal of protection due to a breach of

---

[847] *World Duty Free* v. *Kenya*, *supra* footnote 44, para. 181.

[848] P. Muchlinski, *supra* footnote 175, pp. 539 *et seq.*

[849] *Inceysa* v. *El Salvador*, *supra* footnote 174, para. 249.

[850] H. Lauterpacht, *Recognition in International Law*, Cambridge, Cambridge University Press, 1947, p. 421.

an "in accordance with law" requirement: a breach of the applicable law may be different than a breach of the principle of good faith or a breach of public policy. Furthermore, unlike the commercial context, it is not possible to declare a treaty "void" in the same way as a contract might be declared "invalid" or "void" due to fraud or corruption. Thus, corruption of the investor does not affect the validity of the treaty, but rather its procedural ability to rely on substantive treaty rights, which "remain intact"[851].

### (c) *The Unclean Hands Doctrine and "equal fault" or "mutual fault"*

Depending upon the particular circumstances, the question arises whether the Unclean Hands Doctrine or maxims derivative of it can and should be applied to dismiss a claim tainted by corruption even if, in the investment context, the host State were manifestly or admittedly "equally at fault" by having participated in the corruption.

Indeed, it fell to the arbitral tribunal in *World Duty Free* to consider, in the face of an allegation or finding that the respondent host State might have been at fault in accepting a bribe, whether it had equally offended the applicable law, including international public policy. The arbitral tribunal unanimously held that even in such case it would not be unfair to the claimant investor to dismiss its claims on the grounds that they arose out of or in connection with an investment related to an act of bribery. The award cites amply to Lord Mansfield, who wrote in relevant part:

---

[851] B. M. Cremades, "Corruption and Investment Arbitration", in G. Aksen *et al.* (eds.), *Global Reflections on International Law, Commerce and Dispute Resolution: Liber Amicorum in Honour of Robert Briner*, ICC Publication, 2005, p. 214.

"[T]he objection that a contract is immoral or illegal as between plaintiff and defendant, sounds at all times very ill in the mouth of the defendant. It is not for his sake, however, that the objection is ever allowed; but it is founded in general principles of policy, which the defendant has advantage of, contrary to the real justice, as between him and the plaintiff, but accidentally, if I may say so. The principle of public policy is this: *ex dolo malo non oritur actio. No court will lend its aid to a man who founds his cause of action upon an immoral or illegal act.* If, from the plaintiff's own stating or otherwise, the cause of actions appears to arise *ex turpi causa*, or the transgression of a positive law of this country, *there the court says he has no right to be assisted.* It is upon that ground the court goes; not for the sake of the defendant, but because they will not lend their aid to such a plaintiff. So if the plaintiff and defendant were to change sides, and the defendant was to bring its action against the plaintiff, the latter would then have the advantage of it; for where both are equally at fault, *potior est conditio[n] [sic] defendentis.*" [852]

Notably, the foregoing approach does not perceive any obligation to apply a "balancing test". Such a test

---

[852] *World Duty Free* v. *Kenya, supra* footnote 44, para. 181 (emphasis added) (citing to *Holman* v. *Johnson*, (1775) 1 Cowp. 341, 343 (Mansfield J) (England)). See also International Law Association, *Ascertaining the Contents of the Applicable Law in International Commercial Arbitration*, Rio de Janeiro Conference, August 2008, at 20 ("parties cannot by agreement between themselves legitimately seek through international arbitration to enforce contracts to pay bribes, to commit criminal acts, or to engage in prohibited cartel or similar anti-competitive business practices" (citing to R. Kreindler, *supra* footnote 245, p. 239).

might include quantitatively or qualitatively "weighing" the respective degrees of egregiousness of the illicit conduct of the claimant investor on the one hand and respondent host State on the other[853]. It might also include a consideration of the extent to which the respondent host State subsequently investigated the allegation of bribery and, if applicable, sanctioned its own government officials for having accepted bribes[854].

---

[853] For a policy-based argument in favour of a balancing test which argues that the burden of dealing with the negative effects of corrupt activities should not be borne solely by the host State, see H. Raeschke-Kessler and D. Gottwald, "Korruption und internationales Vertragsrecht: Rechtliche Aspekte der Korruption im Bau- und Infrastruktursektor mit Auslandsbezug", in W. Moll (ed.), *Festschrift für Hans-Jochem Lüer zum 70. Geburtstag*, Munich, Verlag C.H. Beck, 2008, pp. 39, 49 (advocating as a burden-shifting mechanism possible adaptation of any contract binding the two). Query whether the burden-shifting mechanism advocated herein has any firm grounding in public international law and in view of the Unclean Hands Doctrine. In any event, such remedy may have no place when the investment tainted with fraud was not *contract*-based.

[854] This argument was also indirectly discussed in *World Duty Free* v. *Kenya*, *supra* footnote 44, para. 180. While the arbitral tribunal did not make the balance of interests part of its reasoning, it stated,

> "It remains nonetheless a highly disturbing feature in this case that the corrupt recipient of the Claimant's bribe was more than an officer of state but its most senior officer . . . *it appears that no attempt has been made by Kenya to prosecute him for corruption or to recover the bribe in civil proceedings*. It is not therefore surprising that Mr. Ali feels strongly the unfairness of the legal case . . ." (Emphasis added.)

However, as cited above the arbitral tribunal then resolved this conflict of interest by holding that the balance should tip in favour of the public interest, i.e., the people of Kenya.

In *World Duty Free*, the arbitral tribunal concluded that even assuming a balance of interest between the respective interests, the balance would still tip in favour of the respondent host State representing the interests of the public, namely the people of Kenya: "the law protects not the litigating parties but the public; or in this case, the mass of tax-payers and other citizens making up one of the poorest countries in the world"[855].

Ultimately,

> "while the conduct of the investor may be weighed against the conduct of the host country authorities in determining whether the latter had indeed acted wrongly, . . . that conduct must meet a threshold level of unconscionability to negate the improper conduct of the host authorities"[856].

The Unclean Hands Doctrine can be comparably considered for application in *non*-contractual relationships. Neither the wording nor the intended legal consequences of the Unclean Hands Doctrine or related maxims commands or recommends a limitation to contractual relationships. The laws of both civil- and common-law jurisdictions extend the scope of the Unclean Hands Doctrine or comparable doctrines in national law to disputes in tort and *non*-contractual contexts[857].

---

[855] *World Duty Free* v. *Kenya*, see footnote 44, para. 181.

[856] P. Muchlinski, *supra* footnote 175, pp. 539-540 (stating further that "investment tribunals should not countenance illegal behavior by investors or government officials").

[857] With respect to German law, see, e.g., Sec. 242, Bürgerliches Gesetzbuch [German Civil Law Code] [BGB] (being applicable to every "Sonderverbindung", i.e., to qualified social contacts, relationships based on void contracts or relationships based on statutory law; C. Grüneberg, *supra* footnote 809. For an example from

Thus the legal consequence of its application is and should be the same in a contractual or non-contractual context: denial of relief because of the claimant's illicit acts, whether they originate from a contractual or a factual context. Moreover, as in the contractual context so also in the non-contractual context, depending on the circumstances it should generally not be considered unfair to the claimant investor to dismiss its claims on the grounds that they arose out of or in connection with a non-contractual investment tainted by acts of bribery.

### (d) *Arbitrability and acts of bribery*

The issue of arbitrability, properly defined, can arise in international commercial arbitration in the context of whether and when alleged or proven illegal acts serve to render either void *ab initio* or voidable the underlying contract or the agreement to arbitrate, or indeed both[858]. It is submitted that generally the issue of arbitrability should not pose a problem in investment disputes involving bribery.

In this context, it is useful and accurate to distinguish between and among *(a)* commercial arbitration disputes based on privity of contract including an agreement to arbitrate *(clause compromissoire)*; *(b)* investment arbitration disputes having the same basis; *(c)* investment arbitration disputes based on an invest-

---

the law of the State of California, see, e.g., *Camp* v. *Mangels*, 35 Cal. App. 4th 620, 638 (1995) (USA); *Blain* v. *Doctor's Co.*, 222 Cal. App. 3d 1048, 1060 (1990) (USA).

[858] For a discussion of voidness and voidability of the contract or the agreement to arbitrate on the grounds of corruption or other illegality, see generally R. Kreindler, *supra* footnote 41, p. 225, and, with a comparative discussion from a German law perspective, R. Kreindler, *supra* footnote 826.

ment contract and providing for treaty-based arbitration (e.g., *World Duty Free*); and *(d)* investment arbitration disputes based on non-contractual investment and providing for treaty-based arbitration. Accordingly, in such situations as *(d)* and in the face of illegality there can be no discussion of the "voidness" or "voidability" of the treaty or of its dispute resolution provisions. In this sense, I essentially agree with Professor Cremades, who states in relevant part:

> "The effect of corruption on an investor's treaty rights must therefore be procedural. The corrupt investor will be estopped from claiming the benefit of the substantive rights in the BIT. This view is supported by the doctrine of 'clean hands' or *ex injuria jus non oritur* in public international law."[859]

For, in investment disputes the legal basis for a claimant's right to institute legal proceedings against the respondent generally derives directly from an international treaty, for example the ECT. The validity of such treaty *per se* cannot be affected by alleged illegal behaviour of the investor in the way the validity of an arm's-length contract could be impugned in a contract-based arbitration; the investor has no contractual privity to the treaty. Likewise, the validity of the dispute resolution mechanism in a treaty cannot be impugned by such illegal behaviour. In treaty-based investment arbitration, the treaty giving rise to the arbitral proceedings and the illegal acts of the investor are unrelated.

Whether an arbitration commenced thereunder will suffer any defects of lack of jurisdiction or admissibility is, however, a separate question. To be clear, the affirmation of the "arbitrability" of the dispute means that the investment tribunal retains residual procedural competence to negatively affirm the lack of jurisdiction

---

[859] B. M. Cremades, *supra* footnote 851, p. 214.

and/or inadmissibility of claims made, including, for example, on the basis of lack of "consent" to submit the dispute to ICSID jurisdiction in the first place.

Accordingly, an arbitral tribunal in a treaty-based investment dispute should have no hesitation in affirming the "arbitrability" of a dispute in which allegations or admissions of illegality accompany the treaty-based claims. The illegality, even if manifest and uncontested, should not vitiate the validity of the treaty or of its dispute-resolution mechanism.

Indeed, in a treaty-based investment arbitration accompanied by uncontested illegality, it is submitted that it is incumbent upon the arbitral tribunal perhaps all the more to uphold the separability between, on the one hand, any illegality of the investment or operations relation to the investment and/or the investor's conduct and, on the other hand, the ongoing sanctity of the treaty. It is also incumbent upon the arbitral tribunal to take cognizance of a manifest or acknowledged illegality and — either *sua sponte* or pursuant to an application — decide on the legal consequences of such illegality.

*First*, in the face of a manifest or acknowledged illegality of an egregious nature, it behooves the arbitral tribunal to declare the illegality and ascertain the negative consequences for jurisdiction and admissibility. A failure or refusal to do so could be considered to be an instrumentalizing of the arbitral tribunal by one or more illicitly behaving parties [860].

*Second*, it would be contrary to international public policy for an arbitral tribunal to fail to consider an investor's manifest or acknowledged acts of bribery as

---

[860] For a general discussion of possible rights and duties of the arbitral tribunal in the face of manifest illegality by one of the parties, see R. Kreindler, *Aspects of Illegality*, *supra* footnote 634.

offences of international law and international public
policy. This reasoning was also confirmed by the arbitral tribunal in *Inceysa* v. *El Salvador*, which was
asked to consider the investor's violations of public
policy by having obtained the underlying investment
contract by fraud:

> "In light of the foregoing, not to exclude
> Inceysa's investment from the protection of the BIT
> would be a violation of international public policy,
> which this Tribunal cannot allow. Consequently, this
> Arbitral Tribunal decides that *Inceysa's investment
> is not protected by the BIT because it is contrary to
> international public policy*."[861]

*Third*, taking cognizance of the legal consequences
of illegality on the part of the investor is especially
important in ICSID Convention proceedings. The
grounds for annulment pursuant to Article 52, ICSID
Convention, do not expressly include international
public policy violations. This is to be contrasted with
the grounds for annulment based on a violation of
international public policy available under Article 34
*(b)* (ii) of the UNCITRAL Model Law[862] and for

---

[861] In interpreting the Spain-El Salvador BIT, the arbitral tribunal found that El Salvador's consent had been
subject to the condition that the investment was made in
accordance with its domestic law. The arbitral tribunal
denied jurisdiction on the grounds that the investment had
not been made in accordance with El Salvador's law since
the underlying concession contract had been procured
by fraud. *Inceysa* v. *El Salvador*, *supra* footnote 174,
para. 252 (emphasis added).

[862] United Nations Commission on International Trade
Law, UNCITRAL Model Law on International Commercial Arbitration, UN doc. A/40/17, Annex I (21 June 1985),
and A/61/17, Annex I (7 July 2006), available at http://
www.uncitral.org/pdf/english/texts/arbitration/ml-arb/07-
86998_Ebook.pdf.

refusal of enforcement under Article V (2) *(b)* of the New York Convention[863] and Article 36 *(b)* (ii) of the UNCITRAL Model Law. Accordingly, if an arbitral tribunal failed to consider whether the claimant investor's acts of bribery were contrary to international law and public policy and what consequences these acts had for justiciability and admissibility of the claims, this issue would never be examined by a trier of fact who had enjoyed first-hand access to the admission of illegality[864].

Thus where a claimant investor even admits acts of bribery, such illegality does not affect the arbitrability of the claimant's underlying claims in terms of the residual procedural competence of the Arbitral Tribunal to negatively declare the lack of jurisdiction and/or inadmissibility as a consequence of, for example, lack of consent. Thus it is all the more incumbent on the arbitral tribunal to consider the legal consequences, particularly in terms of jurisdiction or admissibility *vel non*. A failure or refusal to do so could be seen as a condoning of illicit investor behaviour. In any event, it could mean forsaking a unique opportunity to take action against the illegality where the admission or proof of the illegality has effectively been presented, under oath or affirmation, with immediacy to the arbitral tribunal as the ultimate trier of fact.

---

[863] New York Convention on the Recognition and Enforcement of Foreign Arbitral Awards, 10 June 1958, 21 *UST* 2517, 330 *UNTS* 38, available at http://www.uncitral.org/pdf/english/texts/arbitration/NY-conv/XXII_1_e.pdf.
[864] Under the UNCITRAL Model Law and the New York Convention, there is no opportunity for a *révision au fond*. See also B. Cremades, *supra* footnote 851, p. 213. See also R. Kreindler, *Aspects of Illegality*, *supra* footnote 41, p. 22 (opining that since the arbitral tribunal has unique access to the facts during the arbitration, it must not forsake the opportunities to assess them).

## 2. *The commercial arbitration context and claimant illegality*

We now turn to the legal consequences and effects of a positive finding of illegality or corruption in the commercial arbitration context. In so doing, the issues are addressed in terms of a comparison and contrast to investment treaty arbitration.

### (a) *Possible denial of benefits of arbitration agreement, resulting in lack of* jurisdiction *?*

In the commercial arbitration context with privity of contract, there is no concept of "consent" governed by transnational public policy in the sense of investment treaty-based arbitration. "Consent" to the arbitration agreement is governed normally by the stipulated or determined national rules of law. Under competence-competence and separability, illegality and corruption not likely to deprive the arbitrator of jurisdiction[865]. Let us also recall *World Duty Free* v. *Kenya*, ICSID (2006)[866], which involved an investment contract under English law. There, while the bribe was admitted, no contention was made that the bribe specifically procured the *arbitration agreement* in the contract, with the result that the "arbitration agreement remained subsisting valid and effective"[867].

Under the expanded arbitrability doctrine, illegality and corruption are likewise not likely to deprive the arbitrator of jurisdiction. This current and correct position largely discredits the position taken by Lagergren in the well-known, previously discussed ICC Case No. 1110 (1963)[868].

---

[865] Judgment of the House of Lords, *supra* footnote 530, paras. 16 *et seq*.

[866] *World Duty Free* v. *Kenya*, *supra* footnote 44.

[867] *Ibid*., para. 187.

[868] *Supra* footnote 3.

(b) *Where the contract was "made" illegally, is jurisdiction affected?*

Where the dispute relates to a commercial contract which was "made" illegally in the sense of either procured or also possibly maintained illegally, what may be the result for *jurisdiction*?

The legality of a commercial contract is not an express jurisdictional prerequisite for the adjudication of disputes arising out of the contract. Indeed fraud, misrepresentation or corruption in the contractual bidding process do not normally result, under the competence-competence and separability doctrines, in a lack of jurisdiction *ratione materiae*. See, for example, *Fiona Trust* v. *Privalov* (2007)[869] and *World Duty Free* v. *Kenya*, ICSID (2006): the "arbitration agreement remains subsisting valid and effective"[870]. Furthermore, commercial contracts made in breach of fundamental principles of applicable law, which normally outlaw fraud and corruption, also do not necessarily result in a lack of jurisdiction[871]. This outcome is interesting, in the comparison with the previous discussion of investment treaty arbitration, insofar as the principle of "No one can benefit from his own wrong" *(nemo auditor propriam turpitudinem allegans)* surely applies equally to the commercial context.

(c) *Inadmissibility or voidness on the basis of "unclean hands"*

Where jurisdiction has been upheld and the investor committed illegality in relation to a commercial contract, may the contract's substantive protections be

---

[869] See *supra* footnote 865.
[870] *World Duty Free* v. *Kenya*, *supra* footnote 44, para. 187.
[871] G. B. Born, *supra* footnote 4, pp. 357 *et seq.*

denied, resulting in *inadmissibility or voidness*, including on the basis of "unclean hands"?

Again, legality is not an express jurisdictional prerequisite, but it may be seen as still being an implied admissibility prerequisite. The contracting party likewise cannot seek redress through protection of substantive legal rights in a contract if it has "unclean hands", as an equitable limitation forming part of the applicable national law. Thus an unlawful act cannot serve as the basis of an action in law *(ex turpi causa non oritur actio)*. This concept was originally developed at common law, but today is found in the laws of many jurisdictions, as already addressed above[872].

Where the parties are *both* blameworthy in the commercial context, the defendant has the stronger position *(in pari delicto potior est conditio possidentis)*, as in the investment context[873]. Thus the corrupt intermediary cannot claim a commission from the corrupt principal. As stated in the Final Report of the 2008 ILA Rio de Janeiro Conference[874], "parties cannot by agreement . . . legitimately seek through international arbitration to enforce contracts to pay bribes . . ."[875].

Moreover, a finding of inadmissibility is to be distinguished from a finding of voidness of the commer-

---

[872] See *supra* Chapter IX.D.1.b.

[873] B. A. Garner (ed.), *supra* footnote 145, Appendix B (p. 1838): "*In pari delicto potior est conditio defendentis.* Where both parties are equally in the wrong, the position of the defendant is the stronger." See also H. G. Beale (ed.), *Chitty on Contracts*, Vol. 1 — *General Principles*, 31st ed., London, Sweet & Maxwell, 2012, paras. 16-007 and 16-180.

[874] Final Report — Ascertaining the Contents of the Applicable Law in International Commercial Arbitration. Available at http://www.ila-hq.org/en/committees/index.cfm/cid/19.

[875] *Ibid.*, p. 21, with footnote 63, citing to R. Kreindler, *supra* footnote 245, pp. 239 *et seq.*

cial contract: contracts procured by corruption are merely voidable at the instance of the innocent party, but are otherwise intrinsically valid: *World Duty Free* v. *Kenya*, ICSID (2006), discussing English law[876]. By contrast, contracts providing for corruption are null and void *ab initio* under most European national laws[877], but not necessarily under English law: "illegal contracts are not devoid of legal effect, but the *ex turpi causa* maxim entails that no action on the contract can be maintained"[878]. This distinction between nullity on the one hand and inability to be "maintained" on the other — the "maintained" nomenclature was precisely used in the decision in *World Duty Free*[879] — may be a distinction without a difference, but it is one which up to now has been maintained, so to speak, in English law.

(d) *Inadmissibility or voidness on the basis of breach of public policy*

Where jurisdiction has been upheld and the investor committed illegality in relation to a commercial con-

---

[876] *World Duty Free* v. *Kenya*, *supra* footnote 44, para. 164, discussing English law.

[877] Art. 8 (2) of the Council of Europe Civil Law Convention on Corruption:

"Each Party shall provide in its internal law for the possibility of all parties to a contract whose consent has been undermined by an act of corruption to be able to apply to the court for the contract to be declared void, notwithstanding their right to claim for damages."

[878] H. G. Beale (ed.), *supra* footnote 873, para. 16-007.

[879] *World Duty Free* v. *Kenya*, *supra* footnote 44, para. 188:

"The Claimant is not legally entitled to maintain any of its pleaded claims in these proceedings as a matter of ordre public international and public policy under the contract's applicable laws."

tract, may its claims may be deemed to breach transnational public policy, resulting in *inadmissibility or voidness*?

It is possible to apply transnational public policy against fraud and corruption to a commercial contract, as an extension of or component of the otherwise applicable rules of national law. Moreover, unlike in the investment treaty context, in the commercial context it is possible to declare a contract "invalid" or "void" for illegality. In this regard, there has been consistency in the willingness to apply local and international law concurrently, but inconsistency in the outcomes.

Thus, it will be rare that a finding of corruption offending public policy will be deemed to result in a denial of jurisdiction, as was decided by *Lagergren* in ICC Case No. 1110 (1963)[880]. More common will be a possible denial of admissibility: for example, *SIREXM* v. *Burkina Faso*, ICSID (2000) — corruption and fraud in relation to an investment *contract*, leading to voidness at law and "breach of public order". And a further possibility will be a finding of voidness of the contract: for example, *World Duty Free* — claims not "maintainable" as a "matter of ordre public international and public policy under the contract's applicable laws".

In all of these cases, there is an equal application of the fundamental maxim that illegality cannot become a source of legal right to the wrongdoer, either as a component of national law or of international law informing national law[881].

---

[880] See *supra* footnote 3.
[881] H. Lauterpacht, *Recognition in International Law*, Cambridge, Cambridge University Press, 1947, p. 421.

CHAPTER X

# JUSTIFICATIONS, EXCUSES AND DEFENCES FOR ILLEGAL CONDUCT

## A. *Introduction*

When might corruption or illegality be legally excused or justified? Claimants occasionally claim that they engaged in acts of bribery or corruption as a means of "self-help" or even "self-defence". They also may contend that the only way to obtain the contract or the investment, particularly in a competitive situation, was to engage in acts of illegality and that such acts are essentially par for the course, and therefore not egregious, in the particular country or environment at issue.

We first look at the conceptual challenges generally and then at the specific illegality and corruption context, including issues common to commercial and investment treaty context and differences. We also look at specific defences in the context of illegality and corruption, such as intentionality, facilitation, (un)lawfulness, self-help or self-defence, duress, necessity, and the pervasiveness of corruption.

## B. *Conceptual Challenges Generally*

### 1. *Issues common to the commercial and investment treaty context*

*First*, justifications, defences and excuses can be used as a "sword", whether generally or specific to the corruption context. The sword can be wielded by the claimant to ensure an entitlement to contractual or treaty benefits, even in the face of and despite its possible own fault or illegality. The sword can also be wielded by the claimant to ensure a denial of a defence by the respondent to the claimant's possible fault.

*Second*, justifications, defences and excuses can be used as a "shield", again either generally or specific to the corruption context. The shield can be held up by the respondent to ensure denial of benefits to claimant because of the claimant's fault or by the respondent to ensure the legitimacy of its own defence to liability, despite its own possible fault.

Depending on the circumstances, the sword or the shield may give rise to an issue of jurisdiction, admissibility or the merits. Depending on the situation, it may serve as a complete bar to a claim or only a partial bar, or perhaps no bar at all. It may be an absolute bar on its own or it may require a balancing or proportionality test, as was addressed above in the context of *World Duty Free* v. *Kenya*[882]. The ability to use the sword or the shield may be contingent upon the applicable rules of law or may instead reside in equity, or both, or indeed it may be a mixture.

In this regard, despite a certain convergence in national laws respecting an interdiction of corruption and bribery, as addressed earlier in the context of intermediary contracts and particularly Swiss law[883], there is not by any means uniformity in domestic civil and criminals laws respecting the different kinds of acts which may give to corruption. Furthermore, despite a certain convergence, there is also a lack of full uniformity in the implementation of international instruments and customary international law in this area.

---

[882] See *supra* Chapter IX.D.1.b and Chapter IX.D.1.c.
[883] See *supra* Chapter II.G.3.

## 2. *Differences between the commercial and investment treaty context*

It is more likely that such a sword will be able to be used successfully in the investment treaty context than the commercial context to defeat a claim on jurisdictional or admissibility grounds, as addressed above[884]. As a shield, it is also more likely that such defences will be able to be used successfully in investment disputes to evade a full merits-based analysis. In investment disputes, there will also be a possibly higher hurdle to obtain application of equitable principles than in commercial disputes.

With regard to competence, jurisdiction, arbitrability, separability and admissibility requirements, there will also be possible notable difference. In the investment context, absent a classical *lex arbitri* verification will be made under the respective treaty requirements and principles of international law. And absent privity of contract, verification will focus on "consent" through treaty accession.

A distinction may also be made between a kind of personal jurisdiction *(ratione voluntatis)* and a kind of subject matter jurisdiction *(ratione materiae)* in a manner not necessarily applicable in commercial arbitration.

And the characterization of the objection or defence as preliminary or rather as a merits question may be more critical in the investment context.

Furthermore, in terms of the enforceability of any adjudication of the preliminary issue depending on the form of the decision, in the investment context the petition for annulment of the preliminary award by either party will be a more likely step than in the commercial context.

---

[884] See *supra* Chapter X.B.1.

## C. The Specific Context of Illegality and Corruption

### 1. Issues common to the commercial and investment context

There are a number of common features of such justifications, excuses and defences in the specific context of illegality and corruption.

*First*, illegality and corruption justifications and defences are normally alleged early on, either because they must be so in order not to be waived, as discussed above[885], or because they figure from an early stage as part of the respective claim or defence.

*Second*, competence, jurisdiction, arbitrability, separability and admissibility requirements generally give rise to an *ex officio* right or duty of verification on the part of the arbitrator to consider such corruption defences, as also addressed above[886].

*Third*, problems of the appropriate burden and standard of proof may apply[887].

*Fourth*, despite the convergence on this point, there will be a lack of uniformity in implementing international instruments/law, as mentioned above[888].

*Fifth*, also despite convergence, there will be a lack of full uniformity in domestic anti-corruption and criminal laws.

### 2. Differences between the commercial and investment treaty context

There are also a number of differences in the treatment of justifications, excuses and defences between commercial and investment arbitration.

---

[885] See *supra* Chapter IX.C.1.a and Chapter IX.B.1.d.
[886] See *supra* Chapter VIII.B.4.
[887] M. A. Raouf, *supra* footnote 9, p. 122.
[888] See *supra* Chapter VI.

*First*, in the investment area reciprocal invocations of excuse and defence are being made with increasing frequency by both claimant and respondent, as addressed above[889].

*Second*, as mentioned investment treaties, including ICSID and ECT, do not expressly address legal effects whereas national laws may do.

*Third*, a claimant allegation in the investment context may serve as the basis for a breach of treaty or international obligations and a respondent State allegation as a justification, defence or excuse.

*Fourth*, in investment arbitration such defences may serve as a sword used by the respondent against corruption by the investor in an effort to defeat the claim on jurisdictional or admissibility grounds or as shield in order to evade a full merits-based analysis.

*Fifth*, in the investment context there will usually be a greater stringency applied to factors such as reasonableness, proportionality and clean hands.

## D. *Specific Defences in the Context of Illegality and Corruption*

Certain specific defences may be highlighted in view of the foregoing observations.

### 1. *Unintentional acts of bribery by the claimant or respondent*

The OECD Convention definition leaves little room for exceptions to the illegality of bribery. It provides that "Article 1 . . . should be implemented in such a way that it does not provide a defence or exception where the foreign public official solicits a bribe." A possible exception may exist where the bribe was not

---

[889] See *supra* Chapter IX.C.2.a.

intentional, but this is to be compared with the respective local law definitions. No express justifications for payments are enumerated within the Convention.

## 2. *"Facilitation payments" by the claimant to the respondent*

As addressed above[890], the US Foreign Corrupt Practices Act (FCPA) contains an exception to bribery for payments made "to expedite or to secure the performance of a routine governmental action by a foreign official . . ."[891]. This provision

> "intends to distinguish between payments which cause an official to exercise other than his free will . . . and those payments which merely move a particular matter toward an eventual act or decision or which do not involve any discretionary action"[892].

The application of this exception has been relatively stringent as far as can be ascertained, with "very limited categories of permissible payments"[893]. This exception is also to be contrasted with more recent statutory approaches, such as the 2010 UK Anti-Bribery Convention, which provides for strict liability for a corporation for bribery by those associated with it, including failure to prevent the bribery[894]. Facilitation payments are in principle forbidden under

---

[890] See *supra* Chapter II.G.1.

[891] 15 USC § 78dd-1 *(b)*, § 78 dd-2 *(b)* and § 78dd-3 *(b)*.

[892] Report of the US House of Representatives, 28 September 1977, HR Rep. No. 95-640, sub. "Section by Section Analysis" — "Facilitation Payments", p. 4. Available at http://www.justice.gov/criminal/fraud/fcpa/history/1977/houseprt-95-640.pdf.

[893] *U.S.* v. *Kay*, 359 F. 3d 738, 745 (5th Cir. 2004).

[894] See Sec. 7-10 of the 2010 UK Bribery Act. See also *supra* footnote 169 and *supra* Chapter II.G.1.

the UK Act, but non-criminal cases may not be prosecuted[895].

## 3. *Lawfulness of activity of the claimant in the respondent host State as an excuse*

The lawfulness of the activity of the claimant in the respondent host State may be invoked as an excuse, even if the activity is unlawful under the *lex causae* and/or the *lex arbitri*, if there is one. As was discussed above in the context of the applicable law, this may raise challenges for the arbitrator both in the commercial and the investment context[896].

An interesting approach is to be found in the Australia anti-bribery law, providing a differentiated table in which several possibilities of successful defences of lawful conduct in the State of the foreign public official are shown[897]. Furthermore, the UK Anti-

---

[895] See the "Bribery Act 2010: Joint Prosecution Guidance of the Director of the Serious Fraud office and the Director of Public Prosecutions", pp. 8 *et seq.*, listing several public interest factors which are relevant to the issue of prosecution (e.g. size and repetition of the facilitation payment). Pursuant to this Guidance, "[a] prosecution will usually take place unless the prosecutor is sure that there are public interest factors tending against prosecution which outweigh those tending in favour". Available at http://www.sfo.gov.uk/media/167348/bribery_act_2010_joint_prosecution_guidance_of_the_director_of_the_serious_fraud_office_and_the_director_of_public_prosecutions.pdf.

[896] See *supra* Chapter I.B.

[897] The lawful conduct defence initially applied where it could be established that the conduct would not have constituted an offence against a law in place in the foreign official's country, but was amended in 2007, following criticism from the OECD. The defence now applies only where it can be established that a written law of the foreign official's country requires or permits the provision of the benefit. See C. Barker, "Background Note on

Bribery Convention provides that even if a payment
was allowed under the laws of the host State, the payment may be deemed illegal under UK law[898]. At the
same time, there may be a legitimate defence to show
that under the written laws of the host State applicable
the foreign public official was permitted to be influenced in the manner in which the act occurred[899].

## 4. *Unlawfulness of activity of the claimant in the respondent host State as a justification*

The claimant's illegal act may justify State interference with the investment, without resulting in State
liability for a violation of substantive protections of
treaty. One example was a justified revocation of a
banking licence in *Genin* v. *Estonia*, ICSID (2001), in
which the tribunal held that the revocation of the
licence did not "rise to the level of a violation of the
[United States-Estonia] BIT or of the international law
principles enshrined therein"[900]. The tribunal reasoned

---

Australia's implementation of the OECD Anti-Bribery
Convention", dated 7 February 2012 (available at http://
parlinfo.aph.gov.au/parlInfo/download/library/prspub/1403
446/upload_binary/1403446.pdf;fileType=application/
pdf#search=%222010s%20background%20note%20(par-
liamentary%20library,%20australia)%22).

[898] F. J. Warin, C. Falconer and M. S. Diamant, "The
British Are Coming ! : Britain Changes Its Law on Foreign
Bribery and Joins the International Fight against Corruption", *Texas International Law Journal*, Vol. 46 (2010),
pp. 17 *et seq.*

[899] Sec. 6 (3) *(b)* of the 2010 UK Bribery Act.

"P [a person] bribes F [a foreign public official] if,
and only if . . . F is neither permitted nor required by
the written law applicable to F to be influenced in
F's capacity as a foreign public official by the offer,
promise or gift."

[900] *Alex Genin et al.* v. *The Republic of Estonia*, Award,
Case No. ARB/99/2, 25 June 2001, para. 373.

that the revocation had to be considered "in its proper context — a context comprised of serious and entirely reasonable misgivings"[901] regarding Claimant's (mis-) conduct. Another example was a justified closing of gambling facilities in *Thunderbird* v. *Mexico*, NAFTA (2006), in which the tribunal held "that Chapter Eleven of the NAFTA recognizes in principle the right of a Contracting Party to regulate conduct that it considers illegal"[902].

At the same time, a *knowing* acceptance of the illegality by the host State can cure a breach by the claimant of local law or estop the State from relying on the illegality as a defence. Thus in *SwemBalt* v. *Latvia*, UNCITRAL (2000), the tribunal held that that

> "it is surprising that the authorities waited for more than four months before taking any measures in that regard, if really the whole enterprise was illegal. In these circumstances we find that SwemBalt has shown, that in all likelihood it has complied with Latvian law, that the Respondent has not shown that the investment was not made in accordance with the laws and regulations of Latvia, and that in any event the actions of the Respondent were out of proportion with any non-compliance that may have existed. We conclude, therefore, that SwemBalt has made an investment in Latvia, which fulfils the requirements made by the Investment Agreement for being protected by that agreement."[903]

---

[901] *Supra* footnote 900, para. 361.

[902] *Thunderbird* v. *Mexico*, *supra* footnote 604, para. 123. Para. 126, *ibid.*, the tribunal stated that it only "examine[s] whether the conduct of Mexico [was] consistent with its obligations under Chapter Eleven of the NAFTA".

[903] *SwemBalt AB* v. *The Republic of Latvia*, Decision by the Court of Arbitration, 23 October 2000, paras. 34-35.

In *Tokios Tokeles* v. *Ukraine*, ICSID (2007), it was concluded that

> "Ukraine had registered Taki Spravy as a valid enterprise in 1994 and had not raised any concern as to form at that time or subsequently, until the dispute arose. This indicated that the investment in question was made in accordance with the laws and regulations of Ukraine." [904]

In *Tecmed* v. *Mexico*, ICSID (2003), the tribunal reasoned that in an auction for the sale of assets relating to a landfill of hazardous industrial waste the permits allowing for the landfill's operation were a central part of the tender and acquisition of the assets. The municipality's request to the competent authority for assisting Tecmed to comply with all formal requirements evidenced that the State itself considered the operation of the landfill and the granting of the required licences "to be the lawful, normal and logical procedure" [905]. The denial by the Federal Government of an extension to operate the landfill was therefore deemed unlawful.

And in *Kardassopoulos* v. *Georgia*, ICSID (2010), the tribunal concluded that Georgia could limit this protection by excluding investments made illegally by the investor, but it could not avoid jurisdiction under the BIT by invoking its own failure to comply with its domestic law [906].

Ultimately, if there is no knowledge of the illegality

---

[904] *Tokios Tokelés* v. *Ukraine*, Decision on Jurisdiction (and Dissent), ICSID Case No. ARB/02/18, 29 April 2004, para. H10.

[905] *Tecnicas Medioamientales Tecmed S.A.* v. *The United Mexican States*, Award, ICSID Case No. ARB (AF)/00/2, 29 May 2003, paras. 89 *et seq.*

[906] *Kardassopoulos* v. *Georgia*, Decision on Jurisdiction, *supra* footnote 491, para. 182.

on the part of the host State, or if there is knowledge but it is *not* attributed to the State, then no waiver or estoppel is likely to be found[907].

## 5. *Self-help or self-defence, duress, economic necessity by the claimant*

Occasionally, a claimant may contend that it committed acts of bribery as an act of self-defence. Self-defence in international law is codified in Article 51 of the UN Charter. Article 51 grants the right of self-defence in case of an armed attack to a UN Member State under certain circumstances[908]. In addition to and co-existing with this treaty source of law, the International Court of Justice has recognized a customary right to self-defence pursuant to Article 38 (1) *(b)*, ICJ Statute, in the *Nicaragua* case[909]. Self-defence is an

---

[907] *World Duty Free* v. *Kenya*, *supra* footnote 44, paras. 169 and 181.

[908] UN Charter, Art. 51, provides that:

"Nothing in the present Charter shall impair the inherent right of individual or collective self-defence if an armed attack occurs against a Member of the United Nations, until the Security Council has taken measures necessary to maintain international peace and security."

[909] ICJ, *Military and Paramilitary Activities in and against Nicaragua (Nicaragua* v. *United States of America)*, *supra* footnote 585, concerning an alleged violation of customary law by the United States when it applied direct force against Nicaragua and also assisted the *Contra* rebels). On one essential point, this treaty itself refers to pre-existing customary international law; this reference to customary law is contained in the actual text of Art. 51, which mentions the "inherent right" (in the French text the *"droit naturel"*) of individual or collective self-defence, which "nothing in the present Charter shall impair" and which applies in the event of an armed attack. *Ibid.*, para. 176.

exceptional right granted to States, which may be exercised only if no other means are available[910].

The question arises of whether a contracting party or investor is entitled to invoke any such right to self-defence against a respondent, including a respondent host State, as a justification, or excuse, for acts of bribery committed by the claimant.

Here, it is submitted that there is a fundamental difference between situations where an individual is endangered and a State is under attack by another State[911]. A State can generally take protective measures only upon prior authorization of the UN Security Council pursuant to Chapter VII of the UN Charter. By contrast, the means foreseen under international law to protect an *individual* against illegal acts committed by a State is the principle of diplomatic protection by the individual's home State[912] or treaty-based protections.

---

[910] Before the entry into force of the UN Charter, the test for customary self-defence already had been strict. See also separate opinion of Judge Simma, *Oil Platforms (Iran v. United States)*, 6 November 2003, available at http://www.icj-cij.org/docket/ ?p1=3&p2=3&k=0a&case=90&code=op&p3=4:

> "I find it regrettable that the Court has not mustered the courage of restating, and thus reconfirming, more fully fundamental principles of the law of the United Nations as well as customary international law (principles that in my view are of the nature of *jus cogens*) on the use of force, or rather the prohibition on armed force, in a context and at a time when such a reconfirmation is called for with the greatest urgency." *Ibid.*, para. 6.

[911] K. Doehring, *Völkerrecht*, 2nd ed., Heidelberg, C.F. Müller, 2004, para. 1043 (discussing the differences between self-defence in national laws and public international law).

[912] I. Brownlie, *Principles of Public International Law*, 7th ed., Oxford University Press, 2008, pp. 477 *et seq.* (discussing diplomatic protection in general).

Alternatively, the individual can seek redress through the good offices of international organizations such as the United Nations or non-governmental organizations. Furthermore, allowing an individual generally to invoke a right to self-defence against a State would render it difficult for a State to exert its police power over citizens and non-citizens alike. In numerous jurisdictions, resistance against the exercise of State authority is even criminalized under certain circumstances[913].

Thus, absent special circumstances, normally a claimant non-State actor should not be entitled to invoke the concept of self-defence against a respondent as a possible means of justifying, or excusing, acts of bribery.

If a claimant could invoke self-defence under such circumstances, the requirements of justified self-defence would still need to be met. Thus the measures undertaken must have been in response to an immediate attack as well as necessary and proportionate. Even accepting an analogy of armed attack to the *non*-military context, a claimant will normally not be able to show that it contemplated that there was an "immediate" attack posed which was attributable to the respondent. There is also the further question of whether the acts of bribery by claimant, which at this point are likely to have been admitted, were legally necessary or proportionate.

With regard to immediacy, as evidenced in Article 51, UN Charter, and ICJ decisions interpreting customary law on the use of force, the invocation of self-defence

---

[913] Sec. 113, Strafgesetzbuch [German Criminal Code] [StGB]; Arts. 433-436, Code Pénal [French Penal Code] [C.Pén.]; Art. 337, Codice penale [Italian Penal Code] [CP]; Washington State Criminal Code § 9A.76/020; Florida Statutes § 843.01; Chap. 17, s. 1, Brottsbalken [Swedish Criminal Code] [BrB].

requires an immediate armed attack[914]. As for the protection of nationals abroad, an analysis of precedents of State practice indicates that the intervening States relied exclusively on danger to life and health in justifying their interventions[915]. A general situation of pressure is not sufficient, as a matter of public international law, to entitle an invocation of self-defence[916]. As for immediacy, the requirement was established by the ICJ in the *Nicaragua* case[917]. If some time passed between the occurrence of alleged threats toward a claimant

---

[914] The ICJ requires the following high standard for an "armed attack" under customary law on the use of force: as the Court observed in the case concerning *Military and Paramilitary Activities in and against Nicaragua*, *supra* footnote 585, para. 191, it is "necessary to distinguish the most grave forms of the use of force (those constituting an armed attack) from other less grave forms".

[915] Examples are the measures taken by the United States in the Congo and the Dominican Republic in 1964 and 1965 or by Belgium in the Congo in 1960 and 1964. For further examples, see W. Ader, *Gewaltsame Rettungsaktionen zum Schutz eigener Staatsangehöriger im Ausland*, Munich, VVF, 1988, pp. 269-271.

[916] See, e.g., the Partial Award, Claims Commission in Jus Ad Bellum Ethiopia's Claims 1-8 (Eth. v. Eri.), 19 December 2004, available at http://www.pca-cpa. org/upload/files/FINAL%20ET%20JAB.pdf, in which Eritrea's argument that Ethiopia's actions were part of a continuing aggression was rejected.

[917] ICJ, *Military and Paramilitary Activities*, *supra* footnote 585, para. 237:

"On the question of necessity, the Court observes that the United States measures . . . cannot be said to correspond to a 'necessity' justifying the United States action against Nicaragua on the basis of assistance given by Nicaragua to the armed opposition in El Salvador. First, these measures were only taken, and began to produce effects, several months after the major offensive of the armed opposition against the Government of El Salvador had been completely repulsed, . . ."

and the initiation of payments the payments would for that reason alone not appear to qualify as on-the-spot reactions to any alleged threats. With regard to necessity and proportionality, these requirements have the character of a rule of customary international law[918]. Thus, no other legitimate means of averting the danger or threat may exist and the action must be limited to what is necessary and proportionate.

In considering proportionality, one should in any event compare and weigh the alleged threat, for example, exercise of pressure to make certain statements in the context of a criminal investigation (which is not on its face illegal), and the response, for example, the admitted bribery of governmental officials (which is manifestly illegal).

## 6. *Justification or excuse on the basis of alleged widespread corruption*

Query whether a claimant's prohibited acts of bribery can be justified, or excused, on the grounds that allegedly corruption is widespread in the country where the acts took place, notably the host State in the investor context.

From time to time, a claimant will contend he was entitled, or had no other alternative, but to engage in bribery because it was the accepted *lingua franca* in the relevant country.

It is submitted that invariably this argument should fail. Even if bribery in a certain country were considered to be widespread, this should not excuse an acknowledged act of bribery. It can be considered a general rule of public international law pursuant to Article 38 (1) *(c)*, ICJ Statute, that it will not excuse an

---

[918] Judgment, *Oil Platforms*, *supra* footnote 910, para. 76; *Military and Paramilitary Activities in and against Nicaragua*, *supra* footnote 909, para. 176.

offender that other offenders violate the law as well. National criminal laws also do not contain a justification to such effect[919].

This general rule was also recently affirmed by the arbitral tribunal in *World Duty Free*, which held:

> "The Tribunal notes that . . . it was alleged that corruption is widespread either within the purchasing country or in the particular sector of activity. However, *all arbitral tribunals concluded that such facts do not alter in any way the legal consequences dictated by the prohibition of corruption* (see ICC case No. 1110 paras. 19-20; ICC case No. 3916, Yves Derains — *Collection of ICC awards* 1974-1985 — Kluwer 1990 — p. 509; ICC case No. 8891 — *Journal du droit international* 2000 No. 4 p. 1083). They recognised that in some countries or sectors of activities, corruption is a common practice without which the award of a contract is difficult — or even impossible — but they always refused to condone such practices. The present Tribunal agrees with such conclusion."[920]

Such propensity for corruption, if true, should not give rise to any legal justification, or excuse, as a matter of the applicable law. A reputation or climate for corrupt commercial or investment activity cannot and should not be invoked for this purpose. Ultimately, "the 'investment climate' cannot be used as an excuse for bad governance where the host country is able to offer high standards of administrative action but fails to do so"[921].

---

[919] To the contrary, aspects of general crime prevention can be an aggravating circumstance in national laws. For German law, see, e.g., Bundesgerichtshof [German Federal Court of Justice], *Neue Juristische Wochenschrift*, 1990, p. 195.

[920] *World Duty Free* v. *Kenya*, *supra* footnote 44, para. 156 (emphasis added).

[921] P. Muchlinski, *supra* footnote 175, p. 546.

### 7. *Economic necessity as the defence by the State to request for a bribe from the claimant*

Finally, where the claimant participated in an act of bribery, then the respondent, which may be a host State, may indeed succeed in invoking a defence. Again, the respondent's illegality has no influence on the (in)admissibility of the corrupt investor's claims.

Where *both* the claimant and the respondent are blameworthy, the respondent will invariably be in the stronger position, as addressed earlier[922]: *ex delicto non oritor actio* ("an unlawful act cannot serve as the basis of an action in law"); *nemo ex suo delicto meliorem suam conditionem facit* ("no one can put himself in a better legal position by means of a delict"): *ex turpi causa non oritur* ("an action cannot arise from a dishonourable cause"); *inadimplenti non est adimplendum* ("one has no need to respect his obligation if the counter-party has not respected its own"); and *nullus commodum capere potest de injuria sua propria* ("no one can be allowed to take advantage of his own wrong")[923].

Where the claimant did *not* participate in the act of bribery, but only the State did, then the State will not succeed with its defence.

Proven bribery or corruption by the State may inform or constitute one or more breaches of subs tantive treaty protections and otherwise applicable national and/or international law.

Can the respondent itself invoke economic necessity as a defence, for example, under Article 25, ILC Draft Articles on State Responsibility? Article 25 (1) provides:

---

[922] See *supra* Chapter IX.D.1.b.
[923] See R. Kreindler, *supra* footnote 782, pp. 317 *et seq.*; B. Cheng, *supra* footnote 812, pp. 149 *et seq.*

"Necessity may not be invoked by a State as a ground for precluding the wrongfulness of an act not in conformity with an international obligation of that State unless the act: *(a)* is the only way for the State to safeguard an essential interest against a grave and imminent peril; and *(b)* does not seriously impair an essential interest of the State or States towards which the obligation exists, or of the international community as a whole."

And Article 25 (2) states:

"In any case, necessity may not be invoked by a State as a ground for precluding wrongfulness if: *(a)* the international obligation in question excludes the possibility of invoking necessity; or *(b)* the State has contributed to the situation of necessity."

Exceptional grounds may exist, see, for example, *CMS* v. *Argentina*, ICSID (2005)[924] and *Enron* v. *Argentina*, ICSID (2007)[925].

However, there should normally not be a possibility of invocation of this defence in the context of bribery or attempted bribery by the State.

---

[924] *CMS Gas Transmission Company* v. *The Argentine Republic*, Award, ICSID Case No. ARB/01/8, 12 May 2005, para. 317:

"While the existence of necessity as a ground for precluding wrongfulness under international law there is no longer disputed, there is also consensus to the effect that this ground is an exceptional one and has to be addressed in a prudent manner to avoid abuse."

[925] *Enron Corporation Ponderosa Assets, L.P.* v. *The Argentine Republic*, Award, ICSID Case No. ARB/01/3, 22 May 2007, para. 304:

"There is no disagreement either about the fact that state of necessity is a most exceptional remedy subject to very strict conditions because otherwise it would open the door to elude any international obligation."

CHAPTER XI

STANDARDS OF REVIEW OF ARBITRAL
AWARDS IN THE CORRUPTION CONTEXT

## A. *Introduction*

An arbitral award, whether in the commercial or the investment context, is not worth the paper it is written on if it cannot be enforced, at least from the perspective of the arbitral tribunal and the "successful" party. When illegality and corruption become part of the mix, then issues of enforceability become all the more problematic, as set forth throughout the earlier chapters.

On the basis of the prior discussion, the following fundamental points can be established generally, without regard to the particularities of the kind of arbitration or the particular law or jurisdiction concerned.

*First*, both commercial and investment-treaty awards are meant to be voluntarily complied with. As obvious and prosaic as this statement may sound, it is not self-evident, insofar as the unsatisfied party may have grounds, exercised in good faith or perhaps in bad faith, to refuse to comply with the terms of the award voluntarily, and particularly its payment terms.

*Second*, the compulsory enforceability of the award will be an issue either of annulment at the place of arbitration or under the ICSID annulment scheme and/or of denial of recognition and enforcement, either at the place of arbitration or elsewhere.

*Third*, while in commercial arbitration the grounds for annulment and denial of enforcement have been increasingly harmonized and converged over the last 20 or so years partly as a result of the UNCITRAL

Model Law, application of those grounds is of course still a matter of local law, including local approaches to such potential enforceability issues as arbitrability, competence, jurisdiction, separability and, especially, public policy.

*Fourth*, allegations, admissions or findings of corruption may implicate each and every one of the above issues, depending on the law or laws applicable and depending on whether the context is commercial arbitration or investment treaty arbitration.

*Fifth*, there are of course certain issues of enforceability which are largely common to the commercial and investment treaty contexts, including in the sense of annulment proceedings at the seat and, in the case of ICSID, ICSID Convention annulment. Procedural defects, due process, the right to be heard, equal treatment, *ultra petita* or *infra petita* are typical grounds for attack and possible set aside in legislation and conventions, whether provided for expressly or impliedly. In both spheres, corruption issues may implicate procedural issues particularly related to the taking of evidence, the standard of proof and burden of proof, elevated to an annulment concern. In both spheres, a violation of domestic or more particularly transnational or international public policy serves as the major imponderable, even while the ICSID Convention annulment grounds do not foresee public policy *per se* as a ground for objection.

And in both spheres, heretofore "private" or "confidential" arbitral proceedings may largely become a matter of public record at the annulment or enforcement stage, through the involvement of the local courts or the ICSID annulment committee mechanism. Furthermore, prior case law on annulment under the *lex arbitri* may be binding or at least persuasive depending on the jurisdiction, while prior case law in the investment treaty context will likewise be persuasive but not binding. Finally, in both settings there may be competing mandates: on the one hand, a general weighing of public policy against corruption, on the other hand a more specific weighing of due process, the finality of the award, and the prohibition against double jeopardy *(nemo debet bis vexari)*[926], especially where "new fresh" evidence of illegality is alleged or even sought to be admitted after the award has been rendered and at the annulment or enforcement stage.

*Sixth*, there are also certain issues of enforceability which have important differences between the commercial and investment treaty contexts, including in the sense of annulment proceedings at the seat and, in the case of ICSID, ICSID Convention annulment. This starts with the premise that most commercial arbitration awards are in fact not subject to a challenge to enforcement, and are complied with voluntarily, whereas investment treaty-based awards, at least in the relatively accessible ICSID sphere, are routinely challenged in the form of ICSID annulment proceedings. Furthermore, in commercial arbitration the application of annulment grounds under the respective *lex arbitri* is circumscribed by and rooted in local law and in concepts of *res judicata* or *stare decisis*, or at least persuasive precedent. By contrast, in investment treaty arbitration the application of annulment grounds under the ICSID Convention is potentially more fluid, as it is rooted in public international law principles and international/ICSID "precedent".

Moreover, corruption seldom implicates arbitrability or other "gateway issues" in commercial arbitration whereas in investment treaty cases it almost always implicates gateway issues. In addition, the public policy violation is expressly enumerated in the Model

---

[926] M. Hwang and K. Lim, *supra* footnote 8, p. 51; B. Cheng, *supra* footnote 812, pp. 364 *et seq.*

Law and other national arbitration laws, even while its application is dependent upon case law and commentary which may or may not be munificent or helpful from country to country. In ICSID investment case, "public policy" will be subject to public international law to the one or other extent and will invariably be subsumed under the "manifest excess of powers" ground for ICSID Convention annulment. Finally, in commercial matters the standards of public policy may be local or a mixture of local and international while in investment disputes public policy is usually viewed as an international analysis, subject to any "in accordance with local law" issues.

### B. *Public Policy-Related Enforceability Issues in the Corruption Context*

#### 1. *Which public policy?*

Which public policy can or should apply in the context of enforceability issues in the corruption context. Should it be the public policy at the seat or as defined by the seat, if any? Should be the public policy under public international law principles, pursuant to, for example, ICSID Convention, Article 52 (1) *(b)* ("manifest excess of powers")? Or should it be at the place or places of attempted enforcement, if any, pursuant to the New York Convention or some other national or international basis for enforcement?

##### (a) *Public policy at the seat or as defined by the seat, if any*

Article 34 (2) *(b)* (i) of the UNCITRAL Model Law provides as a ground for annulment of a commercial award at the seat of arbitration that the award would be "in conflict with the public policy *of this State*". Exceptionally, and if it follows from the applicable conflicts rules, this provision could conceivably lead to the application of the public policy of a foreign State[927]. Major jurisdictions such as France, Switzerland and Germany apply a restrictive concept of "international public policy" as opposed to a broader concept of domestic public policy, whether under the Model Law in the case of Germany[928] or outside of the Model Law framework in the case of France[929] and Switzerland[930] respectively.

Ultimately, in such jurisdictions it is the national concept of an international public policy, and not a provincial local policy in the sense of a *loi de police*[931], which needs to be offended in order to justify set aside, particularly in the case of an award considered to be "international". While public policy will be connected to the fundamental norms of the society, for example, in the case of Germany to its Basic Law or Constitution[932], the public policy at issue is usually international in scope and content[933]. Corruption will normally need to fit within such a conception. In the case of an investment-treaty award under ICSID, corruption will need to fit within international law principles, in the context of a "manifest excess of powers".

---

[927] G. B. Born, *supra* footnote 4, p. 2623.

[928] German Code of Civil Procedure, Sec. 1059 (2) (2) *(b)*.

[929] French New Code of Civil Procedure, Art. 1502 (5).

[930] Swiss Law on Private International Law, Art. 190 (2) *(e)*.

[931] Bundesgerichtshof [German Federal Court of Justice], III ZR 269/88, 18 January 1990, *XIX Yearbook Commercial Arbitration*, 1994, pp. 503 *et seq.*

[932] Oberlandesgericht [Court of Appeal] Celle, 8 Sch 06/06, 31 May 2007, *XXXIII Yearbook Commercial Arbitration*, 2008, pp. 524 *et seq.*

[933] ILA Report on Public Policy as Bar to Enforcement of International Arbitral Awards, *TDM,* Vol. 1 (2004), p. 3.

(b)  *Public policy at the place or places of attempted enforcement, if any*

To a certain extent, Article V (2) *(b)* of the New York Convention, which will usually be the relevant measure for cross-border enforcement of commercial awards, is the mirror-image of Article 34 (2) *(b)* (i) of the UNCITRAL Model Law. This is not at all surprising, since both are United Nations instruments, the former from 1958 and the latter from 1985. Article V (2) *(b)* provides:

> "Recognition and enforcement of an arbitral award may also be refused if the competent authority *in the country where recognition and enforcement is sought* finds that: . . . *(b)* The recognition or enforcement of the award would be contrary to the public policy *of that country*."

Interestingly, the Convention speaks of the "public policy of that country", which might suggest that local public policy could serve as an obstacle to enforcement, whether raised by the award debtor or *sua sponte* by the enforcing court. As stated, this is entirely possible, whereas the current trend in leading jurisdictions is to apply the provision to block enforcement only when the award violates the national concept of a higher transnational or international public policy[934]. While this trend is by no means universal or even widespread, it is solidly established in certain leading jurisdictions and it is submitted that it should be emulated by other jurisdictions in the years to come. Of course, the Convention does not apply to ICSID Convention awards, which have their own self-executing enforcement mechanism under Article 54[935].

---

[934]  *Supra* footnote 933.
[935]  See generally C. H. Schreuer, *supra* footnote 402, pp. 1115 *et seq*.

## 2. *Competing mandates of public policy and finality*

As addressed earlier, it may be difficult or indeed impossible for the arbitrator to equally and fully comply with the mandate of public policy and the mandate of finality, and therefore the one will need to cede to the other for purposes of enforceability. That the challenge is a difficult and important one, and that both the process and the outcome are not always the same, is apparent in the commercial arbitration context by reviewing certain leading decisions which arose in close proximity to each other in the English courts.

### (a) Westacre

In *Westacre Investments Inc.* v. *Jugoimport — SPDR Holding Co. Ltd. & Others*[936], the claimant sought to enforce, in England, an ICC international arbitral award rendered in Switzerland. The basis for the opposition to enforcement was that the award related to a consultancy agreement, expressly governed by Swiss law, which the defendant alleged was a vehicle for influence peddling. He contended that the claimant was to undertake the influence peddling in Kuwait to procure contracts for the sale of military hardware to the Government of Kuwait.

The contract was not subject to English law, nor did the alleged illicit conduct take place in England, nor for that matter did it take place in the country of the seat of arbitration (Switzerland) or the country of the applicable substantive law (also Switzerland). The ICC tribunal had addressed the allegation of illegality in the contract. It had held that neither illegality nor violation

---

[936] Court of Appeal, *Westacre* v. *Jugoimport*, *supra* footnote 206, upholding the decision of the High Court in *Westacre* v. *Jugoimport*, *supra* footnote 319, pp. 570 *et seq.*

of international public policy had been established. The award also survived a challenge before the Swiss Federal Tribunal[937].

Subsequently, new evidence was adduced respecting the true meaning and scope of the parties' "consultancy agreement". Then the English court had to decide whether such evidence gave rise to a defence to enforcement of the foreign award. The English court *granted* enforcement of the award, upholding the jurisdiction of the original Swiss arbitral tribunal to have decided whether illegality existed in the first place:

> "The opportunity for erroneous and uncorrectable findings of fact arises in all international arbitration. If much weight were to be attached to that consideration it is difficult to see that arbitrators would ever be accorded jurisdiction to determine issues of illegality."[938]

The enforcing court recognized that some forms of illegal contracts might not be susceptible of arbitration under English public policy. It gave a contract for illegal importation and distribution of cocaine as an example. Here, the foreign award had arguably been based on an illicit contract, but not of such an egregious nature. Whatever the amplitude of the illegality, the allegedly illicit nature of a commission scheme and its consequences had been amply argued before the prior ICC tribunal with its seat in Switzerland. The tribunal then considered and dismissed the allegation. The defendant's challenge to enforcement in England, based on illegality, thus failed and the award was enforced. Thus, in the face of potentially new and dam-

---

[937] The judgment is published in *ASA Bulletin*, Vol. 13 (1995), pp. 217-226.
[938] High Court, *Westacre* v. *Jugoimport*, *supra* footnote 319, p. 595.

aging evidence indicating that the underlying contract had indeed been for purposes of corruption, the first instance court held in 2000 as follows:

> "However, although commercial corruption is deserving of strong judicial and governmental disapproval . . . On balance . . . the public policy of sustaining international arbitration awards on the facts of this case outweighs the public policy in discouraging international corruption."[939]

It ruled in favour of finality.

A year later, the Court of Appeal (1999) then addressed further the aspect of reopening the matter based on allegedly new facts and found:

> "The seriousness of the alleged illegality . . . is not . . . a factor to be considered at the stage of deciding whether or not to mount a full-scale inquiry. It is something to be taken into account as part of the balancing exercise between the competing public policy considerations of finality and illegality which can only be performed in response to the second question, if it arises, namely, should the award be enforced? . . . I would dismiss the appeal."[940]

While this wording is not entirely clear, it would appear to stand for the proposition that the public policy in favour of the finality of arbitral awards outweighs the public interest "in preventing the (indirect) enforcement of possibly corrupt commercial practices"[941].

---

[939] *Supra* footnote 938, p. 598.
[940] Court of Appeal, *Westacre* v. *Jugoimport*, *supra* footnote 206, pp. 775-776.
[941] A. Johnson, "Illegal Contracts and Arbitration Clauses", *International Arbitration Law Review*, Vol. 2 (1999), p. 36.

The public policy in favour of finality, subject to legitimate grounds for recourse, of course exists in relation to any arbitral award, both commercial and investment treaty-based. Here, the mandate of finality apparently seemed all the more compelling to the enforcing court as grounds not to consider "new" evidence of illegality since illegality had already been squarely pleaded and considered by the ICC arbitral tribunal at the Swiss seat. On this basis alone, also in view of the general prohibition against *de novo* review of the facts in the context of recognition and enforcement proceedings [942] as well as the general prohibition against denial of enforcement on the basis of a "mistake of law" [943], the *Westacre* decision would appear not to be objectionable. At the same time, its rationale is not inconsistent with the conclusion, which it is submitted is the correct one, that the mandate of public policy *per se* should weigh more heavily in the balance than the mandate of finality if and when they are perceived to be in conflict.

Indeed, subsequent to *Westacre* the English courts have correctly held, based on *Westacre*, essentially to this effect. The rationale that the public policy of sustaining international arbitration awards on the facts outweighs the public policy in discouraging international corruptions was also applied as binding by Justice David Steel of the Royal Court of Justice. His judgment concerned a challenge, on grounds of violations of English public policy as well as public policy at common law, of an ICC arbitral award which had upheld a claim for payments under a consultancy agreement [944]. Here, the competent judge found, based

---

[942] G. B. Born, *supra* footnote 4, pp. 2726 *et seq.* and G. B. Born, *International Arbitration: Law and Practice*, The Hague, Kluwer Law International, 2012, pp. 382 *et seq.*
[943] *Ibid.*
[944] See R v. V., [2008] EWHC (Comm) 1531.

on the arguments set out in the *Westacre* decisions that the applicant had failed to establish that the award or its enforcement could be challenged on public policy grounds[945].

The foregoing outcome is also well imaginable in investment treaty-based arbitrations having a classical seat and subject to enforceability tests under national law. Indeed it is also imaginable even in ICSID Convention cases without a classical juridical seat insofar as the "manifest excess of powers" standard for annulment of an ICSID award has generally been used to encompass violations of public policy[946]. Thus where an ICSID tribunal or an ICSID annulment committee is confronted with a perceived conflict between the mandate of finality and the mandate of public policy, in the absence of a public policy violation finality can tip the scales. Where a public policy violation is established in the context of a "manifest excess of powers", then clearly finality will need to cede to this higher value[947].

(b) Soleimany

The same year as the decision in *Westacre*, 1998, in *Soleimany* v. *Soleimany*[948] ([1998] 3 WLR 811, CA) the English courts were called upon to decide whether to enforce a somewhat different award, this time a

---

[945] See R v. V., [2008] EWHC (Comm) 1531, paras. 32, 34.

[946] Art. 52 (1) *(b)* of the ICSID Convention. See Y. Banifatemi, "Defending Investment Treaty Awards: Is There an ICSID Advantage?", in A. J. van den Berg (ed.), *50 Years of the New York Convention: ICCA International Arbitration Conference*, ICCA Congress Series, 2009, Dublin, Vol. 14, Kluwer Law International, 2009, pp. 324 *et seq*.

[947] Y. Banifatemi, *ibid*.

[948] [1998] 3 WLR 811, 13 Int'l Arb. Rep. A1 (March 1998) (CA 1998).

domestic English one. To that extent, there was no competing public policy concern between the law of the seat and the law of the place of attempted enforcement, which were both English law. The basis for the opposition to enforcement was that the award related to an illegal carpet importation agreement, expressly governed by Jewish law, which the defendant alleged violated Iranian export regulations.

The contract was once again not subject to English law, nor did the alleged illicit conduct take place in England, the seat of arbitration. The English arbitral tribunal before the Beth Din was called upon to resolve a dispute over the division of profits from the agreement. The submission to the Beth Din was agreed after the dispute had arisen, and not by an arbitration agreement in the original contract.

The parties agreed to apply Jewish law and stipulated — apparently validly as a matter of the applicable substantive law — that any illegality of the underlying contract would be irrelevant to their rights and duties in the arbitration. The English tribunal addressed and acknowledged that the parties had been involved in an "illicit" enterprise involving "smugglers' fees". However, under the agreed Jewish law it awarded damages to the claimant notwithstanding the admittedly illegal contract. The tribunal thereby considered the illegality to be of no relevance since it was applying Jewish law, under which any alleged illegality would have no effect on the rights of the parties.

This time, the English court *refused* enforcement of the award:

> "The court declines to enforce an illegal contract . . . The parties cannot . . . by procuring an arbitration conceal that they, or rather one of them, is seeking to enforce an illegal contract." [949]

---

[949] *Supra* footnote 948, at 824 A-B.

Thus the defendant successfully challenged enforcement of a domestic award which had admittedly been based on an illicit contract. As in *Westacre*, the court also recognized that some forms of illegal contracts might not be susceptible of arbitration at all under English public policy:

> "The English Court would not recognise an agreement between . . . highwaymen to arbitrate their difference any more than it would recognise the original agreement to split the proceeds."[950]

Here, in contradistinction to *Westacre*, the question of illegality of the agreement had not been argued before the tribunal, and therefore not been rejected by it. On the contrary, illegality had been conceded to and acknowledged by the tribunal. Interestingly in this regard, although the enforcing court did not need to query whether illegality truly attached, in dictum it suggested, contrary to *Westacre*, that in the face of an allegation of illegality less stark than the carpet smuggling contract at issue there, the English court might see fit to enquire further, *on its own motion*, as to the illegality:

> "an enforcement judge, if there is *prima facie* evidence from one side that the award is based on an illegal contract, should inquire further to some extent. Is there evidence on the other side to the contrary? Has the arbitrator expressly found that the underlying contract was not illegal? Or is it a fair inference that he did reach that conclusion? Is there anything to suggest that the arbitrator was incompetent to conduct such an inquiry? May there have been collusion or bad faith, so as to procure an award despite illegality?[951]

---

[950] *Supra* footnote 948, at 821 G.
[951] *Ibid.*, at 824 E-F.

This dictum may be seen as running in a somewhat divergent direction from the *Westacre* court's concern that the "opportunity for erroneous and uncorrectable findings of fact arises in all international arbitration"[952]. It also runs somewhat far afield from the conclusion in that decision that the enforcing court should therefore avoid unwarranted revisiting of facts and evidence which had been before an arbitral tribunal. On the other hand, the *Soleimany* decision is consistent with the notion that English public policy forbids the courts from being used to directly or indirectly enforce corrupt commercial practices.

As the court held:

> "Where public policy is involved, the interposition of an arbitration award does not isolate the successful party's claim from illegality which gave rise to it."[953]

> "The court is in our view concerned to preserve the integrity of its process, and to see that it is not abused. The parties cannot override that concern by private agreement. They cannot by procuring an arbitration conceal that they, or rather one of them, is seeking to enforce an illegal contract. Public policy will not allow it."[954]

Ultimately, the difference in the two outcomes — *Soleimany* and *Westacre* — may be explained in large part by the *failure* to prove illegality in the one case and by the *admission* of the same in the other. Thus the *Soleimany* court concluded that admitted smuggling fell into a category of illegality where as a matter of

---

[952] High Court, *Westacre* v. *Jugoimport*, *supra* footnote 319, p. 595.
[953] *Soleimany* v. *Soleimany*, *supra* footnote 948, pp. 823-824.
[954] *Ibid.*

public policy no arbitral award relating to such illegality would be enforced by an English court.

## (c) Hilmarton

One year later, the *Hilmarton* saga reached English shores. Unlike *Soleimany*, the *Hilmarton* court *granted* enforcement[955].

In *Hilmarton*, the basis for the opposition to enforcement was that the Swiss ICC award related to an illegal contract for the payment of fees due under an agreement to lobby for the awarding of a public works contract in Algeria. That agreement was expressly governed by Swiss law. The defendant alleged that the agreement violated Algerian law as that of the place of performance. Like *Westacre* and *Soleimany*, the contract here was not subject to English law, nor did the alleged illicit conduct take place in England. Nor did the alleged illicit conduct take place in Switzerland, the seat of arbitration.

The ICC arbitral tribunal had addressed and acknowledged that the underlying agreement was illegal — under the Algerian law of performance. Notwithstanding, the tribunal had found that under the agreed Swiss law the contract was licit and not tainted by overseas illegality. This time, as in *Westacre* but unlike in *Soleimany*, the English court granted enforcement of the award[956]. It did so after the Swiss Federal

---

[955] High Court of Justice, *Hilmarton* v. *Omnium de Traitement*, *supra* footnote 321.

[956] The *Hilmarton* dispute had in fact already been the subject of two ICC arbitration awards rendered in Geneva, a decision by the Swiss Federal Tribunal upholding a lower Swiss court's annulment of the first ICC award, and two decisions of the French Cour de Cassation which refused to give effect to the prior Swiss annulment of the first ICC award and instead granted it exequatur in France.

Tribunal had upheld a lower Swiss court's annulment of a first ICC award in the matter[957] and after the French Cour de Cassation twice refused to give effect to the prior Swiss annulment of the ICC award and instead granted it exequatur in France[958].

The decision to grant enforcement in England of the prior Swiss ICC award provides a clear distinction between an action to enforce a *contract* in England and an action to enforce an *arbitral award* in England. The *Hilmarton* enforcing court found that its decision as to enforcement of the Swiss award was not an adjudication of the underlying (allegedly illicit) contract. Accordingly, the court held that in the absence of patent evidence of corruption which would give rise to mandatory public policy considerations, it was irrelevant whether the finding as to illegality would have been the same had English law applied[959].

The *Hilmarton* court relied on the views expressed by Waller LJ in the Court of Appeal in *Westacre*[960]. It found that contracts for the "purchase of influence" offend English public policy[961]. However, it also concluded that their illicit nature would not be "enough" to justify refusal of enforcement of a foreign award by an English court where such contracts were to be performed outside England and the foreign award had found that such contracts were not illegal under the foreign law applicable to the contracts in the arbitration[962].

---

[957] Tribunal Fédéral [Swiss Federal Tribunal], *supra* footnote 195.

[958] Cour de Cassation, 23 March 1994, *Revue de l'arbitrage* (1994), p. 327.

[959] High Court of Justice, *Hilmarton* v. *Omnium de Traitement*, *supra* footnote 321, pp. 372-373.

[960] *Ibid.*

[961] *Ibid.*

[962] *Ibid.*

The *Hilmarton* court thus enforced a foreign (Swiss) arbitral award which had stated explicitly that the underlying contract was illegal under the law of performance (Algeria), but had concluded that under the proper law of the contract (Switzerland) the contract was licit and not tainted by overseas illegality. The enforcing court was also not in a position to second-guess the correctness of the ICC tribunal's conclusion that the illegal contract did not offend public policy at the foreign seat; this was perhaps not surprising inasmuch as this was not the issue before the court. Moreover, in the *Hilmarton* court's view, fraud or corruption would be sufficiently offensive to refuse enforcement of such an award in England, but a contract for the "purchase of personal influence" such as here would not[963]. In short, the English court would appear to have given no great deference to any notion of transnational or international public policy, while clearly giving greater weight to the *lex contractus* and to the law of the place of performance. And the court clearly was prepared to distinguish between outright corruption on the one hand and "purchase of personal influence" on the other, but in a manner which did not provide any real explanation for such distinction.

### (d) *Reconciling* Westacre, Soleimany *and* Hilmarton

Can or should *Westacre, Soleimany* and *Hilmarton* be reconcilable one with the other? It would appear that they are, largely so.

An action to enforce an illegal *contract* shall be subject to English public policy, and shall normally not be successful. This would appear to be correct, and worthy of emulation in commercial and investment arbitration generally. An action to enforce a *domestic*

---

[963] *Supra* footnote 959, p. 372.

*award* which upheld an illegal contract to which *English* law applied and/or to which was to be performed in England shall likewise normally not be successful. This too would appear to be unobjectionable and sound. Furthermore, an action to enforce a domestic award which upheld an illegal contract to which a *foreign* law applied may be enforceable, unless the illegality is such as to make the underlying arbitration a sham and/or to make enforcement of rights arising out of the illegal contract a violation of the integrity of the English judicial process[964].

Ultimately, in the commercial arbitration context an action to enforce a foreign *award* which upheld an illegal contract to which a foreign law applied but which did not offend that foreign law's public policy shall normally be successful. An exception would be where the illegality is of such a nature as itself to offend English public policy and such offence outweighs the "competing mandate" of ensuring the finality of international arbitral awards. What kind of illegality would suffice to cause such an offence? Again, presumably contracts promoting or facilitating corruption, drug trafficking, prostitution, torture, slavery, etc. Such matters may be seen as involving transnational or international public policy. They therefore justify striking down a foreign award not for its incompatibility with a "mere" *loi de police* of another State, but for its irreconcilability with transnational *lois de police*. Such matters would also justify striking down an investment treaty-based award in the context of the ICSID Convention.

---

[964] See also E. Brown, "Illegality and Public Policy — Enforcement of Arbitral Awards in England: Hilmarton Limited v. Omnium de Traitement et de Valorisation S.A.", *International Arbitration Law Review*, Vol. 3 (2000), pp. 31-35.

Last but not least is *O'Callaghan* v. *Coral Racing Ltd.*, 1998, (unreported, *The Times*, 26 November 1998)[965], a case demonstrating the kind of illegality which both the *Westacre* and *Soleimany* courts held would not even be susceptible to a reference to arbitration at all. In that decision, the English Court of Appeal held that an arbitration clause in an indisputably illegal gaming agreement could not be regarded as a valid arbitration agreement since any "arbitration" under the circumstances, meant to be submitted to the editor of *The Sporting Life*, would be devoid of legal consequences. In short, the arbitration agreement itself was a sham, if also not necessarily intentionally a sham[966].

*O'Callaghan* was decided under the Arbitration Act 1950. Had it been decided under the 1996 Act, the outcome would presumably have been the same since no arbitrator could have make a valid monetary award. Focusing on separability, the Court of Appeal held that the arbitration agreement could not be severed from the overall agreement: it "must be treated as part and parcel of the void agreement, and so cannot survive independently"[967].

In fact, the real explanation for the outcome was likely that the undertaking of the parties was not really to be considered as an arbitration agreement in the first place. The rejection of validity was not based so much on heinousness as on arbitrability and practicability. This is perhaps the best way to explain to Mr. O'Callaghan why the public policy condemnation of would-be agreements respecting betting on English football matches is harsher than the public policy

---

[965] See also B. Harris, *et al.*, *The Arbitration Act 1996: A Commentary*, 2nd ed., Blackwell Science Ltd., 2000, pp. 76-77 and 79-80.

[966] R. Kreindler, *supra* footnote 41, p. 246.

[967] B. Harris, *et al.*, *supra* footnote 965.

condemnation of would-be agreements respecting corruption of public officials, influence peddling and the like[968].

## 3. Public policy as a content- or results-oriented approach

Should the reviewing court or annulment committee assess merely whether the outcome of the award would be contrary to public policy, for example, that the conduct compelled by the award or the damages awarded contradicts the relevant public policy? Or, rather should it also consider, possibly by reopening or re-examining the underlying facts, whether the substantive claim granted by the award violates public policy, for example, by imposing liability for failure to engage in illegal practices? Generally speaking, the former is to be endorsed and only in narrow circumstances the latter. Relatively recent cases in commercial arbitration in the English courts, either in the context of annulment or enforcement, have illustrated the challenges present here, including certain of the cases already addressed above.

Thus in *Soleimany* the court set aside an award that had enforced a joint venture for smuggling goods out of Iran in violation of Iranian customs laws:

> "Where public policy is involved, the interposition of an arbitration award does not insulate the successful party's claim from illegality which gave rise to it."

---

[968] Cf. A. Johnson, *supra* footnote 941, p. 37:

"It may appear slightly odd to Mr. O'Callaghan . . . that those involved (or allegedly involved) in international corrupt trading practices and carpet smuggling should be permitted to refer their disputes to arbitration, but perfectly respectable gamblers should not. But there it is. Public policy is a funny thing."

"The court is in our view concerned to preserve the integrity of its process, and to see that it is not abused. The parties cannot override that concern by private agreement. They cannot by procuring an arbitration conceal that they, or rather one of them, is seeking to enforce an illegal contract. Public policy will not allow it."

At the same time, there is a regrettable lack of consistency as to whether enforcement of an award itself must violate public policy or whether a public policy violation would be implicated where the underlying claims are contrary to public policy.

In England, for example, before entry into effect of the 1996 English Arbitration Act in *Deutsche Schachtbau* v. *Ras Al Khaimah*, English Court of Appeal (1987)[969], that non-enforcement requires

"some element of illegality or that the enforcement of the award . . . be clearly injurious to the public good or, possibly, that enforcement would be wholly offensive to the ordinary reasonable and fully informed member of the public on whose behalf the powers of the state are exercised".

In *Westacre*, after entry into effect of the 1996 Act, the English Court of Appeal held that non-enforcement requires that an arbitral award would have to "ignore palpable and indisputable illegality"[970]. However, it is to be noted that where a *foreign* arbitral tribunal already examined — and rejected — an argument based on public policy or illegality, the English courts will usually not reconsider at the enforcement stage

---

[969] Court of Appeal, *Deutsche Schachtbau-und Tiefbohrgesellschaft mbH* v. *Ras Al Khaimah Nat'l Oil Co.*, [1987] 2 Lloyd's Law Reports, p. 254.

[970] High Court, *Westacre* v. *Jugoimport*, *supra* footnote 319, p. 593 (QB), approved in *Westacre* v. *Jugoimport*, *supra* footnote 206 (English Court of Appeal).

again. Thus in *Hilmarton* and in *Westacre* the English Court of Appeal enforced a *foreign* arbitral award irrespective of the illegality of the underlying claims, holding that the policy of giving effect to arbitral awards outweighed policies against conduct deemed illegal under the applicable substantive law.

In Switzerland, generally annulment will follow only if the result, rather than merely the reasoning, is incompatible with Swiss international public policy[971]. The first annulment of an international award to which the 1987 Swiss Private International Law Act applied on the grounds of public policy did not occur until over 20 years later, in 2010, in a case where the award has been rendered in disregard of a judgment involving the same parties, the same dispute and the same action[972]. And in 2009, the Swiss Federal Tribunal held that exceptional "revision" was possible where criminal proceedings after the arbitration concluded provided fresh evidence of fraud which had been unavailable during the arbitration[973].

In France, annulment has generally been found only in the case of a "manifest violation of a rule of law that is deemed essential or of a fundamental principle" —

---

[971] See, e.g., the most recent decisions of the Tribunal Fédéral [Swiss Federal Tribunal] on 27 March 2012 (BGE 138 III 327) and on 19 April 1994 (BGE 120 II 167). See also E. Geisinger and A. Mazuranic, "Chapter 11: Challenge and Revision of the Award", in E. Geisinger and N. Voser (eds), *International Arbitration in Switzerland: A Handbook for Practitioners*, 2nd ed., Kluwer Law International, 2013, p. 249.

[972] Tribunal Fédéral [Swiss Federal Tribunal], 10 April 2010, BGE 136 III 345.

[973] Decision of the Tribunal Fédéral [Swiss Federal Tribunal], 6 October 2009, *Thales (anciennement Thomson CSF)* v. *Frontier AG Bern en liquidation et Brunner Sociedade Civil de Administraçao Limitada*, *ASA Bulletin*, Vol. 28 (2010), pp. 318 *et seq.*

Paris Court of Appeal (2004)[974]. The stringency of this approach should not be underestimated, all the more so since the entry into effect of the new French Decree in 2011[975]. There are rare cases of non-enforcement including cases involving bribery: Paris Court of Appeal (1993)[976]. At the same time, there would appear to be a shift back to a minimalist re-examination of allegedly new facts, as reflected in such cases during the period 1993-2009 as *Westman*[977], *Thomson*[978], *Thalès*[979], *Cytec*[980] and *Schneider*[981].

---

[974] Cour d'appel de Paris (1re Ch. C), *SA Thalès Air Défense* v. *GIE Euromissile*, 18 November 2004, *Revue de l'arbitrage* (2005), p. 757 (French): "l'atteinte devant constituer une violation manifeste d'une règle de droit considérée comme essentielle, ou d'un principe fondamental, . . .".

[975] Decree No. 2011-48 of 13 January 2011. An English translation is provided by E. Gaillard, *et al.* at http://www.iaiparis.com/pdf/FRENCH_LAW_ON_ARBITRATION.pdf.

[976] Cour d'appel de Paris (1 Ch. C), *European Gas Turbines SA* v. *Westman International Ltd.*, 30 September 1993, *Revue de l'arbitrage* (1994), pp. 359 *et seq.*

[977] *Ibid.* and Cour de Cassation (1 Ch. civ.), *Westman International Ltd* v. *European Gaz Turbines*, 19 December 1995, *Revue de l'arbitrage* (1996), p. 49.

[978] Cour d'appel de Paris (1 Ch. C), *SA Thomson CSF* v. *Brunner, Sociedade Civil de Administracao Limitada* v. *Frontier AG Bern*, 10 September 1998 and 7 September 1999, *Revue de l'arbitrage* (2001), pp. 583, 586.

[979] Cour d'appel de Paris (1re Ch. C), *supra* footnote 974.

[980] Cour d'appel de Paris (1re Ch. C), *SNF SAS* v. *Cytec Industries BV*, 23 March 2006, *XXXII Yearbook Commercial Arbitration*, 2007, pp. 282 *et seq.*, and Cour de Cassation (1 Ch. civ.), *Cytec Industries BV* v. *SNF sas*, 4 June 2008, *XXXIII Yearbook Commercial Arbitration*, 2008, pp. 489 *et seq.*

[981] Cour d'appel de Paris (1re Ch. C), *M Schneider Schaltgerätebau und Elektroinstallationen GmbH* v. *CPL Industries Limited*, 10 September 2009, *Revue de l'arbitrage* (2010), pp. 548 *et seq.*

In the United States, no consensus has emerged in this regard. This notwithstanding certain case law in favour of the position that "the public policy exception is implicated when enforcement of the award compels one of the parties to take action which directly conflicts with public policy". See, for example, *Brown* v. *Rauscher* (1993)[982]; *Revere* v. *OPIC* (1980)[983].

## C. Conclusion

We return to our point of departure. An arbitral award, whether in the commercial or the investment context, is not worth the paper it is written on if it cannot be enforced, at least from the perspective of the arbitral tribunal and the "successful" party. When illegality and corruption become part of the mix, then issues of enforceability become all the more problematic, as set forth throughout the earlier chapters. This leads to five concluding questions and an attempt at answers.

*First*, should a reviewing court rehear the merits of the parties' arguments on the legality of the underlying agreement under the choice of law when the question has been reserved to and decided upon the arbitral tribunal? Only upon a presentation of "fresh" evidence, or even without such evidence?

It is submitted that the scope of review of an arbitral award by a reviewing court or, in the case of an ICSID award, by an annulment committee must be considered narrowly defined by the applicable *lex arbitri* or respective ICSID Convention standards. In both cases, a "rehearing" *per se* of prior arguments already made

---

[982] *Brown* v. *Rauscher Pierce Refsnes, Inc.*, 994 F. 2d 775, 782 (11th Cir. 1993).
[983] *Revere Copper & Brass Inc.* v. *Overseas Private Inv. Corp.*, 628 F. 2d 81, 82-83 (DC Cir. 1980).

to and considered by the arbitral tribunal is conceivable only if and to the extent that such arguments are relevant to those standards. In most cases, those standards will likely not permit a "rehearing" as such, although it is conceivable that the manner in which the arbitral tribunal reached its decision or the outcome of the decision may overlap with one or more annulment grounds, including on the basis of violation of public policy or manifest excess of powers. In this regard, the reviewing court or committee is by no means necessarily shut out of some form of reconsideration, and an arbitral tribunal should appreciate that this possibility exists.

On the other hand, the arbitrator has a heavy responsibility to address such questions properly since in most cases the standard for review will be high and the likelihood of successful annulment remote.

In the case of "fresh" evidence not known and not considered at the arbitral stage, and through no fault of the party relying on the evidence, the threshold may indeed be lower. While finality is a crucial mandate, it is not necessarily an end in itself, particularly where fresh evidence of illegality surfaces later on for which an excuse is available and which if ignored would run counter to the prohibition of illegality as a matter of public policy. The question of whether evidence is fresh and whether its delayed disclosure is sufficiently excused will be a fact question to be resolved by the reviewing court or annulment committee. Assuming that the evidence is a legitimate *novum* and that it could not legitimately have been considered earlier, it is submitted that there is no reason to disregard its possible implication for the enforceability of the award. Thus for example in a commercial arbitration subject to the New York Convention, a violation of public policy at the place of attempted enforcement may be raised by the reviewing court *ex officio*, and there is no reason why it should not do so in the case of a true *novum*[984].

The admittedly infrequent experience in ICSID revision proceedings is instructive in this regard[985]. Article 51 (1), ICSID Convention, permits a party to apply for revision of an award

> "on the ground of discovery of some fact of such a nature as decisively to affect the award, provided that when the award was rendered that fact was unknown to the Tribunal and to the applicant and that the applicant's ignorance of that fact was not due to negligence".

Pursuant to Article 51 (2), ICSID Convention, such application must be made "within 90 days after the discovery of such fact and in any event within three years after the date on which the award was rendered".

While certain provisions in international conventions such as Article 51, ICSID Convention, or statutes such as Article 61 of the Statute of the International Court of Justice ("ICJ Statute") allow for revision of a final decision or award, revision proceedings remain an extraordinary remedy[986]. Only in very limited circum-

---

[984] Hwang, *supra* footnote 8, p. 54.

[985] See, generally, R. Kreindler, "Applications for 'Revision' in Investment Arbitration: Selected Current Issues", Miguel Ángel Fernández-Ballesteros and David Arias (eds), *Liber Amicorum Bernardo Cremades* (La Ley, 2010), pp. 679-697.

[986] A. Zimmermann and R. Geiss, "Article 61", in A. Zimmermann *et al.* (eds.), *The Statute of the International Court of Justice: A Commentary*, Oxford, Oxford University Press, 2006, pp. 1299, 1301, para. 2; D. Bardonnet, "De l'équivoque des catégories juridiques: la révision des sentences arbitrales pour 'erreur de fait' ou 'fait nouveau' dans la practique latino-américaine", in C. A. A. Barea *et al.* (eds.), *Liber Amicorum "In Memoriam" of Judge José María Ruda*, 2000, pp. 189, 194, stating, in relevant part, as follows:

stances, if a fact which had already existed at the time the award was rendered but which fact had been unknown to the revision applicant and the arbitral tribunal is discovered after the award was rendered, may an application for revision be admissible, and then only if also this fact would have had a decisive impact on the award. Indeed a finding of the admissibility of a revision application results in the denial of and deviation from the fundamental principle of *res judicata* and the finality of an award. Therefore, it follows from the outset that the relevant prerequisites for a revision application must be interpreted and applied restrictively[987].

Such restrictive interpretation and application must be maintained both at the admissibility stage and, should a revision application be admitted, at the subsequent merits stage[988].

The exceptional character of revision proceedings is also reflected in Article 61 (1) of the ICJ Statute. Article 61 (1) expressly states that

"an application for revision may be made *only* when it is based upon the discovery of some fact of such

---

"Mais il doit être bien entendu que, pour assurer l'autorité et le caractère définitif des décisions arbitrales (ou judiciaires), la révision ne peut être admise que dans des cas exceptionnels."

"But it must be well understood that, in order to ensure the authority and the final character of arbitral (or judicial) decisions, revision cannot be admitted but in exceptional cases." (Translation of convenience.)

[987] See, e.g., K. H. Kaikobad, *Interpretation and Revision of International Boundary Decisions*, Cambridge, Cambridge University Press, 2007, p. 257; R. Geiß, *Revision Proceedings before the International Court of Justice*, Vol. 63 (2003), pp. 167, 172; A. Zimmermann and R. Geiss, *supra* footnote 986.

[988] See, e.g, K. H. Kaikobad, *op. cit.*

a nature as to be a decisive factor, which fact was, when the judgment was given, unknown to the Court and also to the party claiming revision, always provided that such ignorance was not due to negligence"[989].

Therefore, revision in particular is not a form of rehearing which might permit an applicant to question the legal reasoning upon which the award was based[990]. Accordingly, the ICJ has held that the requirements of Article 61 of the ICJ Statute must be interpreted restrictively[991]. Moreover, in order for revision proceedings to be admissible, each and every one of the prerequisites of the relevant statutory or convention provision on revision must be fulfilled[992]. The ICJ has confirmed this on various occasions in relation to revision proceedings pursuant to Article 61, ICJ Statute[993].

In short, revision constitutes an extraordinary remedy that can be admissible only in exceptional and

---

[989] Art. 61 of the Statute of the International Court of Justice (emphasis added).

[990] A. Zimmermann and R. Geiss, *supra* footnote 986, pp. 1299, 1315, (referring to *Epoux Ventense c. Etat S.H.S.*, Yugoslav-German Mixed Arb. Trib., VII RDTAM 79 (1923); ICJ, *Application of the Convention on the Prevention and Punishment of the Crime of Genocide (Bosnia and Herzegovnia* v. *Yugoslavia)*, separate opinion of Judge Koroma, *ICJ Reports 2003*, p. 34.

[991] A. Zimmermann and R. Geiss, *supra* footnote 986, pp. 1299, 1301, para. 2.

[992] See also with respect to international boundary disputes K. H. Kaikobad, *supra* footnote 987, p. 265.

[993] *Land, Island and Maritime Frontier Dispute (El Salvador* v. *Honduras)*, *ICJ Reports 2003*, p. 392. Here, the ICJ relied on its earlier judgment in *Application of the Convention on the Prevention and Punishment of the Crime of Genocide (Bosnia and Herzegovnia* v. *Yugoslavia)*, *ICJ Reports 2003*, pp. 7, 12.

stringent concrete circumstances[994]. The concept of revision adversely affects and undermines the fundamental principle of *res judicata*. For that reason alone, if applied incorrectly or without the requisite stringency the concept of revision is capable of impairing the stability of juridical relations and legal security[995]. In this regard, the ICSID Convention, as in the case of the ICJ Statute[996], generally gives priority to the fundamental principle of *res judicata*. Thus Article 53, ICSID Convention, expressly excludes any ordinary remedies against ICSID awards: "The award shall be binding on the parties and shall not be subject to any appeal or to any other remedy except those provided for in this Convention."[997]

As a general principle, the ICSID Convention, also as in the case of the ICJ Statute[998], ranks the importance of the finality of the award over and above the justice of the award. Accordingly, the principle of finality of international awards may be deviated from only if and insofar as the restrictive prerequisites pursuant to Article 51, ICSID Convention, are individually and collectively satisfied. In light of the foregoing, it is not surprising that revision proceedings generally have

---

[994] See, e.g., K. H. Kaikobad, *supra* footnote 987, p. 257: "revision, not unlike interpretation, is a judicial remedy which must be exercised restrictively and as such cannot lightly be provided".

[995] See also, e.g., S. Rosenne, *The Law and Practice of the International Court, 1920-2005*, 4th ed., 2006, p. 1671.

[996] See I. Kaufmann, *Wiederaufnahme von Verfahren vor dem Internationalen Gerichtshof*, Nomos, 2005, p. 116.

[997] Convention on the Settlement of Investment Disputes between States and Nationals of Other States, 18 March 1965, 17 *UST* 1270, 575 *UNTS* 159, at Art. 53, available at http://icsid.worldbank.org/ICSID/ICSID/RulesMain.jsp.

[998] See I. Kaufmann, *supra* footnote 996, p. 116.

been scarcely used in international adjudication[999]. There have been only three applications for revision under Article 51, ICSID Convention.

Consequently, in view of the dearth of prior ICSID revision experience and the fact that Article 51, ICSID Convention, is modelled on Article 61, ICJ Statute, jurisprudence and literature relating to Article 61, ICJ Statute, may be seen as relevant and apposite when considering an application for revision under Article 51, ICSID Convention.

The central element for the admissibility of revision proceedings pursuant to Article 51, ICSID Convention, is the "discovery of some fact". In order to determine whether there actually is "discovery of some fact", it is important to consider the standards of evidence applicable to establishing whether the alleged corruption indeed amounts to a "fact" in the sense of Article 51, ICSID Convention. Thus, the applicant in ICSID revision proceedings has the burden of proving, *first*, that a "fact" exists; *second*, that such fact was "discovered"; *third*, that such fact is of such a nature as "decisively to affect" the award; *fourth*, that such fact was "unknown" to the Tribunal; *fifth*, that such fact was "unknown" to the applicant; *sixth*, that the applicant's lack of knowledge was not "negligent"; and *seventh*, that the application for revision has been made within 90 days after the "discovery" and in any event within three years after the award was rendered[1000].

*Second*, assuming a public policy goal of pro-enforcement, finality or even *res judicata* which should prevail — in commercial arbitration, in investment treaty arbitration — when should that overriding goal

---

[999] See C. H. Schreuer, *supra* footnote 402, Art. 51, para. 1.

[1000] See, with respect to Article 61, ICJ Statute, I. Kaufmann, *supra* footnote 996, p. 231.

prevail over the public policy of discouraging and hindering unsavoury business practices including corruption, when not?

This question is essentially an offshoot of the prior question, and its answer is essentially similar. Finality is a goal but not a means to an end on its own, and should not be aspired or adhered to at the expense of violating transnational or international norms. The reasoning put forward by Justice Colman in *Westacre* is to be taken with a grain of salt. The enforcing court held that where enforceability was revisited on the basis of facts, not placed before the arbitral tribunal, which demonstrated that the contract was illegal, the court would then consider whether the public policy against the enforcement of illegal contracts was outweighed by the countervailing public policy in support of finality of awards:

> "However, although commercial corruption is deserving of strong judicial and governmental disapproval, few would consider that it stood in the scale of opprobrium quite at the level of drug trafficking. On balance I have come to the conclusion that *the public policy of sustaining international arbitration awards on the facts of this case outweighs the public policy in discouraging international corruption.*"[1001]

Justice Colman thus ruled in favour of the enforceability of the award. The judgment was upheld by the Court in the subsequent appeal proceedings[1002]. There, Justice Mantell rebuffed the attempt to reopen the case, stating as follows:

---

[1001] High Court, *Westacre* v. *Jugoimport*, *supra* footnote 319, p. 598 (emphasis added).

[1002] Court of Appeal, *Westacre* v. *Jugoimport*, *supra* footnote 206; also cited to by Judgment in *R.* v. *V.*, [2008] EWHC (Comm) 1531, at para. 32.

"The seriousness of the alleged illegality . . . is not, in my judgment, a factor to be considered at the stage of deciding whether or not to mount a full-scale inquiry. It is something to be taken into account as part of the *balancing exercise between the competing public policy considerations of finality and illegality which can only be performed in response to the second question, if it arises, namely, should the award be enforced?* Accordingly, I would dismiss the appeal." [1003]

Equally important, international tribunals have applied a balancing test which applies when two conflicting public policy interests, such as the principle of the finality of the award and the principle of prosecuting corruption, are in conflict with each other. When confronted with such a balancing exercise, certain arbitral tribunals have concluded that the public policy of sustaining international arbitration awards on the facts outweighs the public policy in discouraging international corruption [1004]. This is correct insofar as mere corruption allegations do not constitute sufficient evidence to have the balance in favour of finality shift in favour of refusal of enforcement or even revision. It will surely not always be correct where the allegations are in fact admitted or otherwise proven, and in particular where the revelation of corruption was not fully considered or not at all considered in the underlying arbitration.

*Third*, should a reviewing court be allowed to reopen an arbitrator's prior decision on legality solely when the arbitrator disregarded or wrongly decided a

---

[1003] Court of Appeal, *Westacre* v. *Jugoimport*, *supra* footnote 206, pp. 775-776 (emphasis added).

[1004] High Court, *Westacre* v. *Jugoimport*, *supra* footnote 319, p. 571; also cited to by Judgment in *R. v. V.*, [2008] EWHC (Comm) 1531, at para. 32.

palpable and indisputable illegality, or even when the illegality is more subtle and obscure?

The answer to the first part of the question is surely as obvious as the question is loaded. At the same time, the outcome under most modern arbitration laws as well as the New York Convention is not necessarily as clear as one would imagine. A prior disregard, whether wanton or mistaken, of illegality or a prior wrong decision on illegality does not necessarily translate into a ground for denying enforceability to an award. Again, the disregard or mistake would need to be linked to one of the typical grounds for refusal of enforcement, which are largely procedural in nature apart from the ground of violation of substantive public policy. The more "subtle" or "obscure" the illegality, presumably the higher the hurdle will be.

*Fourth*, should the seriousness of the alleged illegality be taken into account at the stage of preliminary enquiry of whether to enforce, or rather only in deciding the ultimate question as to whether the award should be enforced after the court has decided to reopen the issue and finds the underlying transaction illegal?

It will be recalled that in *Westacre* [1005] the claimant sought to enforce, in England, an ICC international arbitral award rendered in Switzerland. The basis for the opposition to enforcement was that the award related to a consultancy agreement, expressly governed by Swiss law, which the defendant alleged was a vehicle for influence peddling. He contended that the claimant was to undertake the influence peddling in Kuwait to procure contracts for the sale of military

---

[1005] Court of Appeal, *Westacre* v. *Jugoimport*, *supra* footnote 206, upholding the decision of the High Court in *Westacre* v. *Jugoimport*, *supra* footnote 319, pp. 570 *et seq.*

hardware to the Government of Kuwait. When new evidence was adduced respecting the true meaning and scope of the parties' "consultancy agreement", the English court had to decide whether such evidence gave rise to a defence to enforcement of the foreign award.

The English court *granted* enforcement of the award, upholding the jurisdiction of the original Swiss arbitral tribunal to have decided whether illegality existed in the first place:

> "The opportunity for erroneous and uncorrectable findings of fact arises in all international arbitration. If much weight were to be attached to that consider-ation it is difficult to see that arbitrators would ever be accorded jurisdiction to determine issues of illegality." [1006]

A year later, the Court of Appeal then addressed further the aspect of reopening the matter based on allegedly new facts and found:

> "The seriousness of the alleged illegality . . . is not . . . a factor to be considered at the stage of deciding whether or not to mount a full-scale inquiry. It is something to be taken into account as part of the balancing exercise between the compet-ing public policy considerations of finality and ille-gality which can only be performed in response to the second question, if it arises, namely, should the award be enforced? . . . I would dismiss the appeal." [1007]

So should the seriousness of the alleged illegality be

---

[1006] High Court, *Westacre* v. *Jugoimport*, *supra* foot-note 319, p. 595.

[1007] Court of Appeal, *Westacre* v. *Jugoimport*, *supra* footnote 206, pp. 775-776.

taken into account at the stage of preliminary enquiry of whether to enforce, or rather only in deciding the ultimate question as to whether the award should be enforced after the court has decided to reopen the issue and finds the underlying transaction illegal? The solution in *Westacre* will surely not fit all circumstances. While there must be compelling reasons to overcome the primacy of finality and mere allegations of illegality may not suffice, not all allegations are to be regarded automatically as second-class citizens. Depending upon the severity of the allegation and the overall circumstances, a full-scale enquiry, within the confines of the respective enforceability standards, may indeed be called for. For this reason alone, the proposition that the public policy in favour of the finality of arbitral awards outweighs the public interest "in preventing the (indirect) enforcement of possibly corrupt commercial practices"[1008] is not deserving of blanket endorsement.

Finally, which is to be preferred? The English view that certain "errors of law" in the arbitrator's determination of illegality are not immune from later review and can themselves even constitute violations of public policy, irrespective of the quality of the illegality? Or rather the overwhelming majority view including under the New York Convention, namely that errors of law or disregard of law are not *per se* grounds for non-enforcement and that the dispositive public policy is a matter of the law of the place of enforcement or annulment, not the law of the place of performance of the (illegal) contract?

In reality, the choice may not be as stark and mutually exclusive as it at first blush sounds. The possibility under the English Arbitration Act 1996 to review awards rendered in English on the grounds of a serious

---

[1008] A. Johnson, *supra* footnote 941, pp. 35-37.

irregularity under Section 68[1009] is perhaps unusual in terms of the elaborateness of the textual provision, especially when compared to the Model Law grounds for annulment[1010].

At the same time, the "serious irregularity" which might arise in the context of illegality or corruption is no less well encompassed by the more spare Model Law provisions. The possibility under the English Arbitration to appeal on a point of law under Section 69[1011] is of course another matter, and does not find a direct counterpart either in Model Law jurisdictions or for that matter in most important non-Model Law countries such as, for example, France, Switzerland or the United States. Indeed even in the United States, in which the perception or misperception has long reigned that the non-statutory ground of "manifest disregard of the law" can reliably be invoked to set aside or even oppose enforcement of an award[1012], at

---

[1009]  Sec. 68, para. 1, provides:

"A party to arbitral proceedings may (upon notice to the other parties and to the tribunal) apply to the court challenging an award in the proceedings on the ground of serious irregularity affecting the tribunal, the proceedings or the award . . ."

Paragraph 2 provides various examples of "serious irregularity".

[1010]  See Art. 34 of the UNCITRAL Model Law titled "Application for Setting Aside as Exclusive Recourse against Arbitral Award."

[1011]  See generally B. Harris *et al*., *supra* footnote 965.

[1012]  See, e.g., S. Wilske and N. Mackay, "The Myth of the 'Manifest Disregard of the Law' Doctrine: Is this Challenge to the Finality of Arbitral Awards Confined to U.S. Domestic Arbitrations or Should International Arbitration Practitioners Be Concerned?", *ASA Bulletin*, Vol. 24 (2006), pp. 216 *et seq*. See also the New York City Bar Report (Committee on International Commercial Disputes) on "The "Manifest Disregard of Law" Doctrine

the latest with the US Supreme Court decision in *Hall Street* v. *Mattel*[1013] it has been clarified that this ground is not a panacea and should rarely be applied, including in the illegality setting[1014].

In any event, it remains that to the extent a disregard or error of law can be equated with a violation of procedural due process or a violation of procedural and/or substantive public policy at the place of attempted enforcement, then non-enforcement may result. It is submitted that this is the correct, stringent standard for review including in the corruption and bribery setting, as any other or more lenient standard, including a *de novo* review of the merits, would generally speaking be inconsistent with the common intention to limit the scope of review of an arbitral award essentially to grounds not related to the underlying merits.

---

and International Arbitration in New York", August 2012, available at http://www2.nycbar.org/pdf/report/uploads/20072344-ManifestDisregardofLaw—Doctrineand InternationalArbitrationinNewYork.pdf.

[1013] *Hall Street Associates, L.L.C.* v. *Mattel Inc.*, 552 US 576, 25 March 2008. H. Weisburg and C. Ryan, "Hall Street v. Mattel", *The National Law Journal*, dated 12 May 2008; T. Kautz, "What Is 'Manifest Disregard of the Law'?", *SchiedsVZ*, 2011, p. 20; J. Greenblatt and C. Ryan, "Forum Non Conveniens Defeats Enforcement of International Arbitration Award: Figueiredo Ferraz E Engenharia de Projeto Ltda v. The Republic of Peru *et al.* 665 F. 3d 384 (2d Cir. 2011)", *International Arbitration Law Review*, Vol. 15 (2012), p. 56.

[1014] *Ibid.*

# BIBLIOGRAPHY

*Books*

Ader, W., *Gewaltsame Rettungsaktionen zum Schutz eigener Staatsangehöriger im Ausland*, Munich, VVF, 1988.

Amerasinghe, C. F., *Evidence in International Litigation*, Leiden/Boston, Martinus Nijhoff Publishers, 2005.

—, *Diplomatic Protection*, Oxford, Oxford University Press, 2008.

Arnaldez, J.-J., *et al.*, *Collection of ICC Awards, Recueil des sentences arbitrales de la CCI : 1996-2000*, The Hague, Kluwer Law International, 2003.

Arfazadeh, H., *Ordre public et arbitrage international à l'épreuve de la mondialisation*, Zurich, Schulthess, 2005.

Arnoldt, T., *Praxis des Weltbankübereinkommens (ICSID)*, Baden-Baden, Nomos Verlagsgesellschaft, 1997.

Beale, H. G. (ed.), *Chitty on Contracts, Volume 1 — General Principles*, 31st ed., London, Sweet & Maxwell, 2012.

Blackaby, N., and C. Partasides, with A. Redfern and M. Hunter, *Redfern and Hunter on International Arbitration*, 5th ed., Oxford, Oxford University Press, 2009.

Born, G. B., *International Commercial Arbitration*, The Hague, Kluwer Law International, 2009.

—, *International Arbitration : Cases and Materials*, The Hague, Kluwer Law International, 2011.

—, *International Arbitration : Law and Practice*, The Hague, Kluwer Law International, 2012.

Brownlie, I., *Principles of Public International Law*, 7th ed., Oxford University Press, 2008.

Cheng, B., *General Principles of Law as Applied by International Courts and Tribunals*, Cambridge, Cambridge University Press, 2006.

Collier, J., and V. Lowe, *The Settlement of Disputes in International Law : Institutions and Procedures*, Oxford, Oxford University Press, 1999.

Derains, Y., and E. A. Schwartz, *A Guide to the ICC Rules of Arbitration*, 2nd ed., The Hague, Kluwer Law International, 2005.

Doehring, K., *Völkerrecht*, 2nd ed., Heidelberg, C.F. Müller, 2004.

Dolzer, R., and C. H. Schreuer, *Principles of International Investment Law*, Oxford, Oxford University Press, 2008.

Fitzmaurice, G., *The Law and Procedure of the International Court of Justice*, Cambridge, Grotius Publications, 1986.

Freedman, M. R., *Lawyers' Ethics in an Adversary System*, Indianapolis, Bobbs-Merrill, 1975.

Gaillard, E., and J. Savage (eds.), *Fouchard, Gaillard, Goldman on International Commercial Arbitration*, The Hague, Kluwer Law International, 1999.

Garner, B. A. (ed.), *Black's Law Dictionary*, 9th ed., West Group, 2009.

Greenblatt, J., and C. Ryan, "Forum Non Conveniens Defeats Enforcement of International Arbitration Award: Figueiredo Ferraz E Engenharia de Projeto Ltda v The Republic of Peru et al. 665 F. 3d 384 (2d Cir. 2011)", *International Arbitration Law Review*, Vol. 15 (2012), p. 56.

Happ, R., *Schiedsverfahren zwischen Staaten und Investoren nach Artikel 26 Energiechartavertrag*, 2000.

Harris, B., *et al.*, *The Arbitration Act 1996: A Commentary*, 2nd ed., Blackwell Science Ltd., 2000.

Kaikobad, K. H., *Interpretation and Revision of International Boundary Decisions*, Cambridge, Cambridge University Press, 2007.

Kaufmann, I., *Wiederaufnahme von Verfahren vor dem Internationalen Gerichtshof*, Nomos, 2005.

Kegel G., and Schurig, K., *Internationales Privatrecht*, 9th ed., Munich, Beck Verlag, 2004.

Knoepfler, F., Corruption et arbitrage international, Publication CEDIDAC, Lausanne, 1998.

Kreindler, R., *Strafrechtsrelevante und andere anstößige Verträge als Gegenstand von Schiedsverfahren: Zum Vorgehen von Schiedsgerichten bei Rechtsverletzungen von Vertragsparteien — ein rechtsvergleichender Beitrag zur nationalen und internationalen Schiedsgerichtsbarkeit" (Illegal and Other Objectionable Contracts as the Subject of Arbitration: A Comparative Law Contribution to National and International Arbitration)*, Schriftenreihe Abhandlungen zum Recht der Internationalen Wirtschaft, Band 71, Verlag Recht und Wirtschaft, 2005.

Lauterpacht, H., *Recognition in International Law*, Cambridge, Cambridge University Press, 1947.

Lew, J., *et al.*, *Comparative International Commercial Arbitration*, Alphen aan den Rijn, Kluwer Law International, 2003.

McLachlan, C., L. Shore and M. Weiniger, *International Investment Arbitration — Substantive Principles*, Oxford, Oxford University Press, 2007.

McLachlan, C., *Lis pendens in International Litigation*,
    Pocketbooks of the Hague Academy of International Law,
    Leiden/Boston, Martinus Nijhoff, 2009.
Musielak, H.-J. (ed.), *Musielak Kommentar zur Zivilpro-
    zessordnung*, 9th ed., Munich, Verlag Franz Vahlen, 2012.
Nicchols, C., *et al.*, *Corruption and Misuse of Public Office*,
    2nd ed., Oxford, Oxford University Press, 2011.
Pieth, M., L. A. Low and P. J. Cullen, *The OECD Convention
    on Bribery — A Commentary*, Cambridge, Cambridge
    University Press, 2007.
Rauscher, Th., P. Wax and J. Wenzel (eds.), *Münchener
    Kommentar zur Zivilprozessordnung*, 3rd ed., Munich,
    Beckverlag, 2008.
Rosenne, S., *Law and Practice of the International Court,
    1920-1996*, Vol. 2, 3rd ed., M. Nijhoff, 1997.
Sasson, M., *Substantive Law in Investment Treaty Arbitra-
    tion: The Unsettled Relationship between International
    Law and Municipal Law*, Kluwer Law International, 2010.
Sayed, A., *Corruption in International Trade and Commer-
    cial Arbitration*, The Hague, Kluwer Law International,
    2004.
—, "The Legal Basis for Arbitrations Respecting State
    Contracts", Thesis (LL.M.), Harvard Law School, 1993,
    *Hein's Legal Theses and Dissertations*, 002-00058.
Schreuer, C. H., L. Malintoppi, A. Reinisch and A. Sinclair,
    *The ICSID Convention: A Commentary*, 2nd ed.,
    Cambridge, Cambridge University Press, 2009.
Stein, F., and M. Jonas, *Stein/Jonas Kommentar zur Zivil-
    prozessordnung*, 22nd ed., Tübingen, Mohr Siebeck, 2002.
*United Nations Anti-Corruption Toolkit*, 3rd ed., Vienna,
    2004.
Wendel, P., *State Responsibility for Interferences with the
    Freedom of Navigation in Public International Law*,
    London, Springer, 2007.
Zimmermann, A., *et al.* (eds.), *The Statute of the Inter-
    national Court of Justice: A Commentary*, Oxford, Oxford
    University Press, 2006.

### Articles and Book Chapters

Al-Sadig, A., "The Effects of Corruption on FDI Inflows",
    *Cato Journal*, Vol. 29 (2009), p. 267.
Argandoña, A., "Private-to-Private Corruption", *Journal of
    Business Ethics*, Vol. 47 (2003), p. 253.
Aronson, B. M., "A New Framework for ICSID Annulment

Jurisprudence: Rethinking the 'Three Generations'", *ICL Journal*, Vol. 6 (2012), p. 1.

Baker, A., "Customary International Law in the 21st Century: Old Challenges and New Debates", *European Journal of International Law*, Vol. 21 (2010), p. 173.

Banifatemi, Y., "Defending Investment Treaty Awards: Is There an ICSID Advantage?", in A. J. van den Berg (ed.), *50 Years of the New York Convention: ICCA International Arbitration Conference*, ICCA Congress Series, 2009, Dublin, Vol. 14, Kluwer Law International, 2009, p. 318.

Bardonnet, D., "De l'équivoque des catégories juridiques: la révision des sentences arbitrales pour 'erreur de fait' ou 'fait nouveau' dans la pratique latino-américaine", in C. A. A. Barea *et al.* (eds.), *Liber Amicorum "In Memoriam" of Judge José María Ruda*, 2000, p. 189.

Beechey, J., "Arbitrability of Anti-trust/Competition Law Issues — Common Law", *Arbitration International*, Vol. 12 (1996), p. 179.

Bernardini, P., "Arbitration Clauses: Achieving Effectiveness in the Law Applicable to the Arbitration Clause", in A. J. van den Berg (ed.), *Improving the Efficiency of Arbitration Agreements and Awards: 40 Years of Application of the New York Convention*, ICCA Congress Series, 1998, Paris, Vol. 9, Kluwer Law International, 1999, p. 197.

Blessing, M., "Regulations in Arbitration Rules on Choice of Law", in A. J. van den Berg (ed.), *Planning Efficient Arbitration Proceedings, the Law Applicable in International Arbitration*, ICCA Congress Series, Vienna, Vol. XII, Kluwer Law International, 1996, p. 391.

Brower, C. N., "Evidence before International Tribunals: The Need for Some Standard Rules", *International Lawyer*, Vol. 28 (1994), p. 47.

Brown, E., "Illegality and Public Policy — Enforcement of Arbitral Awards in England: Hilmarton Limited v. Omnium de Traitement et de Valorisation S.A.", *International Arbitration Law Review*, Vol. 3 (2000), p. 31.

Bottini, G., "Legality of Investments under ICSID Jurisdiction", in M. Waibel *et al.* (eds.), *The Backlash against Investment Arbitration*, Kluwer Law International, 2010, p. 297.

Buchanan, M. A., "Public Policy and International Commercial Arbitration", *American Business Law Journal*, Vol. 26 (1988), p. 511.

Chatterjee, C., "The Reality of the Party Autonomy Rule in

International Arbitration", *Journal of International Arbitration*, Vol. 20 (2003), p. 539.

Cremades, B. M., "Corruption and Investment Arbitration", in G. Aksen *et al.* (eds.), *Global Reflections on International Law, Commerce and Dispute Reso-lution: Liber Amicorum in Honour of Robert Briner*, ICC Publication, 2005, p. 203.

Crivellaro, A., "Arbitration Case Law on Bribery: Issues of Arbitrability, Contract Validity, Merits and Evidence", in K. Karsten and A. Berkeley, *Arbitration, Money Laundering, Corruption and Fraud*, Dossiers — ICC Institute of World Business Law (September 2003), p. 109.

Das, R., and A. Keyal, "Judicial Intervention in International Arbitration", *National University of Juridical Sciences Law Review*, Vol. 2 (2009), p. 585.

de Boisséson, M., "L'arbitrage et la fraude (A propos de l'arrêt Fougerolle, rendu par la Cour de cassation le 25 mai 1992)", *Revue de l'arbitrage* (1993), p. 3.

de Cossio, F. G., "The Competence-Competence Principle, Revisited", *Journal of International Arbitration*, Vol. 24 (2007), p. 231.

Delaume, G. R., "ICSID and the Transnational Financial Community", *ICSID Review — Foreign Investment Law Journal*, Vol. 1 (1986), p. 237.

—, "How to Draft an ICSID Arbitration Clause", *ICSID Review — Foreign Investment Law Journal*, Vol. 7 (1992), p. 168.

—, "The Proper Law of State Contracts Revisited", *ICSID Review — Foreign Investment Law Journal*, Vol. 12 (1997), p. 1.

de Laurentiis, E., "Institutional Strengthening of Public Sector Procurement", in D. D. Bradlow and A. Escher (eds.), *Legal Aspects of Foreign Direct Investment*, The Hague, Kluwer Law International, 1999, p. 241.

Derains, Y., "Public Policy and the Law Applicable to the Dispute in International Arbitration", in P. Sanders, *Comparative Arbitration Practice and Public Policy in Arbitration, VIIIth International Arbitration Congress, New York, 6-9 May 1986*, ICCA Congress Series No. 3, Munich, Beck Verlag, 1987, p. 227.

—, "La lutte contre la corruption — Le point de vue de l'arbitre international", *Contribution au Congrès AIJA*, Montreux, 1996.

Dessemontet, F., "Arbitration of Intellectual Property Rights and Licensing Contracts", in E. Gaillard and D. di Pietro (eds.), *Enforcement of Arbitration Agreements and International Arbitral Awards — The New York Convention in Practice*, London, Cameron May Ltd., 2008, p. 553.

Dickinson, A., "The Role of Public Policy and Mandatory Rules within the Proposed Hague Principles on the Law Applicable to International Commercial Contracts", *Sydney Law School Legal Studies Research Paper*, No. 12/81, p. 1.

Di Rosa, P., "The Recent Wave of Arbitrations against Argentina under Bilateral Investment Treaties: Background and Principal Legal Issues", *The University of Miami Inter-American Law Review*, Vol. 36 (2004), p. 41.

Ferrante, M., "Enforcement of Foreign Arbitral Awards in Italy and Public Policy", in *Hommage à Frederic Eisemann, Liber Amicorum*, ICC Publishing, 1978, p. 84.

Fitzmaurice, G., "The General Principles of International Law Considered from the Standpoint of the Rule of Law", *Recueil des cours*, Vol. 92 (1957), p. 1.

Fortunet, E., "Arbitrability of Intellectual Property Disputes in France", *Arbitration International*, Vol. 26 (2010), p. 281.

Fouchard, P., "Note — Cour d'appel de Paris (1$^{re}$ Ch. suppl.) 10 mars 1988 — Société Crocodile Tourist Project Company (Egypte) v. Aubert, ès qual. et autres", *Revue de l'arbitrage* (1989), p. 269.

Francescakis, P., "Quelques précisions sur les 'lois d'application immédiate' et leurs rapports avec les règles de conflits de lois", *Revue critique de droit international privé*, Vol. 55 (1996), p. 1.

Friedman, M., "Treaties as Agreements to Arbitrate — Related Dispute Resolution Regimes: Parallel Proceedings in BIT Arbitration", in A. J. van den Berg (ed.), *International Arbitration 2006: Back to Basics?*, ICCA Congress Series, Vol. XIII, Montreal, Kluwer Law International, 2007, p. 545.

Gaillard, E., "Landmark in ICSID Arbitration: Committee Decision in 'Wena Hotels'", 3 *New York Law Journal* 4 (2002).

Garcia-Arias, L., "La doctrine des 'Clean Hands' en droit international public", *Yearbook. Association of Attenders of Alumni of the Hague Academy of International Law*, Vol. 30 (1960), p. 14.

García de Enterría, J., "The Role of Public Policy in International Commercial Arbitration", *Law and Policy in International Business*, Vol. 21 (1989-1990), p. 389.

Garnett, R., and L. Nottage, "The 2010 Amendments to the International Arbitration Act: A New Dawn for Australia?", *Asian International Arbitration Journal*, Vol. 7 (2011), p. 29.

Geisinger E., and A. Mazuranic, "Chapter 11: Challenge and Revision of the Award", in E. Geisinger and N. Voser (eds), *International Arbitration in Switzerland: A Handbook for Practitioners*, 2nd ed., Kluwer Law International, 2013, p. 223.

Goldman, B., "Le droit applicable selon la Convention de la BIRD, du 18 mars 1965, pour le règlement des différends relatifs aux investissements entre Etats et ressortissants d'autres Etats", in *Investissements étrangers et arbitrage entre Etats et personnes privées − La Convention BIRD*, 1969, p. 133.

Gorskie, J. L., "US Courts and the Anti-Arbitration Injunction", *Arbitration International*, Vol. 28 (2012), p. 295.

Grantham, W., "The Arbitrability of Intellectual Property Disputes", *Berkeley Journal of International Law*, Vol. 14 (1996), p. 173.

Greenwood, L., "Does Bifurcation Really Promote Efficiency?", *Journal of International Arbitration*, Vol. 28 (2011), p. 105.

Gross, P., "Competence of Competence: An English View", *Arbitration International*, Vol. 8 (1992), p. 205.

Hanotiau, B., and O. Caprasse, "Public Policy in International Commercial Arbitration", in E. Gaillard and D. di Pietro (eds.), *Enforcement of Arbitration Agreements and International Arbitral Awards: The New York Convention in Practice*, London, Cameron May Ltd., 2008, p. 787.

Healy, P. M., and K. G. Palepu, "The Fall of Enron", *Journal of Economic Perspectives*, Vol. 17 (2003), p. 3.

Hefendehl, R., "Enron, WorldCom, and the Consequences: Business Criminal Law between Doctrinal Requirements and the Hopes of Crime Policy", *Buffalo Criminal Law Review*, Vol. 8 (2004), p. 51.

Henderson, M. C., M. G. Oakes and M. Smith, "What Plato Knew about Enron", *Journal of Business Ethics*, Vol. 86 (2009), p. 463.

Heuzé, V., "La morale, l'arbitre et le juge", *Revue de l'Arbitrage* (1993), p. 179.

Hobér, K., "State Responsibility and Investment Arbitration", *Journal of International Arbitration*, Vol. 25 (2008), p. 545.

—, "State Responsibility and Attribution", in R. Muchlinski *et al.* (eds.), *The Oxford Handbook of International Investment Law*, New York, Oxford University Press, 2008, p. 549.

Horsmans, G., "L'arbitrage et l'ordre public interne belge", *Revue de l'arbitrage* (1978), p. 79.

Horvath, G. J., "The Duty of the Tribunal to Render an Enforceable Award", *Journal of International Arbitration*, Vol. 18 (2001), p. 135.

Hunter, M., and G. Conde e Silva, "Transnational Public Policy and Its Application in Investment Arbitrations", *The Journal of World Investment*, Vol. 4 (2003), p. 367.

Hwang, M., and K. Lim, "Corruption in Arbitration — Law and Reality", *Asian International Arbitration Journal*, Vol. 8 (2012), p. 1.

ICC (ed.), "Final Report on the Status of the Arbitrator", *ICC Bulletin*, Vol. 7 (1996), p. 27.

Johnson, A., "Illegal Contracts and Arbitration Clauses", *International Arbitration Law Review*, Vol. 2 (1999), p. 35.

Kahn, P., "The Law Applicable to Foreign Investments: The Contribution of the World Bank Convention on the Settlement of Investment Disputes", *Indiana Law Journal*, Vol. 44 (1968), p. 1.

Karrer, P., "Commentary to Article 187 of Swiss Private International Law Act", in H. Honsell *et al.* (eds.), *International Arbitration in Switzerland — An Introduction and Commentary on Articles 176-194 of the Swiss Private International Law Statute*, The Hague, Kluwer Law International, 2000, p. 479.

Kautz, T., "What Is 'Manifest Disregard of the Law'?", *SchiedsVZ*, 2011, p. 20.

Kessedjian, C., "Transnational Public Policy", in A. J. van den Berg (ed.), *International Arbitration 2006: Back to Basics?*, ICCA Congress Series, Vol. XIII, Montreal, Kluwer Law International, 2007, p. 857.

Kosheri, A. S., and P. Leboulanger, "L'arbitrage face à la corruption et aux trafics d'influence", *Revue de l'arbitrage* (1984), p. 3.

Kreindler, R., "Pitfalls and Pratfalls in the Launching of an ICC Arbitration: Practical Guidelines and Substantive Solutions", *Arbitration & Dispute Resolution Law Journal*, 1993, p. 145.

—, "Impending Revision of the ICC Arbitration Rules — Opportunities and Hazards for Experienced and Inexperienced Users Alike", *Journal of International Arbitration*, Vol. 13 (1996), p. 45.

—, "Approaches to the Application of Transnational Public Policy by Arbitrators", *Journal of World Investment*, Vol. 4 (2003), p. 239.

—, "Aspects of Illegality in the Formation and Performance of Contracts", in A. J. van den Berg (ed.), *International Commercial Arbitration: Important Contemporary Questions*, ICCA Congress Series, 2002, London, Vol. 11 (2003), p. 225.

—, "The Law Applicable to International Investment Disputes", in N. Horn and S. Kröll (eds.), *Arbitrating Foreign Investment Disputes*, Kluwer Law International, 2004, p. 401.

—, "Schiedsgerichte und Rechtsverstöße der Vertragsparteien: Das für die Beurteilung von Rechtsverletzungen anzuwendende Recht", in B. Bachmann *et al.* (eds.), *Grenzüberschreitungen, Beiträge zum Internationalen Verfahrensrecht und zur Schiedsgerichtsbarkeit, Festschrift für Peter Schlosser zum 70. Geburtstag*, Mohr Siebeck Verlag, 2005, p. 429.

—, "Public Policy and Corruption in International Arbitration: A Perspective for Russian Related Disputes", *Arbitration*, Vol. 72 (2006), p. 236.

—, "Die Schiedsfähigkeit von Streitigkeiten über die Rechtsbeständigkeit von eingetragenen Schutzrechten im internationalen Vergleich — aus US-amerikanischer Sicht", *Schiedsgerichtsbarkeit und Gewerblicher Rechtsschutz*, Bonn, Deutsche Institution für Schiedsgerichtsbarkeit e.V., DIS-MAT XIII, 2006, p. 81.

—, "Perspectives on State Party Arbitration: The Future of BITs — The Practitioner's Perspective", *Arbitration International*, Vol. 23 (2007), p. 43.

—, "Standards of Procedural International Public Policy", *Stockholm International Arbitration Review*, Vol. 2 (2008), p. 143.

—, "Applications for 'Revision' in Investment Arbitration: Selected Current Issues", in M. Á. Fernández-Ballesteros and D. Arias (eds.), *Liber Amicorum Bernardo Cremades*, La Ley, 2010, p. 679.

—, "Corruption in International Investment Arbitration: Jurisdiction and the Unclean Hands Doctrine", K. Hobér *et al.* (eds.), *Between East and West: Essays in Honour of Ulf Franke*, Huntington, Juris, 2010, p. 309.

—, "Parallel Proceedings: A Practitioner's Perspective", in

M. Waibel *et al.* (eds.), *The Backlash against Investment Arbitration*, Kluwer Law International, 2010, p. 127.

Kreindler, R., and T. J. Kautz, "Agreed Deadlines and the Setting Aside of Arbitral Awards", *ASA Bulletin*, Vol. 15 (1997), p. 576.

Kreindler, R., and A. Tevini, "The Impact of Public Policy Considerations", in T. D. Halket (ed.), *Arbitration of International Intellectual Property Disputes*, JurisNet, LLC, 2012, p. 437.

Kühn, W., "Practical Problems Related to Bilateral Investment Treaties in International Arbitration", *ASA Special Series 2002*, No. 19.

Lahlou Y., and M. Matousekova, "Le rôle de l'arbitre dans la lutte contre la corruption", *Revue du droit des affaires internationales*, Vol. 6 (2012), p. 621.

Laird, I. A., "A Destinction without a Difference? An Examination of the Concepts of Admissibility and Jurisdiction in Salini v. Jordan and Methanex v. USA", in T. Weiler (ed.), *International Investment Law and Arbitration: Leading Cases from the ICSID, NAFTA, Bilateral Treaties and Customary International Law*, London, Cameron May, 2005, p. 201.

Lalive, P., "Ordre public transnational (ou réellement international) et arbitrage international", *Revue de l'arbitrage* (1986), p. 329.

—, "Transnational (or Truly International) Public Policy and International Arbitration", in Pieter Sanders (ed.), *Comparative Arbitration Practice and Public Policy in Arbitration*, ICCA Congress Series No. 3, New York, Kluwer Law International, 1987, p. 257.

Lamm, C. B., H. Pham *et al.*, "Fraud and Corruption in International Arbitration", M. Á. Fernández-Ballesteros and D. Arias (eds.), *Liber Amicorum Bernardo Cremades*, La Ley, 2010, p. 699.

Lando, O., "The Lex Mercatoria in International Commercial Arbitration", *International and Comparative Law Quarterly*, Vol. 34 (1985), p. 747.

Leboulanger, P., "The Arbitration Agreement: Still Autonomous?", in A. J. van den Berg (ed.), *International Arbitration 2006: Back to Basics?*, ICCA Congress Series, Vol. XIII, Montreal, Kluwer Law International, 2007, p. 3.

Liebscher, C., "Arbitration of Antitrust Disputes", in E. Gaillard and D. di Pietro (eds.), *Enforcement of Arbitration Agreements and International Arbitral Awards —*

*The New York Convention in Practice*, London, Cameron May Ltd., 2008, p. 523.

Mantilla-Serrano, F., "Towards a Transnational Procedural Public Policy", *Arbitration International*, Vol. 20 (2004), p. 333.

Matray L., and P. Martens, "Arbitrage et ordre public interne", *Revue de l'arbitrage* (1978), p. 95.

Mayer, P., "La règle morale dans l'arbitrage international", *Études Pierre Bellet* (1991), p. 379.

—, "Le contrat illicit", *Revue de l'arbitrage* (1984), p. 205.

Méon, P.-G., and K. Sekkat, "Does Corruption Grease or Sand the Wheels of Growth?", *Public Choice*, Vol. 122 (2005), p. 69.

Miles, C. A., "Corruption, Jurisdiction and Admissibility in International Investment Claims", *Journal of International Dispute Settlement*, Vol. 3 (2012), p. 1.

Mirzayev, R., "International Investment Protection Regime and Criminal Investigations", *Journal of International Arbitration*, Vol. 29 (2012), p. 71.

Moss, G. C., "Tribunal's Powers versus Party Autonomy", in R. Muchlinski *et al.* (eds.), *The Oxford Handbook of International Investment Law*, New York, Oxford University Press, 2008, p. 1207.

Muchlinski, P., "'Caveat Investor'? The Relevance of the Conduct of the Investor under the Fair and Equitable Treatment Standard", *International & Comparative Law Quarterly*, Vol. 55 (2006), p. 527.

Oguz, A., "The Role of Comparative Law in the Development of Turkish Civil Law", *Pace International Law Review*, Vol. 17 (2005), p. 373.

Ong, C., *et al.*, "The Meaning of 'Corruptly'", *Singapore Academy of Law Journal*, Vol. 11 (1999), p. 147.

Oppetit, B., "Le paradoxe de la corruption à l'épreuve du droit du commerce international", *Journal du droit international* (1987), p. 5.

Otto, D., and O. Elwan, "Article V (2)", in H. Kronke, *et al.* (eds.), *Recognition and Enforcement of Foreign Arbitral Awards: A Global Commentary on the New York Convention*, Kluwer Law International, 2010, p. 345.

Parra, A. R., "Provisions on the Settlement of Investment Disputes in Modern Investment Laws, Bilateral Investment Treaties and Multilateral Instruments on Investment", *ICSID Review — Foreign Investment Law Journal*, Vol. 12 (1997), p. 287.

—, "Applicable Substantive Law in ICSID Arbitrations

Initiated under Investment Treaties", *ICSID Review — Foreign Investment Law Journal*, Vol. 16 (2001), p. 20.

Paulsson, J., "The ICSID Klöckner v. Cameroon Award: The Duties of Partners in North-South Economic Development Agreements", *Journal of International Arbitration*, Vol. 1 (1984), p. 145.

—, "Jurisdiction and Admissibility", in *Global Reflections on International Law, Commerce and Dispute Resolution — Liber Amicorum in Honour of Robert Briner*, ICC Publishing, 2005, p. 601.

Pinsolle, P., and R. Kreindler, "Les limites du rôle de la volonté des parties dans la conduite de l'instance arbitrale", *Revue de l'arbitrage* (2003), p. 41.

Premeaux, S., "The Link between Management Behavior and Ethical Philosophy in the Wake of the Enron Convictions", *Journal of Business Ethics*, Vol. 85 (2009), p. 13.

Racine, J.-B., avant-propos de Laurence Boy, préface de Philippe Fouchard, *L'arbitrage commercial international et l'ordre public*, Paris, LGDJ, 1999.

Raeschke-Kessler, H., and D. Gottwald, "Corruption", in R. Muchlinski *et al.* (eds.), *The Oxford Handbook of International Investment Law*, New York, Oxford University Press, 2008, p. 584.

Raeschke-Kessler, H., and D. Gottwald, "Korruption und internationales Vertragsrecht: Rechtliche Aspekte der Korruption im Bau- und Infrastruktursektor mit Auslandsbezug", in W. Moll (ed.), *Festschrift für Hans-Jochem Lüer zum 70. Geburtstag*, Munich, Verlag C.H. Beck, 2008, p. 39.

Raouf, M. A., "How Should International Arbitrators Tackle Corruption Issues?", *ICSID Review — Foreign Investment Law Journal*, Vol. 24 (2009), p. 119.

Redfern, A., "The Practical Distinction between the Burden of Proof and the Taking of Evidence — An English Perspective", in A. Redfern, C. Reymond *et al.*, "The Standards and Burden of Proof in International Arbitration", *Arbitration International*, Vol. 10 (1994), p. 317.

Reiner, A., "Burden and General Standards of Proof", in A. Redfern, C. Reymond *et al.*, "The Standards and Burden of Proof in International Arbitration", *Arbitration International*, Vol. 10 (1994), p. 327.

Reinisch, A., "The Issues Raised by Parallel Proceedings and Possible Solutions", in M. Waibel *et al.* (eds.), *The Backlash against Investment Arbitration*, Kluwer Law International, 2010, p. 113.

Reisman, W. M., "The Regime for *Lacunae* in the ICSID Choice of Law Provision and the Question of Its Threshold", *ICSID Review — Foreign Investment Law Journal*, Vol. 15 (2000), p. 362.

—, "Law, International Public Policy (So-called) and Arbitral Choice in International Commercial Arbitration", in A. J. van den Berg (ed.), *International Arbitration 2006: Back to Basics?*, ICCA Congress Series, Vol. XIII, Montreal, Kluwer Law International, 2007, p. 849.

Robertson, C. J., and A. Watson, "Corruption and Change: The Impact of Foreign Direct Investment", *Strategic Management Journal*, Vol. 25 (2004), p. 385.

Rosell, J., and H. Prager, "Illicit Commissions and International Arbitration: The Question of Proof", *Arbitration International*, Vol. 15 (1999), p. 329.

Salacuse, J. W., and N. P. Sullivan, "Do BITs Really Work? An Evaluation of Bilateral Investment Treaties and Their Grand Bargain", *Harvard International Law Journal*, Vol. 46 (2005), p. 67.

Sattar, S., "National Courts and International Arbitration: A Double-edged Sword?", *Journal of International Arbitration*, Vol. 27 (2010), p. 51.

Scherer, M., "Introduction to the Case Law Section", *ASA Bulletin*, Vol. 30 (2012), p. 770.

Schill, S. W., "Private Enforcement of International Investment Law: Why We Need Investor Standing in BIT Dispute Settlement", M. Waibel *et al.* (eds.), *The Backlash against Investment Arbitration*, Kluwer Law International, 2010, p. 29.

Schreuer, C. H., and M. Weiniger, "A Doctrine of Precedent?", R. Muchlinski *et al.* (eds.), *The Oxford Handbook of International Investment Law*, New York, Oxford University Press, 2008, p. 1188.

Shihata, I. F. I., and A. R. Parra, "The Experience of the International Centre for Settlement of Investment Disputes", *ICSID Review — Foreign Investment Law Journal*, Vol. 14 (1999), p. 299.

Shihata, I. F. I., "Applicable Law in International Arbitration: Specific Aspects in Case of the Involvement of State Parties", in I. F. I. Shihata (ed.), *The World Bank in a Changing World*, Vol. II, The Hague, Kluwer Law International, 1995, p. 595.

Shihata, I. F. I., and A. R. Parra, "Applicable Substantive Law in Disputes between States and Private Foreign Parties: The Case of Arbitration under the ICSID Convention", *ICSID Review — Foreign Investment Law Journal*, Vol. 9 (1994), p. 183.

Spiermann, O., "Individual Rights, State Interests and the Power to Waive ICSID Jurisdiction under Bilateral Investment Treaties", *Arbitration International*, Vol. 20 (2004), p. 179.

Stern, B., "Treaties as Agreements to Arbitrate: Comments", in A. J. van den Berg (ed.), *International Arbitration 2006: Back to Basics?*, ICCA Congress Series, Vol. XIII, Montreal, Kluwer Law International, 2007, p. 569.

Tawil, G., "International Centre for Settlement of Investment Disputes. Applicable Law" (UNCTAD, Course on Dispute Settlement, January 2003, Thailand, to be found at http://r0.unctad.org/dispsett/course.htm), p. 7.

—, "The Distinction between Contract Claims and Treaty Claims", in A. J. van den Berg (ed.), *International Arbitration 2006: Back to Basics?*, ICCA Congress Series, Vol. XIII, Montreal, Kluwer Law International, 2007, p. 492.

Tomuschat, C., "International Law: Ensuring the Survival of Mankind on the Eve of a New Century", *Receuil des cours*, Vol. 281 (1999), p. 9.

Tytell, P. V., "The Detection of Forgery and Fraud", in A. J. van den Berg (ed.), *International Commercial Arbitration: Important Contemporary Questions*, ICCA Congress Series, 2002, London, Vol. 11, Kluwer Law International, 2003, p. 314.

von Hoffman, B., "Der internationale Schiedsrichtervertrag — eine kollisionsrechtliche Skizze", *Festschrift für Ottoarndt Glossner zum 70. Geburtstag*, Heidelberg, Verlag Recht und Wirtschaft, 1993, p. 143.

von Mehren, G. M., and C. Salomon, "Submitting Evidence in an International Arbitration: The Common Lawyer's Guide", *Journal of International Arbitration*, Vol. 20 (2003), p. 285.

von Mehren, R. B., and M. E. Patterson, "Recognition and Enforcement of Foreign-Country Judgments in the United States", *Law and Policy in International Business*, Vol. 6 (1974), p. 37.

Wälde, T. W., "Investment Arbitration under the Energy Charter Treaty. From Dispute Settlement to Treaty Implementation", *Arbitration International*, Vol. 12 (1996), p. 429.

Warin, F. J., C. Falconer and M. S. Diamant, "The British Are Coming!: Britain Changes Its Law on Foreign

Bribery and Joins the International Fight against Corruption", *Texas International Law Journal*, Vol. 46 (2010), p. 2.

Wei, S.-J., "Negative Alchemy? Corruption and Composition of Capital Flows", *OECD Development Center*, Working Paper No. 165 (2000).

Weisburg, H., and C. Ryan, "Hall Street v. Mattel", *The National Law Journal*, dated 12 May 2008.

Wetter, J. G., "Issues of Corruption before International Arbitral Tribunals: The Authentic Text and True Meaning of Judge Gunner Lagergren's 1963 Award in ICC Case No. 1110", *Arbitration International*, Vol. 10 (1994), p. 277.

Wilske, S., and T. J. Fox, "Corruption in International Arbitration and Problems with Standard of Proof: Baseless Allegations or Prima Facie Evidence?", in S. Kröll, L. Mistelis *et al*. (eds.), *International Arbitration and International Commercial Law: Synergy, Convergence and Evolution*, The Hague, Kluwer Law International, 2011, p. 489.

Wilske, S., and N. Mackay, "The Myth of the 'Manifest Disregard of the Law' Doctrine: Is this Challenge to the Finality of Arbitral Awards Confined to U.S. Domestic Arbitrations or Should International Arbitration Practitioners be Concerned?", *ASA Bulletin*, Vol. 24 (2006), p. 216.

Wirth, M., "Rechtsbegehren in internationalen Schiedsverfahren — Wie bestimmt müssen sie sein?", in M. Jametti Greiner *et al*. (eds.), *Festschrift für Franz Kellerhals zum 65. Geburtstag*, Bern, Stämpfli Verlag, 2005, p. 145.

Yackee, J. W., "Investment Treaties & Investment Corruption: An Emerging Defense for Host States", *Virginia Journal for International Law*, Vol. 52 (2012), p. 723.

# ABOUT THE AUTHOR

BIOGRAPHICAL NOTE

*Richard Kreindler*, born New York, United States of America, in 1959.

Prof. Dr. Honorary Professor (since 2009) and regular instructor (since 1999), Westfälische Wilhelms University, Münster, Germany, Transnational Litigation and International Commercial and Investment Arbitration.

Adjunct Professor, Johannes-Gutenberg University, Mainz, Germany, lecture and seminar courses on Transnational Litigation and Arbitration (2005-2007).

Lecturer in Private International Law, Hague Academy of International Law, Summer Course (Summer 2012); Lecturer in Diploma in International Commercial Arbitration, Chartered Institute of Arbitrators, Keble College, Oxford, Hong Kong and Singapore (1994-2009); Lecturer in ICC Institute of World Business Law, Paris (since 1993).

Various other periodic teaching/guest lecturing and speaking at university law faculties, including American, Columbia, Frankfurt, Harvard, Heidelberg, Rotterdam, Stockholm, Tokyo, Uppsala, Yale.

Member, New York and Paris Bars; Rechtskundiger, Frankfurt; Fellow and Chartered Arbitrator, Chartered Institute of Arbitrators (CIArb), London.

Partner, International Arbitration and Litigation, Shearman & Sterling LLP, Frankfurt; specialized in international arbitration and litigation matters since 1985.

Counsel, party-appointed arbitrator, sole arbitrator, chairman and expert witness in numerous commercial, construction and investment arbitrations throughout the world.

Served in an editorial or advisory capacity for *Arbitration International, International Arbitration Law Review, SchiedsVZ (German Arbitration Journal), International Legal Materials, Arab Law Quarterly, Arbitration & Dispute Resolution Law Journal, World Arbitration and Mediation Report, Revue de droit des affaires internationales*, the ICC Institute of World Business Law, and

Restatement 3d — US Law of International Commercial Arbitration, among others.

Chairman of the IBA working group charged with review of the 1999 IBA Rules on the Taking of Evidence in International Commercial Arbitration, resulting in the enactment of the revised IBA Rules as of May 2010.

## PRINCIPAL PUBLICATIONS

### Books

*Evaluation of Damages in International Arbitration*, Co-Editor (with Y. Derains), Dossier IV, ICC Institute of World Business Law, 2006.

*Schiedsgerichtsbarkeit — Kompendium für die Praxis (Arbitration — A Practitioner's Compendium)* (with J. Schaefer and Dr. R. Wolff), BB-Handbuch/Bücher des Betriebs-Beraters, Verlag Recht und Wirtschaft, Frankfurt, 2006.

*Strafrechtsrelevante und andere anstößige Verträge als Gegenstand von Schiedsverfahren: Zum Vorgehen von Schiedsgerichten bei Rechtsverletzungen von Vertragsparteien — ein rechtsvergleichender Beitrag zur nationalen und internationalen Schiedsgerichtsbarkeit (Illegal and Other Objectionable Contracts as the Subject of Arbitration: A Comparative Law Contribution to National and International Arbitration)*, Schriftenreihe Abhandlungen zum Recht der Internationalen Wirtschaft, Band 71, Verlag Recht und Wirtschaft, Doctoral Dissertation, Westfälische Wilhelms University, Münster, Germany, 2005.

*Transnational Litigation: A Practitioner's Guide* (General Editor, 3 vols., Oxford/Oceana), including 300-page Introduction and some 25 country chapters by leading international litigation practitioners worldwide, 1999/1997.

*Transnational Litigation: A Basic Primer* (Oxford/Oceana), desktop guide to transnational litigation issues for practitioners and law faculties, 1998.

### Selected Articles and Book Chapters

"Legal Consequences of Corruption in International Investment Arbitration", in L. Lévy and Y. Derains (eds.), *Liber Amicorum en l'Honneur de Serge Lazareff*, Paris, Editions Pedone, 2011, p. 383.

"The 2010 IBA Rules on the Taking of Evidence in International Arbitration", in C. Müller and A. Rigozzi (eds.), *New Developments in International Commercial Arbitration*, Neuchâtel, 2011.

"Das neue französische Schiedsverfahrensrecht und die neue schweizerische ZPO", *Shearman & Sterling LLP Client Publication*, March 2011.

"Abwehrstrategien gegen unerwünschte Rezeptionen US-amerikanischen Rechts in der Schiedsgerichtsbarkeit", in W. F. Ebke *et al.* (eds.), *Das deutsche Wirtschaftsrecht unter dem Einfluss des US-amerikanischen Rechts*, Verlag Recht und Wirtschaft, Frankfurt am Main, 2011, p. 171.

"The Impact of Public Policy Considerations" (with A. Tevini), *Arbitration of International Intellectual Property Disputes*, Th. D. Halket (ed.), JurisNet, 2011, p. 437.

"The 2010 Revisions to the IBA Rules on the Taking of Evidence in International Arbitration", *Les cahiers de l'arbitrage (The Paris Journal of International Arbitration)*, 2011, pp. 23-32.

"Wahl zwischen ordentlichem Gerichtsverfahren und Schiedsverfahren" (with O. Rust and K. Bimboese), in *Beck'sches Rechtsanwalts-Handbuch*, 2011/2007/2004.

"Die Überarbeitung der IBA-Regeln zur Beweisaufnahme in der Internationalen Schiedsgerichtsbarkeit", *Shearman & Sterling LLP Client Publication*, July 2010.

"Are Tribunals Setting New Limits on Access to International Jurisdiction?", *ICSID Review — Foreign Investment Law Journal*, Vol. 25 (2010), p. 37.

"Rechtsschutz für ausländische Direktinvestitionen im Energiesektor: Neue Möglichkeiten in der Investitionsschiedsgerichtsbarkeit", in F. C. Genzow, B. Grunewald and H. Schulte-Nölke (eds.), *Zwischen Vertragsfreiheit und Verbraucherschutz, Festschrift für Friedrich Graf von Westphalen*, Cologne, Otto Schmidt Verlag, 2010, p. 433.

"Application for 'Revision' in Investment Arbitration: Selected Current Issues", in M. A. Fernández-Ballesteros and D. Arias (eds.), *Liber Amicorum for Bernardo Cremades*, La Ley, 2010, p. 679.

"Corruption in International Investment Arbitration: Jurisdiction and the Unclean Hands Doctrine", in

K. Hobér *et al.* (eds.), *Between East and West: Essays in Honour of Ulf Franke*, JurisNet, 2010, p. 309.

"Die Internationale Investitionsschiedsgerichtsbarkeit und die Korruption: Eine alte Herausforderung mit neuen Antworten", *SchiedsVZ (German Arbitration Journal)*, Vol. 8 (2010), p. 2.

"Parallel Proceedings in Investment Arbitration: A Practitioner's Perspective", in M. Waibel *et al.* (eds.), *The Backlash against Investment Arbitration — Perceptions and Reality*, Kluwer Law International, 2010, p. 127.

"Chapter 12: International Arbitration (Preliminary Matters)", in J. M. Gaitis (ed.), *The College of Commercial Arbitrators Guide to Best Practices in Commercial Arbitration*, 2nd ed., JurisNet, 2010.

"The 2010 Revision to the IBA Rules on the Taking of Evidence in International Commercial Arbitration: A Study in Both Consistency and Progress", *International Arbitration Law Review*, Vol. 13 (2010), p. 157.

"Possible Future Revisions to the IBA Rules on the Taking of Evidence in International Commercial Arbitration", K.-H. Böckstiegel *et al.* (eds.), *Schriftenreihe der Deutschen Institution für Schiedsgerichtsbarkeit*, Band 26, Cologne, Carl Heymanns Verlag, 2010.

"Die Investitionsschiedsgerichtsbarkeit und die Korruption", *Shearman & Sterling LLP Client Publication*, December 2009.

"Standards of Procedural International Public Policy", *Stockholm International Arbitration Review*, No. 2 (2008), p. 143.

Chapter "Arbitration" (with A. Cohen and C. Schuetz), in Th. Wegerich (ed.), *Business Laws of Germany*, October 2009.

"Schiedsverfahren mit chinesischen Parteien", Teil 2, *Shearman & Sterling LLP Client Publication*, September 2009.

Chapter "International Commercial Arbitration" (with R. Heinemann), in R. Wolfrum *et al.* (eds.), *Max Planck Encyclopedia of Public International Law*, September 2009.

"Investment Treaties and the Evolution in Their Negotiation and Application: The New Germany-China BIT and Its Relevance to International International Financial Law Trends", *Transnational Dispute Management (TDM)*, Vol. 6, No. 1 (2009).

"Neue Möglichkeiten in der Investitionsschiedsgerichtsbarkeit: Der Vertrag über die Energiecharta", *Shearman & Sterling LLP Client Publication*, January 2008.

"Schiedsverfahren mit chinesischen Parteien", Teil 1, *Shearman & Sterling LLP Client Publication*, December 2008.

"Grenzüberschreitende privatisierte Korruptionsermittlungen", Freundeskreis Rechtswissenschaft, "Schlaglichter 8", *Ansprachen und Reden an der Rechtswissenschaftlichen Fakultät Münster im Akademischen Jahr 2008/ 2009.*

"Wenn foul gespielt wird", Supplement to *Financial Times Deutschland*, 4 November 2008.

Chapters "§ 1033 — Arbitration Agreement and Interim Measures by Court" and "§ 1041 — Interim Measures of Protection" (with J. Schaefer), in K.-H. Böckstiegel *et al.* (eds.), *Arbitration in Germany — The Model Law in Practice*, Kluwer Law International, 2007.

"Herausforderungen für die Internationale Schiedsgerichtsbarkeit: Gestern, heute und morgen — Laudatio für Prof. K.-H. Böckstiegel", *SchiedsVZ (German Arbitration Journal)*, Vol. 5 (2007), p. 316.

"The Importance and Urgency of the Energy Charter Treaty", *International Arbitration Law Review*, Vol. 10, No. 3 (2007).

"Inconsistent ICSID Awards — Is There a Need for an Appellate Structure?", in R. Hofmann and C. J. Tams (eds.), *The International Convention for the Settlement of Investment Disputes (ICSID): Taking Stock after 40 Years*, Schriften zur Europäischen Integration und Internationalen Wirtschaftsordnung, Baden-Baden, Nomos, 2007.

"Investitionen in China und ihre rechtliche Absicherung", *Shearman & Sterling LLP Client Publication*, May 2007.

"Perspectives on State Party Arbitration: The Future of BITs — The Practitioner's Perspective", *Arbitration International — The Journal of the London Court of International Arbitration*, Vol. 23 (2007), p. 43.

"Is the Arbitrator Obligated to Denounce Money Laundering, Corruption of Officials, etc.? The Arbitrator as Accomplice — Sham Proceedings and the Trap of the Consent Award", *Center for Global Development (CGD) Working Group on Corrupt Payments*, February 2007.

"Mit rechtzeitiger Beratung Verstöße gegen FCPA vermeiden", *Börsen-Zeitung*, No. 221, 16 November 2007.

"Strukturierung von Auslandsinvestitionen im Hinblick auf Investitionsförderungsabkommen", *Shearman & Sterling LLP Client Publication*, September 2006.

"Aktuelle Entwicklungen in der Investitionsschiedsgerichtsbarkeit", *Mitteilungsblatt der Arbeitsgemeinschaft für Internationalen Rechtsverkehr im Deutschen Anwaltverein*, 1/2006.

"Fair and Equitable Treatment — A Comparative International Law Approach", *Transnational Dispute Management (TDM)*, Vol. 3 No. 3 (2006).

"Final Rulings on Costs: Loser Pays All?", *ASA Bulletin, Association suisse de l'arbitrage*, Special Series, No. 26 (2006).

"Seeking a Happy Medium in Document Disclosure", *Guide to the World's Leading Experts in Commercial Arbitration*, Euromoney, 2006.

"Schiedsgerichte und Rechtsverstöße der Vertragsparteien: Das für die Beurteilung von Rechtsverletzungen anzuwendende Recht", *Transnational Dispute Management (TDM)*, Vol. 3, No. 2 (2006).

"Public Policy and Corruption in International Arbitration: A Perspective for Russian-Related Disputes", *Arbitration: The Journal of the Chartered Institute of Arbitrators*, Vol. 72 (2006), p. 236.

"Die Schiedsfähigkeit von Streitigkeiten über die Rechtsbeständigkeit von eingetragenen Schutzrechten im internationalen Vergleich — aus US-amerikanischer Sicht", German Institution of Arbitration (Deutsche Institution für Schiedsgerichtsbarkeit), *DIS-MAT XIII*, 2006.

"Gerichtliche Verfahren um gewerbliche Schutzrechte im internationalen Vergleich und grenzüberschreitende Strategien – aus US-amerikanischer Sicht", German Institution of Arbitration (Deutsche Institution für Schiedsgerichtsbarkeit), *DIS-MAT XIII*, 2006.

"Approaches to the Application of Transnational Public Policy by Arbitrators", *Mezhdunarodny Kommerchesky Arbitrazh*, 2006.

"Aktuelle Entwicklungen in der Investitionsschiedsgerichtsbarkeit", *Shearman & Sterling LLP Client Publication*, December 2005.

"Arbitral Forum Shopping", *American Review of International Arbitration*, Vol. 16 (2005), p. 157.

"Arbitral Forum Shopping", in B. M. Cremades and J. D. M. Lew (eds.), *Parallel Arbitration Tribunals and Awards in International Arbitration*, Dossier III, ICC Institute of World Business Law, 2005, p. 153.

"Cross-Border Purchase Price Adjustment Provisions" (with G. Zuber *et al.*), *The Journal of Private Equity*, Vol. 8 (2005), p. 82.

"Die Kostenentscheidung im Schiedsgerichtsverfahren aus US-amerikanischer Sicht", German Institution of Arbitration (Deutsche Institution für Schiedsgerichtsbarkeit), *DIS-MAT X*, 2005.

"Arbitrators and Illegality: The Challenge of Determining the Proper Applicable Law", *The International Who's Who of Commercial Arbitrators*, 2005.

"Schiedsgerichte und Rechtsverstöße der Vertragsparteien: Das für die Beurteilung von Rechtsverletzungen anzuwendende Recht", in B. Bachmann (ed.), *Grenzüberschreitungen: Beiträge zum Internationalen Verfahrensrecht und zur Schiedsgerichtsbarkeit; Festschrift für Peter Schlosser zum 70. Geburtstag*, Tübingen, Mohr Siebeck, 2005, p. 429.

"Recht und Sprache", Schlaglichter 4, *Ansprachen und Reden an der Rechtswissenschaftlichen Fakultät Münster im Akademischen Jahr 2004/2005*, Westfälische Wilhelms University Münster, 2005.

"The Law Applicable to International Investment Disputes", N. Horn and S. M. Kröll (eds.), *Studies in Transnational Economic Law*, Vol. 19: *Arbitrating Foreign Investment Disputes*, Kluwer Law International, 2004, p. 401.

"Germany" Chapter (with R. Heinemann), in M. Falls (ed.), *International Arbitration: A Country-by-Country Look at Alternative Dispute Resolution Methods around the Globe*, Boston, Aspatore, 2005.

"Weighing up Arbitration Options in Germany", Guide to the World's Leading Experts in Commercial Arbitration, 2004.

"Aspects of Illegality in the Formation and Performance of Contracts", *Transnational Dispute Management (TDM)*, Vol. 1, No. 3 (2004).

"Benefiting from Oral Testimony of Expert Witnesses: Traditional and Emerging Techniques", in L. Lévy and V. V. Veeder (eds.), *Arbitration and Oral Evidence*, Dossier II, ICC Institute of World Business Law, 2004, p. 87.

"Aspects of Illegality in the Formation and Performance of Contracts", *OGEL, Oil, Gas & Energy Law*, Vol. I, No. 5 (2003).

"Allemagne: les cinq premières années d'application de la

nouvelle législation" (with J. Schaefer), *Revue de l'arbitrage (Bulletin du Comité français de l'arbitrage )*, No. 2 (2003), p. 495.

"Les limites du rôle de la volonté des parties dans la conduite de l'instance arbitrale" (with P. Pinsolle), *Revue de l'arbitrage (Bulletin du Comité français de l'arbitrage)*, No. 1 (2003), p. 41.

"Aspects of Illegality in the Formation and Performance of Contracts", *International Council for Commercial Arbitration (ICCA), Congress Series No. 11*, 2003.

"Aspects of Illegality in the Formation and Performance of Contracts", *International Arbitration Law Review*, Vol. 6, No. 1 (2003), p. 1.

"Die Anerkennung und Vollstreckung ausländischer Schiedssprüche unter besonderer Berücksichtigung des New Yorker Übereinkommens von 1958", *Mitteilungsblatt der Arbeitsgemeinschaft für Internationalen Rechtsverkehr im Deutschen Anwaltverein*, 1/2003.

"Approaches to the Application of Transnational Public Policy by Arbitrators", *The Journal of World Investment*, Vol. 4 (2003), p. 239.

"Standpunkt: Internationale Schiedsverfahren", *International Journal of Dispute Resolution*, November 2002.

"Aktuelle (Streit-)Fragen bei der Anwendung der ICC-Schiedsgerichtsordnung 1998 — Praxisüberblick", *Recht der Internationalen Wirtschaft* (2002), p. 249.

"Book Review: Die ICC Schiedsgerichtsordnung in der Praxis", *Arbitration International*, Vol. 18 (2002), p. 99.

"Overview: Arbitration — Germany", *International Law Office, Online Newsletter*, January 2002.

"The Enforcement of Foreign Arbitral Awards in the German Courts", *International Law Office, Online Newsletter*, October 2002.

"Validity of Mandatory Pre-Arbitration Negotiation Clauses", *International Law Office, Online Newsletter*, May 2002.

"An Overview of Key Rights and Duties at the Beginning Stage of an International Arbitration", *International Arbitration Law Review*, Vol. 4, No. 3 (2001), p. 77.

"Das neue deutsche Schiedsverfahrensrecht aus ausländischer Sicht", in R. Briner *et al.* (eds.), *Law of International Business and Dispute Settlement in the 21st Century, Liber Amicorum Karl-Heinz Böckstiegel*, Cologne, Carl Heymanns Verlag, 2001, p. 401.

"Legislation in Germany — A New Era for Arbitration", *Legalease Special Report*, April 2001.

"Practical Issues in Drafting International Arbitration Clauses in the Engineering Context", *International Arbitration Law Review*, Vol. 4, No. 4 (2001).

"Mandatory Negotiation or Mediation Clauses and Arbitration" (with S. Berruti), *IBA Section on Business Law, Arbitration and ADR*, October 2001.

"Recent Issues in the Application of the 1998 ICC Rules of Arbitration", *Table Talk, International Arbitration Club*, London, 2000.

"Das neue deutsche Schiedsverfahrensrecht: Eine ausländische Betrachtung", in K. P. Berger (ed.), *Festschrift für Otto Sandrock zum 70. Geburtstag*, Heidelberg, Verlag Recht und Wirtschaft, 2000, p. 515.

"Internationale Schiedsverfahren: Deutschland als 'Entwicklungsland'?", *Recht der Internationalen Wirtschaft*, No. 5 (2000), p. 1.

"Procedural Issues in International Engineering Arbitration from the Tribunal's Perspective", *ADR & the Law*, American Arbitration Association, 2000.

"Nachgefragt bei . . .", *Frankfurter Allgemeine Zeitung*, 19 November 1999.

"Foreign Perspective on Arbitration, Litigation", *New York Law Journal*, 8 November 1999.

"The New (1998) German Arbitration Act: Its Relevance to Foreign Practitioners", *News and Notes from the Institute for Transnational Arbitration*, Vol. 13 (1999).

"Arbitration versus Litigation in Transnational Contracts", in S. B. Meek and D. Campbell (eds.), *Comparative Law Yearbook of International Business*, Vol. 21, London, Kluwer Law International, 1999.

"Transaction et arbitrage dans le cadre du règlement d'arbitrage de la CCI", *Bulletin de la cour internationale d'arbitrage*, Vol. 9, No. 2 (1998), p. 22.

"Arbitration under the G.C.C. Commercial Arbitration Center Rules in the Context of Banking and Finance Disputes", *Lebanese Review of Arab and International Arbitration*, Vol. 8, 1998, p. 9.

"Settlement Agreements and Arbitration in the Context of the ICC Rules", *ICC International Court of Arbitration Bulletin*, Vol. 9 (1998), p. 22.

"Speedier Arbitration as a Response to Changes in World Trade: A Necessary Goal or a Threat to the Expectations of the Parties?", in B. G. Davis (ed.), *Improving*

*International Arbitration: The Need for Speed and Trust, Liber Amicorum for Michel Gaudet*, Paris, International Chamber of Commerce, 1998, p. 180.

"Das neue deutsche Schiedsverfahrensrecht aus ausländischer Sicht" (with T. Mahlich), *Neue Juristische Wochenschrift* (1998), p. 563.

"A Foreign Perspective on the New German Arbitration Act" (with T. Mahlich), *Arbitration International — The Journal of the London Court of International Arbitration*, Vol. 14 (1998), p. 65.

"Arbitration: A Creative Alternative to Intellectual Property Litigation in Light of Two Recent U.S. Supreme Court Decisions", *World Arbitration and Mediation Report (WAMR)*, Vol. 9 (1998), p. 13.

"Consultant's Corner: Key Distinguishing Jurisdictional Issues in Transnational Litigation", *The Metropolitan Corporate Counsel*, October 1998.

"Schiedsverfahren oder Staatliche Gerichtsbarkeit in Internationalen Verträgen: Neue Relevante Entwicklungen in den USA" (with P. Nacimiento), *Recht der Internationalen Wirtschaft*, No. 9 (1998), p. 674.

"International Arbitration and the U.S. Courts: Recent Developments in Selected Areas Relevant to Foreign Parties", *Arbitration and Dispute Resolution Law Journal*, Part 3, September 1998.

"Obtaining Jurisdiction Abroad: Party Autonomy and Choice-of-Forum Clauses", *New York Law Journal*, 29 June 1998, p. 1.

"European and Foreign-Based Litigation", *New York Law Journal*, 10 April 1998.

"Arbitrage et recours juridictionnels: l'attitude des parties étrangères ayant à opter entre un arbitrage et un procès aux Etats-Unis", *Revue du droit international des affaires*, No. 2, 1998, p. 173.

"Issues in Drafting and Performance of Arbitration Agreements in the Context of Bilateral Investment Treaties and Energy Projects" (with T. Kautz), *International Arbitration Report*, Vol. 12 (1997), p. 25.

"Arbitrating Banking and Finance Disputes under GCC Arbitration Centre Rules", *Middle East Executive Reports*, Vol. 20, No. 9 (1997).

"Arbitration under the Rules of the G.C.C. Commercial Arbitration Centre Rules in the Context of Banking and Finance Disputes", *G.C.C. Commercial Arbitration Centre Bulletin*, Bahrain (1997) (in Arabic translation).

"The GCC Commercial Arbitration Centre", *Arab Region Newsletter*, July 1997.

"The GCC Commercial Arbitration Centre Rules in the Context of Banking and Finance Disputes", *G.C.C. Commercial Arbitration Bulletin*, No. 5 (1997).

"An Overview of the Arbitration Rules of the Recently Established GCC Commercial Arbitration Center, Bahrain", *Arab Law Quarterly*, Vol. 12, Part I (1997), p. 3.

"International Arbitration Clauses", *In-House Counsel International*, March/April (1997).

"Practical Issues in Drafting International Arbitration Clauses", *Knowles Quarterly Review*, International Supplement, March (1997).

"Practical Issues and Problems in the Drafting of International Arbitration Clauses", *Japan Commercial Arbitration Journal*, No. 11 (1996) (in Japanese translation).

"Practical Issues in Drafting International Arbitration Clauses", *Arbitration: Journal of the Chartered Institute of Arbitrators*, Vol. 63, No. 1 (1997), p. 47.

"Aspects pratiques et difficultés de rédaction des clauses d'arbitrage international", *Série sur l'arbitrage et les contentieux internationaux*, Vol. I, No. 1 (1997).

"The Influence of the ICC Rules, UNCITRAL Rules and UNCITRAL Model Law in Addressing Procedural Pitfalls at the Commencement Stage of an International Arbitration", *International Business Law Journal* (in two parts), Nos. 1 and 2 (1997), pp. 117 and 236.

"Particularities of International Financial Arbitration in the Context of Challenges to Arbitral Awards", in J. J. Norton (ed.), *Yearbook of International Financial and Economic Law*, The Hague, Kluwer Law International, 1997, p. 201.

"Agreed Deadlines and the Setting Aside of Arbitral Awards" (with T. Kautz), *ASA Bulletin*, Association suisse de l'arbitrage, No. 4 (1997), p. 576.

"Schiedsverfahren oder Staatliche Gerichtsbarkeit in Internationalen Verträgen: Neue Relevante Entwicklungen in den USA (Erster von Zwei Teilen)", *Schriftenreihe zur Internationalen Schiedsgerichtsbarkeit und Internationalen Rechtsstreitigkeiten*, Band I, No. 2, 1997.

"Arbitration versus Litigation in Transnational Contracts: Recent Trends in the United States Relevant to Foreign Parties Faced with the Choice (Part Two of Two Parts)",

*International Arbitration and Litigation Briefing*, Vol. I, No. 3 (1997).

"Orders for Security for Costs: US and Germany", *Arbitration and ADR*, September 1997.

"Plumbing the Depths of Germany's Jurisdictional Rules" (with T. Mahlich), *International Commercial Litigation Supplement: Litigation Strategy Yearbook*, Euromoney Publications, 1997.

"Arbitration versus Litigation in Transnational Contracts: Recent Trends in the United States Relevant to Foreign Parties Faced with the Choice (Part One of Two Parts)", *International Arbitration and Litigation Briefing*, Vol. 1, No. 2 (1997).

"Arbitration or Litigation? ADR Issues in Transnational Disputes", *Dispute Resolution Journal*, Vol. 52, No. 4 (1997).

"A New Impetus for ADR in France?: The New French Law on Mediation and Conciliation", *World Arbitration & Mediation Report (WAMR)*, Vol. 7, No. 2 (1996).

Praktische Fragen und Probleme beim Entwurf internationaler Schiedsvereinbarungen", *Schriftenreihe zur Internationalen Schiedsgerichtsbarkeit und Internationalen Rechtsstreitigkeiten*, Band I, No. 1, 1996.

"Impending Revision of the ICC Arbitration Rules — Opportunities and Hazards for Experienced and Inexperienced Users Alike", *Journal of International Arbitration*, Vol. 13, No. 2 (1996), p. 45.

"Practical Issues and Problems in the Drafting of International Arbitration Clauses", *International Arbitration and Litigation Briefing*, Vol. 1, No. 1 (1996).

"A French Perspective toward the Debate on Revising the ICC Rules of Arbitration", *International Arbitration Report*, Vol. 11, No. 1 (1996).

"Legislating for ADR", *International Commercial Litigation*, December 1995/January 1996.

"Some French Lessons for the ICC's Rules of Arbitration", *International Commercial Litigation*, September 1995.

"Pitfalls and Pratfalls in the Launching of an ICC Arbitration", *Japan Commercial Arbitration Journal* (1995) (in Japanese translation).

"Comments and Proposals to the U.S. Council for International Business Regarding Revision of the Rules of Arbitration of the International Chamber of Commerce", January 1995.

"German Court: Missed Deadline Doesn't Affect

Claimant's Right to Have Appointing Authority Designate Arbitrator", *International Arbitration Report*, Vol. 10, No. 5 (1995).

"International Arbitration and Local Law", *Arab Region Newsletter*, August 1995.

"Divided by the Same Rules", *The Lawyer*, Vol. 9, No. 11 (1995).

"Notes on the Early Stages of an International Arbitration: A Practical View for the Arabian Gulf", *World Arbitration & Mediation Report (WAMR)*, Vol. 6, No. 1 (1995).

"The Arbitration Agreement — Its Multifold Critical Aspects", *ASA Bulletin, Association suisse de l'arbitrage*, Special Series, No. 8 (1994).

"Filing Claims Arising out of the Gulf War", *International Financial Law Review*, No. 31 (1993).

"Claiming against Iraq", *Insurance Law & Claims*, August 1993.

"Pitfalls and Pratfalls in the Launching of an ICC Arbitration", *Arbitration and Dispute Resolution Law Journal* (1993), p. 145.

"Judicial Proceedings to Set Aside Arbitral Awards: Circumscribing Challenges in Continental Europe", *World Arbitration & Mediation Report (WAMR)*, Vol. 4, No. 9 (1993).

"Swiss Federal Supreme Court Rules on Scope of Award Review", *News & Notes from the Institute for Transnational Arbitration*, Vol. 8, No. 2 (1993).

"Swiss Federal Supreme Court Interprets New Arbitration Law to Circumscribe Judicial Review", *News & Notes from the Institute for Transnational Arbitration*, Vol. 8, No. 1 (1993).

"Court Intervention in Commercial and Construction Arbitration: Approaches in the U.S. and Europe", *Japan Commercial Arbitration Journal* (1993) (in Japanese translation).

"Court Intervention in Commercial and Construction Arbitration: Approaches in the U.S. and Europe", *Construction Lawyer*, Vol. 13, No. 4 (1993).

"Supervision and Support of Arbitration by Courts: A Comparative Approach", *Japan Commercial Arbitration Journal* (1993) (in Japanese translation).

"Litigation versus Arbitration: Recent Trends in the U.S. Courts: A Comparative Approach", *International Arbitration Report*, Vol. 8, No. 5 (1993).

"ICC-Schiedsgerichtsordnung: 'Rechte' und 'Pflichten'

des Beklagten im Anfangsstadium", *Recht der Internationalen Wirtschaft*, No. 8 (1992).

"Supervision and Support of Arbitration by Courts: A Comparative Approach", *International Arbitration Report*, Vol. 7, No. 8 (1992).

"A Defendant's Initial Rights and Duties in International Arbitration on the Basis of the ICC Rules", *International Arbitration Report*, Vol. 6, No. 9 (1991).

"A Defendant's Initial Rights and Duties in an ICC Arbitration", *International Financial Law Review*, August 1991.

**PUBLICATIONS
OF THE HAGUE ACADEMY
OF INTERNATIONAL LAW**

## COLLECTED COURSES

Since 1923 the top names in international law have taught at the Hague Academy of International Law. All the volumes of the *Collected Courses* which have been published since 1923 are available, as, since the very first volume, they are reprinted regularly in their original format. There is a complete and detailed catalogue.

Since 2008, certain courses have been the subject of a pocketbook edition.

In addition, the total collection now exists in electronic form. All works already published have been put "on line" and can be consulted under one of the proposed subscription methods, which offer a range of tariffs and possibilities.

## WORKSHOPS

The Academy publishes the discussions from the Workshops which it organizes. The latest title of the Workshops already published is as follows : *Topicality of the 1907 Hague Conference, the Second Peace Conference* (2007). (See below.)

## CENTRE FOR STUDIES AND RESEARCH

The scientific works of the Centre for Studies and Research in International Law and International Relations of the Hague Academy of International Law, the subjects of which are chosen by the Curatorium of the Academy, have been published, since the Centre's 1985 session, in a publication in which the Directors of Studies reported on the state of research of the Centre under their direction. This series has been discontinued and the title of the latest booklet published is as follows: *Rules and Institutions of International Humanitarian Law Put to the Test of Recent Armed Conflicts*. Nevertheless, when the work of the Centre has been of particular interest and originality, the reports of the Directors of Studies together with the articles by the researchers form the subject of a collection published in the series The Law Books of the Academy.

---

**Requests for information must be addressed to**

HAGUE ACADEMY OF INTERNATIONAL LAW

Peace Palace, Carnegieplein 2, 2517 KJ The Hague
The Netherlands

communication@hagueacademy.nl

Printed in August 2013
by Triangle Bleu,
59600 Maubeuge (France)

Setting : R. Mirland,
59870 Warlaing (France)

£2.00
27-12